Energy Law in Australia

Energy Law in Australia

Alexandra Wawryk
Carolyn Vigar
Paul Bradley
Tina Hunter

This book was originally published as a monograph in the International Encyclopaedia of Laws/Energy Law.

Founding Editor: Roger Blanpain
General Editor: Frank Hendrickx
Volume Editors: Kurt Deketelaere & Bram Delvaux

Wolters Kluwer

Published by:
Kluwer Law International B.V.
PO Box 316
2400 AH Alphen aan den Rijn
The Netherlands
E-mail: international-sales@wolterskluwer.com
Website: lrus.wolterskluwer.com

Sold and distributed in North, Central and South America by:
Wolters Kluwer Legal & Regulatory U.S.
7201 McKinney Circle
Frederick, MD 21704
United States of America
Email: customer.service@wolterskluwer.com

Sold and distributed in all other countries by:
Air Business Subscriptions
Rockwood House
Haywards Heath
West Sussex
RH16 3DH
United Kingdom
Email: international-customerservice@wolterskluwer.com

ISBN 978-90-411-9629-3

e-Book: ISBN 978-90-411-9630-9
web-PDF: ISBN 978-90-411-9641-5

The Authors

Alex Wawryk received first class degrees in Economics and Law and a PhD in Law from the University of Adelaide, Australia. She is currently a Senior Lecturer in Contract Law, Mining and Energy Law, and Climate Change Law at the University of Adelaide Law School. She also taught Environmental Law and International Energy Law, for a number of years at Adelaide University.

As well as conducting research into petroleum law, Alex's areas of research have focused on renewable energy law, including measures to encourage renewable energy generation, and wind energy, and mining and environmental law.

In 2014 she was awarded a Barbara Kidman Research Fellowship to pursue her research into petroleum law and regulation. Alex has published articles in a range of journals, including Lloyds Maritime and Commercial Law Quarterly, the Oxford Journal of Environmental Law, the Journal of Energy and Natural Resources Law, the Australia and New Zealand Maritime Law Journal, the University of New South Wales Law Journal, the Melbourne University Law Review, the Australasian Journal of Natural Resources Law and Policy, and the Environmental and Planning Law Journal. She is an associate editor for renewable energy for OGEL, a specialist online database and journal for Oil, Gas and Energy Law, and, with Professor Tina Hunter, is co-editing a special issue for OGEL in 2016–2017 on *Decommissioning of Offshore Installations*.

Alex is a barrister and solicitor of Supreme Court of South Australia. She is on the Board of Management of the Environmental Defenders Office (SA) and is a member of the World Conservation Union's Specialist Group on Energy Law. Alex is also a member of the Australian Resources and Energy Law Association (AMPLA); the Institute for Mining, Energy and Resources at the University of Adelaide; and is currently a member of the Academic Advisory Panel to the South Australian government's 2016–2017 *Leading Practice Mining Acts Review*. She is the author of the parts Introduction, Part IV. Regulatory Framework Concerning Coal, Part V. Interaction between Energy Law and Environmental Law and Part VI. Interaction between Energy Law and Tax Law of this monograph.

The Authors

Carolyn Vigar has twenty years' experience as a specialist adviser on public law and regulation. Carolyn commenced her career with the Crown Solicitor's Office (SA) in 1997 as an adviser on the implementation of National Competition Policy. From 2002–2012, Carolyn was employed by Miner Ellison (Melbourne) as a specialist public law, regulation and competition law adviser. In 2013, Carolyn joined Wallmans Lawyers (Adelaide) as the leader of the public law and regulation practice. Carolyn currently is the principal of Tanom Legal.

During her career, Carolyn provided legal services to both the public and private sectors on systems of regulation. Carolyn was a key advisor on the establishment of the National Electricity Market in 1998 and has had significant roles in respect of other fundamental developments Australia's energy markets. Other regulatory focuses include water, gas, waste, public lighting, renewable and embedded generation, geosequestration, ports and airports.

Carolyn understands the correlation between the interpretation of regulatory frameworks and the physical and commercial realities of operating in regulated markets. Her practice has involved advising on established systems of regulation and whether these are 'fit for purpose' for the deployment of new or novel technologies. Aside from advising on established regulatory systems, Carolyn has been engaged to advise on regulatory design and deployment utilising a range of regulatory tools and strategies to achieve public policy and commercial objectives. She is the author of the parts, Part I. Regulatory Framework Concerning Electricity
Part VII. Interaction Between Energy Law and Competition Law, of this monograph.

The Authors

Paul Bradley received his Bachelor of Science from Flinders University, SA and his Postgraduate Diploma of Law and Postgraduate Diploma in Legal Services from Nottingham Trent University, United Kingdom. He received a Master of Laws from the University of Strathclyde, Glasgow, United Kingdom.

Paul is currently a consultant in the Energy & Resources and Corporate and Commercial business units of the specialist commercial law firm, Cowell Clarke, in South Australia. He joined the firm in 2011 to establish the Energy, Resources and Environment practice group, and was partner and team leader of that group for a number of years.

Paul's work as a legal practitioner has predominantly focussed on corporate, commercial and compliance work primarily for ASX listed energy and resource companies in Australia. He has acted as a legal adviser to clients within the gas sector in Australia for the past nine years, and regularly acts in matters involving large Australian energy companies.

Paul has taken a particular interest in the developing legal landscape of oil and gas regulation in Australia. He spent many years as a committee member of the South Australian Branch of the Australian Energy and Resources Law Association (AMPLA) SA Branch, three years as a committee member of the Association of International Petroleum Negotiators (AIPN) and has been a committee member of The Minerals Institute (AusIMM). He has authored Part II. Regulatory Framework Concerning Gas of this monograph.

The Authors

Professor Hunter specialises in Energy and Petroleum Law and is the Director of the Aberdeen University Centre for Energy Law (AUCEL). She teaches and researches in the areas of National and International Petroleum Law, Unconventional Petroleum Regulation, Arctic Petroleum Law and Governance, International Investment Protection in the Energy Sector, and Resources Law and Policy. She has received academic qualifications in marine sediments, geology, political science, applied science, and law, completing her PhD at the University of Bergen, Norway.
She has been a visiting scholar at the University of Bergen, the University of Aberdeen, Murdoch University, and the University of Texas, Austin. She has taught in many countries, including Norway, Finland, Iceland, Greece, Russia, and Australia.
Professor Hunter has presented at over fifty conferences on four continents, and written over forty peer reviewed articles. Her expertise has been sought by many national and state/regional governments, where she has been engaged to analyse petroleum laws, draft legislation and advise on technical, policy and governance issues relating to conventional and unconventional petroleum. She has also consulted to governments, industry groups and NGOs in several jurisdictions including Australia, New Zealand, the UK, Russia, the Philippines and Canada. In June 2014, Professor Hunter participated in an unconventional gas learning symposium at the World Bank, Washington DC.
Professor Hunter was previously a member of the South Australian Roundtable for Unconventional Gas Projects, and the working group for the Queensland Modernising Queensland Resources Acts Program. She is currently the Deputy Chair of the Marketing and Communication Committee of the Aberdeen Chapter of the SPE, a co-editor of the Oil, Gas and Energy Law Journal (OGEL), and co-editor of the upcoming OGEL Journal special on *Decommissioning of Offshore Installations* with Dr Alex Wawryk. She is the author and editor of several books, including the *Handbook of Shale Gas Law and Policy* (Intersentia), *Regulation of the Upstream Petroleum Sector* (Edward Elgar) and *Petroleum Law in Australia* (LexisNexis). She is currently researching and writing a book on the prevention of oil spills in the Arctic Region. She has contributed the part, Part III. Regulatory Framework Concerning Petrol, of this monograph.

Table of Contents

Table of Contents

List of Abbreviations

ACCC	Australian Competition and Consumer Commission
ACCU	Australian Carbon Credit Unit
ACT	Australian Capital Territory
ADR	Australian Design Rules
AEMC	Australian Energy Market Commission
AEMO	Australian Electricity Market Operator
AER	Australian Energy Regulator
ALP	Australian Labor Party
ATC	Australian Transport Council
ATO	Australian Tax Office
BAS	Business Activity Statement
BEEC	Building Energy Efficiency Certificate
c/kWh	cents per kilowatt hour
CACA	Conduct and Compensation Agreement
CCA	Climate Change Authority
CCS	carbon capture and storage
CER	Clean Energy Regulator
CGT	capital gains tax
CNG	compressed natural gas
COAG	Council of Australian Governments
CO_2	carbon dioxide
CO_2-e	carbon dioxide equivalent
CPI	Consumer Price Index
CPM	Carbon Pricing Mechanism
CPRS	Carbon Pollution Reduction Scheme
CSG	coal seam gas, also known as coal seam methane
DA	Designated Authority

DAFGS	Diesel and Alternative Grants Fuel Scheme
DEE	Department of the Environment and Energy
DFRS	Diesel Fuel Rebate Scheme
DIIS	Department of Industry, Innovation and Science
DNSP	Distribution Network Service Provider
DRE	Resources and Energy Division of the NSW Department of Industry
DtS	Deemed-to-Satisfy
EDR	Economic Demonstrated Resources
EEIS	Energy Efficiency Improvement Scheme
EES	Energy Savings Scheme
EEZ	Exclusive Economic Zone
EGCS	Energy Grants (Credits) Scheme
EITE	emissions-intensive trade-exposed
EPAA	*Environmental Planning and Assessment Act 1979* (NSW)
EPBC Act	*Environment Protection and Biodiversity Conservation Act 1999* (Cth)
EPHC	Environment Protection and Heritage Council
ERF	Emissions Reduction Fund
ERL	Energy Rating Label
ESC	Energy Savings Certificate
ESCOSA	Essential Services Commission of South Australia
ETS	emissions trading system
FBT	fringe benefits tax
FiT	feed-in tariff
GEMS Act	*Greenhouse and Energy Minimum Standards Act 2012* (Cth)
GHG	greenhouse gas
GJ	gigajoule
GMV	gross vehicle mass
GST	goods and services tax

List of Abbreviations

HPSCT	Hay Point Services Coal Terminal
IESC	Independent Expert Scientific Committee on Coal Seam Gas and Large Coal Mining Development
ILUA	Indigenous land use agreement
IPART	Independent Pricing and Regulatory Tribunal
ITAA97	*Income Tax Assessment Act 1997* (Cth)
JA	Joint Authority
JCB	Joint Coal Board
JPDA	Joint Petroleum Development Area
kt	kilotonnes
kVA	1,000 volt amps
LNG	liquefied natural gas
LPG	liquid petroleum gas
LRET	Large-scale Renewable Energy Target
MCE	Ministerial Council on Energy
MCMPR	Ministerial Council on Mineral and Petroleum Resources
MEPS	Minimum Energy Performance Standards
MNES	Matters of national environmental significance
MPCCC	Multiparty Climate Change Committee
mmbbl	million barrels
MMRT	Minerals Resources Rent Tax
Mt	megatonnes
MWh	megawatt hours
NABERS	National Australian Built Environment Rating System
NatHERS	Nationwide House Energy Rating Scheme
NCC	National Construction Code, or National Competition Council
NDC	Nationally Determined Contribution
NECF	National Energy Customer Framework
NEM	National Electricity Market
NERL	National Energy Retail Law

NERR	National Energy Retail Rules
NGER Act	*National Greenhouse and Energy Reporting Act 2007* (Cth)
nm	nautical miles
NNTT	National Native Title Tribunal
NOPSA	National Offshore Petroleum Safety Authority
NOPSEMA	National Offshore Petroleum Safety and Environmental Management Authority
NOPTA	National Offshore Petroleum Title Administrator
NPA	National Partnership Agreement on Coal Seam Gas and Large Coal Mining Development
TNSP	Transmission Network Service Provider
NSW	New South Wales
NT	Northern Territory
OCS	Offshore Constitutional Settlement
OPA	*Offshore Petroleum Act 2006* (Cth)
OPGGSA	*Offshore Petroleum Greenhouse Gas Storage Act 2006* (Cth)
OPGGS(E)R	Offshore Petroleum and Greenhouse Gas Storage (Environment) Regulations 2009
OPGGSR	Offshore Petroleum and Greenhouse Gas Storage Regulations 2011
OPGGS(S)R	Offshore Petroleum and Greenhouse Gas Storage (Safety) Regulations 2009
OOA	Opt-Out Agreement
PGERA	*Petroleum and Geothermal Energy Resources Act 1967* (WA)
PRRT	petroleum resource rent tax
PSLA	*Petroleum (Submerged Lands) Act 1967* (Cth)
PSLA (WA)	*Petroleum Submerged Lands Act 1982* (WA)
PJ	petajoule

List of Abbreviations

PM&C	Department of the Prime Minister and Cabinet
PSO	Product Stewardship for Oil Scheme
Qld	Queensland
QCA	Queensland Competition Authority
R&D	Research and Development
REC	Renewable Energy Certificate
REES	Retailer Energy Efficiency Scheme
RES-E	Electricity generated from renewable energy sources
RET	Renewable Energy Target
RIDA	regional interests development approval
RRRA	resource rent royalty agreement
SA	South Australia
SCER	Standing Council on Energy and Resources
SCPO	stabilised crude petroleum oil
STC	Small-Scale Technology Certificate
STTM	Short Term Trading Market
Tas	Tasmania
tcf	trillion cubic feet
TJ	terajoules
tWh	terawatt hours
UNCLOS	United Nations Convention on the Law of the Sea
UNFCCC	United Nations Framework Convention on Climate Change
VDGTS	Victorian gas transmission system
VDWGM	Victorian declared wholesale gas market
Vic	Victoria
WA	Western Australia
WICET	Wiggins Island Coal Export Terminal

General Introduction

Chapter 1. General Background

§1. Overview of Australia's Energy Sources

1. Australia is a large country, with mainland Australia covering an area of 7.69 million km². Despite its size, Australia is sparsely populated, with a population of just over 22.5 million people, and a population density of 2.6 persons per km², one of the lowest in the world. This reflects the geography of Australia as the lowest, flattest and the driest of the continents (excepting Antarctica), with a large arid centre. Most of the population live along the eastern, southeastern and to a lesser extent, the west coast of Australia, with very few people living in the centre.[1] Before settlement by the British in 1788, Aboriginal and Torres Strait Islander peoples inhabited most areas of Australia. The current estimated resident Aboriginal and Torres Strait Islander population of Australia as at 30 June 2011 was estimated to be about 3% of the total Australian population.[2]

2. Australia is blessed with vast and diverse natural resources. Agriculture and mining have traditionally been crucial industries, in terms of employment and export income. Australia is the world's eighth largest energy producer, accounting for around 2.4% of the world's energy production. Australia's energy production was 18,715 PJ in 2014–2015. Australia has abundant resources of coal, conventional gas and coal seam gas (CSG), uranium, and renewable energy resources, including wind, solar, geothermal, hydro, wave, tidal and bioenergy. In 2014–2015, the major energy sources produced (on an energy content basis) were coal (66.4%), uranium (13.9%) and gas (13.2%). Australia is a net energy exporter. Australia exported 76% of the energy it produced in 2015, and generated AUD 67 billion of energy exports in 2014–2015.[3]

1. International Energy Agency, Energy Policies of IEA Countries: Australia 2012 Review, 15 (OECD/IEA, 2012).
2. Australian Bureau of Statistics, *3238.0.55.001 - Estimates of Aboriginal and Torres Strait Islander Australians, June 2011*, http://www.abs.gov.au/ausstats/abs@.nsf/mf/3238.0.55.001 (accessed 1 Nov. 2016).
3. Geoscience Australia and the Bureau of Resources and Energy Economics, *Australian Energy Resource Assessment* (2nd ed, 2014) (interim update 2016), *Executive Summary*, http://www.ga.gov.au/aera/executive-summary (accessed 6 Nov. 2016).

3. In 2013, Australia was the world's 20th largest consumer of energy, and the 17th largest in per capita energy use. In 2014–2015, Australia's primary energy consumption was 6,016 PJ. After being strongly positive for decades, Australia's energy demand fell slightly in 2014–2015, for a number of reasons, including improvements in energy efficiency, a decline in energy-intensive industries, and higher electricity prices. However, Australia's demand for energy is projected to increase to 8,541 PJ in 2049–2050.[4]

4. Coal is Australia's largest energy resource. Australia has the fourth largest reserves of coal in the world, and is the fourth largest producer and the second largest exporter of coal. At the end of 2014, Australia's recoverable Economic Demonstrated Resources (EDR) of coal were 63.3 Gt of black coal and 62.0 Gt of brown coal. At 2014 production levels, Australia has approximately 112 years of recoverable black coal EDR and 1022 years of brown coal EDR. Australia's large, low-cost onshore reserves of coal has meant that coal mining has played a dominant role in Australia's energy mix, with about 80% of Australia's electricity currently generated from coal.[5] The majority of Australia's coal (some 96%) is mined in Queensland and New South Wales.

5. Gas is Australia's third largest energy resource, after coal and uranium. Total identified gas resources are approximately 279,819 PJ (257 trillion cubic feet, or tcf), equating to around 106 years of gas at current production rates. Around 95% of Australia's conventional gas resources are located in offshore basins off the northwest and southeast coasts of Australia. These resources have been progressively developed for domestic use and liquefied natural gas (LNG) export. At the end of 2014, Australia's total identified conventional gas resources were estimated at 186,200 PJ (169 tcf). At current production rates, Australia has sufficient conventional gas reserves (77,200 PJ; 70 tcf) to last another thirty-four years.

6. Australia also has a large unconventional gas resource, including coal seam gas, shale gas and tight gas. Significant CSG resources have been identified in the major coal basins of eastern Australia. These are being developed for domestic use and LNG export, particularly in Queensland, which holds more than 93% of reported CSG reserves. Large amounts of shale gas resources (about 11 tcf of contingent resources) have been identified onshore, although as shale gas resources are in the early stages of exploration, the size of resources requires further definition. Production of shale gas resources in the Cooper Basin, which began in 2012, accounts for about 80% of total reported contingent shale gas resources. Total contingent resources of tight gas are estimated at 44 tcf, with reserves identified in three established conventional gas-producing basins (the Perth, Cooper and Gippsland Basins) located relatively close to infrastructure, and being considered for commercial production. The rest of the

---

4. *Ibid.*
5. GA/BREE, *Australian Energy Resource Assessment* (2nd ed, 2014) (interim update 2016), *Coal*, http://www.ga.gov.au/aera/coal (accessed 6 Nov. 2016); Geoscience Australia, *Coal Resources*, http://www.ga.gov.au/scientific-topics/energy/resources/coal-resources (accessed 6 Nov. 2016).

contingent tight gas resources are in basins without infrastructure and are currently not being considered for commercial production.[6]

7. Oil is an important source of energy, supplying most of Australia's transport needs. Australia has limited domestic supplies of crude oil, and the imports the majority of its crude oil and refined petroleum liquids. In 2014, Australia ranked 25th in the world in terms of proven oil reserves, with only around 0.2% of world oil reserves. Australia’s primary oil production (crude oil, condensate and LPG) was 1,022 PJ or 174 million barrels (mmbbl) in 2014. Around 90% of oil production comes from only a few major offshore fields. Australia has a large potential for unconventional oil resources, including oil shale and shale oil. Although exploration and development of oil shales has a long history, and large contingent resources have been reported for oil shale deposits in Queensland, there is as yet no significant production. Australia also has the potential to find large shale oil resources.[7]

8. Australia has more than one third of the world's known uranium resources. At December 2015, Australia has the world's largest reasonably assured resources of uranium recoverable at less than USD 130/kg of uranium, at an estimated 1,267 kt. ‘Reasonably Assured Resources’ (RAR) refers to uranium that ‘occurs in known mineral deposits of delineated size, grade and configuration such that the quantities which could be recovered within the given production cost ranges with currently proven mining and processing technology, can be specified’.[8] At current Australian uranium production levels, this will last more than 200 years. Australia has 532 kt of uranium in inferred resources recoverable at less than USD 130/kg of uranium. A further 34 kt of uranium in RAR and 58 kt in inferred resources are recoverable at a cost range of USD 130–260/kg of uranium. Australia has three producing uranium mines: Olympic Dam, and the Four Mile mine, both in South Australia; and Ranger in the Northern Territory.[9] Also, various projects in Western Australia have received environmental approval or are proceeding through the assessment and approval process. Australia has no nuclear power industry, and exports the uranium it produces. Australia

6. GA/BREE, *Australian Energy Resource Assessment* (2nd ed, 2014) (interim update 2016), *Gas*, http://www.ga.gov.au/aera/gas (accessed 6 Nov. 2016).
7. GA/BREE, *Australian Energy Resource Assessment* (2nd ed, 2014) (interim update 2016), *Oil*, http://www.ga.gov.au/aera/oil (accessed 6 Nov. 2016).
8. GA/BREE, *Australian Energy Resource Assessment* (2nd ed, 2014) (interim update 2016), *Appendix B, Resource Classification*, http://www.ga.gov.au/aera/appendix-b-resource-classification (accessed 6 Nov. 2016). ‘Inferred resources’ refers to uranium that is inferred to occur ‘based on direct geological evidence, in extensions of well-explored deposits, or in deposits in which geological continuity has been established but where specific data, including measurements of the deposits, and knowledge of the deposit's characteristics, are considered to be inadequate to classify the resource as RAR’.
9. Ranger will close down in 2021, when the lease expires. The operator, Energy Resources of Australia, has been exploring an underground extension of the mine. However, Rio Tinto, the owner of the Mine, and the Mirarr traditional owners, do not support an extension to the Authority.

also has significant thorium reserves but no production, nor is large-scale production likely in the next few decades.[10]

9. Australia also has a rich diversity of renewable energy resources. In 2015, renewable energy provided 14.6% of Australia's electricity, with hydroelectric power providing 5.9% of Australia's electricity, wind energy 4.9%, solar energy 2.4%, and bioenergy 1.3%. Geothermal energy for electricity generation remains minimal, and ocean energy resources remain largely undeveloped. In 2015, Tasmania sourced 99.9% of its electricity from renewable energy sources (predominantly hydroelectricity), South Australia 41.3% (wind and solar energy), Western Australia 12.1%, Victoria 12.1%, New South Wales 7.7% and Queensland 4.4%.[11] A major driver for the uptake of renewable energy, in particular wind and solar energy, was the introduction of the national Renewable Energy Target (RET) in 2001, with cumulative wind installed capacity growing from under 100 MW in 2000 to 4,187 MW in 2015.[12] State government policies, such as feed-in tariffs for solar power, have also supported the growth in renewable energy (*see* Part V below).

10. Australia's primary fuel mix is expected to change in the future. Although coal is currently the major source of Australia's electricity generation, reduced electricity demand since 2008 has led to significant fossil-fuel powered generation plants being permanently or temporarily removed from the market, with capacity withdrawals exceeding new generation entry by wind and solar facilities. Coal is expected to continue to play a major role the future, but a shift to lower emissions fuels is expected to result in a reduction in coal's share in electricity production, with more electricity generated from gas and renewable energy.[13]

§2. Legal and Political Structure

11. Australia has a federal system of government, comprised of the Commonwealth or federal government, six States (Western Australia, New South Wales, Queensland, South Australia, Victoria and Tasmania) and two Territories (the Northern Territory and the Australian Capital Territory (ACT)). Australia is a constitutional monarchy: the Queen of England is the Australian Head of State. However, the power to make laws resides with the Australian Commonwealth and State parliaments. The Queen has no role in making laws, although the Queen's representative, the Governor-General, does have a limited role in the parliamentary process.

12. The Commonwealth Parliament (also called the legislature) consists of a House of Representatives representing electorates in all States and Territories, and a Senate. The party with a majority in the House of Representatives provides a ministry from its members in both Houses of Parliaments. The federal government has historically been formed by one of the two major political parties: either the Australian Labor

10. Geoscience Australia and the Bureau of Resources and Energy Economics, *Australian Energy Resource Assessment* (2nd ed, 2014) (interim update 2016), *Uranium and Thorium*, http://www.ga.gov.au/aera/uranium-and-thorium (accessed 6 Nov. 2016).
11. Clean Energy Council, *Clean Energy Australia Report 2015*, 6 (Clean Energy Council, 2015).
12. *Ibid.*, 50, 55.
13. GA/BREE, *supra* n. 3.

Party (ALP), or the Liberal Party in political alliance with the National Party, referred to as the 'Coalition'. The people do not vote directly for the Prime Minister; the leader of the ALP or Liberal Party will become the Prime Minister (unless they fail to be elected to Parliament). The Prime Minister has no direct role in making federal legislation: this is the role of the Commonwealth Parliament. The State and Territory parliaments also exercise legislative powers.

13. The Commonwealth government came into being after Federation on 1 January 1901. The Constitution of the Commonwealth of Australia (also called the Australian Constitution, the Commonwealth Constitution, or simply 'the Constitution') sets out the powers of the federal government. Under the doctrine of the separation of powers, the Commonwealth Parliament exercises legislative power, the executive exercises executive power, and the courts exercise judicial power.[14] However, the various Australian Government Ministers must also be members of both the executive and Parliament. In practice, Parliament delegates wide regulatory powers to the executive. Each federal government Minister is responsible to Parliament for the operation of a department, and the regulatory powers of government Ministers to administer legislation are usually delegated to the various government departments over which the Ministers preside.

14. Because of the way in which the Constitution divides legislative power between the State/Territory and the Commonwealth Parliaments, there is considerable complexity in Australia's onshore and offshore energy, natural resources and environmental legislation.

I. The Regulation of Natural Resource Exploitation Onshore

15. Following British settlement, the Westminster model was used as the basis of government in the six Australian colonies established in the nineteenth century. The Australian States, as former British colonies, have inherited the plenary power of the British Parliament to make laws for the peace, order and good government of their people. Upon Federation in 1901, the Commonwealth was given power to make laws only with respect to matters expressly set out in the Commonwealth Constitution.

16. Section 51 of the Constitution lists a number of matters over which the States and the Commonwealth have concurrent legislative power.[15] As there was little doubt in 1901 that the regulation of natural resources was the province of the States, there is no specific 'head of power' giving the Commonwealth Parliament legislative power with respect to onshore mining, petroleum, energy and/or the environment. However, other heads of power are able to support Commonwealth legislation concerning natural resources. These include the power to pass legislation with respect to: interstate

14. Although the Constitution vests the executive powers of government in the Governor-General representing the English monarch, by tradition these powers are exercised by the elected government.
15. Where there is an inconsistency between a Commonwealth and State law, the State law is invalid to the extent of the inconsistency: Commonwealth Constitution, s. 90.

and overseas trade and commerce;[16] foreign, trading, financial and corporations;[17] external affairs;[18] taxation;[19] defence;[20] and the power to pass legislation with respect to 'the people of any race'.[21]

17. Following a number of divisive constitutional law cases in the 1980s, it is now generally recognised that the Commonwealth could legislate over most aspects of the mining, petroleum and energy industries if it chose to do.[22] However, The Commonwealth has not exercised these powers. The States retain regulatory control over nearly all aspects of the mining and energy industries, including exploration, production, transport, and the processing/refining of minerals and hydrocarbons. Matters such as the ownership of onshore minerals and petroleum, authorisations and approvals, environmental protection, and health and safety are regulated by the States, as is the generation, transport and supply of electricity. The States also levy royalties, which are a price for the right to produce or extract minerals or petroleum, or a charge for the acquisition of a right to property.[23] However, the Commonwealth Parliament has exclusive power to levy duties of custom and duties of excise, which are taxes on any step before consumption in the production, manufacture, sale or distribution of goods, whether of domestic or foreign origin.[24]

18. The States regulate most of the environmental aspects of mining and petroleum exploration and extraction. To avoid expensive and divisive federal-state conflicts, in the 1990s the States and Commonwealth adopted a strategy of 'co-operative federalism' through adoption of two political agreements: the 1992 *Intergovernmental Agreement on the Environment*,[25] and 1997 *Heads of Agreement on Commonwealth/ State Roles and Responsibilities for the Environment*.[26] These form the basis for the *Environment Protection and Biodiversity Conservation Act 1999* (Cth) ('EPBC Act'), pursuant to which the Commonwealth regulates environmental matters that are of international and national concern. The EPBC Act is of relevance to the natural resources industries to the extent that mining and energy developments affect these matters. The States continue to regulate a wide range of environmental matters of state or local

16. Commonwealth Constitution, s. 51(i).
17. Section 51(xx).
18. Section 51(xxix).
19. Section 51(ii).
20. Section 51(vi). This provides the constitutional basis for the federal control of uranium mining and nuclear power.
21. Section 51(xxvi). This provides the constitutional basis for the *Native Title Act 1993* (Cth).
22. *Commonwealth v. Tasmania* (1983) 158 CLR 1; *Richardson v. Forestry Commission* (1988) 164 CLR 261. *See* Crawford J, 'The Constitution and the Environment' (1991) 13 *Sydney Law Review* 11; Bate G, *Environmental Law in Australia* (8th ed, Lexis Nexis/Butterworths, 2013); Fitzgerald F, *Mining Agreements: Negotiated Frameworks in the Australian Minerals Sector* (Lexis Nexis, 2001).
23. *Harper v. Minister for Sea Fisheries* (1989) 168 CLR 314.
24. Commonwealth Constitution, s. 90; *Ha & Anor v. State of New South Wales & Ors* (1997) 189 CLR 465.
25. *National Environment Protection Council Act 1994* (Cth), Sch.
26. *Heads of Agreement on Commonwealth and State Roles and Responsibilities for the Environment* (Council of Australian Governments, 1997).

concern, such as planning, conservation and heritage, native vegetation and water resources law.

II. The Regulation of Offshore Natural Resource Exploitation

19. The regulation of offshore mining and petroleum is more complex. In 1973, the federal Labor government asserted Commonwealth sovereignty over offshore areas in the *Seas and Submerged Lands Act 1973* (Cth). The validity of this legislation was upheld by the High Court,[27] in a decision handed down just days after the Liberal Party won the federal election after campaigning on the basis of States' rights. The Commonwealth and States negotiated a political agreement known as the Offshore Constitutional Settlement (OCS),[28] and passed mirror Commonwealth and State legislation, by virtue of which the States maintain title to, and power to legislate in respect of, resources from the low water mark seaward to 3 nautical miles (nm), this being the breadth of the territorial sea at that time.[29]

20. Thus, very generally speaking, the States' offshore mining and petroleum laws, and environment laws, apply from the low water mark seaward to 3 nm, that is, in 'coastal waters'.[30] The Commonwealth's offshore mining and petroleum Acts apply in 'Commonwealth Waters', that is, from 3 nm seaward to 200 nm (the outer boundary of the Exclusive Economic Zone (EEZ)), or to the outer edge of the continental shelf, whichever is greater. In Commonwealth waters, the States and Commonwealth jointly administer the Commonwealth's offshore petroleum and mining laws. The EPBC Act applies in all offshore waters.

III. Key Areas of Commonwealth Involvement in the Regulation of Natural Resources

21. Because most aspects of the mining and energy industries are regulated by the States, the federal government is directly involved in only limited areas. Some key matters which are the subject of Commonwealth Regulation are:

- federal competition law, which applies to all industries;
- offshore petroleum and minerals development, and carbon sequestration, in Commonwealth waters;

27. *New South Wales v. Commonwealth* (1975) 135 CLR 337.
28. *Offshore Settlement. A Milestone in Co-operative Federalism* (AGPS, Canberra, 1980) and *Offshore Constitutional Settlement: Selected statements and documents 1978-79* (Commonwealth of Australia, 1980).
29. The States passed the mirror *Coastal Waters (State Powers) Act 1980* and the *Coastal Waters (State Title) Act 1980*.
30. The States' power to legislate over, and their title to, offshore resources remains to 3 nm, although the breadth of Australia's territorial sea is now 12 nm from the baseline.

- through the EPBC Act, protection of the environment for matters of national and international concern, including World Heritage Areas, and nationally and internationally listed and migratory threatened species;
- federal climate change and renewable energy and energy efficiency laws, including 'Direct Action' (comprised of the Emissions Reduction Fund (ERF) and the Safeguard Mechanism) and the RET;[31]
- the regulation of native title under the *Native Title Act 1993* (Cth), including provisions requiring negotiation with indigenous peoples living on, and/or or maintaining connections with, their traditional lands;
- various financial matters, including: duties of custom and excise in relation to petroleum and minerals; taxation, including taxes specific to mining and energy, such as the Petroleum Resource Rent Tax (PRRT); and subsidies and financial assistance, for example, for research and development (R&D) of new renewable energy technologies; and
- the control of foreign investment.

31. The Renewable Energy Target (RET) is established through the *Renewable Energy (Electricity) Act 2000* (Cth).

Chapter 2. Basic Principles of Energy Law

§1. Public Ownership of Mineral and Petroleum Resources

22. One of the fundamental principles underlying energy law in Australia is the public ownership of natural resources, including coal, oil, gas, and uranium. The natural resources legislation of the States and Territories generally reserves the ownership of minerals (including coal and uranium) and petroleum (oil and gas) to the Crown in right of the State.[32] However, the private sector, not the government sector, undertakes the exploitation of minerals and petroleum. Exploration for, and production of, minerals and petroleum is regulated in the various Australian jurisdictions under statutory schemes whereby exploration and production is prohibited without the necessary authorisation issued by the relevant resources Minister. As the owner, the State charges a royalty for the right to produce the mineral or petroleum resource. Ownership of minerals and petroleum is transferred to the holder of the authorisation after production of the resource.

§2. The Introduction of Competition to Achieve Efficiency in Supply

23. Australia's electricity infrastructure, including the transmission and distribution network, was constructed in the twentieth century by the large, vertically integrated, monopolistic electricity companies, owned by the State governments. These were responsible for all aspects of electricity supply, including generation, transmission, distribution and retail functions. Historically, each State operated its own, physically separate electricity supply system, regulated under State law. Similarly, in the gas industry, while private petroleum companies produced gas, state-owned businesses held monopolies over transmission, distribution and retail functions. Long-term contracts between producers and consumers, rather than trading markets, have governed the supply (and pricing) of gas.

24. From the 1990s, as part of a process of broader microeconomic reform taking place under the National Competition Policy, the States and federal governments have sought to reform the monopolistic energy industries of each State, in a process that is ongoing today. The fundamental rationale underlying the reform of energy markets, and which governs energy law and policy today, is a belief in the benefits of competitive markets in providing efficient market outcomes. Competitive markets achieve an efficient allocation of resources as the market balances energy demand and supply, and allow energy products and services to be delivered at the lowest cost to consumers. One of the fundamental aims underlying energy law and policy is to increase competition in Australia's energy markets, in order to achieve efficient outcomes, in particular low prices for consumers.

32. *See* further Ch. 3: Historical Background; and Parts II and III, below.

25. To introduce competition, from the mid-1990s, the state-owned electricity companies were disaggregated into generation, transmission, distribution and retail functions. Competition was introduced into the generation and retail levels. Along with disaggregation, the state-owned businesses were progressively corporatised and/or privatised. While most generation and retail businesses in SA, NSW and Victoria are under private ownership, state ownership of energy companies continues to exist in other States. The further privatisation of state-owned energy corporations, to drive innovation and productivity, is one of the stated policies of the current Federal Coalition government in the *Energy White Paper 2015*.[33]

26. As part of the introduction of competition, in the mid-1990s, the Council of Australian Governments (COAG) agreed to establish one competitive electricity market in Australia, called the National Electricity Market (NEM). Queensland, New South Wales, Victoria, Tasmania, South Australia and the Australian Capital Territory are participating jurisdictions in the NEM. Western Australia and the Northern Territory are too remote to participate in the physical market for electricity, although Western Australia participates to a certain degree, for example, through the operation of the WA market by the Australian Energy Market Operator. The market is established and regulated through the *National Electricity Law* and *National Electricity Rules*. There are three distinct gas markets in Australia – the Northern, Western and Southeastern gas markets – regulated through the *National Gas Law* and *National Gas Rules*.

27. The *National Electricity Law* and *National Gas Law* clearly demonstrate an emphasis on efficiency as a primary objective underlying the national legislative regimes. The stated objective of the *National Gas Law* is to 'promote efficient investment in, and efficient operation and use of, natural gas services for the long term interests of consumers of natural gas with respect to price, quality, safety, reliability and security of supply of natural gas'.[34] Similarly, the objective of the *National Electricity Law* is to 'promote efficient investment in, and efficient operation and use of, electricity services for the long term interests of consumers of electricity with respect to— (a) price, quality, safety, reliability and security of supply of electricity; and (b) the reliability, safety and security of the national electricity system'.[35]

28. Although some levels of the electricity and gas industries are competitive, transmission and distribution are natural monopolies. Another key principle of Australia's energy law today is that the parts of the energy supply system that are natural monopolies are to be regulated in such a way as to be consistent with the competitive markets within which they operate. One example of this is electricity network revenue determinations. A particularly important application of this principle is the regulation of third-party access to electricity and gas pipelines and electricity networks to prevent the owners of infrastructure from using their market power to raise barriers to entry and undermine competition, for example, by charging unjustifiably high prices for access, or imposing unreasonable terms and conditions on access to critical infrastructure.

33. Australian Government, Department of Industry and Science, *Energy White Paper 2015*, 8 (Commonwealth of Australia, 2015).
34. *National Gas Law*, s. 23, contained in *National Gas (South Australia) Act 2008* (SA) (and the application legislation of participating jurisdiction), Sch.
35. *National Electricity Law*, s. 7, contained in *National Electricity (South Australia) Act 1996* (SA) (and the application legislation of participating jurisdiction), Sch.

Thus, access to nationally significant infrastructure, including electricity and gas infrastructure, is regulated under Part IIIA of the *Competition and Consumer Act 2010* (Cth) while a general access regime for pipelines (not limited to nationally significant infrastructure) is contained within the *National Gas Law*, and for network access in the electricity industry, in the *National Electricity Law*.[36]

29. Retail contestability is a fundamental feature of the NEM. The market rules are designed to empower consumers through requirements for the provision of required information, and to protect small consumers through requirements for retailers to provide basic or standard retail contracts, as well as providing the opportunity for negotiated contracts.[37] As part of the drive to increase competition and achieve efficiency, the current federal government is committed to removing unnecessary regulatory barriers that distort competition and price signals. For example, the federal government is committed to abolishing the existing two-part electricity tariff structure, whereby consumers are charged a fixed connection fee, and pay a variable charge for the amount of electricity consumed. Current federal government policy is to introduce cost-reflective tariffs, to minimise the cross-subsidisation between consumers, reduce prices and lower network costs. Consumers would pay the cost of electricity supply at the time of use, using price signals to reduce demand at times of peak electricity use, when demand for electricity is at its highest and power most expensive.[38] To achieve the benefits of cost-reflective tariffs, advanced or smart metering technology will need to be rolled out across the country.

30. The various Australian governments, through the COAG Energy Council (*see* Chapter 4, §1 below), are committed to increasing competition and efficiency in the supply of gas. The gas market has traditionally relied on long-term contracts between the suppliers and consumers of gas, and although trading markets and hubs have emerged in recent years, a number of these are still in their infancy.[39] With massive investment and increased exports of LNG over the past five-ten years, the market has been undergoing significant change. In 2014, the Energy Council, through the release of its Australian Gas Market Vision, committed to continuing gas market reform, seeking to establish a liquid wholesale gas market with a transparent gas reference price, to provide market signals for gas investment and supply, and which will, with access and connection to infrastructure, enable market participants to trade gas more readily at various locations across Australia.[40] On 19 August 2016, the Energy Council released its comprehensive Gas Market Reform Package, comprised of four priority areas (gas supply, market operation, gas transportation and market transparency), to drive the achievement of its Australian Gas Market Vision.

---

36. These third-party access regimes are discussed in more detail in Parts I and II below.
37. *See* Part I, below.
38. *Energy White Paper 2015*, *supra* n. 33, 11.
39. *See* Part II, below.
40. COAG Energy Council, *Australian Gas Market Vision*, 1 (COAG, 2014).

§3. Consistency Across Australia

31. Because energy law and policy has historically been a matter for the States and Territories, there has been, and continues to be, disparate legislation and policy across the country. One of the key principles underlying energy law and regulation is to decrease or remove inefficiencies in energy regulation and unnecessary regulatory barriers, in particular costs and inefficiencies arising from overlapping or duplicated State and Commonwealth regulatory requirements. Thus, for example, a fundamental aim underlying the formation of the national energy market is that of improving consistency in laws and regulations, to 'remove the costs consumers pay to support different jurisdictional regulatory environments, improve reliability and introduce more competition to lower costs'.[41] To achieve consistency in law and policy, the States/Territories have entered into a range of National agreements, partnerships, strategies, principles, frameworks, under the auspices of COAG (*see* Chapter 4, §1 below). These political agreements are incorporated into law through Commonwealth legislation and/or the use of mirror Commonwealth/State/Territory legislation.

§4. Energy Security and Reliability of Supply

32. As a net exporter of energy, with vast reserves of coal, gas, and renewable energy resources, Australia has not had to contend with concerns regarding the security of supply to the same extent as nations that are heavily reliant on imported energy. In an Australian context, 'energy security' is defined as the 'adequate, reliable and competitive supply of energy', where adequacy is the provision of sufficient energy to support economic and social activity; reliability is the provision of energy with minimal disruptions to supply; and competitiveness is the provision of energy at an affordable price.[42] That energy security is a key concern is reflected in the *National Electricity Law* and *National Gas Law,* which expressly include among their objectives the promotion of efficiency to ensure: the reliability and security of supply of natural gas; the reliability and security of supply of electricity; and the reliability, safety and security of the national electricity system.

33. There are certain issues of concern regarding the reliability of gas supply and the reliability of the electricity grid. At the end of 2016, a major issue of concern to the federal government is the security of gas supply to the Eastern States, as Australia's natural gas is increasingly processed and exported as LNG to meet international contracts. A related concern is the increasing domestic price of gas, as the price becomes linked to higher international prices. This has raised the issue of whether the States and/or federal government should hold gas reservation policies. The West Australian and Queensland Governments have policies that support the reservation of gas for supply to domestic users, although the policy has not yet been applied in Queensland. In Queensland, the government may, when granting a tenement, require that gas produced from the tenement area be supplied only to the Australian market. The

41. *Energy White Paper 2015*, *supra* n. 33, 9.
42. Australian Government, Department of Resources, Energy and Tourism, *National Energy Security Assessment 2011*, 2 (Commonwealth of Australia, 2011).

Western Australia gas reservation policy aims to secure domestic gas commitments up to the equivalent of 15% of LNG production from each export gas project, with the government and individual LNG project proponents negotiating the means by which the proponents will meet their domestic gas commitments.[43]

34. The Australian government and the governments of New South Wales, South Australia, Victoria, Tasmania, the Northern Territory and the ACT, do not support gas reservation. The stated policy of the Australian federal government, expressed in the Energy White Paper 2015, is to pursue gas market reform to encourage additional investment and gas supply.[44] This approach has been supported by the Australian Competition and Consumer Commission (ACCC) in its 2016 East Coast Gas Inquiry report, in which the ACCC recommended that domestic gas reservation policies should not be introduced, because 'artificially reduced prices weaken the economic incentives for further gas exploration and appraisal' and 'reduce the likelihood of new sources of gas being developed, to the detriment of the level and diversity of supply for domestic gas users'.[45]

35. The issue of security of gas supply has led to divergence between the Commonwealth and States/Territories over the issue of State/Territory-imposed moratoria on the production of unconventional gas, which been imposed because of community concerns regarding the environmental impacts of unconventional gas developments (*see* Part II below). The federal government has criticised the moratoria, as these will restrict gas supplies and place further pressure on gas prices.

36. A second issue of concern is the security and reliability of the national electricity grid, particularly as more variable power such as wind energy is brought into the system, and as consumers increasingly move off the grid, using PV installations with battery storage. Australian Energy Market Operator (AEMO) is responsible for overseeing power system security of the NEM and the South West Interconnected System in Western Australia. AEMO has established a 'Future Power System Security' work programme to identify opportunities and challenges to power system security and stability that could arise in the short term (three years) and the long term (ten years), with more variable power, and less synchronous generation, in the electricity system.

37. A third potential issue is security of oil supply. However, Australia has suffered minimal disruption to its imported fuel supplies for many years. The Australian liquid fuel supply chain has 'considerable span and diversity, including crude and petroleum product shipments into and around Australia, refinery throughput, bulk fuel storage tanks, extensive terminal and distribution networks, over 6000 retail outlets, and substantial fuel storage facilities of major fuel users', which delivers a high level of security and reliability by global standards.[46]

43. Warburton A and Reid J, 'Government reserves on domestic gas policy, but the pressure mounts … ' (2 May 2014) http://m.minterellison.com/publications/domestic-gas-policy/ (accessed 30 Nov. 2016).

44. *Energy White Paper 2015*, *supra* n. 33, 20.

45. Australian Competition and Consumer Commission, *Inquiry into the East Coast Gas Market*, 6-7 (ACCC, April 2016).

46. Australian Petroleum Institute, *Maintaining supply security and reliability for liquid fuels in Australia*, 6 (API, 2013).

38. Australia is party to the International Energy Agency (IEA) treaty, under which it is obliged to hold crude oil stocks equivalent to at least ninety days of net oil imports.[47] Historically, Australia has relied on commercial industry stocks and significant domestic production of crude oil to meet its stockholding obligations, but increasing imports of oil has caused the country to be in breach of its stockholding obligations since 2009.[48] Australia's last National Energy Security Assessment, conducted in 2011, did not find evidence that these breaches are an indication of a decline in Australia's domestic energy security, and the current Australian government considers that supply reliability will be maintained in Australia because of the 'depth, liquidity and diversity of international crude and fuel markets, combined with the existing Australian stockholding and at-sea tanker arrangements of commercial companies'.[49] Nevertheless, the Australian Government has agreed a plan to return to compliance, providing AUD 23.8 million over four years from 2016, to establish the Energy Security Office and support its activities in meeting the stockholding requirements.[50]

39. As part of other IEA obligations, Australia's National Oil Supplies Emergency Committee has developed and manages the National Liquid Fuel Emergency Response Plan, to ensure a co-ordinated response by Australian governments and industry to any liquid fuel or oil supply emergency at a national or international level.

§5. Sustainability of Energy Supply

40. As a party to both the United Nations Framework Convention on Climate Change (UNFCCC) and the Kyoto Protocol to the Convention,[51] and having ratified the Paris Agreement on 9 November 2016,[52] Australia is committed to a reduction of greenhouse gas (GHG) emissions of 26–28% below 2005 levels by 2030.[53] With around 76% percent of Australia's GHG emissions arising from energy use, the commitment to reduce these emissions can be described as an entrenched principle of energy law. However, the key Acts that regulate Australia's national electricity and gas markets

47. OECD, *Decision of the Council establishing an International Energy Agency of the Organisation*, 15 Nov. 1974, C(74)203/FINAL; *Agreement on an International Energy Program*, as amended 5 Feb. 1975 and by subsequent Governing Board decisions to May 1979, Paris, 18 Nov. 1974, 1979 ATS 7 (in force 19 Jan. 1976).
48. *National Energy Security Assessment 2011*, *supra* n. 42, 13, 16.
49. *Ibid.*, 13; *Energy White Paper 2015*, *supra* n. 33, 26.
50. Australian Government, Department of Energy and Environment, *IEA International Energy Program Treaty*, http://www.environment.gov.au/energy/energy-security-office/international-engagement/iea-treaty (accessed 30 Nov. 2016).
51. United Nations Framework Convention on Climate Change, adopted 14 Jun. 1992, UNCED Doc A/CONF.151/5/Rev.1, (Vol I), Annex I, 13 Jun. 1992, 31 *ILM* 874 (1992); Kyoto Protocol to the United Nations Framework Convention on Climate Change, *Report of the Conference of the Parties at its Third Session, 1-11 Dec. 1997*, U.N. Doc FCCC/CP/1997/7/Add.1, 18 Mar. 1998, Annex.
52. United Nations Framework Convention on Climate Change, Report of the Conference of the Parties at its Twenty First Session, 30 Nov.–11 Dec. 2015, FCCC/CP/2015/L.9/Rev.1, 12 Dec. 2015, Annex.
53. *See* Part V, below.

– the *National Electricity Law* and *National Gas Law* – do not include the environmental sustainability of supply as an objective of the legislation. Federal government policy and aims in respect of climate change, including the reduction of GHG emissions in the energy sector, are dealt with in separate legislation.

41. Although Australia is committed to the reduction of GHG emissions, there has been considerable uncertainty and change in relation to federal climate change policy, and the appropriate means of achieving emissions reductions. Very generally speaking, the more conservative Coalition governments have preferred voluntary means of achieving Australia's emissions target, while the Labor Party has been committed to mandatory measures, including the introduction of an emissions trading scheme. Whether mandatory or voluntary, both parties have shown a preference for market-based tradeable certificate schemes, such as the RET, the Carbon Pricing Mechanism (CPM) (now abolished), and the ERF, complemented by State market-based tradeable certificate schemes in relation to achieving energy efficiency. These schemes are supported by mandatory requirements, for example, in relation to greenhouse emissions reporting, and energy labelling scheme and energy efficiency standards. Climate change law and policy are discussed further at Chapter 3, §5 [I] below, and Part V, below.

Chapter 3. Historical Background

§1. Oil and Gas Exploration and Development

I. Conventional Oil and Gas Resources

A. Onshore

42. Exploration for conventional oil and gas resources onshore began in Australia much earlier than exploration for offshore resources, with initial exploration activities in South Australia commencing as far back as 1886. Conventional oil resources contribute little to Australia's energy requirements, with natural gas resources far more abundant.

43. The Cooper and Eromanga Basins, which straddle northern South Australia and southeastern Queensland, are the most important onshore petroleum basins in South Australia. The Moomba gas fields were extensively developed in the 1960s and 1970s, and connected through the construction of pipelines to gas markets in Adelaide (1969), New South Wales (1976) and Queensland (1993). In the Northern Territory, the Mereenie oil and natural gas fields and the Palm Valley gas field, discovered in the 1960s in the highly prospective Amadeus Basin, have been developed since the 1980s, and conventional/natural gas is the major fuel for electricity generation in the Northern Territory. Natural gas is also an important fuel in Western Australia, comprising 70% of the State's energy supply, although much development takes place offshore.[54]

44. In Queensland, while conventional gas has been developed since the 1970s, the exploitation of unconventional gas, in particular CSG, has skyrocketed since the early 2000s, and now provides over 75% of the domestic gas market. In both New South Wales and Queensland, while coal remains the dominant fuel for electricity generation, the exploration for CSG has increased dramatically. In Victoria, onshore exploration for oil and gas takes place in the Otway Basin and the onshore part of the Gippsland Basin, although most onshore petroleum activity in Victoria relates to the transport of gas.[55]

45. Petroleum exploration and production has been conducted under statutory regimes, and there has been no development of common law principles in relation to petroleum in Australia.[56] All petroleum and gas is the property of the Crown. Because of the constitutional situation in Australia, the regulation of nearly all facets of the onshore minerals, petroleum and gas industries, including exploration, production, transport and processing/refining of minerals, gas and petroleum, has taken place under

54. Hunter T and Chandler J, *Petroleum Law in Australia,* 40, 58, 191, 196 (LexisNexis Butterworths, 2013).
55. *Ibid.,* 40, 193, 195 (LexisNexis Butterworths, 2013).
56. Hunt M, *Minerals and Petroleum Law* 4 (Butterworths, 1996).

State and Territory law. As hydrocarbons, both petroleum and natural gas exploration and production are regulated under the same Act.

46. The first statutory recognition of petroleum occurred in early (and since repealed) State mining legislation, including the *Mining Act 1893* (SA), *Mining Act 1904* (WA), *Mining Act 1905* (Tas) and the *Mining Act 1906* (NSW), where the definition of 'minerals' included reference to mineral oils, oil and/or petroleum. In the Northern Territory, Queensland and Victoria, the statutory recognition of petroleum resources began with the passage of special purpose petroleum legislation (since repealed), being the *Petroleum Act 1915* (Qld), *Mines (Petroleum) Act 1935* (Vic) and the *Petroleum (Prospecting and Mining) Act 1954* (NT). Eventually the other States and Territories (except the ACT and Tasmania) also passed special purpose petroleum legislation, being the *Petroleum Act 1935* (SA), *Petroleum Act 1936* (WA) and the *Petroleum Act 1955* (NSW).

47. As of 1 November 2016, the current State/Territory legislation governing the exploration and production of petroleum and conventional gas is: the *Petroleum Act 1923* (Qld) and the *Petroleum and Gas (Production and Safety) Act 2004* (Qld); *Petroleum and Geothermal Energy Act 2000* (SA); *Petroleum Act 1998* (Vic); *Petroleum and Geothermal Energy Resources Act 1967* (WA); *Petroleum (Onshore) Act 1991* (NSW); *Petroleum Act* (no date) (NT). In Tasmania, petroleum is dealt with under the *Mineral Resources Development Act 1995* (Tas). The ACT does not have petroleum mining legislation.

B. *Offshore*

48. Oil and conventional gas development in Australia predominantly takes place in offshore basins. Australia holds less than 1% of the world's crude oil reserves, but holds significant resources of gas, with Australia the sixth largest exporter of LNG in the world.

49. Offshore petroleum was first discovered in the Bass Strait between Victoria and Tasmania in the 1960s. Three fields in the Bass Strait – the Marlin, Halibut and Kingfisher oil fields, in the Gippsland and Otway Basins – began production in the early 1970s, and the Bass Strait became the most important region for the production of crude oil in Australia from the 1960s. Since the 1960s, significant hydrocarbon reserves have been discovered on the North West Shelf off the northwestern coast of Western Australia. The Browse, Bonaparte and Carnarvon Basins contain oil reserve and vast gas reserves, including some 80% of Australia's conventional gas reserves, and most of Australia's LNG resources come from the North West Shelf. Significant exploration has also occurred in the Timor Sea, with the Greater Sunrise oil and gas fields holding vast amounts of conventional gas. Australia also has three under-explored offshore sedimentary basins, including the Perth Basin and Mentelle Basin off the coast of WA, and the Bight Basin in the Great Australian Bight.[57]

50. When oil was discovered in the Bass Strait in the 1960s, it was not clear whether the Commonwealth or the States had jurisdiction over Australia's offshore

57. Hunter and Chandler, *supra* n. 54, 38–39.

areas. In 1967, the Commonwealth and States entered into a political agreement,[58] as consequence of which the States and Commonwealth enacted mirror legislation, the Petroleum (Submerged Lands) Acts of 1967, to govern offshore oil exploitation. However, after the enactment of the *Seas and Submerged Lands Act 1973* (Cth), the constitutional validity of which was upheld by the High Court in *New South Wales v. The Commonwealth*,[59] the Commonwealth and States entered a new political agreement, the OCS.

51. As a result of the OCS, the States enacted new Petroleum (Submerged Lands) Acts in 1982. These Acts, with the *Petroleum (Submerged Lands) Act 1967* (Cth), introduced a system of governance for Australia's offshore areas whereby the States enact and administer petroleum legislation, applying in State coastal waters (the baseline of the territorial sea to three nm seaward); and the Commonwealth enacts offshore petroleum legislation regulating petroleum activities in Commonwealth waters (3 nm seaward to 200 nm) and on the continental shelf where it extends beyond the EEZ, but with joint State/Territory and Commonwealth administration of the statutory scheme. The system remains in place today, although the legislation has changed, and details of the current offshore petroleum legislation and regulatory regime are discussed further in Parts II and III, below.

II. Unconventional Resources

52. Australia is estimated to have vast reserves of unconventional hydrocarbon resources. To date, oil and gas companies in Australia have targeted three forms of unconventional resources: shale gas, extracted from shale formations; tight gas, extracted from sandstones of low porosity and permeability; and coal seam gas (also known as coal bed methane), extracted from coal formations.[60]

53. It has been estimated that Australia could have more than 1000 tcf in recoverable shale gas.[61] Although some production of shale gas has occurred in the Cooper Basin, the shale and tight gas industries are as yet in their infancy, and more research needs to be done to confirm Australia's reserves of these resources.[62] In contrast, the CSG industry is relatively well established. Most CSG reserves are located in the Bowen and Surat Basins in central Queensland (92%), with smaller reserves in the Gunnedah, Gloucester and Sydney Basins in New South Wales, and the Clarence-Moreton Basin on the NSW-Queensland border.[63]

58. *1967 Agreement Relating to the Exploration for, and the Exploitation of, the Petroleum Resources, and Certain Other Resources, of the Continental Shelf of Australia and of certain Territories of the Commonwealth and of certain other Submerged Land.*
59. (1975) 135 CLR 337.
60. Hunter T and Chandler J, *supra* n. 54, 181.
61. Australian Council of Learned Academies, *Engineering Energy: Unconventional Gas Production: A study of shale gas in Australia*, 50 (ACOLA, 2013).
62. *Ibid.*; Hunter T and Chandler J, *supra* n. 54, 59–60.
63. Geoscience Australia and the Bureau of Resources and Energy Economics, *Australian Energy Resource Assessment*, 96 (2nd ed, 2014).

54. The CSG industry has developed only recently in the history of Australia's hydrocarbon exploitation. From the early 1900s–1940s, efforts were made to manage gas emanating from underground coal mining activities. Most notably, methane gas extracted from the Sydney Harbour colliery at Balmain was compressed and sold as an industrial and motor fuel. However, at this time most CSG was simply vented. From the 1950s, more attention was given to draining mines of gas before coal extraction, primarily for mine safety.[64]

55. The first exploration for CSG as a resource in its own right began in Queensland's Bowen Basin in 1976, and although by the mid-1980s a number of wells had been drilled, it was not until 1996 that Australia's first CSG extraction began, in central Queensland. NSW began CSG production in 2001. The exponential growth in CSG mining has occurred in the Bowen and Surat Basins in Queensland. Annual CSG production in 1995 was zero, increasing to 1 PJ in 1996 to 296 PJ (0.2 tcf) in 2011–2012, and accounting for around 13% of Australia's total gas production. Queensland produced 97% of CSG production, and NSW the remaining 3%. In 2011–2012, 735 CSG exploration and production wells were drilled.[65] Currently, over 30% of the eastern Australian gas network is fed by CSG.[66]

56. All exploration and development of unconventional fuels in Australia has occurred onshore, and thus is regulated by State/Territory legislation. New South Wales, the Northern Territory, South Australia and Western Australia use their existing petroleum legislation to regulate the grant of authorisations for unconventional gas exploration and production, namely the *Petroleum (Onshore) Act 1991* (NSW); *Petroleum Act* (no date) (NT); *Petroleum and Geothermal Energy Act 2000* (SA); and the *Petroleum and Geothermal Energy Resources Act 1967* (WA). Queensland also uses its general petroleum legislation, the *Petroleum and Gas (Production and Safety) Act 2004* (Qld), to regulate the grant of CSG authorisations. This legislation rewrote and updated the Petroleum Act of 1923, which was inadequate to deal with the rapidly expanding CSG industry. In Victoria, specific legislation has been passed to regulate the development of unconventional gas and oil resources, namely the *Mineral Resources (Sustainable Development) Act 1990* (Vic).

57. The development of unconventional gas has faced community objection and concerns over the environment impacts of hydraulic fracturing (in relation to the extraction of shale and tight gas) and water use for CSG extraction, particular the depletion of aquifers. As a result, the NSW and Queensland governments have implemented a number of legislative reforms concerning land access, community engagement, environment protection, water and well activities. Other States have introduced bans or moratoriums on unconventional resources, including a moratorium on hydraulic fracturing in Tasmania and the Northern Territory, and in Victoria, a ban

---

64. Enever J, Jeffrey R and Wold M, *The Birth of the Coal Seam Gas Industry in Australia: the Role of Research* (no page numbers) (Australasian Mining History Association, 2014), http://www.mininghistory.asn.au/wp-content/uploads/2014/08/the-birth-of-the-coal-seam-gas-industry-in-australia.pdf (accessed 12 Nov. 2016).
65. Geoscience Australia and the Bureau of Resources and Energy Economics, *supra* n. 63, 101.
66. New South Wales Department of Industry, Division of Resources and Energy, *What is coal seam gas?*, http://www.resourcesandenergy.nsw.gov.au/landholders-and-community/coal-seam-gas/the-facts/what-is-coal-seam-gas (accessed 12 Nov. 2016).

on the exploitation of unconventional resources and a moratorium on onshore gas exploration and extraction until 2020.[67]

§2. Coal Mining

58. Black coal was first discovered in NSW near the site of Newcastle in 1791. A subsequent discovery in 1797 at the north of the Hunter River led to the production and export of coal from 1799, and the establishment of a convict settlement – later to become Australia's first industrial town, Newcastle – near the mouth of the Hunter River in 1802.[68] Commercial production of coal began at Lithgow in NSW in 1865 and, from 1867, a systematic attempt was made by the government to investigate the colony's coal resources. In 1897, the Sydney Harbour Colliery opened at Balmain. By 1908, NSW dominated Australia's coal production and export, producing 9.1 million tons of coal, out of a national yield of 10.1 million tons, and exporting 2.55 million tons out of an Australian export total of 2.56 million tons in that year.[69] Historically, NSW coal has supplied generation of electricity in that State, underpinning industrial development including the steel industry, with export markets growing from the 1960s. New South Wales remained the dominant producer of coal until the 1990s, when it was surpassed by Queensland.[70]

59. Black coal was discovered in Queensland near Ipswich in 1825, with the first mine beginning production in 1846. Ipswich became an important industrial town in the second half of the nineteenth century. Increased mapping and investigations of coal resources took place after the discovery of coal at Blair Athol in 1846, although the years of the depression in the 1930s restricted exploration and development. Rapid growth in exploration and development occurred in Queensland from the 1960s, with production of coal surpassing NSW from the 1990s. Much of Queensland's coal has been exported.[71]

60. In Victoria, black coal was first discovered in 1826, but not mined until 1908 at Wonthaggi. Brown coal was discovered in 1857, with the Yallourn North open cut mine beginning production in 1889. The competition from brown coal in Victoria caused the Wonthaggi mine to close in 1968, and there is currently no black coal production in Victoria. Victoria's brown coal has been used for electricity generation.[72]

61. Black coal was discovered at the Irwin River in Western Australia in 1846. In 1883 the important Collie deposits were discovered and mined from 1898. This

67. *See* Part II.
68. Knight P and Hood M (eds), *Coal and the Commonwealth: The Greatness of an Australian Resource*, 46 (University of Queensland, October 2009).
69. New South Wales Department of Industry, *Exploration and production in NSW*, http://www.resourcesandenergy.nsw.gov.au/landholders-and-community/coal-seam-gas/the-facts/exploration-and-production#_history-of-mining__002c-oil-and-gas-production (accessed 12 Nov. 2016).
70. Knights and Hood, *supra* n. 68.
71. Australian Bureau of Statistics, *1301.0 –Year Book Australia 1982*, 'Black Coal in Australia' (no page numbers) (Commonwealth of Australia, 1982); Knights and Hood, *supra* n. 68.
72. Australian Bureau of Statistics, *ibid.*; Australian Government, Geoscience Australia, *Coal Resources* (accessed 12 Nov. 2016).

coal was used in the State's railways and for electricity generation. Black coal was discovered at Leigh Creek in South Australia in 1888. However, it was not until 1944 that mining began at the Telford open cut mine at Leigh Creek. This coal was once used by the railways and industry as well as electricity generation, but the entire production came to be consumed at SA's Port Augusta power station, until its closure. Coal was first discovered in Tasmania in 1703, but with hydroelectricity supplying most of the State's energy needs, coal exploration and mining has not played a major role in the State.[73]

62. While all petroleum resources are owned by the Crown, the situation is not as simple in regard to the ownership of coal resources, which were discovered well before oil and gas. Coal is a 'mineral' resource, not a hydrocarbon. From the first settlement in Australia in 1788 until the mid-nineteenth century, the British government exercised control over Australia's natural resources. When the colonial Governors granted title to land, ownership to minerals passed to the grantee according to the rules of the common law, which presumed resources to be part of the land.[74] The exception was ownership of precious metals, gold and silver, which remained vested in the Crown by virtue of the Royal Prerogative.[75] In 1855, control over Crown lands in Victoria and NSW was vested in those colonies through their Constitutions; with other States following.[76] This allowed the colonial parliaments to legislate for the Crown to retain ownership of minerals in future grants of land.[77]

63. The principle of private ownership of minerals has been virtually abolished by statute. This has been achieved through legislation requiring all new grants of freehold to reserve minerals to the Crown, which had been enacted in all the States by 1909.[78] However, in respect of land granted prior to this legislation, the landowner retained private ownership of the minerals (except gold and silver) unless they or their predecessor had transferred ownership to someone else. More recently, the States have appropriated ownership of minerals through their mining legislation. The Crown owns all minerals, including coal, in South Australia and Victoria.[79] In 1981, the ownership of all unmined coal in New South Wales was reserved to the Crown by the *Coal Acquisition Act 1981* (NSW), with the New South Wales Coal Compensation Board

73. *Ibid.*
74. The common law maxim '*cujus est solum, ejus est usque ad inferos*' applied: that 'to whomsoever the soil belongs, he owns also to the sky and to the depths'.
75. This applies in Australia as part of the common law: *Woolley v. A-G (Vic) (1877)* 2 App Cas 163 at 167-8.
76. *New South Wales Constitution Act 1855* (Imp), s. 2; *Victoria Constitution Act 1855* (Imp), s. 2; *Australian Waste Lands Act 1855* (Imp), s. 5; *UK Constitution Act 1867* (UK); *Western Australia Constitution Act 1890* (Imp), s. 3.
77. Hunt M, *Minerals and Petroleum Law*, *supra* n. 56, 8.
78. *Crown Lands Act 1884* (NSW), s. 7; *Crown Lands Act 1888* (SA), s. 9; *Crown Lands Act 1891* (Vic), s. 12; *Crown Lands Act 1898* (WA), s. 15; *Crown Lands Act 1905* (Tas), s. 27; *Mining on Private Land Act 1909* (Qld), ss 6, 21A; *Minerals (Acquisition) Ordinance 1953* (NT) and the *Northern Territory Self-Government Act* 1978 (Cth); *Leases Act 1918* (ACT) and the *Land (Planning and Environment) Act 1991* (ACT), ss 211, 218, 219.
79. *Mining Act 1971* (SA), s. 16; *Mineral Resources (Sustainable Development) Act 1990* (Vic), s. 9.

given responsibility for determining compensation payable for this compulsory acquisition.

64. There is still some private ownership of coal in Queensland. Subsection 8(2) of the *Mineral Resources Act 1989* (Qld) vests ownership of coal in the Crown (a) where the coal is on or below the surface of land that was acquired by the Crown as provided in the *Agricultural Lands Special Purchase Act 1901* and subsequently alienated in fee simple by the Crown; and (b) where the coal is on or below the surface of land (other than land referred to in paragraph (a)) except where that land was alienated in fee simple by the Crown before 1 March 1910, and the grant of that land did not contain a reservation to the Crown of the property in that coal. Thus, where ownership of coal was obtained as part of a grant of land prior to 1910, it remains in private ownership unless acquired by the Crown under the *Agricultural Lands Special Purchase Act 1901*. To determine the ownership of the coal in Queensland, the date of alienation of the land must be obtained from the initial deed of grant.

65. In Western Australia, paragraph 9(1)(b) of the *Mining Act 1978* (WA) provides that all minerals (other than precious metals) 'existing in their natural condition on or below the surface of any land that was not alienated in fee simple from the Crown before 1 January 1899 are the property of the Crown'. Thus, the Crown owns all coal resources not alienated from the Crown before 1 January 1989.

66. In the Australian States and the Northern Territory, coal is defined as a 'mineral' and managed within minerals legislation. The first Australian mining laws were enacted in 1851.[80] While most States and Territories have regulated coal mining through general mining legislation, for a period of time in the twentieth century, the two major mining States of NSW and Queensland enacted separate legislation governing coal mining. Both passed a raft of legislation covering various aspects of coal mining, including mines health and safety, mining authorisations, and other legislation. However, the separate legal regimes for the authorisation of exploration and production of coal were abolished in Queensland in 1974 and New South Wales in 1992.[81] As of 1 November 2016, the current State/Territory legislation governing the exploration and production of coal is: *Mining Act 1992* (NSW); *Mining Act* (no date) (NT); *Mineral Resources Act 1989* (Qld); *Mining Act 1971* (SA); *Mineral Resources (Sustainable Development) Act 1990* (Vic); *Mineral Resources Development Act 1995* (Tas); and the *Mining Act 1978* (WA).

---

80. The Governors of Victoria and NSW issued Proclamations asserting the Crown's right to gold in 1851. Early general mining legislation includes: in Victoria, the 1852 *An Act to restrain by summary Proceeding unauthorised Mining on Waste Lands of the Crown* (15 Vic. No. 35), and the *Mining Statute 1865*, being 'An Act to provide for the Management of and the Administration of Justice in relation to Mining Interests' (29 Vic. No. 291); in NSW, the *Mining Act 1874* (37 Vic. No. 13); in SA, the *Mining Act 1893* (No. 587 of 56 and 57 Vic. 1893); in Queensland, the *Mining Act of 1898* (62 Vic. No. 24); in WA, the *Mining Act 1904* (3 Edw. VII No. 30); in Tasmania, *The Gold Fields Regulation Act 1859* (23 Vic. No. 26) and *The Mining Act 1893* (57 Vic. No. 24).

81. In Queensland: *see* the *Mining for Coal and Mineral Oil Act of 1912* (3 Geo. V. No. 6), repealed by the *Coal Mining Act of 1925* (16 Geo. V No. 30), which was repealed by the *Mining Act and Another Amendment Act 1974* (Qld) and the *Coal Mining Safety and Health Act 1999* (Qld), s. 298. In New South Wales, the *Coal Mining Act 1973* (NSW) governed the granting of coal authorisations, until its repeal by the *Mining Act 1992* (NSW).

67. Because of the strategic importance of coal to energy and production, in the twentieth century, the coal industry in both NSW and Queensland were subject to government control through powers granted to government coal Boards. The Queensland Coal Board, established in 1948, was given extensive powers in relation to the production and distribution of coal in Queensland; while the Joint Coal Board (JCB), established by the New South Wales and Commonwealth governments in 1946, was given very wide powers over virtually every aspect of the NSW coal industry.[82] However, by the end of the twentieth century, the system of private exploration, production and distribution of coal had become well developed in both States, and the coal boards were abolished.

§3. Uranium Mining

68. The existence of uranium deposits in Australia has been known since the 1890s. Uranium was first mined in the 1930s at Radium Hill and Mount Painter in South Australia, mainly for medical uses. Systematic exploration began in 1944 at the request of the British and United States' governments. Discoveries at various sites led to the production of uranium from five mines from 1951–1974: Radium Hill in SA from 1954; Rum Jungle in the Northern Territory from 1954, and two sites in the South Alligator Valley in the NT; and Mary Kathleen in Queensland from 1958. Uranium from these mines was exported to satisfy contracts with the British and US, primarily for weapons testing, but was also exported for nuclear power. However, four of these mines had closed by 1964, except Rum Jungle which closed in 1971, because the contracts were fulfilled or the ore bodies exhausted.[83]

69. The global development of nuclear power led to a new wave of exploration in the 1960s. The Ranger deposits were discovered in the NT in 1969, and after the Ranger Uranium Environmental Inquiry from 1975–1977, the federal government granted approval for the Ranger open pit mine, which began operations in 1981. The Nabarlek mine opened in the NT in 1980, although it ceased production in the mid-1980s when the ore resource was depleted, and has been rehabilitated. Mary Kathleen was reopened in 1975, but closed in 1982 when the ore resource was depleted and has also been rehabilitated. The Olympic Dam underground mine (copper, gold and uranium) began operations in South Australia in 1988.[84]

70. Australia currently has three mines in operation, from which all production is exported. These are the Ranger mine; Olympic Dam; and the Four Mile mine in

82. *See Coal Industry (Control) Act of 1948* (Qld) (repealed); *Coal Industry Act 1946* (Cth) (repealed); *Coal Industry Act 1946* (NSW) (repealed). For the history of the Joint Coal Board, *see* Coal Services, *About Us*, http://www.coalservices.com.au/saboutus.aspx//History.aspx (accessed 17 Nov. 2016). The body 'Coal Services' in New South Wales maintains functions in relation to health and safety.

83. World Nuclear Association, *Australia's Uranium*, Appendix: A brief history of Australian uranium mining (updated November 2016) http://www.world-nuclear.org/information-library/country-profiles/countries-a-f/australia.aspx (accessed 23 Nov. 2016).

84. *Ibid.* and Geoscience Australia and the Bureau of Resources and Energy Economics, *Australian Energy Resource Assessment*, 178 (2nd ed, 2014).

South Australia, which began operations on 14 April 2014. Open pit mining at Ranger ceased in 2012 when the ore body was mined out, and although the operator explored the option of underground mining, with opposition from the traditional Aboriginal owners and the lease due to expire in 2021, the owner (Rio Tinto) has announced the mine will close down. Two other uranium mines have been developed recently in South Australia: the Beverley and Honeymoon mines. Beverley opened in 2001, but mining ceased there in 2013, and at Beverley North in 2014. The Honeymoon mine, which began production in 2011, has been in care and maintenance since 2013.[85]

71. Australia does not have a uniform and consistent law or policy regarding uranium mining. Uranium mining and nuclear power have had a long history of community opposition in Australia. There is no nuclear power in Australia, and although uranium mining occurs, it is still opposed by some parts of the community. At the federal level, the policy of the Liberal Party and Coalition from the 1970s has been to expedite the production and export of uranium. However, in 1977, with increasing anti-nuclear and anti-uranium protests across Australia, the ALP adopted a policy of declaring a moratorium on uranium mining and treatment, or the 'no new mines' policy. From 1984, the policy of the ALP was to oppose the development of any new uranium mines beyond existing operations (Ranger, Nabarlek, and from 1988, Olympic Dam), known as the 'three mine policy'. This policy was briefly abandoned and reintroduced at the 'no new mines' policy in the 1990s, and then abolished permanently in 2007. Any limits on uranium mining now come from the States.[86]

72. State law and policy varies between the States, and has varied between the political parties within the States. Currently, South Australia, the Northern Territory, Western Australia and Tasmania allow the exploration and mining of uranium. WA imposed a ban on uranium mining in 2002 when the WA Labor party was in government, which was lifted in 2008 when the WA Liberal Party came into office. Queensland and New South Wales permit exploration for uranium only. Uranium exploration and production were both prohibited in Queensland in the 1980s. The ban on production in Queensland was briefly lifted in 2012, but then reintroduced in 2014. Uranium exploration and production were also prohibited in New South Wales in the 1980s, but exploration has been permitted since 2012.[87] Victoria does not permit uranium exploration or mining.[88]

73. The regulatory framework governing uranium mining in Australia is complex. The States and the Northern Territory approve mining licences and regulate the day-to-day operations of uranium mines in their jurisdictions. In the Northern Territory, uranium exploration and production is governed under the *Mining Act* (NT). In South Australia, uranium exploration and production is governed under the *Mining Act 1971* (SA), although special legislation, the *Roxby Downs (Indenture Ratification) Act 1982* (SA) governs the Olympic Dam mine. In Western Australia, exploration and production is governed under the *Mining Act 1978* (WA), although certain projects under development are covered by specific legislation, such as the *Uranium (Yeelirrie) Agreement Act*

85. World Nuclear Association and Geoscience Australia/BREE, *ibid.*
86. World Nuclear Association, *ibid.*
87. *Uranium Mining and Nuclear Facilities Prohibition Act 1986* (NSW); *Mining Legislation Amendment (Uranium Exploration) Act 2012* (NSW).
88. *Nuclear Activities (Prohibitions) Act 1983* (Vic).

1978 (WA). In Tasmania, uranium mining is regulated under the *Mineral Resources Development Act 1995* (Tas), although there are no operating mines in Tasmania. Exploration for uranium in NSW and Queensland is governed under *Mining Act 1992* (NSW) and the *Mineral Resources Act 1989* (Qld). As with other resources such as coal and petroleum, a range of other legislation is also relevant, in particular State environmental laws, and native title law.

74. A number of federal Acts also apply to uranium mining. Australia is a party to the Treaty on the Non Proliferation of Nuclear Weapons, according to which Australian uranium may only be exported for peaceful purposes.[89] The *Atomic Energy Act 1953* (Cth) requires the Minister for Resources, Energy and Northern Australia to be notified upon discovery of uranium.[90] Under the *Nuclear Non-Proliferation (Safeguards) Act 1987* (Cth), approval from the Australian Safeguards and Non-Proliferation Office is required for the possession and transport of uranium. The export of refined uranium is prohibited under the Customs (Prohibited Exports) Regulations 1958 without a permission granted by the Minister for Resources, Energy and Northern Australia.[91]

75. Transportation of uranium and its by-products is regulated through the *Australian Radiation Protection and Nuclear Safety Act 1998* (Cth). State legislation regulates health and safety, for example, the *Radiation Protection and Control Act 1982* (SA). Commonwealth environmental assessment and approval under the *Environment Protection and Biodiversity Conservation Act 1999* (Cth) is required where an action has, will have or is likely to have, a significant impact on a 'matter of national environmental significance'. As 'Nuclear Actions' are a matter of national environmental significance, uranium mining will usually trigger the assessment and approval provisions of this Act.

§4. Regulation of Electricity and Gas Markets

76. Electrification began in Australia in the late nineteenth century, with the small-scale provision of electricity in capital cities by private or municipal electricity companies. However, in the twentieth century, these bodies were taken over by State utilities. For many decades until the 1990s, the large-scale supply of Australia's electricity was undertaken by large, vertically integrated, monopolistic electricity companies, owned by the State governments. The economic theory of economies of scale provided a rationale for vertical integration and the monopolistic supply of large-scale electricity; while state ownership stemmed from a belief in the role of government in 'promoting economic development, social welfare, employment, equity, justice and community interests', and the necessity of governments providing cheap, safe and

89. Treaty on the Non-Proliferation of Nuclear Weapons (1 Jul. 1968), London, United Kingdom, Moscow, Russia and Washington DC, US; 729 UNTS 161; 7 ILM 8809 (1968); 21 UST 483; [1973] ATS 3 (in force 5 Mar. 1970).
90. *Atomic Energy Act 1953* (Cth), s. 36.
91. Customs (Prohibited Exports) Regulations 1958 reg. 9, made under the *Customs Act 1901* (Cth).

efficient power given a lack of capital funding and expertise in infrastructure provision in the private sector.[92]

77. The state-owned electricity utilities were responsible for all functions of electricity supply, including generation, transmission and distribution networks, and retail/marketing activities. With electricity generation and consumption historically dominated by coal, electricity infrastructure in Australia is concentrated in areas where energy consumption is highest, and coal resources are located. The public utilities constructed large coal-fired generation plants near major population centres, and constructed electricity transmission and distribution lines to distribute power to the State. The electricity systems of the States and Territories were physically separate and were not interconnected. Each State governed and regulated its own electricity industry under State legislation.

78. The modern, large-scale supply of gas developed later than large coal-fired electricity generation and hydropower, although gas has a long history in some cities in Australia. Victoria, for example, began to use gas in the 1840s, when gas lights were introduced to Melbourne, and the 1940s and 1950s saw the widespread use of gas for illumination in cities such as Sydney and Melbourne. However, large-scale natural gas production and supply did not occur in Australia until the late 1960s. Gas is now used for direct applications such as residential heating and cooking and for electricity generation at gas-fired power stations.

79. The first large-scale supply of natural gas began in South Australia in 1969, following construction by the state of the Moomba-Adelaide pipeline after major onshore discoveries were made at the Cooper Basin in 1963 and 1966. In Queensland, gas was discovered in the Surat Basin in 1960, and was supplied by pipeline to Brisbane from 1969. In the Northern Territory, the fist gas discoveries were made in the 1960s, and gas was first piped to Alice Springs in 1983, with a link to Darwin completed in 1987. Large offshore oil and gas resources were discovered in Bass Strait in the 1960s, and gas from the Gippsland Basin became the major source of Victoria's gas supply. In Western Australia, massive gas/condensate discoveries off the northwestern coast of Western Australia were made in the 1970s, and are the main source of that State's gas supply.

80. Until the 1990s, while the production of gas has been undertaken by a small number of private petroleum/gas companies, the transmission and distribution of gas occurred through pipelines owned by the State, which had a monopoly over the transport of gas. The retail sector was also dominated by the large state-owned gas companies. In many States, vertically integrated state-owned companies controlled the transmission, distribution and retail sectors. Given the very large distances across Australia, three separate gas 'markets' developed, whereby gas fields were linked to consumers by pipelines; the Western gas market (in WA); the Northern gas market, in the Northern Territory; and the Eastern gas market, with pipelines linking SA, Queensland, NSW and Victoria. As with electricity, until the 1990s, the gas industry was largely governed

92. Abbott M, 'The Performance of an Electricity Utility: The Case of the State Electricity Commission of Victoria, 1925-93', 46(1) *Australian Economic History Review* 23, 25 (2006); Sharma D, 'The Multi-Dimensionality of Electricity Reform – An Australian Perspective', 31 *Energy Policy* 1093 (2003).

by State legislation. Most domestic gas trade has taken place, and continues to take place, through contracts between producers and major users, and producers and retailers.

81. Reform of both Australia's electricity and gas markets began in the 1990s, and took place as part of a much broader platform of microeconomic reform under national competition policy (*see* Part VII). The reform process included the following elements: restructuring of the publicly owned gas, electricity and other monopoly businesses; the introduction of competitive neutrality, so that state-owned enterprise do not have unfair advantages in business; facilitating access to nationally significant infrastructure, including pipelines and electricity infrastructure, in order to promote competition; and the regulation of state-owned enterprises which retain a market monopoly, such as transmission and distribution in electricity and gas supply.[93]

82. From the mid-1990s, the large, vertically integrated, state-owned electricity enterprises were disaggregated into generation, transmission, distribution and retail functions, and progressively corporatised and/or privatised. The degree of privatisation differs across the country. Private businesses now own most generation capacity in Victoria, NSW and Victoria, and the retail sector has been privatised. In contrast, government-owned corporations own control the majority of capacity in Queensland and Tasmania.[94] However, recent years have seen the emergence of 'gentailers' – the vertical integration of retailers and generators – both by private enterprise and among state-owned enterprises, to internally manage risk in the spot market.[95] Transmission and distribution networks are regulated as natural monopolies, and may be under state or private ownership.

83. COAG also replaced the separate state electricity markets with the NEM, governed by the *National Electricity Law* (*see* Part I, below). With construction of the national Grid through interconnectors, the NEM began operations in 1998. Key features were as follows: market rules were set out in the National Electricity Code, which was enforced by the National Electricity Code Administrator; a new network access regime was established under Part IIIA of the *Trade Practices Act 1974* (Cth) (now the *Competition and Consumer Act 2010* (Cth)), to be regulated by the Trade Practices Commission (now the ACCC); and the NEM Management Company was created to manage the wholesale market.

84. The reform of Australia's gas markets also began in the 1990s, and as with electricity, saw the restructuring of the vertically integrated gas utilities into separate transmission, distribution and retailing arms, and various degrees of private ownership of these functional businesses introduced across the States and Territories. New arrangements for access to gas pipelines were introduced through the *National Third Party Access Regime for Natural Gas Pipelines,* as part of which the *National Gas Code* set out the principles for access. In addition, legislative barriers to interstate and overseas trade were removed.[96]

---

93. Lyster R and Bradbrook A, *Energy Law and the Environment* 118–119 (Cambridge University Press, 2006).
94. Australian Energy Regulator, *State of the Energy Market 2015*, 39 (Commonwealth of Australia, 2015).
95. *Ibid.*
96. Lyster and Bradbrook, *supra* n. 93, 130–131.

85. Despite the reforms in the 1990s, it became evident significant challenges in the gas and electricity industries remained to be addressed. In June 2001, the then COAG Ministerial Council on Energy (MCE) was established, to 'provide effective policy leadership to meet the opportunities and challenges facing the energy sector in Australia', and to focus on a number of priority tasks, relating to the review of Australia's energy policy and energy market reform.[97] The MCE appointed the Hon. Warwick Parer to conduct the review of Australia's energy policy, and the 2002 Report, *Towards A Truly National and Efficient Energy Market* (the 'Parer Review') contained a number of recommendations regarding energy policy and electricity and gas market reform. Many of these were adopted by the MCE in its 2003 report to COAG, entitled *Reform of Energy Markets*.[98]

86. In June 2004, COAG signed the *Australian Energy Market Agreement*, which provided a comprehensive response to the Parer Review and MCE Report.[99] This formed the basis for changes to the regulatory framework for the NEM, including the establishment of two new regulatory bodies for the NEM and gas markets, the Australian Energy Market Commission (AEMC) and the Australian Energy Regulator (AER), and the introduction of new *National Electricity Rules* by the AEMC. In 2008, new principles and legislation for reform of the gas markets – the *National Gas Law* and *National Gas Rules* – were adopted.

87. The work programme of the MCE (now the COAG Energy Council) has been critical in the development and reform of Australia's electricity and gas markets. The electricity and gas reform agenda of the Energy Council is ongoing.

§5. Climate Change: Renewable Energy and Energy Conservation

I. General

88. 'Climate change' law has been, and continues to be, characterised by policy uncertainty, with diverging approaches to climate change law and policy between the two major political parties at the federal level, the ALP and Liberal Party/Coalition over the past twenty-five years. Australia ratified the *UNFCCC* in 1992, but Australia's national GHG emissions target, and the measures by which it should achieve the target, continue to be an area of policy difference between the ALP and Coalition, and between the States and the Commonwealth, and of political controversy. This has seen a raft of diverse programmes relating to renewable energy and energy conservation in transport, and electricity generation and use, adopted across the States, Territories and Commonwealth. The ongoing uncertainty and constant change in relation to energy and climate change is in contrast to the adoption of market reforms in relation to the security and efficiency of supply of electricity and gas, which have been pursued by both parties.

97. *Ibid.*, 124.
98. Ministerial Council on Energy, Report to the Council of Australian Governments, *Reform of Energy Markets* (11 Dec. 2003).
99. *Australian Energy Market Agreement* (30 Jun. 2004) (as amended 9 Dec. 2013).

89. The federal Liberal Party/Coalition has essentially supported the adoption of voluntary approaches to climate change. In 1997, the Howard Liberal government, which refused to ratify the Kyoto Protocol, adopted a 'no regrets' policy to reducing GHG emissions. The 'Safeguarding the Future Strategy' (1997) and the 'Measures for Building a Better Environment' tax measures of 1999 introduced a range of largely voluntary measures to address GHG emissions, such as incentives for solar power, remote power generation, and R&D in renewable energy technology, and the establishment of the Australian Greenhouse Office in 1998. However, the ability of these initiatives to achieve meaningful emissions reductions were criticised.[100] Although the possibility of an emissions trading scheme had been flagged in Australia since the 1980s, the Howard government consistently refused to introduce such a scheme.

90. Nonetheless, in 2001, the Howard government, through the COAG MCE, initiated an important mandatory scheme to reduce GHG emissions: the RET, the objective of which was to increase the uptake of renewable energy in electricity generation by 2% above 1998 levels. This is described in more detail in Part VI.

91. In the absence of strong federal leadership, from the 1990s the States and Territories adopted their own GHG Strategies, and a number of state-based programmes and initiatives from the 1990s, such as the New South Wales GHG Benchmarks Scheme, a voluntary baseline-and-credit scheme to decrease emissions in the electricity industry, which commenced in January 2003.[101] The States also conducted their own inquiry into the possibility of a state-legislated nationwide emissions trading scheme in the early 2000s.[102] This was conducted at the same time as a federal government Task Force inquiry into emissions trading, which recommended the establishment of an emissions trading scheme.[103] After this, both the Liberal Party, under the Prime Ministership of John Howard, and the ALP under the leadership of Kevin Rudd, promised as part of their 2007 election campaigns to implement a scheme.

92. With the ALP winning the federal election in 2007, a change in policy took place. The Labor government under Primate Minister Keven Rudd ratified the Kyoto Protocol, introduced emissions reporting legislation, and sought to introduce an emissions trading scheme, the Carbon Pollution Reduction Fund. Although this was defeated in the Senate, in 2011, the ALP under Prime Minister Julia Gillard introduced

100. Australian Senate, Report of the Environment, Communications, Information, Technology and the Arts References Committee, *The Heat is On: Australia's Greenhouse Future* (7 Nov. 2000). *See also* Hon. Warwick L. Smith, *Independent Review of the Australian Greenhouse Office* (June 2002, released 4 Feb. 2003); Australian National Audit Office, *Australian Greenhouse Office Audit Report* No. 34 (2003–2004).

101. *Electricity Supply Act 1995* (NSW), Pt. 8A. The Scheme imposed obligations on all NSW electricity retailers, known as Benchmark Participants, to reduce a portion of the greenhouse gas emissions attributable to their sales/consumption of electricity in NSW. Participants had to purchase and surrender NSW Greenhouse Abatement Certificates, created by accredited Abatement Certificate Providers. The scheme was abolished in 2012 when the Carbon Pricing Mechanism was introduced. The ACT introduced a Greenhouse Gas Benchmarks Scheme in 2004, but it too was abolished when the Carbon Pricing Mechanism commenced.

102. National Emissions Trading Taskforce, *Possible design for a national greenhouse gas emissions trading scheme: Final framework report on scheme design* (NETT, 2007).

103. Prime Ministerial Task Force on Emissions Trading, *Report of the Task Force on Emissions Trading* (Australian Government, 2007).

the 'Clean Energy Package'. This established a number of new mechanisms, including the establishment of the CPM, a federal emissions trading scheme; the Climate Change Authority, an independent statutory body which conducts research and reviews; the Australian Renewable Energy Agency, which brought together a range of disparate programmes for R&D into renewable energy technologies, and has USD 2 billion in funding; the Clean Energy Finance Corporation, created to leverage private sector funding for renewable technologies; and the Climate Commission, established to provide public information on the effects of and potential solutions to global warming. The Gillard government also created a national, Commonwealth framework for electrical product energy efficiency in 2012.

93. The Clean Energy Package was introduced over the opposition of the conservative Liberal Party, now led by Tony Abbott. Upon re-election in 2013, the Coalition government under the Prime Minister Tony Abbott abolished the CPM and the Climate Commission, and sought to abolish the CEFC, a plan which was abandoned upon strong opposition. Federal policy returned again to an emphasis on voluntarism, with the introduction of the voluntary ERF as the main scheme to reduce GHG emissions. The existence of the RET remained in doubt under Prime Minister Tony Abbott, and although it has been undermined to an extent by constant reviews and changes, it has proved crucial to the uptake of wind energy and solar energy in Australia. While the Liberal Party remain opposed to the introduction of emissions trading, the reintroduction of an emissions trading scheme remains part of the policy of the ALP. In the absence of a bipartisan approach at the federal level, and with the various States and Territories continuing to provide their own programmes for energy efficiency and renewable energy (examine in more detail in Part VI below), climate change law and policy in relation to energy remains divided and uncertain.

II. Background to Selected Major Renewable Energy Sources

A. Hydropower

94. In 2013, Australia had over 120 operating hydroelectric power stations, with a total generation of almost 20 GWh or 8% of total energy generated.[104] As water availability is a key constraint on the future growth of hydroelectricity generation in Australia, most major large-scale hydro energy opportunities have already been realised, although there may be some growth in use of 'mini-hydro' schemes in the future. Ninety percent of Australia's installed capacity is shared between Tasmania, New South Wales and Victoria, although Queensland has some hydroelectricity and mini-hydro project operates in South Australia.

95. Tasmania is the only that State that uses hydroelectricity as the major form of electricity generation, and is the major generator of hydropower in Australia. Hydroelectricity was first used in Tasmania in 1895. In 1914, the State Government set up the Hydro-Electric Department, which became the Hydro-Electric Commission in 1929, and then Hydro Tasmania. Hydro Tasmania is a government-owned utility,

104. Australian Renewable Energy Agency, *Hydropower*, http://arena.gov.au/about-renewable-energy/hydropower/ (accessed 23 Nov. 2016).

operating under the *Government Business Enterprises (GBE) Act* 1995 (Tas) and the *Hydro-Electric Corporation Act* 1995 (Tas). It operates the hydroelectricity system in Tasmania, supplying electricity to the NEM: first to Tasmania, then to the Australian mainland through the Basslink interconnector.

96. The Snowy Mountains Hydro-Electric Scheme is one of the largest and most complex hydroelectric schemes in the world. Construction started in 1949 and finished in 1974. The Snowy Hydro Company is jointly owned by the New South Wales (58%), Victorian (29%) and Federal (13%) governments.[105] It operates as a company under the Corporations Law, with an independent Board of Directors. The water operations of the Scheme are regulated by a licence issued under Part 5 of the *Snowy Hydro Corporation Act 1997* (NSW), which gives effect to the *Snowy Hydro Water Inquiry Outcomes Implementation Deed* (3 June 2002), agreed between the New South Wales, Victorian and Federal governments.

B. Wind and Solar Energy

97. Australia has some of the best wind resources in the world, particularly in the south, southwest and southeast of the country. Australia experienced a rapid rise in installed wind energy capacity and solar energy installations since 2001, when the RET was introduced. Falling costs of solar photovoltaic panels, combined with State policies and incentives for solar energy in the decade from 2000, in particular feed-in tariffs, stimulated the growth of installation of small-scale solar energy systems in Australia, although the country's vast solar resources still remain largely untapped. To date, solar water heating has been the primary type of solar energy used.

98. Many of the issues concerning the construction of wind energy are governed by the State and Territories' detailed planning and environment laws. Apart from Tasmania, where Hydro Tasmania is involved in wind energy, wind energy development usually takes place by private companies. Common issues of concern, including the impact of turbines on birds and bats, visual impact, and noise impacts, are addressed through the States' planning and environmental laws. These were amended from the early-mid 2000s, when the onshore wind energy started to develop rapidly in Australia, to include guidelines and requirements for wind energy facilities, for example, setback requirements from dwellings, and noise limits set by the relevant State's Environmental Protection Authority. Conditions may be placed on planning authorisations to address concerns about impacts of turbines.

99. One of the main issues in relation to the expansion of the solar energy industry in Australia has been consumer protection in relation to the quality of solar energy systems or their parts, and correct installation. Solar energy products must meet mandated Australian Standards; and to ensure that solar energy systems are installed correctly, mandatory licensing requirements for undertaking electrical/plumbing work are required. Australia has introduced a co-regulatory scheme, run by the Clean Energy Council (CEC), the peak industry association for renewable energy. The CEC deals with complaints involving a breach of the CEC's voluntary Accreditation Code of Conduct for installers, as well as the Australian Standards relating to solar PV systems.

105. Snowy Hydro, *Who We Are*, http://www.snowyhydro.com.au/our-business/who-we-are/ (accessed 23 Nov. 2016).

The accreditation and complaints scheme has been approved by the ACCC and given some legal effect through the *Renewable Energy (Electricity) Act 2000* (Cth).

C. Geothermal Energy

100. There is significant potential for geothermal energy in Australia, primarily from unconventional geothermal energy resources. These include Hot Rock (Enhanced Geothermal Systems/EGS) geothermal energy, and Hot Sedimentary Aquifer (HSA) geothermal energy. Currently, geothermal energy is a relatively new and emerging industry, with exploration being conducted in all States and the Northern Territory. Significant resources have been identified and there are several companies in advanced stages of exploration, with 400 geothermal tenements granted across Australia and around AUD 1.5 billion in work programmes underway.[106] However, as of 23 November 2016, there is no commercial production, with most projects at proof-of-concept or early demonstration stage. The regulation of geothermal exploration and development is undertaken by the States/Territories, either through petroleum legislation, minerals legislation, or stand-alone geothermal energy legislation.[107]

§6. Native Title

101. When the British colonised Australia, the settlers dispossessed the Aboriginal peoples of their traditional lands. Land rights for Aboriginal and Torres Strait Islander peoples refers to the 'ongoing struggle to gain legal and moral recognition of ownership of lands and waters they called home prior to colonisation of Australia in 1788'.[108] After the Federal Court in *Milirrpum v. Nabalco Pty Ltd* in 1971 held that the common law did not recognise Aboriginal land ownership or rights to land, the Commonwealth and some of the States passed specific land rights legislation to legally recognise the Aboriginal ownership of land.[109] Examples of land rights legislation are the *Aboriginal Land Rights (Northern Territory) Act 1976* (Cth), the *Anangu Pitjantjatjara Yankunytjatjara Land Rights Act 1981* (SA), and the *Maralinga Tjarutja Land Rights Act 1984* (SA). This legislation returned lands to the Aboriginal people, as inalienable freehold title. Among other things, consistently with the rights of any land held in fee simple, the legislation restricts rights of entry to land under the land rights legislation.

102. Despite this specific land rights legislation, Aboriginal ownership of their traditional lands was not recognised by the common law until 1992, in the seminal case *Mabo v. Commonwealth* (No. 2).[110] In this case, the High Court found the common

106. Australian Geothermal Energy Association, http://www.agea.org.au/ (accessed 23 Nov. 2016).
107. As of 1 Nov. 2016, the current legislation is: *Mining Act 1992* (NSW); *Geothermal Energy Act 2009* (NT); *Geothermal Energy Act 2010* (Qld); *Petroleum and Geothermal Energy Act 2000* (SA); the *Mineral Resources Development Act 1995* (Tas); *Geothermal Energy Resources Act 2005* (Vic); and the *Petroleum and Geothermal Energy Resources Act 1967* (WA).
108. Australian Institute of Aboriginal and Torres Strait Islander Studies, *Land Rights*, http://aiatsis.gov.au/explore/articles/land-rights (accessed 25 Nov. 2016).
109. *Milirrpum v. Nabalco Pty Ltd* (1971) 17 FLR 141.
110. *Mabo v. Commonwealth* (No. 2) (1992) 175 CLR 1.

law of Australia recognises that 'native title' may exist, where Aboriginal people have maintained an ongoing cultural connection with the land and/or waters, from the time preceding European settlement. The native title rights of a particular group will depend on the traditional laws and customs of those people. Native title rights include (but are not limited to) rights to hunt, fish, access land for camping, and rights to conduct traditional ceremonies. However, native title rights do not include the right to exploit minerals or petroleum. Native title may have been extinguished before *Mabo*, where State or federal action inconsistent with the continuation of native title rights occurred; and native title can be extinguished by federal or State actions, but since 1975, this requires compliance with the *Racial Discrimination Act 1975* (Cth).

103. After the decision in Mabo, the Commonwealth Parliament passed the *Native Title Act 1993* (Cth).[111] This is a large and complex Act, and is now the main source of law governing native title rights and interests. Consistently with the common law, it requires a traditional connection with the land to have been maintained for native title to exist. Native title has been recognised or claimed over much of Australia, and the National Native Title Tribunal is the determining body for native title claims. The legislation requires certain procedures to be followed to gain consent from native titleholders for 'future acts' on native title lands (such as granting mineral and petroleum tenements, or access to land for electricity infrastructure, including renewable energy installations) and puts in place procedures regarding resolution of access to native title lands for future acts where consent cannot be negotiated. These procedures are described further in Part IV below, in relation to coal.

104. The Native Title Act allows the States and Territories to develop their own procedures with respect to mineral and petroleum acts, although there are subject to government approval, to ensure they do not offer diminished protection. Procedures regarding native title are contained in the resources legislation of some States, notably Part 9B of the *Mining Act 1971* (SA) and Parts 12–19 of the *Mineral Resources Act 1989* (Qld).

111. The States also passed Native Title legislation.

Chapter 4. Role of Government Institutions in the Shaping and Administration of Energy Law and Policy

§1. Council of Australian Governments (COAG)

105. As a federation, with legislative responsibility for all aspects of energy and natural resources law and policy divided between one Commonwealth, six State and two Territory governments, there is considerable diversity between the States, and between the Commonwealth and States, in the approach to energy and natural resources law and policy. Achieving a nationally consistent approach to energy law and regulation across Australia faces considerable challenges.

106. In the 1990s, to avoid costly and divisive federal-state conflicts regarding jurisdiction over environmental and natural resources, the States and Commonwealth adopted a strategy of co-operative federalism. Not only has this approach allowed the Commonwealth and States to avoid constitutional legal challenges, but it has seen the development of national strategies, policies and legislation on a wide range of matters concerning the environment, energy and natural resources. The Commonwealth's role has been to co-ordinate the development of consistent national policies, often offering funding as an incentive for the implementation of programmes of reform.

107. The processes of consultation are undertaken through the use of ministerial forums. COAG, established in 1992, is the peak intergovernmental forum in Australia for the promotion of policy reforms which are of national significance or which need co-ordinated action by all Australian governments. Its members are the Prime Minister, State and Territory Premiers and Chief Ministers and the President of the Australian Local Government Association.

108. The use of COAG ministerial councils is an important aspect of co-operative federalism. Ministerial councils are comprised of State and federal government ministers, supported by standing committees and specialist subcommittees to provide information and advice. In June 2001, COAG established two standing councils of particular relevance to natural resources and energy law. The Ministerial Council on Mineral and Petroleum Resources (MCMPR) was established 'to ensure the safe, responsible, and competitive development of the nation's mineral and energy resources to optimise long-term economic, social and environmental benefits to the community'.[112] The MCE was established to 'provide effective policy leadership to meet the opportunities and challenges facing the energy sector in Australia', and to focus on a number of priority tasks, relating to the review of Australia's energy policy and energy market reform.[113]

109. Following a decision by COAG to reform the system of Ministerial Councils in June 2011, the MCCPR and the MCE were amalgamated and replaced by the COAG

112. http://govtree.io/departments/14d53f08-ministerial-council-on-mineral-and-petroleum-resources-mcmpr.

113. Bradbrook and Lyster, *supra* n. 93, 124.

Standing Council on Energy and Resources (SCER). The SCER was responsible for pursuing priority issues of national significance in the energy and resources sectors and progressing the key reform elements of the former MCCPR and the MCE. In December 2013, the SCER was abolished and the COAG Energy Council was formed, to streamline the COAG council system and refocus it on COAG's priorities. The COAG Energy Council is the current Ministerial forum for developing an integrated and coherent national energy policy, and State/Commonwealth co-operation in the pursuit of national energy reforms.[114] The Energy Council and its predecessors has played a crucial role in reform of Australia's electricity and gas market, and has also been responsible for other initiatives such as establishment and review of the RET.

110. Through the Energy Council and its predecessors, COAG has been involved in the development of a number of intergovernmental National Agreements, National Partnership Agreements, national Strategies, Principles and National Frameworks relating to resources and energy law and policy. These agreements signify the commitment of jurisdictions to implement decisions that have been reached or confirmed by COAG. In many cases, they are the precursor to the passage of either Commonwealth legislation or mirror Commonwealth/State/Territory legislation.[115] Examples of the types of agreements that have been reached or endorsed by COAG and/or its ministerial councils include the following:

- the *Australian Energy Market Agreement* (2004);
- the *National Strategy on Energy Efficiency 2009–2020 Memorandum of Understanding*, 30 April 2009; and the *National Partnership Agreement on Energy Efficiency*, 2 July 2009 (Incorporating the *National Strategy on Energy Efficiency*);
- the *Energy Market Reform: Revised National Principles for Feed-In Tariff Arrangements* (2013);
- the *Carbon Dioxide Capture and Geological Storage: Australian Regulatory Guiding Principles* (2005);
- the *National Partnership Agreement on CSG and Large Coal Mining Development* (2012) and the *Nationalised Harmonised Regulatory Framework on Natural Gas from Coal Seams* (2013);
- the *National Mine Safety Framework* (2002) which aims to achieve a nationally consistent legislative and occupational health and safety regime for the Australian mining industry; and
- the *Strategic Framework for Managing Abandoned Mines in the Minerals Industry* (2010), which provides high level guidance on issues to be addressed when managing abandoned mines.

111. The current Energy Council is guided by its Terms of Reference and its work covers the following broad themes: overarching responsibility and policy leadership for Australian gas and electricity markets; promotion of energy efficiency and energy productivity in Australia; Australian electricity, gas and petroleum product energy security; co-operation between Commonwealth, State and Territory governments;

114. http://www.scer.gov.au/.
115. Council of Australian Governments, *Agreements and Reporting*, http://www.coag.gov.au/agreements_and_reports (accessed 4 Nov. 2016).

and facilitating the economic and competitive development of Australia's mineral and energy resources.[116] The Energy Council undertakes reviews into a number of aspects of Australia's resources industry and energy markets, and its work programme is based around six strategic themes: generation, networks, retail, energy productivity, natural gas, and resources productivity and development.[117] The Energy Council also has oversight of, and works in collaboration with, the institutions established to operate and regulate the NEM and gas markets, including the AEMC, AEMO, and the AER.

§2. Commonwealth and State Departments

112. The Commonwealth and State government resources departments play a major role in the administration and development of energy policy and law. These departments administer resources legislation, assessing licences/authorisations for the exploration, production of petroleum, gas and coal under statutory schemes, and undertaking compliance/enforcement activities under the legislation. The departments also undertake legislative reviews, releasing discussion papers, receiving and collating public submissions on legislative reviews and amendments, and providing advice to the relevant Minister. Environmental departments administer a wide range of legislation designed to protect the environment, and undertake reviews and offer policy advice to the relevant Minister.

I. Commonwealth Government Departments

113. **Department of Industry, Innovation and Science.**[118] The Department of Industry, Innovation and Science (DIIS) incorporates the former Department of Resources, Energy and Tourism, which was created in 2007 and dissolved in 2013. The DIIS administers a wide range of industry, research, innovation, science and resources programmes; and administers legislation and offers policy advice, including in relation to a number of key areas relevant to the resources and energy sector. The 2015 White Energy Paper, which sets out the current Australian Government's energy policy framework, was released through the DIIS.[119]

114. A major responsibility of the DIIS is the administration of the legal framework governing petroleum exploration and development in Australia's offshore waters. The Department provides the Australian Government with policy advice in relation to upstream offshore petroleum; assists in the awarding of offshore exploration permits and other titles, through the National Offshore Petroleum Titles Administrator, a departmental branch with responsibility for titles administration and data management functions in relation to offshore petroleum activities in Commonwealth waters; and assists in the regulation of offshore petroleum industry activities. As most of Australia's

116. COAG Energy Council, *About Us*, http://www.scer.gov.au/about-us/our-role (accessed 12 Nov. 2016).
117. *Ibid.*
118. http://www.industry.gov.au/Pages/default.aspx (accessed 12 Nov. 2016).
119. http://ewp.industry.gov.au/ (accessed 12 Nov. 2016).

LNG production takes place in Commonwealth waters, the department also plays a major role in the development of Australia's LNG industry through its role in regulating offshore petroleum development.

115. The DIIS is also engaged in several key mining activities and initiatives. It has national policy responsibility for a number of Australia's mineral commodities, including coal, and is responsible for regular bilateral minerals and energy consultations with Australia's major trading partners and other stakeholders, including China, India, Japan, the Republic of Korea, Taiwan and the USA, and. The department also works with State and Territory governments who have primary responsibility for regulating the CSG industry, and it is involved with implementation of the National Mine Safety Framework. The Department has responsibility for legislation, policy and programme delivery for low-emissions fossil-fuel technologies initiatives, such as Carbon Capture and Storage (CCS).

116. The DIIS also administers programmes for, and offers policy advice on, innovation and R&D, including innovation and R&D in the clean energy industry.

117. **Department of the Environment and Energy.**[120] The Department of the Environment and Energy (DEE) was established on 19 July 2016, when responsibility for energy policy was transferred to the Department of the Environment. The environment department, under its various guises, has had primary responsibility for the administration of Commonwealth environment legislation and policy for many years.[121] The DEE offers policy advice on a range of matters relating to protection of the environment and heritage, and administers a range of Commonwealth Acts concerned with environmental protection.

118. One major environmental law administered by the Minister for Environment and Energy (and delegated to the DEE) is the EPBC Act, which first, sets out a statutory scheme for environment assessment and approval where activities are likely to have a significant impact on certain matters of national and international significance; and second, contains provisions relating to the conservation of biodiversity and heritage, including the establishment of the Commonwealth system of protected areas, and protected species legislation. Other environment legislation administered by the DEE includes: *Aboriginal and Torres Strait Islander Heritage Protection Act 1984* (Cth); *Australian Heritage Council Act 2003* (Cth); the various Great Barrier Reef Marine Park Acts (Cth); *Environment Protection (Sea Dumping) Act 1981* (Cth); *Fuel Quality Standards Act 2000* (Cth); *National Environment Protection Council Act 1994* (Cth); *National Environment Protection Measures (Implementation) Act* 1998 (Cth); and the various Commonwealth Ozone Protection and Synthetic Greenhouse Gas Acts.

119. The DEE also has responsibility for energy policy, and to a limited extent, the NEM. The DEE is responsible for: the development and co-ordination of domestic climate change policy; renewable energy policy, including the RET policy, regulation

120. https://www.environment.gov.au/ (accessed 12 Nov. 2016).

121. The department has constituted under various names, including the Department of the Environment (2013–2016); Department of Sustainability, Environment, Water, Population and Communities (2010–2012); Department of the Environment, Water, Heritage and the Arts (2007–2010); Department of the Environment and Heritage (2002–2007); Environment Australia (1998–2001); Department of the Environment (1997–1998); and Department of the Environment, Sport and Territories (1995–1997).

and co-ordination, and renewable energy technology development; energy efficiency; greenhouse emissions and energy consumption reporting; climate change adaptation strategy and co-ordination; the co-ordination of climate change science activities; and GHG abatement programmes. The Department's role in relation to the NEM is to support the Commonwealth Minister responsible for energy in his or her role as the chair of the COAG Energy Council, and to seek to achieve Australian Government policy objectives in COAG Energy Council decisions.

120. The energy legislation administered by the DEE includes the following: Australian Energy Market Act 2004 (Cth); Australian National Registry of Emissions Units Act 2011 (Cth); Australian Renewable Energy Agency Act 2011 (Cth); Building Energy Efficiency Disclosure Act 2010 (Cth); Carbon Credits (Carbon Farming Initiative) Act 2011 (Cth); Clean Energy Finance Corporation Act 2012 (Cth); Clean Energy Regulator Act 2011 (Cth); Climate Change Authority Act 2011 (Cth); Greenhouse and Energy Minimum Standards Act 2012 (Cth); National Greenhouse and Energy Reporting Act 2007 (Cth); Product Stewardship (Oil) Act 2000 (Cth); and the Renewable Energy (Electricity) Act 2000 (Cth).

121. **Department of Infrastructure and Regional Development.**[122] This department provides policy advice to the Minister for Transport and Infrastructure on issues relating to transport infrastructure, including energy-related policies such as national standards for vehicle emissions.

122. **Department of the Prime Minister and Cabinet.**[123] The Department of the Prime Minister and Cabinet (PM&C) provides policy advice to the Prime Minister and the Cabinet on a range of domestic and international affairs, including the implications of proposals for relations between the Australian government, and State and Territory governments. The PM&C advises the Prime Minister on international policy, including trade agreements and Australia's role in global and regional co-operation, and works to establish free trade agreements, to advance Australia's exports, including resource/energy exports.

123. **Australian Taxation Office.**[124] The Australian Taxation Office administers tax legislation, including income tax, GST, the petroleum rent resource tax, and the fuel tax and fuel tax rebate schemes.

II. State/Territory Government Departments

124. Various State/Territory government departments are responsible for the administration and review of State and Territory natural resources, energy (including renewable energy) and environmental law, and the provision of policy advice to government Ministers. Table 1 lists a number of the key government departments with responsibility in these fields.

122. https://infrastructure.gov.au/ (accessed 12 Nov. 2016).
123. http://www.dpmc.gov.au/ (accessed 12 Nov. 2016).
124. https://www.ato.gov.au/ (accessed 12 Nov. 2016).

Table 1: State/Territory Government Departments with Responsibility for Energy Law and Policy, 1 November 2016

State/Territory	*Government Department*
New South Wales	Department of Industry, Skills and Regional Development (Resources and Energy Division) Department of Planning and Environment
Northern Territory	Department of Mines and Energy Department of Environment and Natural Resources (Lands Resource Management) Department of Lands, Planning and the Environment
Queensland	Department of Natural Resources and Mines Department of Environment and Heritage Protection Department of Energy and Water Supply
South Australia	Department of State Development (Energy Resources Division and Minerals Resources Division) Department of Environment, Water and Natural Resources Department of Planning, Transport and Infrastructure Department of Premier and Cabinet (Office of the Chief Economist, Low Carbon Unit, Renewables SA)
Tasmania	Department of State Growth (Mineral Resources Tasmania) Primary Industries, Parks, Water and Environment
Victoria	Department of Economic Development, Jobs, Transport and Resources (Earth Resources Regulation) Department of Environment, Land, Water and Planning
Western Australia	Government Department of Mines and Petroleum Department of Environmental Regulation Department of Planning Department of Water

§3. Independent Statutory Authorities

125. A range of independent statutory bodies undertake regulatory, rule-making and policy functions in the field of natural resources and energy law. These bodies are constituted under statute, as an agent of the government, and their functions and powers are set out in the statute which creates them. Independent statutory authorities have an independent Board of Management, and are independent of direction or control by the State, or any Minister or officer of the State, in the performance of their functions. However, such Authorities are usually situated with the portfolio of a government Minister, and the relevant Minister may be empowered to give certain directions to the Authority, for example, in relation to general policies, such as financial administration.

Statutory authorities usually have reporting obligations under the statute which created them.

126. Some key independent Commonwealth statutory authorities with regulatory functions in relation to energy are: the AER (national electricity and gas market regulator); the AEMC (rule-making in national electricity and gas markets); the Clean Energy Regulator (CER) (RET, ERF and safeguard mechanism regulator); the National Offshore Petroleum Safety, Environment and Management Authority (offshore petroleum regulator in Commonwealth waters); and the ACCC (federal competition law regulator). Their roles are discussed in more detail in Parts I, II, III, V and VII below.

127. A number of independent statutory authorities also operate at the State/Territory level. These include the State electricity regulators such as the NSW Independent Pricing and Regulatory Tribunal (IPART), the Essential Services Commission of South Australia (ESCOSA), and the Economic Regulation Authority of Western Australia; and the various State Environment Protection Authorities.

§4. Other Independent Bodies

128. A range of other bodies have a role to play in the administration and/or shaping of natural resources and energy law. These may be constituted to undertake legislative reviews and research, offer advice, or play an advisory or consultative role in the assessment and approvals processes. Only a few examples are set out below.

129. First, the Senate may refer certain matters to the Senate Standing Committees for inquiry and report to Parliament. The Senate Standing Committees on Environment and Communications undertakes inquiries into matters concerning energy and the environment. The Environment and Communications Legislation Committee conducts inquiries into Bills referred to it by the Senate on matters relevant to energy or environment law, and oversees the performance of government departments. The Environment and Communications References Committee may conduct broader inquiries in relation to any other matters referred to it by the Senate. For example, in 2014 the Senate established a Select Committee on Wind Turbines to inquire into the application of regulatory governance and economic impact of wind turbines; while in 2016–2017 the Committee has conducted inquiries into the *Retirement of coal fired power stations*, and *Oil or gas production in the Great Australian Bight*.

130. Second, various research institutions and authorities have been established to conduct policy and legislative reviews, and offer advice to government. The Productivity Commission is a major institution providing independent research and advice to Government on economic, social and environmental issues.[125] The Commission conducts inquiries and research as requested by the Australian Government, often focussing on market barriers and inefficiencies, and suggesting legislative reforms. Recent reports and research papers in the area of energy and natural resources include: *Examining Barriers to More Efficient Gas Markets* (2015), the *Mineral and Energy Resource Exploration* Inquiry Report (2014); *Electricity Network Regulation* Inquiry Report (2013), and the *Review of Regulatory Burden on the Upstream Petroleum (Oil and Gas) Sector* (2009).

125. http://www.pc.gov.au/ (accessed 12 Nov. 2016).

131. The Climate Change Authority, established under the *Climate Change Authority Act 2011* (Cth) plays an important role in the governance of Australia's climate change policies and legislation. It undertakes independent research and reviews and makes recommendations on the Carbon Farming Initiative; the ERF and Safeguard Mechanism; the National Greenhouse and Energy Reporting System; and any other matters requested by the Minister responsible for climate change, or the Australian Parliament. It provides independent expert advice to the Government on climate change mitigation initiatives.[126]

132. Third, independent scientific committees conduct research and provide advice into a range of energy-related matters. For example, the Independent Expert Scientific Committee (IESC) on CSG and Large Coal Mining Development, established under the EPBC Act, provides scientific advice to regulators and decision-makers on the potential impacts of CSG and large coal mining developments on Australia's water resources. The Committee also provides advice to the Australian Government on research priorities and projects.[127] The Independent Scientific Committee on Wind Turbines is as an independent, multidisciplinary, expert group, which provides advice on a range of matters concerning the measurement and monitoring of noise from wind energy facilities.[128]

133. Fourth, independent Commissioners may be appointed to deal with complaints and assist in the administration of energy law or policy. For example, the National Wind Farm Commissioner is an independent role appointed by the Australian Government, reporting to the Minister for the Environment. The Commissioner's role is to receive and refer complaints from community residents about wind farms, and to promote best practices for industry and government in regard to the planning and operation of wind farms.[129]

134. Fifth, Expert Panels may be constituted to offer advice or assist in the administration of energy law or policy. An example of an Expert Panel in the area of energy and natural resources is the NSW Mining and Petroleum Gateway Panel, which is an independent body of scientific experts constituted under the NSW *State Environmental Planning Policy (Mining, Petroleum Production and Extractive Industries) 2007*. When a proposed coal mine is on strategic agricultural land, the coal mining project must be submitted to the Gateway Panel for independent, scientific assessment of the impact on strategic agricultural land and its associated water resources, before a development consent application is submitted.[130]

135. Finally, government bodies have been established to administer finance for clean and renewable energy projects. For example, the Clean Energy Finance Corporation (CEFC) was created under the *Clean Energy Finance Corporation Act 2012* (Cth) to leverage private sector funding for renewable energy and clean technology projects and identify and remove barriers to the financing of projects. The Australian Renewable Energy Agency (ARENA), was established as an independent statutory body under the *Australian Renewable Energy Agency Act 2011* (Cth) to provide financial

126. http://climatechangeauthority.gov.au/ (accessed 12 Nov. 2016).
127. http://www.iesc.environment.gov.au/ (accessed 12 Nov. 2016).
128. https://www.environment.gov.au/climate-change/renewable-energy (accessed 12 Nov. 2016).
129. https://www.nwfc.gov.au/ (accessed 12 Nov. 2016).
130. http://www.mpgp.nsw.gov.au/ (accessed 12 Nov. 2016).

assistance for: research into renewable energy technologies; the development, demonstration, commercialisation or deployment of renewable energy technologies; and the storage and sharing of information and knowledge about renewable energy technologies.

Chapter 5. Sources of Energy Law

§1. Treaties

136. Treaties do not automatically become part of Australian law upon ratification by the Executive, as Parliament must enact legislation to give effect to the terms of the convention. Australia is party to a number of treaties, the obligations under which affect the content of national laws relevant to energy and natural resources, as the terms have been incorporated into domestic law through legislation.

137. While there are too many treaties to discuss here, they include multilateral trade and investment treaties, such as the General Agreement on Tariffs and Trade/World Trade Organization, and bilateral treaties such as the China-Australia Free Trade Agreement, the Japan Australia Economic Partnership Agreement, and the Korea-Australia Free Trade Agreement. Australia has signed but not ratified the Energy Charter Treaty. Australia has also ratified a range of environmental treaties that have affected the content of energy and natural resources law in Australia, including the UNFCCC and Kyoto Protocol to the Convention, as well as the Paris Agreement.[131]

138. Other treaties of particular relevance to energy law include those with Timor-Leste, relating to development of petroleum and gas resources in the Timor Sea. The Timor Sea Treaty, Agreement Relating to the Unitisation of The Greater Sunrise and Troubadour Fields, and the Treaty on Certain Maritime Arrangements in the Timor Sea, have been negotiated to allow oil and gas development in the Timor Sea to take place, despite the unresolved dispute between Australian and Timor-Leste over maritime boundary delimitation in the Timor Sea.[132] The provisions of these treaties are incorporated into Australian law through the *Offshore Petroleum and Greenhouse Gas Storage Act 2006* (Cth).

131. *United Nations Framework Convention on Climate Change*, Adopted 14 Jun. 1992, UNCED Doc A/CONF.151/5/Rev.1, (Vol I), Annex I, 13 Jun. 1992, 31 *ILM* 874 (1992); *Kyoto Protocol to the United Nations Framework Convention on Climate Change*, Report of the Conference of the Parties at its Third Session, 1–11 Dec. 1997, U.N. Doc FCCC/CP/1997/7/Add.1, 18 Mar. 1998, Annex; *Paris Agreement*, United Nations Framework Convention on Climate Change, Report of the Conference of the Parties at its Twenty First Session, 30 Nov.–11 Dec. 2015, FCCC/CP/2015/L.9/Rev.1, 12 Dec. 2015, Annex.

132. *Timor Sea Treaty Between the Government of Australia and the Government of East Timor*, (Dili, 20 May 2002), [2003] ATS 13 (entered into force 2 Apr. 2003); *Treaty Between the Government of Australia and the Government of the Democratic Republic of Timor-Leste on Certain Maritime Arrangements in the Timor Sea*, (Sydney, 12 Jan. 2006), [2007] ATS 12 (entered into force 23 Feb. 2007); *Agreement Between the Government of Australia and the Government of the Democratic Republic of Timor-Leste Relating to the Unitisation of The Sunrise and Troubadour Fields* (Dili, 6 Mar. 2003) [2007] ATS 11 (entered into force 23 Jan. 2007).

§2. The Commonwealth Constitution

139. While not a source of energy law itself, the Commonwealth Constitution is of paramount importance to the structure of energy law in Australia, as it governs the division of legislative powers and responsibilities between the Commonwealth, and the States and Territories.

§3. Legislation and Subordinate Legislation

140. The primary source of energy law is Commonwealth and State legislation, that is, Acts of Parliament, and subordinate legislation, or Regulations, made under the relevant Act. Regulations, which are quicker and easier to amend than legislation, usually contain more detailed rules and requirements necessary for successful implementation of the primary legislation. These may include, for example, legal definitions; fees, forms and more detailed environmental and other information required for applications such as for coal, gas and petroleum tenements; and royalty rates. Other types of subordinate legislation include rules, directions, determinations, plans, policies and notices, which are issued by the relevant Minister under the relevant Act and Regulations.

141. Government codes may also be seen as a source of energy law. These have legal effect when legislation requires them to be observed. One example is the Queensland Land Access Code, given legislative force by the *Mining and Energy Resources (Common Provisions) Act 2014* (Qld). Other examples are the various Environmental Codes relevant to mining in New South Wales, namely the *Exploration Code of Practice: Environmental Management*; *Exploration Code of Practice: Produced Water Management, Storage and Transfer*; *Exploration Code of Practice: Rehabilitation*; and the *Exploration Code of Practice: Community Consultation*. These contain mandatory requirements for mineral exploration, and breaching any of these mandatory provisions will automatically be a breach of a condition of an exploration licence, making the tenement holder liable to compliance and enforcement under the relevant mining Act.

142. Industry codes may also become a type of 'hard law' through reference to them in legislation. For example, the Australian Clean Energy Council (CEC), the peak clean energy industry association, runs a Solar Accreditation Scheme to certify installers' competence in design and installation of stand-alone and grid-connected solar PV systems. Only installers accredited under this scheme or the Australian Business Council for Sustainable Energy accreditation scheme, *and* who are bound by *and* have complied with the CEC's Accreditation Code, are entitled to create small-scale technology certificates under the *Small-Scale Renewable Energy Scheme: Renewable Energy (Electricity) Regulations 2001*, made under the *Renewable Energy (Electricity) Act 2000* (Cth).[133]

---

133. *Small-Scale Renewable Energy Scheme: Renewable Energy (Electricity) Regulations 2001*, reg. 20AC.

§4. COMMON LAW

143. When Australia was settled by the British, the colonies inherited the rules of the common law in force in England at the time. This was the law developed by the courts in England from the tenth century onwards. The common law continues to exist and be developed in Australia, although rules of the common law may be abolished or changed by statute. The fields of energy and natural resources law are largely regulated by legislation, and not the common law. However, the rules of the common law are still important in legal areas that interact with energy and natural resources law, in particular contract law, tort law (such as the law of negligence) and property law.

§5. ROLE OF THE COURTS

144. Although legislation and subordinate legislation are the major courses of the rules of energy law, the courts also help to shape the structure and content of energy law in Australia. The decisions of the High Court in relation to issues of constitutional law have proved fundamental in shaping the division of legislative power between the Commonwealth and the States. The High Court also has judicial power to determine the constitutionality of Commonwealth legislation.

145. The courts also influence the application of energy law through statutory interpretation. In individual cases, courts affect the way in which the executive administers the law through applications for judicial review of government decisions, and merits review and appeals. The courts have also been given a key role to play in dispute resolution regarding access to private land for mineral and petroleum exploration. The courts have been given the power under resources legislation to resolve the contentious issue of access to land where mining companies and landowners cannot reach agreement; the courts may deny access to land, or allow access to land on conditions, including the payment of compensation.

Part I. Regulatory Framework Concerning Electricity

Chapter 1. Overview of Regulatory Framework

§1. Introduction

146. Australia's constitutional system provides enumerated powers to the Commonwealth and plenary powers to the States.[134] Due to this constitutional structure, electricity is regulated predominantly under State and Territory laws.

147. Significant change occurred in the regulation of the electricity sector from the mid-1990s as part of microeconomic reform resulting from the National Competition Policy Review which reported to the federal government in 1993.[135] The joint implementation of the National Competition Policy by all Australian jurisdictions occurred pursuant to inter-jurisdictional agreements and was monitored and assessed by a specifically constituted National Competition Council.[136] Each jurisdiction accepted specific obligations to review publicly owned monopolies and to ensure competitive neutrality between government business enterprises and the private sector.[137] These obligations resulted in the review and reorganisation of government business enterprises across many sectors.

148. Reform of the electricity sector resulted in the vertically integrated, government-owned monopolies responsible for electricity supply being disaggregated, reorganised as corporations and, in some jurisdictions, privatised. Disaggregation enabled competition to be introduced within the generation and retailing levels of the electricity sector and targeted regulation to be developed and implemented in respect of the network (distribution and transmission) elements of the sector.

149. The introduction of competition into the electricity sector required different systems of regulation to be introduced. Regulation independent of publicly owned

134. *Commonwealth of Australia Constitution Act* (UK), s. 51.
135. Hilmer F, Rayner M & Taperell G, *National Competition Policy Review* (Commonwealth of Australia, 1993).
136. *Competition Principles Agreement* (11 Apr. 1995), *Conduct Code Agreement* (11 Apr. 1995) and the *Agreement to Implement the National Competition Policy and Related Reforms* (11 Apr. 1995).
137. *Competition Principles Agreement* (11 Apr. 1995), cls 3, 4.

providers in the electricity market was required, along with regulation aimed specifically at the natural monopoly, consumer protection and co-ordination risks inherent in a competitive, disaggregated environment. These regulatory systems were implemented by each State and Territory in respect of the electricity industry operating within its jurisdiction.

150. While a common regulatory approach was taken in respect to some issues, the regulatory framework across Australia was significantly fragmented between the States and Territories. Each State/Territory jurisdiction established independent regulators for the electricity industry within its jurisdiction. Typically, separate regulators were established in respect of economic regulation and technical regulation. Independent economic regulators were generally responsible for licensing, economic regulation of network businesses, consumer protection, co-ordination issues between electricity market participants and network access. Where electricity prices continued to be regulated, this was also a function of the economic regulator.

151. Coincidentally with the disaggregation of the electricity sector, the NEM commenced on 13 December 1998. Initially the NEM was a wholesale electricity market servicing South Australia, Victoria, New South Wales, the ACT and Queensland via an interconnected national grid. In May 2005, Tasmania entered the NEM and became fully active with the commissioning of Basslink (a transmission interconnector between mainland Australia and Tasmania) on 29 April 2006. Western Australia and the Northern Territory are not NEM jurisdictions.

152. The NEM is currently regulated under the *National Electricity Law* and *National Electricity Rules*. This is an 'application of laws' scheme enacted by the South Australian Parliament through the *National Electricity (South Australia) Act 1996* (SA), and applied by each of the other NEM jurisdictions through an application Act passed by their respective Parliaments. Although the design of the regulatory framework promotes consistent application across the NEM jurisdictions, various derogations and differences in application laws result in some variation between jurisdictions. This was more apparent in the early history of the NEM, but still persists.

153. The emergence of new technologies and the maturing of a competitive electricity sector are challenging the existing regulatory frameworks. The growth of renewable energy generation and the availability of embedded generation are challenging assumptions on which the system of regulation is based. Options for significant reform of the regulatory system underlying the NEM are being investigated through the inter-jurisdictional COAG Energy Council.[138]

154. While the regulatory system that underpins the NEM is the most prominent system of electricity sector regulation in Australia, State and Territory '(jurisdictional') regulation remains relevant. For example, notwithstanding detailed regulation under the *National Electricity Rules*, generation of electricity remains subject to jurisdictional regulation.[139] Generators are subject to technical and safety regulation, generally by a

138. COAG Energy Council, Energy *Market Transformation Project Team – 2016 Forward Work Program,* http://www.coagenergycouncil.gov.au/council-priorities/energy-market-transformation (accessed 21 Nov. 2016).

139. *Electricity Act 1996* (SA); *Electricity Safety Act 1971* (ACT); *Electricity Supply Act 1995* (NSW); *Electricity Act 1994* (Qld); *Electricity Safety and Administration Act 1997* (Tas); *Electricity Industry Act 2000* (Vic); *Electricity Safety Act 1998* (Vic).

technical regulator.[140] Jurisdictional licensing may also be required in addition to NEM registration.[141] In addition, Western Australia and the Northern Territory each operate separate systems of electricity regulation.[142] Outlining the jurisdictional regulation of the electricity sector is beyond the scope of this Part. Consequently, the discussion below focuses on the NEM.

§2. National Electricity Market

I. Description of the NEM

155. The NEM can be described by reference to its objective, participating jurisdictions, regulators and operators, registered participants, the national grid and the spot market for electricity and market ancillary services.

A. National Electricity Objective

156. The National Electricity Objective ('NEO') states that the objective of the *National Electricity Law* is to promote efficient investment in, and efficient operations and use of, electricity services for the long-term interests of consumers of electricity with respect to:

(a) price, quality, safety, reliability and security of supply of electricity; and
(b) the reliability, safety and security of the national electricity system.[143]

157. The NEO's emphasis on efficiency and security of supply is reflected in the scope of regulation under the *National Electricity Rules*, which are concerned with:

- participation in the NEM;[144]
- the operation and settlement of the wholesale market for electricity and market for ancillary services;[145]
- system security;[146]
- connection to the national grid;[147]
- economic regulation of distribution and transmission networks;[148] and

140. For example, the Technical Regulator established under the *Electricity Act 1996* (SA), s. 7, with functions relevant to the electricity supply industry under s. 8. Specific technical requirements under the *Electricity (General) Regulations 2012* (SA) apply.
141. For example, licensing by the Essential Services Commission of South Australia under ss 15, 22 of the *Electricity Act 1996* (SA).
142. *Electricity Industry Act 2004* (WA); *Electricity Reform Act* (NT).
143. *National Electricity Law*, s. 7.
144. *National Electricity Rules* (version 85) (1 Nov. 2016), Ch. 2.
145. *Ibid.*, Chapter 3.
146. *Ibid.*, Chapter 4.
147. *Ibid.*, Chapter 5.
148. *Ibid.*, Chapters 6 and 6A.

– metering.[149]

158. Matters relevant to the electricity sector, but falling outside of the policy position encapsulated by the NEO, are subject to separate systems of regulation. Most notably, the promotion of an environmentally sustainable electricity sector is separately regulated under various pieces of Commonwealth legislation (*see* Part V below).

B. Participating Jurisdictions

159. The participating jurisdictions of the NEM are South Australia, Victoria, New South Wales, the ACT, Queensland and Tasmania.[150] South Australia acts as the lead legislator in respect of the application of laws scheme which enacts the *National Electricity Law*.[151] Each of the other participating jurisdictions enacts an application Act which applies the *National Electricity Law*, being the schedule to *National Electricity (South Australia) Act 1996* (SA), as a law of the respective jurisdiction.[152] There is some variation in the terms of the application Acts which is a cause of disparity in the regulation of the NEM between jurisdictions.

160. The Ministers responsible for the legislation enacting the *National Electricity Law* as a law of the respective jurisdiction ('Responsible Ministers') of each participating jurisdiction have specific functions and powers under the *National Electricity Law*, including: seeking reports, information or services from AEMO;[153] initiating jurisdictional derogations from the *National Electricity Rules*;[154] and intervening as of right in a merits review before the Australian Competition Tribunal with respect to reviewable regulatory decisions made by the AER.[155]

161. Oversight of the NEM is undertaken in respect of energy market policy by the COAG Energy Council. The participating jurisdictions continue to influence the development of the NEM and electricity market reform through their participation (along with Western Australian and the Northern Territory) in the COAG Energy Council. The work programme set by the COAG Energy Council includes consideration of policy and regulatory responses to key electricity market issues relating to new technology, innovation and market change.[156]

162. Some government ownership of electricity businesses is retained in all NEM jurisdictions other than South Australia and Victoria. These publicly owned businesses operate distinctly from their government shareholders under corporatised models with independent boards.

149. *Ibid.*, Chapter 7.
150. *National Electricity Law*, s. 5.
151. *National Electricity (South Australia) Act 1996* (SA).
152. *Electricity (National Scheme) Act 1997* (ACT); *National Electricity (New South Wales) Act 1997* (NSW); *Electricity – National Scheme (Queensland) Act 1997* (Qld); *Electricity – National Scheme (Tasmania) Act 1999* (Tas); *National Electricity (Victoria) Act 1997* (Vic).
153. *National Electricity Law*, s. 51.
154. Subsection 91(3).
155. Paragraph 71J(b).
156. COAG Energy Council, *supra* n. 138.

C. Regulators and Operators

163. Three institutions provide specifically for the regulation and operation of the NEM: AEMO; the AER; and the AEMC.

1. AEMO

164. AEMO (previously known as the National Electricity Market Management Company ('NEMMCO')) has been the operator of the NEM since the market commenced in 1998. AEMO is a company limited by guarantee constituted under the *Corporations Act 2001* (Cth). As originally constituted, NEMMCO was wholly owned by the Ministers for Energy of the NEM-participating jurisdictions.

165. NEMMCO was rebadged as 'AEMO' on 1 July 2009 as a reflection of a broadening of NEMMCO's role beyond the operation of the NEM. From this date, AEMO became responsible for a range of operation and planning functions in the electricity and gas markets which had previously been undertaken by six separate entities located in various jurisdictions.[157] The participating jurisdictions share in the membership of AEMO, which is comprised of government members (being the participating NEM jurisdictions) and industry members. Government members exercise 60% of the voting rights with the remaining 40% being exercisable by industry members.[158]

166. In respect of the NEM, AEMO has a range of statutory functions set out in the *National Electricity Law* and the *National Electricity Rules*.[159] AEMO's functions can be broadly classified as concerning: participant registration; market operation; power system security; and network planning.[160] Statutory power to undertake these functions is vested in AEMO by the *National Electricity Law*.[161] Additional functions are vested in AEMO by the application Acts of participating jurisdictions and AEMO's constitution.[162]

2. AER

167. The AER is constituted under the *Competition and Consumer Act 2010* (Cth).[163] Specific functions and powers are conferred on the AER with respect to the NEM regarding: monitoring and enforcing compliance with the *National Electricity Law* and *National Electricity Rules*; and undertaking economic regulatory functions

157. Australian Energy Market Operator, *AEMO in profile*, https://web.archive.org/web/20091014131437/http://www.aemo.com.au/corporate/0000-0002.pdf (accessed 21 Nov. 2016).
158. AEMO *Constitution*, cl. 6.11.
159. *National Electricity Law*, s. 49. AEMO also has statutory functions in respect of gas markets under the *National Gas Law and National Gas Rules* (*see* Part II) and the regulation of energy retailing under the *National Energy Retail Law and National Energy Retail Rules* (*see* Ch. 5, §3 below, and Part III).
160. *National Electricity Rules* (version 85) (1 Nov. 2016), Chs 2–5 respectively.
161. *National Electricity Law*, s. 49A.
162. Section 50.
163. *Competition and Consumer Act 2010* (Cth), Pt. IIIAA.

in respect of transmission and distribution networks.[164] To facilitate its compliance functions, the AER has a range of coercive statutory powers enabling investigation of suspected breaches of the *National Electricity Law* and *National Electricity Rules*.[165]

3. AEMC

168. The AEMC is established by South Australian legislation.[166] The AEMC has responsibility for rule-making in respect of energy markets and energy market development.[167] Specific AEMC functions in respect of the NEM are set out in the *National Electricity Law*.[168] The AEMC is responsible for:

- the amendment of the *National Electricity Rules* in accordance with the process set out in the *National Electricity Law* and the *National Electricity Rules*;[169]
- the establishment of the Reliability Panel vested with responsibility for monitoring, reviewing and reporting on the safety, security and reliability of the national electricity system;[170] and
- undertaking reviews requested by the COAG Energy Council.[171]

D. Registered Participants

169. Participation in the NEM is heavily regulated and limited only to those entities which register with AEMO (or are exempted from registering).[172] Categories of registered participants and criteria for registration are provided in Chapter 2 of the *National Electricity Rules*.[173] Different obligations under the *National Electricity Rules* are attached to different categories of registered participant.[174] The regulatory framework applying to generators, network service providers (transmission and distribution networks), market customers (retailers and other purchasers of electricity from the spot market), and metering providers, is described in Chapters 2–5 below.

---

164. *National Electricity Law*, s. 15.
165. Part 3.
166. *Australian Energy Market Commission Act 2004* (SA), s. 5.
167. Section 6.
168. The AEMC also has functions under the *National Gas Law* and *National Gas Rules*.
169. *National Electricity Law*, s. 34.
170. Section 38.
171. Section 41.
172. Section 11.
173. *National Electricity Rules* (version 85) (1 Nov. 2016), Ch. 2; Australian Energy Market Operator, *Participant categories in the National Electricity Market*, http://www.aemo.com.au/-/media/Files/PDF/Participant-Categories-in-the-National-Electricity-Market.ashx (accessed 21 Nov. 2016); Australian Energy Market Operator, *NEM Current registration and exemption list*, https://www.aemo.com.au/Electricity/National-Electricity-Market-NEM/Participant-information/Current-participants/Current-registration-and-exemption-lists (accessed 21 Nov. 2016).
174. *National Electricity Rules* (version 85) (1 Nov. 2016), cl. 2.1.2©.

II. Regulation of the NEM

A. Role of theNational Electricity LawNational Electricity Rules

170. As explained above, the *National Electricity Law* provides the regulatory framework for the NEM. The *National Electricity Rules* are subordinate legislation made under the *National Electricity Law*. The initial *National Electricity Rules* were made by the South Australian Minister for Energy in June 2005,[175] replacing the *National Electricity Code* which had operated since the commencement of the NEM.

B. Participation in the NEM

171. Participation in the NEM must be sanctioned either by registration or holding an exemption from registration. Generators connected to the national grid, market customers purchasing electricity from the spot market, network service providers and metering providers must either be registered or qualify for an exemption from registration.[176]

172. Chapter 2 of the *National Electricity Rules* sets out categories and subcategories of registered participants. An entity may participate in the NEM in multiple capacities provided that the entity is registered for each capacity.[177] Generators, network service providers, market customers and metering providers are discussed in Chapters 2–5 below. Other categories of registrant under the *National Electricity Rules* are:

- trader: registration enables participation in settlements residue auctions under clause 3.18 of the *National Electricity Rules*;[178]
- reallocator: registration enables participation in reallocation transactions under clause 3.15.11;[179]
- special participant: being either a system operator appointed by AEMO to carry out functions under Chapter 4 of the *National Electricity Rules* or a distribution system operator responsible for controlling or operating any portion of distribution system;[180]
- intending participant: being a person who intends undertaking an activity for which registration is required.[181]

173. Registration obligates the registered participant to comply with the *National Electricity Rules*.[182] Participant fees must be paid by the registered participant as

175. *South Australian Gazette*, 63 (30 Jun. 2005) (Hon Patrick Conlon).
176. *National Electricity Law*, ss 11–14.
177. *National Electricity Rules* (version 85) (1 Nov. 2016), cl. 2.8.1(b).
178. *National Electricity Rules* (version 85) (1 Nov. 2016), r. 2.5A; *see also* clause 3.6.5.
179. Rule 2.5B.
180. Rule 2.6.
181. Rule 2.7.
182. Clause 2.8.1(a1).

determined by AEMO.[183] A market participant must not participate in the NEM unless it satisfies the prudential requirements applying to its NEM activities.[184] These requirements are set out in Chapter 3 of the *National Electricity Rules*.[185] AEMO may only grant registration if it is satisfied that the applicant will meet prudential requirements, will comply with the *National Electricity Rules* (including the payment of fees) and complies with relevant requirements under jurisdictional legislation.[186] Transfer of registration is subject to the approval of AEMO.[187]

C. Market Operation

174. AEMO is required to operate and administer a spot market for the sale and purchase of electricity and market ancillary services.[188] The electricity traded through the NEM is the sent-out generation of market generators. AEMO utilises ancillary services to maintain the frequency and voltage in the NEM in order to operate the system in a safe, secure and reliable manner.[189] Different categories of ancillary services are provided to meet different circumstances in the NEM. Some of these are subject to arrangements with AEMO and others are provided as market ancillary services through the spot market.[190]

175. Market design principles set out in the *National Electricity Rules* are intended to guide AEMO's operation of the spot market. These principles refer to: minimisation of AEMO decision-making to maximise the commercial freedom of market participants; maximising transparency in the interests of achieving a very high degree of market efficiency; avoiding any special treatment of particular technologies; and providing equal access to the market for existing and prospective market participants.[191]

176. The operation of the spot market requires AEMO to establish and manage a system of central dispatch, including facilities for: the receipt of dispatch bids by market generators and dispatch offers by market customers; the issuing of dispatch instructions and the imposition of constraints on central dispatch; settlements; and compilation of statistics, forecasts and reports and dissemination of information to enable the market to operate efficiently.[192]

177. The central dispatch system operated by AEMO must balance power system supply and demand.[193] AEMO is also required to use best endeavours to maintain

---

183. Clause 2.11.
184. Clause 2.4.1.
185. Rule 3.3.
186. *National Electricity Law*, para. 49(1)(c); *National Electricity Rules* (version 85) (1 Nov. 2016), cl. 2.4.2.
187. *National Electricity Rules* (version 85) (1 Nov. 2016), cl. 2.9A.
188. *National Electricity Law*, paras 49(1)(a) and 49(1)(b); *National Electricity Rules* (version 85) (1 Nov. 2016); cls 3.2.2, 3.15.1.
189. Australian Energy Market Operator, *Guide to Ancillary Services in the National Electricity Market*, 4 (April 2015).
190. *Ibid.*, 4 and 8.
191. *National Electricity Rules* (version 85) (1 Nov. 2016), cl. 3.1.4.
192. Clause 3.2.2.
193. Clause 3.8.1(a).

power system security while maximising the value of the spot market.[194] The National Electricity Market Dispatch Engine ('NEMDE') is the electronic system utilised by AEMO to operate central dispatch.[195]

178. The integrity of the central dispatch process is regulated through limitations on rebidding, specific requirements regarding offers and bids not being misleading or deceptive and consequences for failing to comply with dispatch instructions.[196] If a scheduling error occurs, then compensation may be claimed by affected market participants from the participants' compensation fund. The entitlement to compensation and the quantum is subject to determination of a dispute resolution panel established under Chapter 8 of the *National Electricity Rules*.[197]

179. The price paid for electricity in respect of a trading interval is the time weighted average of the electricity dispatched during that trading interval.[198] The price paid for ancillary market services is the marginal cost of those services determined for each region.[199] Prices may fluctuate between the 'market floor' price of AUD 1,000 MWh to the 'market cap' of AUD 12,500.[200] Given the potential financial exposure to spot market prices, market participants hedge their risk through off market transactions. The transactions are not regulated under the *National Electricity Rules*, but a reallocation process is allowed for in the settlements system to facilitate these transactions.[201]

D. System Security, Safety and Reliability

180. AEMO is required to undertake the day-to-day operation of the power system.[202] There are a range of mechanisms available to AEMO to fulfil its obligation to use reasonable endeavours to maintain power system security. The *National Electricity Rules* provides that an escalating series of market interventions may be deployed by AEMO for this purpose.[203]

181. AEMO administers the projected assessment of system adequacy ('PASA') to provide market participants with information as to the short (six trading days) to medium term (two years) adequacy of the power system.[204] Information for the PASA is compiled weekly by AEMO on a rolling twenty-four month basis.[205] Other forecasts are required to be prepared by AEMO in respect of: patterns of network congestion;[206]

194. Clause 3.8.1(a).
195. Clause 3.8.21.
196. Clauses 3.8.22, 3.8.22A, 3.8.23.
197. Clause 3.5.24.
198. Clauses 3.9.1, 3.9.2.
199. Clause 3.9.2A.
200. Clauses 3.9.4, 3.9.6.
201. Clause 3.15.11. Hedging arrangements may be subject to the *Corporations Act 2001* (Cth), Ch. 7.
202. *National Electricity Rules* (version 85) (1 Nov. 2016), cl. 3.2.3(a).
203. Clauses 3.2.3(a) and (b).
204. Clauses 3.7.1, 3.72, 3.7.3.
205. Clause 3.7.1(c).
206. Rule 3.7A.

forecast of available capacity of intermittent generation (e.g., wind and solar);[207] impact of energy constraints;[208] and demand-side participation information.[209]

182. AEMO must also determine the constraints that apply to the power system resulting from network outages and constraints on power flows between or within regions.[210]

183. A Reliability Panel (an institution within the AEMC) is responsible for preparing reliability settings and standards guidelines.[211] AEMO is required to publish guidelines as to how AEMO will implement Reliability Panel guidelines.[212]

---

207. Rule 3.7B.
208. Rule 3.7C.
209. Rule 3.7D.
210. Clause 3.8.10.
211. Clause 3.9.3A. *See also* http://www.aemc.gov.au/About-Us/Panels-committees/Reliability-panel.aspx.
212. Clause 3.9.3D.

Chapter 2. Generation

§1. Overview

184. Coal remains the predominant fuel used for electricity generation in Australia. In 2014–2015, coal generation accounted for 54% of the registered generation capacity in the NEM, but produced 76% of the sent-out generation.[213] Gas is the other predominant fuel with gas-fired generating units accounting for 20% of the registered capacity in the NEM. In 2014–2015, however, gas produced 12% of the sent-out generation.[214] Coal and gas generating units with a nameplate rating of over 30 MW will be registered as scheduled generating units given their ability to respond to dispatch instructions issued by AEMO.[215]

185. Semi-scheduled generating units with a nameplate rating of over 30 MW (such as wind and solar generating units) participate in central dispatch differently due to the intermittent nature of their generation. AEMO is able to limit the sent-out generation from semi-scheduled generating units through the use of network constraints, but at other times the generating unit can supply up to its maximum capacity.[216] Wind generation accounted for 6.6% of capacity and generated 4.9% of output in 2014–2015 (an 8% growth over the previous financial year).[217]

186. Solar generation is predominantly small-scale generation from rooftop solar PV which is not traded in the NEM. Installed rooftop solar generation capacity in 2014–2015 equalled 8% of the generation capacity registered in the NEM (and is anticipated to grow).[218]

§2. Participation in the NEM

I. Registration

187. Unless an exemption applies, all generators attached to the national grid must be registered with AEMO.[219] AEMO may exempt generators from registration provided that this is not inconsistent with the NEO. AEMO issues guidelines for this

213. Australian Energy Regulator, *State of the Energy Market 2015*, 27 (updated February 2016).
214. *Ibid.*
215. Australian Energy Market Operator, *Participant categories in the National Electricity Market*, *supra* n. 173, 2.
216. *Ibid.*
217. Australian Energy Regulator, *supra* n. 213, 29.
218. *Ibid.*, 30.
219. *National Electricity Rules* (version 85) (1 Nov. 2016), cl. 2.2.1(a).

purpose.[220] Generating units with a nameplate rating of less than 5 MW have the benefit of a standing exemption in specific circumstances on the basis that the impact of these units on the NEM is marginal.[221] For generating units with a nameplate rating of greater than 5 MW, application for exemption needs to be made to AEMO. For generating units with a nameplate rating of 30 MW or above, an exemption will only be granted in exceptional circumstances.[222]

188. A person otherwise required to register as a generator may be exempted from registration through the registration of an intermediary. To register an intermediary, AEMO must be satisfied from a technical perspective that the intermediary can be treated for the purpose of the *National Electricity Rules* as the owner or operator of the relevant generating system.[223]

189. Registered generators fall within two categories: market generators and non-market generators. Except where an exemption applies, each generating unit attached to the national grid must be classified as either a market or non-market generating unit.[224] All generating units with a nameplate rating of over 30 MW (unless exempted from registration) will be classified as market generating units, unless the entire sent-out energy from the generating units is purchased by the 'Local Retailer' or a customer located at the same connection point on the national grid to the generating unit. If one of these requirements is satisfied, then the generating unit will be classified as a non-market generating unit.[225]

190. The entire sent-out generation of a market generating unit must be provided through the spot market operated under Chapter 2 of the *National Electricity Rules*. Market generators receive payments from the spot market through the settlements system administered by AEMO.[226]

191. Within the market and non-market classifications, generating units are designated as: scheduled generating units; non-scheduled generating units; or semi-scheduled generating units. These designations signify the ability of the generating unit to receive and comply with dispatch instructions issued by AEMO.[227] In addition, market generating units can be classified by AEMO as being ancillary services generating units.[228] This classification enables the generating units to provide ancillary services (*see* section II below).[229]

192. A 'small generator aggregator' category of registered participant has existed since 1 January 2013.[230] The purpose of introducing this new category of registrant was to facilitate the participation of the owners of small generating units in the NEM by enabling the aggregation of the output of the generating units by a small generation

220. Clause 2.2.1(c); Australian Energy Market Operator, 'Guideline on exemption from registration as a generator', *Guide to NEM generator classification and exemption* (August 2014), Part 3.
221. *Ibid.*, section 3.6.
222. *Ibid.*, ss 3.8 and 3.9.
223. *National Electricity Rules* (version 85) (1 Nov. 2016), cl. 2.9.3.
224. Clause 2.2.1(f).
225. Clauses 2.2.4 and 2.2.5.
226. Clause 2.2.4(c).
227. Clauses 2.2.2, 2.2.3, 2.2.7.
228. Clause 2.2.6.
229. Clause 2.2.6.
230. Clause 2.3A.

aggregator.[231] Prior to the introduction of small generator aggregation, the owners of small generating units needed to individually satisfy the same registration requirements as the owners of large generating units, and this acted as a disincentive to participating in the NEM.[232]

II. Participation in Central Dispatch

193. Market generators are required to participate in the central dispatch process by submitting dispatch offers.[233] The capacity of generating units to participate in central dispatch must be notified to AEMO in accordance with the *National Electricity Rules*.[234] Each market generator must dispatch its generating units in accordance with AEMO's dispatch instructions.[235] A failure to conform to a dispatch instruction is dealt with as a non-conformance under the *National Electricity Rules*.[236]

194. Dispatched electricity is purchased by market customers through the spot market. The financial settlement of these transactions is undertaken by AEMO. In a day there are 48 trading intervals of 30 minutes each with 6 dispatch intervals of 5 minutes. Market generators dispatched by AEMO send out generation according to the dispatch offers provided by the generators. Essentially, the spot price for each trading interval is determined by the highest offer dispatched during the trading interval.[237]

195. Market generators may apply to AEMO to classify a generating unit as a market ancillary services generating unit.[238] The *National Electricity Rules* describe ancillary services as '*services that are essential to the management of power system security, facilitate orderly trading in electricity and ensure that electricity supplies are of acceptable quality*'.[239] There are eight categories of market ancillary services.[240] Dispatch of market ancillary services is according to bid price.[241] As with the spot market for electricity, the marginal price for market ancillary services is set by the highest bid dispatched in a dispatch interval.[242] Payment for market ancillary services is administered by AEMO through the settlement system.[243]

231. Australian Energy Market Commission, *Rule Determination: National Electricity Amendment (Small Generation Aggregator Framework) Rule 2012* (29 Nov. 2012), ss 3.2, 3.3.
232. *Ibid.*, 9.
233. *National Electricity Rules* (version 85) (1 Nov. 2016), cl. 3.8.2.
234. Clause 3.8.4.
235. Clause 3.8.21.
236. Clause 3.8.23.
237. Rule 3.9.
238. Clause 2.2.6.
239. Clause 3.11.1(a).
240. Clause 3.11.2(a).
241. Clause 3.8.7A.
242. Clause 3.11.1(b).
243. Clause 3.15.6A.

196. The prices submitted for dispatch offers and ancillary service offers are firm and cannot be altered. There is a limited ability to alter other aspects of an offer, such as available capacity.[244]

244. Clauses 3.8.22(a), (b).

Chapter 3. Transmission

§1. Overview

197. Market generating units dispatch electricity into the national grid and market customers purchase electricity transported via the national grid.[245] The national grid is the sum of all connected distribution and transmission systems in the NEM-participating jurisdictions.[246] The five transmission networks operating in the NEM-participating jurisdictions are linked by six cross-border interconnectors.[247] The combined length of this transmission system is greater than 43,000 km.[248]

198. Ownership of distribution networks, transmission networks and interconnectors varies between the States and Territories.[249] Victoria has a unique structure for its transmission network with ownership being separated from responsibility for network planning and augmentation.[250] The revenue of owners and operators of transmission networks for network services is regulated by the AER.[251] Connection to the national grid and investment in additional network infrastructure is also regulated.[252]

§2. Participation in the NEM

I. Registration

199. A person must not own or operate a transmission network system connected to the national grid unless registered with AEMO or exempted by the AER.[253] The AER may only grant an exemption from registration where this is consistent with the NEO and after consultation with the jurisdictional authorities administering electricity legislation in the relevant jurisdiction.[254] A person otherwise required to register as a transmission network service provider ('TNSP') may be exempted from registration through the registration of an intermediary. To register an intermediary, AEMO must be satisfied from a technical perspective that the intermediary can be treated for the

245. Clauses 2.2.4(c), 2.3.4(c).
246. Chapter 10.
247. Australian Energy Regulator, *supra* n. 213, 66.
248. *Ibid.*, Table 2.1, 68.
249. *Ibid.*, Tables 2.1 and 2.2.
250. *Ibid.*, Table 2.1, 66.
251. *National Electricity Rules* (version 85) (1 Nov. 2016), Ch. 6A.
252. Chapter 5.
253. Clauses 2.5.1(a), 2.5.1(d), 5.2.3(a); Australian Energy Regulator, *Network Service Provider Registration Exemption Guideline* (27 Aug. 2013).
254. *National Electricity Rules* (version 85) (1 Nov. 2016), cls 2.5.1(d), (f).

purpose of the *National Electricity Rules* as the owner or operator of the relevant transmission system.[255]

II. Economic Regulation

200. Two types of service are subject to regulation by the AER under Chapter 6A of the *National Electricity Law*: prescribed transmission services and negotiated transmission services.[256] TNSPs are obliged to provide prescribed transmission services and negotiated transmission services on terms of access consistent with the requirements of the *National Electricity Rules* to an existing or intending registered participant in the NEM or a person eligible to become a registered participant.[257]

A. Prescribed Transmission Services

201. The maximum annual revenues of TNSPs for prescribed transmission services are regulated by the AER making transmission determinations in accordance with Chapter 6A of the *National Electricity Rules*.[258] The revenues are determined for a regulatory control period of not less than five years.[259] In performing an economic regulatory function, the AER must apply the NEO and the revenue pricing principles set out in the *National Electricity Law*.[260]

202. Each regulatory reset is undertaken by the AER utilising a defined regulatory process. This commences approximately two years prior to the expiry of the existing determination, upon the AER publishing a framework and approach paper with respect to the regulatory reset.[261] The TNSP is required to submit a revenue proposal and proposed pricing methodology to the AER.[262] Provision is made in the *National Electricity Rules* for preliminary consideration of this information by the AER and resubmission if the AER considers there are non-compliances which need to be addressed by the TNSP.[263]

203. The *National Electricity Rules* also provide for public consultation in respect of the information provided by the TNSP and the proposed approach of the AER.[264] Further consultation will occur following the release of a preliminary determination of the AER.[265] A final determination is made taking into account any

255. Clause 2.9.3.
256. Clauses 6A.1.4(a), 6A.2.1.
257. Clause 6A.1.3.
258. Part C, Ch. 6A.
259. Clause 6A.4.2(c).
260. *National Electricity Law*, ss 7, 7A, 16.
261. *National Electricity Rules* (version 85) (1 Nov. 2016), cl. 6A.10.1A; Australian Energy Regulator, *supra* n. 213, Table 2.3, 72; Australian Energy Regulator, *AER forward calendar: Regulatory determinations* (June 2016).
262. *National Electricity Rules* (version 85) (1 Nov. 2016), cl. 6A.10.1; *see* r. 6A.25 in respect of the regulation of pricing methodologies.
263. Clauses 6A.11.1, 6A.11.2.
264. Clause 6A.11.3.
265. Rule 6A.12.

submissions received in relation to the preliminary determination.[266] The contents of a transmission determination are prescribed by the *National Electricity Rules*.[267] The AER is required to provide reasons and rationale justifying its decision.[268]

204. From data submitted by the TNSP, the AER applies a building block methodology to determine the revenue required to meet anticipated capital and operating costs for the next regulatory control period.[269] A post tax revenue model for this purpose has been published by the AER in accordance with the *National Electricity Rules*.[270] Key components of the building block methodology are:

- return on capital: the value of the regulatory asset base is subject to a roll forward model for its valuation from one regulatory control period to the next.[271] An allowed rate of return is determined by the AER;[272]
- depreciation of the regulated asset base must be calculated on the value of the assets as at the beginning of each regulatory year;[273]
- cost of corporate income tax is estimated using a formula provided in the *National Electricity Rules*;[274]
- efficiency benefit sharing scheme for the attribution of efficiency gains or losses occasioned by operating expenditure in a regulatory period being more or less than forecast expenditure;[275]
- capital expenditure efficiency scheme to provide an incentive for efficient capital investment by a TNSP in a regulatory control period;[276]
- forecast operating expenditure;[277] and
- forecast capital expenditure.[278]

205. Specific cost pass through events are prescribed either in the *National Electricity Rules* or by determination of the AER.[279] Costs arising in these circumstances may be able to be passed through in transmission service tariffs.[280] Savings arising from these circumstances may be required to be passed through in tariffs.[281]

266. Rule 6A.13.
267. Clause 6.14.1.
268. Clause 6A.14.2.
269. Clause 6A.5.4.
270. Australian Energy Regulator, *Electricity transmission network service providers, Post-tax revenue model handbook* (29 Jan. 2015); *National Electricity Rules* (version 85) (1 Nov. 2016), cl. 6A.5.1.
271. *National Electricity Rules* (version 85) (1 Nov. 2016), cl. 6A.6.1, Sch. 6A.2.
272. Clause 6A.6.2.
273. Clause 6A.6.3.
274. Clause 6A.6.4.
275. Clause 6A.6.5.
276. Clause 6A.6.5A.
277. Clause 6A.6.6.
278. Clause 6A.6.7.
279. Clauses 6A.6.9, 6A.7.3.
280. Clause 6A.7.3(a).
281. Clause 6A.7.3(b).

206. The AER may reopen a transmission determination on application of a TNSP in limited circumstances.[282] The AER may also revoke or amend a transmission determination if the AER considers that the determination is affected by a material error or deficiency of a type prescribed.[283] A TNSP can seek a review of a transmission determination by the Australian Competition Tribunal.[284]

B. Negotiated Transmission Services

207. Part D of Chapter 6A of the *National Electricity Rules* sets out the regulatory framework for access to negotiated transmission services. Various principles applying to these prices are set out in the *National Electricity Rules*, including that the price for a negotiated transmission service should be based on the cost incurred by the TNSP in providing the service.[285] The costs of the TNSP must be determined in accordance with the principles and policies set out in the 'Cost Allocation Methodology' for the TNSP approved by the AER.[286]

208. The AER determines negotiated transmission service criteria to apply to the terms and conditions of access to negotiated transmission services, including price.[287] A 'Negotiating Framework' (also approved by the AER) applies to negotiations between a TNSP and service applicant in respect of negotiated transmission services.[288] The Negotiating Framework includes obligations on both parties to negotiate in good faith. Exchange of information between the parties to facilitate negotiations is also required by the Negotiation Framework.[289] If prices cannot be negotiated, then the matter can be referred to the AER as a transmission services access dispute under the *National Electricity Rules*.[290] A commercial arbitrator will be appointed to resolve the dispute.[291]

III. Network Connection

209. Access to the national grid is regulated under Chapter 5 of the *National Electricity Rules*. The principles applying to connection include the opportunity for all registered participants to connect to networks on reasonable terms and conditions.[292]

282. Clause 6A.7.1.
283. Rule 6A.15.
284. *National Electricity Law*, s. 71B.
285. *National Electricity Rules* (version 85) (1 Nov. 2016), cl. 6A.9.1(1).
286. Clause 6A.9.1(1); *see also* Rule 6A.19.
287. Clauses 6A.9.2(a), 6A.9.4; *see* , for example, Australian Energy Regulator, *ElectraNet transmission determination 2013–14 to 2017–18* (April 2013), 25.
288. *National Electricity Rules* (version 85) (1 Nov. 2016), cls 6A.9.2(a), 6A.9.3.
289. *See* , for example, *ElectraNet Negotiating Framework for the provision of Negotiated Transmission Services 1 Jul. 2013–30 Jun. 2018*, cls 4–7.
290. *National Electricity Rules* (version 85) (1 Nov. 2016), r. 6A.30.
291. Clause 6A.30.2.
292. Clause 5.1.3.

210. The connection of new or altered facilities or equipment to the transmission network must not occur without an application being made to the TNSP.[293] TNSPs are obliged to review and process connection applications in accordance with the *National Electricity Rules*.[294] The process by which a connection to the transmission network is established or modified is prescribed.[295]

211. A connection enquiry from a person seeking to connect to a transmission network must be considered and responded to by the relevant TNSP.[296] In considering a connection enquiry, the TNSP must liaise with any other network service provider that the TNSP reasonably considers would be affected by the connection.[297] The TNSP may seek additional information from applicants in support of the connection enquiry.[298] Specific information must be provided in response to a connection enquiry.[299] This information can assist a person submitting a connection application to the TNSP.[300]

212. Connection may be on the basis of 'automatic access standards' predetermined by the TNSP or, where these do not apply, negotiated access standards determined by agreement between the TNSP and the connection applicant.[301] Where the automatic access standard or agreed negotiated access standards will apply, then the TNSP must proceed to make an offer to connect.[302] The offer to connect may be negotiated and accepted by the connection applicant.[303] Specific provisions apply in respect of the connection of a generator,[304] network service provider,[305] or customer.[306]

213. To maintain the security of the network, all registered participants are obliged to operate equipment in compliance with the *National Electricity Law*, *National Electricity Rules* and good electricity industry practice.[307] The technical standards in the *National Electricity Rules* and requirements under connection agreements also influence the design and planning of facilities connected to the TNSP.[308] TNSPs must also comply with the technical standards set out in the *National Electricity Rules*.[309]

214. A party to a connection agreement has rights of inspection and testing under the *National Electricity Rules* to determine whether counterparties are complying

---

293. Clauses 5.2.4(b), 5.2.5(b).
294. Clause 5.2.3(d).
295. Rule 5.3.
296. Clauses 5.3.1, 5.3.2.
297. Clause 5.3.3(a).
298. Clause 5.3.2(b) and Sch. 5.5.
299. Clause 5.3.3(b).
300. Clause 5.3.4.
301. Clauses 5.3.3(b1), 5.3.4(e), 5.3.4A; *see also* Sch. 5.2.
302. Clause 5.3.5(a).
303. Clause 5.3.7.
304. Clause 5.3.9; *see also*, Sch. 5.2.
305. Schedule 5.3(a).
306. Schedule 5.3.
307. Clause 5.2.1.
308. Clauses 5.2.4, 5.2.5.
309. Clause 5.2.3(b) and Schs 5.1a, 5.1.

with the technical requirements under the agreement.[310] Commissioning of equipment connected to a transmission network is also regulated.[311]

IV. Network Planning and Investment

215. Network planning is a responsibility of the TNSP.[312] Each year the TNSP will obtain information from registered participants connected to the TNSP regarding generation and load forecasts to enable the TNSP to plan for operation and expansion of the transmission network.[313] Each TNSP must publish an annual transmission planning report.[314] The minimum planning period to be reflected in the report is ten years.[315] TNSPs are obliged to engage in joint network planning with distribution network service providers (DNSP) connected to the transmission network.[316]

216. AEMO has responsibility for national transmission planning.[317] This role includes providing advice and assessment of whether transmission network augmentation will have a material inter-network impact.[318]

217. Network investment is subject to regulation. A 'regulatory investment test' must be undertaken in respect of each proposed network investment which is to be funded through prescribed transmission service tariffs.[319] For transmission network investment this is referred to as the 'RIT-T'. The purpose of the RIT-T is to ensure that investment is efficient because consumers will pay for the costs of the investment through regulated revenues.[320] Where the cost of the network augmentation will not be met through consumer tariffs (e.g., the augmentation is funded by a generator), the RIT-T does not apply.[321]

218. In undertaking the RIT-T, the proponent of the network investment must consider all credible options for achieving the outcome sought through the proposed network investment. The preferred option will be the credible option that maximises the present value of net economic benefit to all those who produce, consume and transport electricity in the NEM.[322] The AER determines the matters to be covered in an RIT-T.[323]

---

310. Rule 5.7.
311. Rule 5.8.
312. Clauses 5.11.2, 5.12.1.
313. Clause 5.11.1 and Sch. 5.7.
314. Clause 5.12.2.
315. Clause 5.12.1(c).
316. Clause 5.14.1.
317. Rule 5.20.
318. Rule 5.21.
319. Rule 5.15; Australian Energy Regulator, *supra* n. 213, 74.
320. COAG Energy Council, *Review of the regulatory investment test for transmission: Consultation paper* (30 Sept. 2016), 7.
321. *National Electricity Rules* (version 85) (1 Nov. 2016), r. 5.18.
322. Clause 5.16.1(b).
323. Clause 5.16.1(a); Australian Energy Regulator, *Regulatory investment test for transmission* (June 2010).

219. The analysis undertaken is a cost-benefit analysis of the future with the credible option implemented compared with no option being implemented.[324] Other mandatory requirements of the RIT-T are set out in the *National Electricity Rules*, including compliance with guidelines issued by the AER and consultation.[325] There are limited exemptions from applying the RIT-T based upon urgent and unforeseen responses, project value, project purpose (i.e., being for maintenance or replacement, rather than augmentation) or where cost recovery will occur other than through prescribed transmission services.[326]

220. Detailed consultation requirements apply to an RIT-T.[327] Conclusions reached in a project assessment report for an RIT-T are also susceptible to challenge with the AER responsible for determining the dispute.[328] On 19 August 2016, the COAG Energy Council set terms of reference for a review of the requirements of the RIT-T.[329]

324. Clause 5.16.1(c)(1).
325. Clauses 5.16.1, 5.16.2.
326. Clauses 5.16.3(a), 5.16.4.
327. Clause 5.16.4.
328. Clause 5.16.5.
329. COAG Energy Council, *RIT-T review – terms of reference* (19 Aug. 2016).

Chapter 4. Distribution

§1. Overview

221. The distribution networks which are components of the national grid are in various public and private sector ownership.[330] The combined length of these distribution networks is 730,642 kms servicing 9,608,292 customers.[331] The revenue of owners and operators of distribution networks for network services is regulated by the AER.[332] Connection to the national grid and investment in additional network infrastructure is also regulated.[333]

§2. Participation in the NEM

I. Registration

222. As with the transmission network system, a person must not own or operate a distribution network system connected to the national grid unless registered with AEMO or exempted by the AER.[334] The AER may only grant an exemption from registration where this is consistent with the NEO and after consultation with the jurisdictional authorities administering electricity legislation in the relevant jurisdiction.[335] A person otherwise required to register as a DNSP may be exempted from registration through the registration of an intermediary. To register an intermediary, AEMO must be satisfied from a technical perspective that the intermediary can be treated for the purpose of the *National Electricity Rules* as the owner or operator of the relevant distribution system.[336]

II. Economic Regulation

223. Two types of services are subject to regulation by the AER under Chapter 6A of the *National Electricity Law*: direct control services and negotiated distribution services.[337] DNSPs are obliged to provide direct control services and negotiated

330. Australian Energy Regulator, *supra* n. 213, Table 2.2, 69.
331. *Ibid.*
332. *National Electricity Rules* (version 85) (1 Nov. 2016), Ch. 6.
333. Chapter 5.
334. Clauses 2.5.1(a), (d); AER, *Network Service Provider Registration Exemption Guideline* (27 Aug. 2013).
335. Clauses 2.5.1(d), 2.5.1(f).
336. Clause 2.9.3.
337. Clause 6.2.1(a).

distribution services on terms of access consistent with the requirements of the *National Electricity Rules* to a person applying for the service.[338]

A. Direct Control Services

224. Direct control services may be split into two subclasses: standard control services and ancillary control services.[339] In determining the classification of a distribution service, the AER is required to consider a number of factors, including the potential for the development of competition in the market for the provision of the service.[340]

225. The AER is obliged to make a distribution determination for each distributor for each regulatory control period (of not less than five years).[341] The distribution determination will set out price or revenue controls (or a combination of these) in respect of direct control services.[342] Various control mechanisms for revenue and price are available to the AER. Specific considerations apply in relation to revenue and price setting for each of standard control services and ancillary control services.[343] Various guidelines are published by the AER in respect of the economic regulation of DNSPs.[344] Again, the AER must apply the NEO and the revenue pricing principles set out in the *National Electricity Law*.[345]

226. The regulation of direct control services is, in effect, largely identical to that described above in Chapter 3 for prescribed transmission services, except that the regulation applies to DNSPs and not TNSPs. Thus, the details regarding regulatory resets;[346] public consultation;[347] the AER's building block methodology;[348] specific cost pass through events;[349] the powers of the AER to reopen, revoke or amend a distribution determination;[350] and the right of a DNSP to seek a review of the distribution determination from the Australian Competition Tribunal,[351] which mirror the provisions described above in relation to prescribed transmission services, will not be set out verbatim here. In essence, the legislative scheme employs the same criteria and principles for regulation of the direct control services, as for prescribed transmission services.

338. Clause 6.1.3(a).
339. Clause 6.2.2(a).
340. Clause 6.2.2(c).
341. Clauses 6.2.4, 6.3.2(b).
342. Clause 6.2.5.
343. Clauses 6.2.5(b), (c), (d).
344. Clause 6.2.8.
345. *National Electricity Law*, ss 7, 7A, 16.
346. *National Electricity Rules* (version 85) (1 Nov. 2016), cls 6.8, 6.8.1A, 6.8.2, 6.9.1, 6.9 and r. 6A.25; Australian Energy Regulator, *supra* n. 213, Table 2.3, 72; Australian Energy Regulator, *supra* n. 261.
347. *National Electricity Rules* (version 85) (1 Nov. 2016), cls 6.9.3, 6.12.1, 6.12.2 and rr 6.10, 6.11.
348. Clauses 6.4.1, 6.5.1–6.5.3, 6.5.5–6.5.8, 6.5.8A, 6.6.2–6.6.4 and Sch. 6.2; Australian Energy Regulator, *supra* n. 270.
349. Clauses 6.5.10, 6.6.1.
350. Clauses 6.6.5, 6.6A.2; r. 6.13.
351. *National Electricity Law*, s. 71B.

B. Negotiated Distribution Services

227. Negotiated distribution services are regulated under Part D of Chapter 6 to the *National Electricity Law*.[352] Again, these provisions largely mirror those applicable to TNSPs. Various principles apply to the setting of prices for negotiated distribution services, including that the price for a negotiated distribution service should be based on the cost incurred by the DNSP in providing the service.[353] The costs of the DNSP in this respect must be determined in accordance with the principles and policies set out in the 'Cost Allocation Methodology' for the DNSP approved by the AER.[354]

228. The AER determines negotiated distribution service criteria to apply to the terms and conditions of access to negotiated distribution services, including price.[355] A 'Negotiating Framework' also approved by the AER applies to negotiations between a DNSP and service applicant in respect of negotiated distribution services.[356] The Negotiating Framework includes obligations on both parties to negotiate in good faith.[357] Exchange of information between the parties to facilitate negotiations is required by the Negotiation Framework.[358] If prices cannot be agreed between a DNSP and a service applicant, the matter can be referred to the AER as a distribution services access dispute under the *National Electricity Rules*. Unlike the regulations relating to TNSPs, here, the AER is responsible for determining the dispute.[359]

III. Network Connection

229. Access to the national grid is regulated under Chapter 5 of the *National Electricity Rules*. The access regime applying to distribution networks is predominately the same as applies to transmission networks (*see* Chapter 3 above). Access arrangements for distribution networks must conform to prescribed requirements of the *National Electricity Rules*.[360] Specific provisions apply to the establishment or alteration of an embedded generation connection.[361]

352. *National Electricity Rules* (version 85) (1 Nov. 2016), cl. 6.2.7 and Pt. D, Ch. 6.
353. Clause 6.7.1(1).
354. Clause 6.7.1(1).
355. Clauses 6.7.2(a), 6.7.4; *see* , for example, Australian Energy Regulator, *SA Power Networks determination 2015–16 to 2019–20 – final decision*, Attachment 17 (October 2015).
356. *National Electricity Rules* (version 85) (1 Nov. 2016), cls 6.7.2(a), 6.7.3.
357. *See* , for example, Australian Energy Regulator, *supra* n. 355.
358. *See* , for example, *ElectraNet Negotiating Framework, supra* n. 289, cls 4–7.
359. *National Electricity Rules* (version 85) (1 Nov. 2016), r. 6.22.1.
360. Rule 5.5.
361. Rule 5.3A and Sch. 5.4B.

IV. Network Planning and Investment

230. DNSPs must undertake an annual distribution planning process.[362] The minimum planning period to be reflected in the report is five years.[363] DNSPs are obliged to engage in joint network planning with TNSPs for the transmission network to which the distribution network is connected.[364]

231. Network investment is subject to regulation. A 'regulatory investment test' must be undertaken in respect of each proposed network investment which is to be funded through prescribed distribution service tariffs.[365] For distribution network investment, this is referred to as the 'RIT-D'. The purpose of the RIT-D is to ensure that investment is efficient because consumers will pay for the costs of the investment through regulated revenues.[366] The requirements applying to an RIT-D are predominately the same as apply to the RIT-T (*see* Chapter 3 above). Where the cost of the network augmentation will not be met through consumer tariffs (e.g., the augmentation is funded by a generator), the RIT-D does not apply.[367]

362. Rule 5.13.
363. Clause 5.13.1(b).
364. Clause 5.14.1.
365. Rule 5.17.
366. Rule 5.17.1.
367. Rule 5.18.

Chapter 5. Consumption

§1. Overview

232. The regulatory frameworks applying to consumers of electricity are not consolidated. The participation of retailers and large industrial users of electricity in the spot market is regulated by the *National Electricity Rules*, including rights of access to network services and metering standards.[368] The national framework for consumer protection is set out in the National Energy Customer Framework ('NECF'), comprised of the *National Energy Retail Law (NERL)*, *National Energy Retail Rules (NERR)* and Chapter 5A of the *National Electricity Rules*. The *NERL* applies as an application of laws scheme under the *NERL (South Australia) Act 2011* (SA).[369] However, this scheme has not been universally adopted. The *NERL* does not apply in Western Australian or the Northern Territory, and only partially applies in Victoria.[370] Furthermore, various modifications to the NECF are made through the application laws of each jurisdiction, and State/Territory regulation continues to operate in respect of consumer protection even within those jurisdictions which have adopted the NECF.

§2. Participation in the NEM

I. Market Customers

233. A person who purchases electricity through the national grid must register as a customer.[371] Categories of registered customers relate to the source of the electricity purchased. Where the customer purchases electricity from the spot market, the person must register as a market customer.[372] Reflecting the nature of the wholesale spot market, market customers are typically electricity retailers and large industrial users

368. Chapters 5A, 7.
369. The *National Energy Retail Law* is the schedule to the *National Energy Retail Law (South Australia) Act 2011* (SA). The *National Energy Retail Law* is applied in each jurisdiction by application Acts: *National Energy Retail Law (South Australia) Act 2011* (SA), *National Energy Retail Adoption Act 2012* (NSW); *National Energy Retail Law (ACT) Act* 2012 (ACT); *National Energy Retail Law (Tasmania) Act* 2012 (Tas); *National Energy Retail Law (Queensland) Act 2014* (Qld).
370. In Victoria, Ch. 5A of the *National Electricity Rules* has applied since July 2016, but the *National Energy Retail Rules* have no application: *see* Australian Energy Market Commission, *Guide to the application of the NECF* (2016).
371. *National Electricity Rules* (version 85) (1 Nov. 2016), cl. 2.3.1(a).
372. Clause 2.3.4(c).

of electricity.[373] Prudential requirements specified in the *National Electricity Rules* must be satisfied in order to register as a market customer.[374]

234. Electricity purchased by market customers can be designated as a scheduled load (meaning that the customer will participate in the central dispatch process co-ordinated by AEMO in respect of the load).[375] Market customers may also apply to have their loads designated as ancillary market loads, enabling the customer to provide ancillary services.[376] Market customers purchase electricity in the spot market by submitting dispatch bids.[377] The prices submitted from dispatch bids are firm and cannot be altered. There is a limited ability to alter other aspects of a bid.[378]

II. Metering

235. Metering and metering data services are regulated by Chapter 7 of the *National Electricity Rules*. Metrology procedures applying in the NEM are determined by AEMO.[379] AEMO also publishes the Market Settlement and Transfer Solution Procedures which are binding on all registered participants.[380] Metering data is used by AEMO in its administration of the settlements system for the spot market.[381]

236. Each market participant is obliged to ensure that a connection point for which it is responsible has a metering installation and that metering installation is registered with AEMO.[382] Security requirements apply to metering installations and data.[383] Technical standards for metering installations and standards for metering data services are prescribed in the *National Electricity Rules*.[384] Inspection, testing and audit of metering installations and verification of metering data are also provided for in the *National Electricity Rules*.[385]

237. Each meter must be assigned to a responsible person. This could be either the relevant market participant or a metering services provider.[386] The responsible person is responsible for the metering installation at each connection point and the collection of metering data by that metering installation. A metering installation must only be provided by a metering provider and the provision of metering data services must only be undertaken by a metering data provider.[387] Any person may apply to

373. Australian Energy Market Operator, *NEM Current registration and exemption list, supra* n. 173.
374. *National Electricity Rules* (version 85) (1 Nov. 2016), cls 2.4.1(c), 3.3.
375. Clause 2.3.4(e).
376. Clause 2.3.5.
377. Clause 3.8.7.
378. Clauses 3.8.22 (a), (b).
379. Clause 7.3.1, r. 7.14.
380. Clause 7.2.8.
381. Rule 7.9.
382. Clauses 7.2.1(a), 7.2.7, 7.3.1(a), 7.5.1 and Sch. 7.5.
383. Rule 7.8.
384. Rules 7.3, 7.11 and Sch. 7.2.
385. Rule 7.6 and Sch. 7.3.
386. Clause 7.2.1(a).
387. Clauses 7.4.1, 7.4.1A.

AEMO for accreditation and registration as a metering provider or metering data provider, however, prescribed qualifications apply to these roles.[388]

238. AEMO is required to publish metering data provision procedures dealing with the provision of information to retail customers.[389]

239. As a consequence of a new framework to apply to metering from 1 January 2017, a new category of registrant – a metering co-ordinator – has been introduced into the *National Electricity Rules*. The objective of the new framework is to facilitate the installation of advanced metering.[390] Advanced metering is a key component of the AEMC's current 'Power of Choice' reforms, which promote consumer awareness of energy consumption and ability to make consumption choices.[391]

240. A person who engages in the co-ordination of metering services at a connection point may register with AEMO as a metering co-ordinator.[392] Generally, the electricity retailer responsible for a connection point on the national grid will need to appoint a metering co-ordinator in respect of that connection point.[393] The metering co-ordinator will be responsible for engaging a metering provider to carry out the installation and maintenance of the metering installation and a metering data provider to provide metering data services. These are distinct roles under the *National Electricity Rules*,[394] but could all be undertaken by the metering co-ordinator.[395]

§3. National Energy Retail Law

241. The *NERL* regulates the retail supply of energy (both electricity and gas) to consumers and applies to retailers and distributors.[396] Retailers must hold authorisations issued by the AER under the *NERL*, or be entitled to an exemption.[397] The national energy retail objective is to '*promote efficient investment in, and efficient operation and use of, energy services for the long term interests of consumers of energy with respect to price, quality, safety, reliability and security of supply of energy*'.[398] Co-ordination between retailers and distributors is required to achieve this objective. The *NERR* provide a framework for this co-operation.[399]

388. Clauses 7.4.2, 7.4.2A and Schs 7.4, 7.6.
389. Clause 7.16.1.
390. Australian Energy Market Commission, *Rule Determination: National Electricity Amendment (Expanding competition in metering and related services) Rule 2015* (26 Nov. 2015), iii.
391. Australian Energy Regulator, *supra* n. 213, 17; Australian Energy Market Commission, *Power of choice review – giving consumers options in the way they use electricity* (30 Nov. 2016); Australian Energy Market Commission, *Rule Determination*, *supra* n. 390, i.
392. *National Electricity Rules* (version 85) (1 Nov. 2016), cl. 2.4A.
393. Australian Energy Market Commission, *Rule Determination*, *supra* n. 390, v.
394. Chapter 7, *National Electricity Rules* (version 85) (1 Nov. 2016).
395. Australian Energy Market Commission, *Rule Determination*, *supra* n. 390, v.
396. *National Energy Retail Law*, s. 16.
397. *National Energy Retail Law*, ss 88, 110; *see* Australian Energy Regulator, *supra* n. 213, Table 5.1, 125.
398. *National Energy Retail Law*, s. 13.
399. *National Energy Retail Rules* (version 6) (23 Jun. 2016), Pt. 5.

242. The focus of the *NERL* is regulating energy supply to small customers connected to the national grid.[400] The *NERL* defines 'small customer' as: a residential customer (being a person who purchases energy principally for personal, household or domestic use at premises); and a business customer which consumes less than 100 megawatt hours (MWh) of electricity or 1 terajoule (TJ) of gas per year.[401] Small customers account for 98% of electricity connections and 99% of gas connections.[402] Electricity and gas distributors are obliged to connect small customers in accordance with the *NERR*.[403] There are two relevant types of connection contracts, these being deemed standard connection contracts and negotiated connection contracts.[404]

243. Full retail contestability applies in all Australian jurisdictions, meaning that customers can choose to contract with any authorised retailer of electricity.[405] The *NERL* provides that only two types of energy contracts may be entered into with small customers: standard retail contracts and market retail contracts.[406]

244. Retailers who are the designated retailer for premises are obliged to offer a small customer at that premise a standard retail contract at the standing offer price.[407] Standing offer prices must be published by the retailer on the retailer's website.[408] The standing offer prices may be varied by the retailer, subject to complying with any jurisdictional requirements.[409] Each retailer and distributor must prepare and publish a standard contract.[410] The *NERR* must provide for model terms to be provided in standard contracts and may also provide for the adoption, form and content of standard retail contracts.[411] A standard contract will be void to the extent that its terms are inconsistent with the model terms.[412]

245. A market retail contract is able to be negotiated between a small customer and a retailer.[413] The *NERR* may set out minimum terms which apply to market retail contracts.[414] Similarly, negotiated connection contracts can be formed between a customer and a distributor.[415]

---

400. *National Energy Retail Law (South Australia) Act 2011*, s. 16(a).
401. *National Energy Retail Law*, ss 3, 5; *National Energy Retail Regulations*, reg. 7.
402. Australian Energy Regulator, *supra* n. 213, 122.
403. *National Energy Retail Law*, s. 66.
404. Section 67.
405. Australian Energy Regulator, *supra* n. 213, 127.
406. *National Energy Retail Law*, s. 20.
407. Section 22; *National Energy Retail Rules* (version 6) (23 Jun. 2016), cl. 16.
408. *National Energy Retail Law*, s. 23.
409. Subsection 23(2).
410. Sections 24, 69.
411. Sections 21, 24(2), 68, 72; *National Energy Retail Rules* (version 6) (23 Jun. 2016), cls 12, 13, 81 and Schs 1, 2.
412. *National Energy Retail Law*, ss 29, 73.
413. Section 33.
414. Sections 34, 36; *National Energy Retail Rules* (version 6) (23 Jun. 2016), cls 14, 15 and Part 7.
415. *National Energy Retail Law*, s. 78; *National Energy Retail Rules* (version 6) (23 Jun. 2016), cl. 81.

246. Energy marketing is subject to regulation under the Energy Marketing Rules.[416] Minimum information requirements which must be satisfied before a retailer enters into a contract with a small customer are prescribed.[417] Direct marketing through door-to-door selling and mail is also regulated.[418] Various other consumer protection mechanisms are incorporated into the *NERL* including:

- the prescription of minimum service standards which must be complied with by energy retailers;[419]
- a requirement for each retailer to maintain a customer hardship policy and provide payment plans;[420]
- requirements for billing;[421]
- a compulsory energy ombudsman scheme for dealing with customer complaints and disputes;[422]
- a retailer of last resort scheme;[423]
- connection and supply obligations (including constraints on de-energisation or disconnection);[424] and
- a regime for small compensation payments to be paid by distributors to customers for compensable incidents.[425]

247. The 'Power of Choice' reforms, currently being implemented through amendments to the *National Electricity Rules*, are designed to enable consumers to understand their electricity consumption and make choices regarding electricity patterns.[426] Rising electricity prices in the NEM have impacted upon consumer behaviour, with consumption falling by an average of 1.7% per annum in the five years prior to 30 June 2014.[427] Reforms facilitating greater competition in meter provision commenced in 2014, with provision for greater transparency for consumption data, and were further progressed in 2015 with requirements for default communications protocols to enable competition between metering providers.[428] By 2017, distributors will need to implement tariffs which reflect the efficient costs of providing electricity to each consumer.[429]

416. *National Energy Retail Law*, s. 53; *National Energy Retail Rules* (version 6) (23 Jun. 2016), Div. 10.
417. *National Energy Retail Rules* (version 6) (23 Jun. 2016), cl. 64.
418. Clauses 65, 66.
419. *National Energy Retail Law*, s. 23.
420. *National Energy Retail Law*, ss 43, 44; *National Energy Retail Rules* (version 6) (23 Jun. 2016), cls 71, 72.
421. *National Energy Retail Rules* (version 6) (23 Jun. 2016), Div. 4.
422. *National Energy Retail Law*, ss 83, 86. The scheme is comprised of an energy ombudsman operating in each participating jurisdiction: *National Energy Retail Regulations*, reg. 5.
423. *National Energy Retail Law*, Pt. 6.
424. *National Energy Retail Rules* (version 6) (23 Jun. 2016), Pt. 4, Divs 5, 6; and Pt. 5, Divs 2, 3.
425. *National Energy Retail Law*, Pt. 7.
426. Australian Energy Market Commission, *Power of choice review*, *supra* n. 391; Australian Energy Market Commission, *Rule Determination, supra* n. 390, i.
427. Australian Energy Regulator, *supra* n. 213, 24.
428. *Ibid.*, 17.
429. *Ibid.*, 18.

248. Aside from the deployment of advanced metering and cost-reflective tariffs, consumers are being empowered through the availability of decentralised technologies and increasing awareness of electricity supply alternatives (including decentralised distribution and renewables).[430] Incentives to shift consumption patterns and adopt alternative electricity supply options are likely to become more prevalent as further technology options emerge and are adopted. The consumption decisions made by electricity customers will impact future regulation and commercial activities in the electricity sector.

430. Wouters C, Vigar C and Van Hende K, 'Increasing consumer choice – the potential impact of prosumers on electricity market regulation', *ICER Chronicle* (ed. 3) (March 2015).

Part II. Regulatory Framework Concerning Gas

Chapter 1. Production

§1. Ownership of Gas Resources

249. Different forms of mineral ownership and development regimes can be identified across the world, as follows:

- the `regalian' system where the State owns all minerals but leases or assigns rights to exploit these resources to private developers under set conditions;
- a system whereby state ownership of minerals is inalienable and where resources are developed either directly by state-owned entities or under contract by the private sector; and
- a system where ownership of minerals is tied to ownership of the land above.[431]

250. In Australia, mineral development generally occurs under the regalian system, although there is some direct public development of resources.

251. The nature of petroleum, being a substance that can exist in a number of forms that can move and migrate beneath the Earth, has led to the need for a unique legal regime to be created. Each Australian Petroleum Act (onshore and offshore) contains a relatively standard definition of petroleum.[432] Petroleum means 'any naturally occurring hydrocarbon in a gaseous, liquid or solid state'. Thus, in Australia, the

431. Mining Industry Commission, *Mining and Minerals Processing in Australia*, Report No. 7, vol. 1, 10 (Australian Government Publishing Service, 1991).

432. *Petroleum (Onshore) Act 1991* (NSW), s. 3; *Petroleum Act* (NT), s. 5; *Petroleum and Gas (Production and Safety) Act 2004* (Qld), s. 10; *Petroleum and Geothermal Energy Act 2000* (SA), s. 4; *Petroleum Act 1998* (Vic), s. 6; *Petroleum and Geothermal Energy Resources Act 1967* (WA), s. 5; *Offshore Petroleum and Greenhouse Storage Act 2006* (Cth), s. 7; *Petroleum (Submerged Lands) Act 1982* (NT), s. 4; *Petroleum (Offshore) Act 1982* (NSW), s. 5; *Petroleum (Submerged Lands) Act 1982* (Qld), s. 4; *Petroleum (Submerged Lands) Act 1982* (SA), s. 4; *Petroleum (Submerged Lands) Act 1982* (Tas), s. 3; *Offshore Petroleum and Greenhouse Gas Storage Act 2010* (Vic), s. 6; *Petroleum (Submerged Lands) Act 1982* (WA), s. 4.

ownership, exploration and production of gas is regulated under various State and Commonwealth Petroleum Acts.

252. In Australia, the statutory schemes regulating the ownership and development of petroleum/gas is separated into the onshore and offshore regimes, with the offshore regime further divided into the offshore regime for State coastal waters (from the low water mark seaward to 3 nm) and Commonwealth waters (being the areas seaward from 3 nm).

I. Ownership of Petroleum: Onshore and Offshore

A. Onshore

253. In Australia, ownership of oil and gas found onshore or within the three-mile territorial limit lies with the Crown (in practice, the State and Territory governments), regardless of who owns the land on the surface. In each of the Australian States and the Northern Territory, legislation declares that petroleum on or below the surface of all land is the property of the Crown.[433] The Crown owns any naturally occurring surface or subsurface petroleum regardless of when the land containing the petroleum passed into private ownership by Crown grant. The effect of the legislative provisions renders entirely inapplicable the common law principle of property ownership: that the owner of the land surface owns the soil beneath the surface down to the centre of the earth.

B. Offshore

254. Under international law, Australia has sovereignty over its territorial sea, that is, waters up to 12 nm from the baseline of the territorial sea. The baseline is normally the low water mark. Until the 1970s, it was not clear whether the Australian States or the Commonwealth Parliament had jurisdiction over the territorial sea, which at that time was 3 nm in breadth. In 1973, in the *Seas and Submerged Lands Act 1973* (Cth), the Commonwealth asserted sovereignty over the territorial sea, and sovereign rights over the continental shelf and the exclusive economic sea. The State governments opposed this assertion of Commonwealth jurisdiction over all offshore areas, and commenced actions in the High Court, challenging the constitutional validity of the legislation. In 1975, the High Court upheld the constitutional validity of the *Seas and Submerged Lands Case*, finding that the Commonwealth has sovereignty over waters from the baseline to the outer limit of the territorial sea, including the seabed beneath these waters.[434]

---

433. *Petroleum (Onshore) Act 1991* (NSW), s. 6; *Petroleum Act* (NT), s. 6 ; *Petroleum and Gas (Production and Safety) Act 2004* (Qld), s. 26; *Petroleum and Geothermal Energy Act 2000* (SA), s. 5; *Mineral Resources Development Act 1995* (Tas), s. 6; *Petroleum Act 1998* (Vic), s. 13; *Petroleum and Geothermal Energy Resources Act 1967* (WA), s. 9.

434. *New South Wales v. The Commonwealth* (1975) 135 CLR 337.

255. Following this decision, the Commonwealth and the States undertook negotiations, which resulted in the OCS of 1979.[435] The OCS deals with Commonwealth and State jurisdiction in the waters to the outer limit of the territorial sea. In general, the States have responsibility for areas up to 3 nm from the territorial sea baseline, which are known as State 'coastal waters'. As part of the OCS, title in the seabed beneath the coastal waters of each State was vested in the State by section 4 of the *Coastal Waters State Title Act 1980* (Cth):

> By force of this Act, but subject to this Act, there are vested in each State, upon the date of commencement of this Act, the same right and title to the property in the seabed beneath the coastal waters of the State, as extending on that date, and the same rights in respect of the space (including space occupied by water) above that seabed, as would belong to the State if that seabed were the seabed beneath waters of the sea within the limits of the State.

256. It was also agreed between the Commonwealth, the States and the Northern Territory that Commonwealth offshore petroleum legislation should be limited to the area that is outside the coastal waters of the States and the Northern Territory, and that for this purpose the outer limits of the State and Northern Territory coastal waters should be 3 nm from the baseline of the territorial sea (which reflected the limit of Australia's territorial sea at the time). On the outer limits of those coastal waters there is no basis, statutory or otherwise, for Crown ownership of subsea oil or gas. Although the Commonwealth has power to legislate in respect to exploration for and exploitation of the resources of the continental shelf it has no property in the continental shelf at common law.[436] The offshore petroleum legislation does not purport to declare that the Commonwealth has property in any petroleum situated on or under the continental shelf. The rights of the Commonwealth are in this respect sovereign rights rather than proprietary rights.

II. Transfer of Ownership

257. The petroleum legislation of the States, the Northern Territory and the Commonwealth all authorise the holders of petroleum production licences or leases to conduct petroleum production operations and recover petroleum from within their lease or licensed area. Although the language is not uniform, the legislation generally provides that upon extraction or recovery the petroleum becomes the property of the

435. *Offshore Settlement. A Milestone in Co-operative Federalism* (AGPS, Canberra, 1980) and *Offshore Constitutional Settlement: Selected statements and documents 1978-79* (Commonwealth of Australia, 1980).
436. *Commonwealth v. WMC Resources Ltd* (1998) 194 CLR 1.

licence holder.[437] It is generally considered that the right to recover petroleum in a licence area creates a statutory pool of capture.[438] This interpretation provides that the production licence entitles the holder to recover not only oil and gas which is in the licence area at the time of grant of the licence, but also petroleum which migrates into the licence area during the course of production operations.

258. The position regarding naturally occurring petroleum situated in State coastal waters is the same as under the onshore legislation, although the constitutional and statutory position is more complex, because of the OCS. Unlike the onshore petroleum legislation, the offshore petroleum statutes do not contain provisions asserting Crown ownership of subsurface petroleum.

§2. Licensing

259. The upstream petroleum sector can be divided into three phases: exploration and appraisal; development and construction; and production.

260. The 'midstream' sector includes the gas transmission sector, where processed natural gas is transported through high pressure pipelines to the distribution system (or to major manufacturing or power generation customers).

261. The downstream activities include refining, distribution, wholesaling and retailing.

262. The State governments have sovereignty and jurisdiction over oil and gas reserves located onshore and within their respective coastal waters. While a vast number of Acts affect the development of oil and gas in Australia (*see* Table 2), each State (except Tasmania) has its own sectoral petroleum legislation and administrative framework.[439] These statutory regimes, which govern upstream petroleum exploration and development in Australia, confer rights by authorisations, variously called titles, tenements, permits, licences, and/or leases. Different licences provide different rights to different activities.

437. *Petroleum Act* (NT), s. 6; *Petroleum and Gas (Production and Safety) Act 2004* (Qld), s. 28; *Petroleum and Geothermal Energy Act 2000* (SA), s. 5; *Petroleum Act 1998* (Vic), s. 17; *Petroleum and Geothermal Energy Resources Act 1967* (WA), s. 11A; *Offshore Petroleum and Greenhouse Storage Act 2006* (Cth), s. 285; *Petroleum (Submerged Lands) Acts 1982*, s. 127. There is no such provision in the *Petroleum (Onshore) Act 1991* (NSW) or the *Mineral Resources Development Act 1995* (Tas).

438. Toskas E, 'A Comparative Review of Unit Development under the Commonwealth Petroleum Act', 26 ARELJ (2007).

439. *See* Table 2, note a. In Tasmania, both mineral and petroleum development are regulated under the *Mineral Resources Development Act 1995* (Tas).

Table 2: Selected Legislation Affecting Upstream Petroleum[440]

<table>
<tr><th rowspan="2">Scope of Legislation</th><th rowspan="2">Onshore</th><th colspan="2">Offshore</th></tr>
<tr><th>Coastal Waters</th><th>Commonwealth Waters</th></tr>
<tr><td rowspan="3">Petroleum and pipelines</td><td>State onshore petroleum legislation[a]</td><td rowspan="5">Petroleum (Submerged Lands) Act 1982 or equivalent[b]</td><td>Petroleum (Timor Sea Treaty) Act 2003 (Cth)</td></tr>
<tr><td>State pipeline-specific legislation[c]</td><td rowspan="4">Offshore Petroleum and Greenhouse Gas Storage Act 2006 (Cth)</td></tr>
<tr><td>Barrow Island Act 2003 (WA)</td></tr>
<tr><td>Occupational health and safety</td><td>Occupational Health and Safety Act 1991 (Cth)</td></tr>
<tr><td></td><td>State OHS or major hazard facilities legislation</td></tr>
<tr><td>Environment, heritage and development</td><td colspan="3">Environment Protection and Biodiversity Conservation Act 1999 (Cth)</td></tr>
<tr><td></td><td colspan="3">Aboriginal and Torres Strait Islander Heritage Protection Act 1984 (Cth)</td></tr>
<tr><td></td><td></td><td colspan="2">Other Commonwealth environment- and heritage-specific legislation</td></tr>
<tr><td></td><td colspan="2">State environment-, heritage- and development-specific legislation</td><td></td></tr>
<tr><td></td><td>Local government legislation</td><td></td><td></td></tr>
<tr><td>Native title and land rights</td><td colspan="3">Native Title Act 1993 (Cth)</td></tr>
<tr><td></td><td colspan="2">Aboriginal Land Rights (Northern Territory) Act 1976 (Cth) (NT only)</td><td></td></tr>
<tr><td></td><td colspan="2">State native title, land rights and other land access legislation</td><td></td></tr>
<tr><td>Other</td><td colspan="3">National Greenhouse and Energy Reporting Act 2007 (Cth)</td></tr>
</table>

440. Australian Productivity Commission, *Review of the Regulatory Burden in the Upstream Petroleum (Oil and Gas) Sector: Research Report* (Productivity Commission, 2009) (updated).

		Australian Maritime Safety Authority Act 1990 (Cth)
		Navigation Act 2012 (Cth)
		Submarine Cables and Pipelines Protection Act 1963 (Cth)
		Maritime Transport and Offshore Facilities Security Act 2003 (Cth)
	Defence Act 1903 (Cth)	
	Customs Act 1901 (Cth)	
	Quarantine Act 1908 (Cth)	

a. *Petroleum (Onshore) Act 1991* (NSW); *Petroleum Act* (NT); *Petroleum and Gas (Production and Safety) Act 2004* (Qld); *Petroleum and Geothermal Energy Act 2000* (SA); *Mineral Resources Development Act 1995* (Tas); *Petroleum Act 1998* (Vic); *Petroleum and Geothermal Energy Resources Act 1967* (WA).

b. *Petroleum (Offshore) Act 1982* (NSW); *Petroleum (Submerged Lands) Act 1981* (NT); *Petroleum (Submerged Lands) Act 1982* (Qld); *Petroleum (Submerged Lands) Act 1982* (SA); *Petroleum (Submerged Lands) Act 1982* (Tas); *Offshore Petroleum and Greenhouse Gas Storage Act 2010* (Vic); *Petroleum (Submerged Lands) Act 1982* (WA).

c. *Pipelines Act 1967* (NSW); *Energy Pipelines Act 2015* (NT); *Gas Pipelines Act 2000* (Tas); *Pipelines Act 2005* (Vic); *Petroleum Pipelines Act 1969* (WA).

263. There are effectively three licensed stages in Australian petroleum regimes:

(1) Exploration permits: these authorise exploration for petroleum and the recovery of petroleum on an appraisal basis in the permit area.
(2) Retention leases: these are used when the blocks contain petroleum but the recovery of that petroleum is not yet commercially viable, but likely to become commercially viable within fifteen years. Retention leases authorise exploration for petroleum and the recovery of petroleum on an appraisal basis in the lease area.
(3) Production licences: the holder of an exploration permit or retention lease applies for a production licence to authorise the recovery of petroleum in the licence area (as well as further exploration).

264. Separate licences attach to pipelines for conveyance of oil and gas (*see* Chapter 3, below).

265. Under each jurisdiction, there is a system of registration of titles. Government approval is required for transacting in those petroleum titles and the register will contain a history of those transactions.

I. Exploration Permit

A. Onshore

266. The exploration process for oil and gas are the same. The legislation provides for a licence to conduct exploration for petroleum, usually called an exploration permit or exploration licence, although in Queensland it is called an authority to prospect. The availability of acreage for exploration is determined under the various Petroleum Acts, and an application for a licence includes evidence of financial standing, technical qualifications and capacity to comply with the Act. Once a licence is granted the holder of it has an exclusive right to explore the area comprised within that licence. Included in the types of exploration activities that might be engaged in are seismic surveys, which allow explorers to view the area below the surface and to identify those areas where they think petroleum may be accumulated.

267. All of the States' petroleum Acts contain a prohibition on conducting an activity other than in accordance with the licence, and all of the Acts provides for a retention licence/lease (other than Queensland), which allows the holder of an exploration permit to hold on to an area because it is not yet commercial to develop it. The names of these licence/leases are set out in Table 3. New South Wales refers to this as an assessment lease. In Queensland, the Minister can declare part of an authority to prospect a 'potential commercial area of the authority', where petroleum production or storage is likely to become viable within fifteen years.[441] In South Australia, provisions regarding the grant of a petroleum retention licence require at least one well to have been drilled to demonstrate the existence of the regulated resource.[442].

268. When the holder of an exploration permit or licence wants to move to commercial production, they must apply for a different type of permit which authorises production in commercial quantities, usually called a production licence, although in New South Wales it is called a production lease. The States, other than Western Australia,[443] do not provide for the declaration of a location or a specific time period within which a production licence or retention licence must be applied for, other than the expiry of an exploration permit.

269. Each of the New South Wales, Northern Territory, Queensland, South Australian and Victorian onshore petroleum Acts empowers the relevant Minister to require the holder of an exploration permit to apply for a production licence.[444] The legislation does not generally contemplate the grant of multiple production licences over an exploration permit area (other than in South Australia).

441. *Petroleum and Gas (Production and Safety) Act 2004* (Qld), s. 90.
442. *Petroleum and Geothermal Energy Act 2000* (SA), s. 30.
443. *Petroleum and Geothermal Energy Resources Act 1967* (WA), s. 48A.
444. *Petroleum (Onshore) Act 1991* (NSW), s. 37; *Petroleum Act* (NT), s. 30; *Petroleum and Gas (Production and Safety) Act 2004* (Qld), s. 96; *Petroleum and Geothermal Energy Resources Act 2000* (SA), s. 36; *Petroleum Act 1998* (Vic), s. 35.

B. *Offshore*

270. Under section 97 of the *Offshore Petroleum and Greenhouse Gas Storage Act 2006* (Cth) ('OPGGSA'), it is an offence to explore for petroleum in the Commonwealth's offshore area unless authorised by a petroleum exploration permit, or otherwise by the Act. An exploration permit confers upon its holder the exclusive right to explore in the permit area.[445] Provisions for exploration permits/licences exist in the States' offshore petroleum legislation, which applies in State coastal waters.

II. Production Licence

A. *Onshore*

271. Once a reservoir has been discovered, field development plans are formulated. After being developed, a field commences the production stage. Primary, secondary and tertiary methods are used to recover hydrocarbons. A production licence is required to produce petroleum.

272. Western Australia introduced the *Petroleum Act 1967* at a similar time as the *Petroleum (Submerged Lands) Act 1967* and used similar principles applying to internal and external waters. These principles define permit areas by graticular blocks and identification of blocks containing a 'discovery'. This in turn starts the clock for a time within which a production licence must be applied for. Although permit areas in Western Australia, New South Wales, the Northern Territory and Queensland are defined by reference to graticular blocks, South Australia and Victoria do not define areas by reference to blocks.

273. In contrast to Western Australia, South Australia conducted a major review of its *Petroleum Act 1940* (SA) at the end of the twentieth century, but did not follow the Commonwealth's offshore petroleum mining code. Rather, there was a shift to a regulatory approach based on principles of certainty, openness, transparency, flexibility, practicality and efficiency. Smaller exploration tenants over shorter terms were included to facilitate competition, and confine the area of a production licence to twice the size of the area underlain by proven and probable reserves of petroleum.

274. Production licences generally contain conditions that the licensee complies with the Act; that royalty is payable; and that insurance or 'financial assurance' is in place for designated amounts, to meet any obligations that might arise under the Act, should the Act be contravened. Table 3 compares some of the key features of the State regimes in relation to production licences, including the name of the production authorisation; whether or not the holder of an exploration permit or retention licence has the right to a production licence upon commercial discovery of petroleum; whether or not a retention lease is available to enable appraisal of the commercial viability of the resource; the term of the production lease; and the royalty imposed on the right to extract petroleum.

445. *Offshore Petroleum and Greenhouse Gas Storage Act 2006* (Cth), s. 98.

Table 3: Selected Key Features of State/Territory Production Licensing Regimes

State	*Automatic Right to PL, or at the Discretion of the Decision-Maker*	*Appraisal*	*Term of PL*	*Royalty*	*Name of Authorisation*
WA	Statutory Right	Retention Lease	21 years	Between 5 and 12.5%	Production Licence
NSW	Discretion of Governor	Assessment Lease	Up to 21 years	Nil – first 5 years, then 6–10% from six to ten years	Production Lease
Vic.	Governor and Council	Retention Lease	No term limit	10%	Petroleum Lease
Qld	Governor and Council	No Retention Lease	Up to 30 years	10%	Petroleum Lease
SA	Statutory Right	Retention Lease	Unlimited	10%	Petroleum Production Licence
NT	Statutory Right	Retention Lease	21–25 years	10%	Production Licence

B. Offshore

275. Provisions for production licences also exist in the States' and Northern Territory's offshore petroleum legislation, which apply to State coastal waters. In the Commonwealth offshore area, section 161 of the OPGGSA provides for a petroleum production licence to authorise the recovery of petroleum, and carrying out exploration and operations necessary for those purposes. An applicant may apply for a production licence over blocks that are subject to a current exploration and/or retention lease. Providing the holder of an exploration permit complies with the OPGGSA, if the permit holder makes a commercial discovery of petroleum a production licence will be issued, authorising the licensee to recovery petroleum from the licence area and granting the permit holder property rights in the petroleum recovered.[446]

446. Section 98 of the OPGGSA confers the right to explore. Section 285 of the OPGGSA states that petroleum recovered in the licence area becomes the property of the petroleum production licensee.

276. If the Joint Authority (JA) decides to grant a production licence, NOPTA will issue an offer document to the applicant and the applicant may accept that offer by submitting a request for grant of a production licence.[447] The OPGGSA imposes a number of standard conditions on production licences, and the JA may also impose whatever conditions it thinks appropriate.[448] The licence is granted for an indefinite period but may be subject to termination of there is no activity for a five-year period.[449]

277. The rights conveyed by production licences have been considered. In the case of *WMC v. Commonwealth*,[450] it was found an exploration permit issued under the offshore Commonwealth petroleum law applying in the Timor Sea was 'property', notwithstanding that it was a right created by statute and not the common law, as an exploration permit can be transferred and dealt with for consideration, is recorded on a register, and is definable. However, the decision of the Federal Court was appealed to the High Court, which reversed the decision.[451]

278. Depending upon the type of production facility used – for example, a mobile offshore drilling unit (MODU) – an applicant may also need to consider whether it will be subject to any Australian Maritime Regulation, including the *Shipping Registration Act 1981* (Cth) and the *Navigation Act 2012* (Cth).

§3. Royalty

279. Petroleum is the property of the Crown, and upon production an obligation to pay royalty arises. The royalty is generally between 10–12.5% and is calculated by reference to actual sale value less treatment, processing, refining and transportation costs.

§4. Unconventional Petroleum

280. 'Unconventional petroleum' is a term used to describe a lack in permeability in the source rock, where the hydrocarbon is trapped, and there is restricted movement of petroleum towards the well. As a result, unconventional means are required to maintain production.

281. To date, all exploration and development of unconventional gas in Australia has occurred onshore, and is therefore regulated by State/Territory legislation. New South Wales, the Northern Territory, South Australia and Western Australia use their existing petroleum legislation to regulate the grant of authorisations for unconventional gas.[452] Only Victoria has enacted specific legislation to regulate the development of

447. *Offshore Petroleum and Greenhouse Gas Storage Act 2006* (Cth), s. 260.
448. Section 162.
449. Section 166.
450. *Commonwealth v. WMC Resources* (1996) 67 FCR 153.
451. *Commonwealth v. WMC Resources* (1998) 194 CLR 1.
452. *Petroleum (Onshore) Act 1991* (NSW); *Petroleum Act* (no date) (NT); *Petroleum and Gas (Production and Safety) Act 2004* (Qld); *Petroleum and Geothermal Energy Act 2000* (SA); *Petroleum and Geothermal Energy Resources Act 1967* (WA).

unconventional petroleum resources, namely the *Mineral Resources (Sustainable Development) Act 1990* (Vic).

282. Australia's petroleum legislation is not drafted to treat petroleum derived from shale or tight rocks differently from petroleum derived from conventional petroleum reservoirs. As a result, the size and duration of permit areas that transition from an exploration permit to a production licence are drafted in a conventional sense, and need to be applied to the unconventional production. This creates issues with their application.

283. As there is no requirement for an impermeable cap rock, the area of an unconventional resource may be considerably larger than a conventional resource. The delineation of an unconventional resource is difficult, and generally requires an extra step based on feasibility of maintaining production. Conventional petroleum operations have set approaches or phases: exploration; appraisal of a well once a discovery is made; and development and production. In conventional petroleum production, an individual well can be used for a considerable proportion of the resource. As a result, the judgment of when commercial production is feasible, and when to transition into a production licence, can be clearer in conventional production than in unconventional production, which may require multiple wells to be drilled and flow rates tested, and the use of a pilot plant.

284. The phases of development can overlap in unconventional operations as a result of the considerable period required for appraisal of the resource. The legislation does not define 'appraisal' in the context of unconventional petroleum, or proof-of-concept type operations. It also does not provide for a pilot plant and the sale of petroleum to test the feasibility of a shale or tight rock project. South Australia and Queensland do provide certain provisions around feasibility testing.

285. In addition, community concerns over the environmental impacts of hydraulic fracturing (fracking), the use of water in CSG development and the impact of water extraction on underground aquifers, and the issue of access to agricultural land, have resulted in unconventional resources attracting their own inquiries and regulation, in the form of bans or moratoriums on the issue of petroleum exploration permits or fracking. These developments include the following:

- In Victoria, there has been a moratorium on unconventional oil and gas activities since 2012. In August 2016, the government established a ban on all unconventional onshore gas development (fracking) and coal seam gas extraction and a moratorium on any other onshore gas operations until 30 June 2020.
- – A moratorium and independent scientific inquiry on fracking, which began in the Northern Territory in September 2016.
- In Tasmania, the government introduced a moratorium on fracking from March 2014 until March 2020, although to date there has been no hydrocarbon production in Tasmania, nor has any hydraulic fracturing been undertaken there. Other exploration activities for unconventional gas resources are allowed.

286. Other States have not banned the development of unconventional gas resources, but have undertaken or commissioned inquiries and/or strengthened environmental regulations. In December 2012, the South Australian Department for

Manufacturing, Innovation, Trade, Resources and Energy (DMITRE) (now the Energy Division of the Department of State Development) published the *Roadmap for Unconventional Gas Projects in South Australia*. The Roadmap contains 125 recommendations covering the full life-cycle of unconventional gas projects, from exploration to production, and possible LNG exports, to encourage the safe exploration and production of unconventional gas under the *Petroleum and Geothermal Energy Act 2000* (SA).[453]

287. In 2011, New South Wales introduced a freeze on applications for onshore petroleum exploration licences. In 2012, the government introduced new requirements for CSG producers, including, as part of a new Strategic Regional Land Use Policy, a two kilometre exclusion zone around residential and village areas, an Aquifer Interference Policy, a Code of Practice for Well Integrity, and a *Code of Practice for Coal Seam Gas Fracture Stimulation*; and a ban on harmful BTEX chemicals (petroleum compounds benzene, toluene, ethylbenzene and xylene) and evaporation ponds.[454] In February 2013, the Premier directed the NSW Chief Scientist and Engineer to conduct a comprehensive review of CSG-related activities, focussing on the human health and environment impacts.[455] The *Final Report of the Independent Review of Coal Seam Gas Activities in NSW* was released on 30 September 2014, after which the government released the *New South Wales Gas Plan* (2014), setting out its response to the Report and plans for strategic regulation of the CSG industry. While the freeze on exploration licences expired in September 2015, the Gas Plan brought about a number of legislative and regulatory changes, including the designation of the Environment Protection Authority as lead regulator for CSG approvals.

288. Queensland has also established a comprehensive governance framework to oversee the development of the State's CSG industry. All applications for major CSG production projects are subject to a strict assessment and approvals process through an environmental impact statement (EIS) process carried out under the *State Development and Public Works Organisation Act 1971* (Qld) or through the *Environmental Protection Act 1994* (Qld). Among other things, the Queensland Government has banned the use of evaporation dams and strengthened conditions around the treatment and use of CSG water; prohibited the use of BTEX chemicals in fracking fluids; established a regional interests development approval (RIDA) requirement under the *Regional Planning Interests Act 2014* for activities proposed in areas of regional interest; and established a CSG Compliance Unit to monitor CSG operators and ensure that they are in compliance with industry laws and regulations; and put in place new provisions regarding access to land and compensation through the *Mineral and Energy Resources (Common Provisions) Act 2014* (Qld).

289. In 2011, the Western Australian Department of Mines and Petroleum (DMP) commissioned an independent report to assess the capacity of the *Petroleum and Geothermal Resources Act 1967* (WA) to regulate shale gas exploration and production

453. Department of State Development, *Unconventional Gas Projects*, http://www.statedevelopment.sa.gov.au/resources/unconventional-gas-projects (accessed 21 Nov. 2016).

454. New South Wales Government, Department of Industry, Resources and Energy Division, *Coal seam gas: Codes, policies and legislation*, http://www.resourcesandenergy.nsw.gov.au/landholders-and-community/coal-seam-gas/codes-and-policies (accessed 21 Nov. 2016).

455. http://www.chiefscientist.nsw.gov.au/reports/coal-seam-gas-review (accessed 21 Nov. 2016).

activities in the State. This report, *Regulation of Shale, Coal Seam and Tight Gas Activities in Western Australia*, was released in 2011. The DMP issued its Response on 31 October 2011, accepting a number of recommendations to improve regulation. However, in August 2013, in response to ongoing community concerns, the WA Parliament's Standing Committee on Environment and Public Affairs undertook an investigation into hydraulic fracturing and its implications for the State, presenting its Report in November 2015.[456] The State currently assesses unconventional production using its law and regulations for conventional oil and gas. The *Guide to the Regulatory Framework for Shale and Tight Gas in Western Australia: A Whole-of-Government Approach* (2015) explains the State's assessment and regulation processes for shale and tight gas projects.

290. None of the licensing regimes of the States and Northern Territory give any special treatment to petroleum in shale or tight rocks. None of them refers specifically to shale or tight rocks, or petroleum extracted from those geological forms. All of the petroleum statutes contain a definition of petroleum that comprises all naturally occurring hydrocarbons, whether in gaseous, liquid or solid state, with some exclusions such as oil shale and coal. Oil shale is an organic rich and fine grained sedimentary rock containing organic compound kerogen. It has to be mined and treated to extract the oil from the kerogen.

§5. Administration of Petroleum Legislation

I. Onshore Petroleum

291. All Australian States and Territories have strong regulatory frameworks in place to manage impacts of petroleum exploration and production. In all Australian jurisdictions, companies intending to carry out drilling and stimulation operations must submit several applications to the relevant departments, including: a drilling application; an environment plan; and a safety management plan. Assessment of these plans will determine any additional measures required during operations, such as monitoring of aquifers.

292. The State and Territory government departments are responsible for the administration of petroleum legislation, including regulation of upstream oil and gas activities. Table 4 lists the relevant State departments responsible for the administration of onshore petroleum law.

Table 4: State and Territory Petroleum Regulators, as at 21 November 2016

Jurisdiction	*Department*
New South Wales	Department of Industry, Division of Resources and Energy: Minerals and Petroleum

456. Standing Committee on Environment and Public Affairs, *Implications for Western Australia Of Hydraulic Fracturing For Unconventional Gas*, Report 42 (November 2015).

Victoria	Department of Environment and Primary Industries
Queensland	Department of Natural Resources and Mines
Western Australia	Department of Mines and Petroleum
South Australia	Department of State Development, Energy Resources Division
Tasmania	Department of Infrastructure, Energy and Resources
Northern Territory	Department of Mines and Energy

II. Offshore Petroleum

293. In State coastal waters, the State and Territory resource departments administer State/Territory offshore petroleum law.[457]

294. Development and modernisation of regulations and administration in the Commonwealth offshore regime is a long-running endeavour, underway since the 1990s. This has seen a prescriptive regulatory structure based on the direction of power of the old *Petroleum (Submerged Lands) Act 1967* progressively replaced by outcomes-based regulations; first in relation to occupational safety, then environment, then data management, and most recently, resources management. In 2006, the *Petroleum (Submerged Lands) Act 1967* (Cth) was rewritten and re-enacted as the *Offshore Petroleum Act 2006* (Cth), and is now the *Offshore Petroleum and Greenhouse Gas Storage Act 2006* (Cth) ('OPGGSA').

295. Following the Montara blowout and oil spill off the coast of Northern Australia in 2009, the system of regulation underwent some fundamental changes. The Report of the Inquiry into the Montara blowout criticised the Northern Territory for its minimalist approach to regulatory tasks, and made a number of criticisms of the offshore regulatory framework.[458] The Commonwealth legislature enacted the *Offshore Petroleum and Greenhouse Gas Storage Legislation Amendment (Miscellaneous Measures) Act 2010* (Cth) to extend the powers of the safety regulator, the National Offshore Petroleum Safety Authority (NOPSA), to regulate the structural integrity of facilities, wells and well-related equipment, which had previously been the responsibility of the Designated Authority (DA). The *Offshore Petroleum and Greenhouse Gas Storage Amendment (National Regulator) Act 2011 (Cth)* made further changes. In 2012, NOPSA was converted by amendment to the National Offshore Petroleum Safety and Environment Management Authority (NOPSEMA), and added environmental management to its portfolio.[459]

296. The process of modernisation, and the strengthening of environmental protection, compliance and enforcement, continued with the passage of the *Offshore*

457. The administration of offshore petroleum law is also discussed in this monograph in Part III 'Petrol', below.

458. Borthwick D, *Report of the Montara Commission of Inquiry*, Executive Summary, 6 (Government of Australia, 2010).

459. *Offshore Petroleum Act 2006* (Cth), s. 645.

Petroleum and Greenhouse Gas (Compliance Measures) Act 2013 (Cth) and the *Offshore Petroleum and Greenhouse Gas (Compliance Measures 2) Act* 2013 (Cth). These Acts introduced a civil penalty regime, increased the level of criminal penalty provisions, and implemented a range of alternative enforcement mechanisms which came into force in October 2014, following the proclamation of the *Regulatory Powers (Standard Provisions) Act 2014*.

297. Today, the key authorities responsible for upstream oil and gas regulation are: the Joint Authorities; the National Offshore Petroleum Titles Administrator (NOPTA); and NOPSEMA. The JA is the primary decision-maker under the *Offshore Petroleum and Greenhouse Gas Storage Act 2006*. The JA for each State and the Northern Territory comprises the responsible Commonwealth Minister of Resources and Energy, and the relevant State or Northern Territory Minister. The Joint Authorities have the power to make certain decisions under the OPGGSA, including (but not limited to) the granting of petroleum titles, the imposition of title conditions and cancellation of titles, as well as decisions about resource management and resource security.

298. The day-to-day administration of the petroleum legislation is vested in NOPTA and NOPSEMA. NOPTA is an administrator, and its functions can be broadly divided into advisory and regulatory. NOPTA prepares key JA decisions on matters such as the grant and termination of titles, approval of work programmes and field development plans, imposition of unitisation requirements and other resource management decisions. The regulatory functions relate to data and information management. NOPSEMA is an independent statutory authority, responsible for regulating all facets of environment and safety.

299. In addition to environmental approval required from NOPSEMA, upstream petroleum projects in the Commonwealth offshore area may require assessment and approval under the *Environment Protection and Biodiversity Conservation Act 1999* (Cth) ('EPBC Act'). Any proposal that has, will have, or is likely to have, a 'significant impact' on one of the nine 'matters of national environmental significance' (MNES) set out in the Act, should be referred to the Commonwealth Minister for Environment for assessment and approval. Petroleum projects in onshore areas and State coastal areas may also require assessment and approval under the EPBC Act.

Chapter 2. Exploitation

§1. 'Rule of Capture'

300. The 'rule of capture' developed in the US. It provides that the person with the right to produce oil and gas from an area owns the oil and gas produced from the wells drilled on that land, even though it may be proved that part of such oil and gas migrated from adjoining lands. At a simplistic level, the rule of capture concept allows property units (in oil and gas) to be lost as a consequence of its subsurface movement, as petroleum belongs to the person who produces it first. As a consequence of the rule of capture, various individuals with tenures on land are placed in competition with each other to produce from a reservoir before the opportunity to do so is lost. That competition can lead to waste.

301. In Australia, the rule of capture can arise between jurisdictions, and within a jurisdiction. Petroleum deposits divided by jurisdictional boundaries, such as between South Australia and Queensland in the Cooper Basin, can give rise to consideration of the rule of capture. In each of the States and the Northern Territory, legislation declares that all petroleum on or below the surface of all land is the property of the Crown.[460] The effect of these declarations of property rights are that they may have been fixed at the period of the declaration, and that all petroleum within the jurisdictional boundaries at that date of enactment are caught; or they may be flexible, in the sense that they include petroleum within the jurisdictional boundary from time to time.

302. The second way in which the rule of capture may be applicable is in determining the rights confined on a petroleum production title holder. When the production title is granted to a particular person, does it include only the petroleum in place prior to the disturbance of any reservoir by drilling, or does it include petroleum which enters that space by way of migration? A reservoir may extend beyond the boundaries of a production title, and a production title(s) may be granted over the lands surrounding one title, thereby granting the rights of production to other separate production title holders. Where there are mutual rights of various holders of titles, the questions of reservoir management and equity are important.

303. Developing countries are usually characterised by systems which allow government to closely control development of oil and gas. As a result of the potential for dispute on 'rule of capture' issues, the Australian legal system developed principles of unit development. If a licence holder discovers petroleum in the licensed area and the reservoir extends to another licence area, the legislation provides for unitisation principles, which allow for common production by separate licence holders.

304. Both compulsory and voluntary unitisation are used in Australia. Voluntary unitisation is the more common route than compulsory unitisation by statute. Voluntary

460. *Petroleum (Onshore) Act 1991* (NSW), s. 6; *Petroleum Act* (NT), s. 6; *Petroleum and Gas (Production and Safety) Act 2004* (Qld), s. 26; *Petroleum and Geothermal Energy Act 2000* (SA), s. 5; *Mineral Resources Development Act 1995* (Tas), s. 6; *Petroleum Act 1998* (Vic), s. 13; *Petroleum and Geothermal Energy Resources Act 1967* (WA), s. 9.

unitisation has economic benefits, because fewer wells need to be drilled to achieve similar recovery, and because secondary recovery techniques may be more effectively planned.

305. The Onshore Petroleum Acts of the States and the Northern Territory (with the exception of Tasmania) contain provision for compulsory unitisation.[461] The underlying purpose of legislative requirements for unitisation is to avoid waste, and to thereby avoid lost royalty income that would otherwise be payable to the State from extraction. The common features of the equivalent provisions throughout mainland Australia are: that at least one production licence has been granted; that the relevant minister may require the licensee to arrange unitisation; that a scheme will be imposed if the licensee does not arrange a unitisation scheme; and that there is no power for a minister to impose a scheme without first giving the licensee the opportunity to do it voluntarily first.[462] While most jurisdictions, including South Australia, Victoria and the Northern Territory, limit unitisation to fields within the boundaries of the State, the petroleum Act of Western Australia specifically addresses the issue of fields within the State that traverse State boundaries.[463]

306. Australia has a number of examples of multi-field unitisation. This is the application of unitisation principles not just to one field lying within two licence areas, but rather, to a number of fields and a number of licensed areas, that are otherwise held within a variety of different joint ventures, to join them into one unitised joint venture which covers the entire area. In South Australia, the *Cooper Basin (Ratification) Act 1975* (SA) and the *Stony Point (Liquids Project) Ratification Act 1981* (SA) are examples of ratification Acts for the unit development of petroleum reserves.

§2. Competition Law

307. Australia's core competition law provisions are contained in Part IV of the *Competition and Consumer Act 2010* (Cth) (previously the *Trade Practices Act 1974* (Cth)). The intent of the Competition and Consumer Act is to enhance the allocation of resources by allowing for competitive rivalry for supply of goods and services to exist. Within the concept of competition in the market, there must be a market with a sufficient number of sellers, to enable the market to price goods and services. If there are sufficient sellers, then no one seller will be able to set the price. If there are insufficient sellers, there is a monopoly (or oligopoly), and sellers are able to set an increased price for the product, above that which would be expected to exist in a competitive market, earning a higher profit at the expense of consumers. This means that there is not a fair allocation of resources.

308. Collaborations amongst industry participants are common in energy and resource projects. This collaboration arises primarily as a result of the need for considerable capital and the need to allocate risk. For example, joint marketing

461. *Petroleum Act 1984* (NT), s. 69; *Petroleum and Geothermal Energy Act 2000* (SA), s. 42; *Petroleum Act 1998* (Vic), s. 79; *Petroleum and Geothermal Energy Resources Act 1967* (WA), s. 69.
462. *See* , for example, *Petroleum and Geothermal Energy Resources Act 2007* (SA), s. 42.
463. *Petroleum and Geothermal Energy Resources Act 1967* (WA), s. 69.

agreements between joint venturers have been a long-term feature of oil and gas projects in Australia. These agreements often have a single purchaser, allowing the joint venturers to leverage economies of scale and the particular expertise of one joint venture party to sell their product. However, the participants in these projects are often competitors, and as a result, such collaboration under the Competition and Consumer Act is 'cartel conduct', which may have the effect of substantially lessening competition in the market.

309. Cartel conduct is a serious offence, with civil and criminal sanctions including fines exceeding AUD 10 million for corporations, and up to ten years in jail for individuals. It is illegal for a corporation to indemnify its officers against legal costs and any financial penalty. The conduct prohibited by the Competition and Consumer Act includes fixing, controlling or maintaining prices. In addition, the Competition and Consumer Act prohibits a corporation from entering into a contract that substantially lessens competition. This is a 'catch-all' provision. Corporations wishing to collaborate to exploit an opportunity will need to consider their Competition and Consumer Act obligations where they are fixing, controlling, or maintaining the price for or a discount allowance, rebate or credit in relation to goods or services supplied, or if they are limiting supplier output or they have certain exclusionary provisions. These are all examples of cartel conduct which is prohibited by the Competition and Consumer Act, regardless of the effect on competition.

310. In relation to cartel conduct, there are three avenues by which oil and gas corporations may manage competition law issues. These are: (a) to apply the 'joint venture' exception; (b) to characterise the conduct as 'exclusive dealing'; or (c) to apply for authorisation.

I. 'Joint Venture' Exception

311. The joint venture exemption applies to joint venture parties who negotiate or enter a joint marketing agreement. Those agreements require consensus as to price and terms, generally amongst competitors. Any such agreements on price will impact upon the competitive process. However, agreements to price arrived at for the purposes of a joint venture are not subject to the prohibition to the extent that they relate to the joint supply, by two or more parties to the joint venture, in proportion to their respective interests in the joint venture. This provides a useful protection from what would otherwise be a strict liability for breach of the Competition and Consumer Act by joint venturers in agreeing a set or fixed price.

312. Despite the joint venture exception, a joint marketing agreement may yet contravene the Competition and Consumer Act if it has the purpose of effecting a substantial lessening of competition in a market. There are two particular types of agreements that cause potential problems. The first is agreements between joint venture parties where they joint market the venture's product and fix or maintain a price for it. This could substantially lessen competition in the market. The second type is agreements between joint venturers and their customers where exclusive-type arrangements may be introduced, which also have the effect of substantially lessening competition.

313. There are differences in relation to the nature of oil and gas from a competition point of view. Natural gas is not easily stored, and needs to be distributed in a continuous flow without a break point that could otherwise be used for separate marketing, so there are operational scale advantages to marketing the output of natural gas joint venture through a single entity. Often separate marketing of natural gas is not found to be feasible. Even if the separate marketing of natural gas was feasible, the anticompetitive effect of the joint marketing agreement would need to be considered against the co-ordination of marketing that would be required between the joint venturers if they were to individually market their share of the output.

II. 'Exclusive Dealing'

314. The Competition and Consumer Act also contains a mechanism that provides that if conduct would otherwise constitute cartel conduct, it can be categorised as exclusive dealing (other than third line forcing), in which case the conduct does not constitute a contravention of the cartel conduct prohibition.

315. Section 47 of the Competition and Consumer Act prohibits various forms of exclusive dealing. A corporation engages in exclusive dealing where it supplies goods or services to a person on the condition that the person does not acquire a competitor's goods or services, or, in the alternate, that it acquires goods or services on the condition that the supplier does not supply products or services to other persons. However, exclusive dealing does not constitute a contravention of the Competition and Consumer Act unless it has the purpose of substantially lessening competition. If conduct is part of exclusive dealing, it is not illegal per se, but must be subjected to a competition test for contravention of the Competition and Consumer Act. Parties may notify the ACCC of conduct that might fall within the various definitions of exclusive dealing and, while the notification stands, they will not be held in breach of section 47. The ACCC can only remove the notification if they consider the conduct substantially lessens competition and that there are no benefits to the public that would outweigh the anticompetitive detriment.

316. It is possible to use this exception if an arrangement can be characterised as a purely vertical rather than horizontal market. Subcontracting can assist in achieving competition law compliance.

III. Authorisation

317. The ACCC may grant authorisation for conduct that would otherwise contravene the prohibitions in the Competition and Consumer Act, if it is satisfied the public benefits of the conduct outweigh any anticompetitive detriment. If authorisation is granted, the conduct is immune from the application of the competition provisions of the Act. Duration of immunity will be decided by the ACCC.

Chapter 3. Transport

318. Preliminary processing of hydrocarbons occurs onsite as part of recovery. Processing involves dividing the product into oil, water and gas.

319. Produced gas is processed to remove natural gas liquids such as ethane, propane, butane and condensates for direct sale to industrial and petrochemical markets. Naturally occurring liquid petroleum gas (LPG) (propane and butane) is separated from natural gas and condensates, compressed and transported in pressurised tanks to domestic or export markets.

320. Natural gas – of which the primary component is methane – is transported to gas processing plants. This is generally done by pipeline. Inert gases, liquid hydrocarbons, sulphur and impurities are removed from the gas, leaving a commercial gas comprised of mainly methane. Processed natural gas can be sold directly, or to a gas retailer. The retailer will require third-party access to transmission and distribution pipelines to distribute gas to domestic consumers.

321. Natural gas can also be converted to liquid natural gas (LNG) to be loaded onto an LNG shipping tanker and exported. By cooling methane to -161.5°C, its volume is approximately 600 times less than the equivalent volume of methane gas. In this way it can be transported by ship, where pipelines are not economic or possible. Liquid methane is then offloaded at its destination, heated and distributed using pipelines. There are currently no explicit limitations on, nor specific regulatory regimes restricting, the export of gas (including LNG), and this is an export industry that has been rapidly expanding as a result of strong demand overseas.

§1. Pipelines

322. There are three gas markets in Australia: the Eastern market, covering Victoria, New South Wales, Queensland, South Australia and Tasmania; the Northern market, covering the Northern Territory and parts of South Australia; and the Western market, covering Western Australia. Australia's major population centres are separated from each other and from the basins by large distances. The product is often a distance from any infrastructure and generally some form of transportation is required. To build a pipeline requires a large capital investment and can traverse land owned by various different entities and individuals. The gas market in Australia is generally served by one major pipeline connecting a basin to the market. Within each basin there are a number of joint ventures, but generally only one of these joint ventures owns the infrastructure that supplies the gas.

323. Each State or Territory has its own pipeline legislation.[464] Land access, easement acquisitions and approval for construction and operation of pipelines vary across the different States and Territories. The State and Territory regulatory regimes generally require that a pipeline licence is obtained to construct and operate a petroleum

464. *Pipelines Act 1967* (NSW); *Energy Pipelines Act 2015* (NT); *Petroleum and Geothermal Energy Act 2000* (SA); *Petroleum and Gas (Production and Safety) Act 2004* (Qld); *Gas Pipelines Act 2000* (Tas); *Pipelines Act 2005* (Vic); and the *Petroleum Pipelines Act 1969* (WA).

pipeline and land access rights or tenure are obtained for the pipeline. Any environmental approvals for a pipeline are complemented by the general environmental approvals required under State or Territory and Commonwealth legislation. Australian Standard 2885 (AS 2885) applies to the design, construction, testing, operations and maintenance of gas and petroleum pipelines. The many other standards used by the pipeline industry are referred to in AS 2885 as the principal document.

I. Land Access for Pipelines

324. There are two different types of petroleum/gas pipelines: those that require a separate licence, and those that can be constructed under a production licence. If a pipeline is located entirely within a production licence, then a separate licence is not required. If a separate pipeline licence is required and is granted, the licensee must acquire the land for the purposes of construction and operation of the pipeline. The pipeline owner will be required to negotiate the terms under which any owner of any private land is willing to grant access for the construction and operation of the pipeline. Often an easement is required over the pipeline route. As the right exists only over the pipeline land and there is no dominant estate, the easement required is an 'easement in gross'. 'Easements in gross' are generally used to benefit a statutory or prescribed authority.

325. Government authorities have powers of compulsory acquisition to facilitate land access. Private landowners can be compelled under the pipelines legislation to grant pipeline easements. Where the pipeline traverses Government land, an easement under the applicable land legislation would generally need to be obtained. Consents may also need to be obtained from other interested parties, including native title parties, heritage stakeholders, local Government, pastoral lessees, and mining titleholders.

II. Third-Party Access Rights to Natural Gas Transportation Pipelines

326. Australia's gas industry really started to develop in the 1960s, and it developed with the assistance of the relevant State governments, which wished to use it to ensure the economic development of their own jurisdiction. Until the 1990s, the Australian gas markets were characterised by the existence of vertically integrated gas companies, with monopolies on production, transmission, distribution and retail gas delivery. Natural gas transmission and distribution pipelines are viewed as natural monopolies, as gas can be transported more cheaply and efficiently along one pipeline system than by two or more operators. It is not cost-efficient to duplicate the pipeline infrastructure. However, this means the incumbent pipeline owner/operator may use their market power to deny third-party access to the system, or impose unreasonably high prices for access, or set other terms and conditions that restrict access.[465] Regulation has been introduced to deal with monopolies on transmission, distribution and retail sales (the upstream oil and gas sector, which is dominated by private companies, is competitive).

327. The reform of Australia's gas markets began in the 1990s, and, as with the reform of electricity markets, this occurred as part of a more general review of Australia's national competition policy. The Gas Pipelines Acts of 1997, which included the *National Third Party Access Code for Natural Gas Pipelines* ('Gas Pipelines Access law'), regulated access to transmission and distribution pipelines. If pipelines were 'covered' under the regime, the service provider had to have an access arrangement in place approved by the ACCC, or by the relevant State or Territory regulator. The access reforms were supported by structural reforms, to break up the vertically integrated gas utilities into separate transmission, distribution and retailing businesses.[466]

328. In its 2003 report to COAG, entitled *Reform of Energy Markets*, the COAG MCE agreed that gas markets required further reform, accepting various recommendations of the 2002 MCE Review into Energy Markets,[467] and later, the 2004 Productivity Commission Inquiry Report *Review of the Gas Access Regime*.[468] Further reforms were introduced when the *National Gas Law* came into effect on 1 July 2008. The *National Gas Law* currently governs the terms and conditions of access to Australia's natural gas transmission and distribution pipelines, replacing the old Gas Pipelines Access law. The objective of the *National Gas Law* is to 'promote efficient investment in, and efficient operation and use of, natural gas services for the long term interests of consumers of natural gas with respect to price, quality, safety, reliability and security of supply of natural gas'.[469]

329. South Australia was lead legislator, enacting the *National Gas (South Australia) Act 2008* (SA), containing the *National Gas Law* and the *National Gas Rules* in the schedule to the Act. All other Australian jurisdictions introduced or passed application acts to apply the National Gas Law in their jurisdictions, except Western Australia.[470] Western Australia became a participating jurisdiction under the *National Gas Law* in January 2010, to the extent set out in the *National Gas Access (WA) Act* 2009 (WA).

---

465. Lyster R and Bradbrook A, *Energy Law and the Environment*, 130 (Cambridge University Press, 2006). The gas access regime was governed by the *Natural Gas Access Inter-government Agreement* (7 Nov. 1997), as result of which the *National Third Party Access Code for Natural Gas Pipelines* was agreed by the Commonwealth, States and Territories. The Code as contained within Schs 1 and 2 to the *Gas Pipelines Access (South Australia) Act 1997* (SA).
466. Lyster and Bradbrook, *supra* n. 465, 131.
467. Parer W, Breslin P, Sims R and Agostini D, *Towards a Truly National and Efficient Energy Market* (Commonwealth of Australia, 2002) ('Parer Review').
468. Australian Productivity Commission, *Review of the Gas Access Regime* (Productivity Commission, 2004).
469. National Gas Law, s. 23.
470. *National Gas (ACT) Act 2008* (ACT); *National Gas (New South Wales) Act 2008* (NSW); *National Gas (Northern Territory) Act 2008* (NT); *National Gas (Queensland) Act 2008* (Qld); *National Gas (Tasmania) Act 2008*; *National Gas (Victoria) Act 2008* (Vic); *National Gas Access (WA) Act 2009* (WA); *Australian Energy Market Act 2004* (Cth).

330. The intent of the *National Gas Law* was for it to be consistent with the regime under the *National Electricity Law*. The *National Gas Law* adopts a decision-making framework and includes the *National Gas Rules*, which set out the process for decision-making. The *National Gas Law* establishes two principle regulatory bodies for gas. First, the Australian Energy Market Commission (AEMC) is responsible for developing the *National Gas Rules*, managing change and reviewing effectiveness.[471] The AEMC reports to the MCE, as required. Second, the AER (in Western Australia the Economic Regulation Authority (ERA)) is the regulator of gas markets, including pipeline access, enforcement and compliance.[472]

A. Access under theNational Gas Law

331. In the *National Gas Law*, 'pipelines' are classified by the National Competition Council ('NCC') as either transmission pipelines or distribution pipelines. Classification determines the obligations to which a pipeline is subject under the law, and which bodies have certain decision-making powers under the law. The primary function of a transmission pipeline is to convey gas to market. The primary function of a distribution pipeline is to reticulate gas within a market. A cross boundary pipeline is one which crosses a State or Territory border.[473] Processing facilities upstream, gathering lines and some pipelines downstream of an end-user's connection point are not included in the definition of pipelines, and accordingly cannot be covered by the *National Gas Law*.[474]

332. The *National Gas Law* applies access regulations to pipelines that are subject to a 'coverage determination'.[475] Access to uncovered pipelines is a matter for commercial negotiation and arrangements, without recourse to the regulators. The purpose of regulating pipelines under a coverage regime is to reduce barriers to entry into gas markets, ensuring that vertically integrated gas companies cannot limit competition by preventing access to pipelines.

333. A pipeline may be covered in a number of ways:

- pipelines which are covered pipelines under the previous gas code are deemed to be covered pipelines under the *National Gas Rules*;
- any person who considers that a pipeline meets certain 'coverage criteria' may apply to the NCC for the pipeline to be covered;[476]
- a pipeline will be covered where a service provider has been awarded a tender to construct and operate a pipeline as a result of a tender approval process approved under the *National Gas Rules*;[477] or

471. National Gas Law, ss 69, 74.
472. National Gas Law, s. 27.
473. National Gas Law, ss 13, 14.
474. National Gas Law, s. 2.
475. Coverage determinations are addressed in the National Gas Law, Ch. 3, Pt. 1.
476. National Gas Law, s. 92. The coverage criteria are set out in s. 15.
477. National Gas Law, s. 126.

– a pipeline will be covered where a service provider voluntarily submits a full access arrangement to the regulator (the AER, or in WA, the ERA) and the regulator makes or approves that voluntary access arrangement.[478]

334. Two forms of regulation are available for a covered pipeline. The first of these is 'full regulation', which requires the service provider to submit an access arrangement to the regulator for approval. The *National Gas Law* sets out the matters the AER must take into account when deciding whether or not to approve an access arrangement, including the 'revenue and pricing principles' contained in section 21 of the *National Gas Law*.

335. The second is 'light regulation', which provides a negotiate/arbitrate model for third-party access, with arbitration by the regulator in the event of an access dispute.[479] Light regulation regime is intended to operate so that not all covered pipelines will necessarily be subject to full regulation; rather, they will be able to avoid the upfront setting of reference tariffs (price regulation) and potentially the need for an access arrangement altogether. The principal concern is to ensure the form of regulation that is appropriate for a particular pipeline service is proportionate to the degree of market power involved.

336. The NCC can determine applications for light regulation and, in considering a determination, will consider whether a service provider's market power allows it to be lightly regulated.[480] Although a service provider subject to light regulation is not subject to price regulation, prices must be published along with terms and conditions for access to those services.[481] The service provided cannot engage in price discrimination, and is subject to arbitration under access dispute provisions in the NGL.[482]

337. The *National Gas Rules* require that the AEMC establish and maintain a register of all pipelines that are, or have been, subject to any form of regulation or exemption from regulation under the *National Gas Law* or under the old Gas Pipelines Access law.[483]

B. Part IIIA of the Climate Change Authority (CCA)

338. Part IIIA of the Competition and Consumer Act establishes a legal regime to facilitate third-party access to certain 'services' provided by means of 'significant infrastructure facilities'. It is also known as the National Access Regime.

339. The starting point for consideration of the application of the Competition and Consumer Act to a transmission pipeline is the determination of what constitutes a 'service'. The definition of 'service' relies on there being a facility which is (a) essential for service provision, and (b) exhibits the features of a natural monopoly. The monopoly may be created because the economies of scale are such that the cost

478. National Gas Law, s. 127.
479. Light regulation is addressed in the National Gas Law, Ch. 3, Pt. 2.
480. National Gas Law, ss 89, 110, 132.
481. National Gas Rules (version 32) (25 Oct. 2016), r. 36.
482. As to the prohibition on price discrimination, *see* National Gas Law, s. 170. Access disputes are regulated in National Gas Law, Ch. 6.
483. National Gas Rules (version 32) (25 Oct. 2016), r. 133.

of service provision falls as the scale of operations increase; and the nature of assets is such that there is no alternative economic value in use, such that any potential entrant that was unsuccessful would have a high unrecoverable cost. These features produce high barriers to entry to potential competitors, so in the absence of government ownership or regulation, the asset or facility owner has substantial power in the choice of pricing and service provision. A pipeline must exhibit these features to be capable of providing a 'service' for the purposes of the Competition and Consumer Act.

§2. SHIPPING

340. The Australian Government regulates the security of Australian maritime transport and offshore facilities through the *Maritime Transport and Offshore Facilities Security Act 2003* (Cth) and the *Maritime Transport and Offshore Facilities Security Regulations 2003*. This legislation was introduced in response to Chapter XI-2 of the 1974 *International Convention for the Safety of Life at Sea* and the *International Ship and Port Facility Security Code 2003*.[484] The *Navigation Act 2012* (Cth) and the *Marine Safety Act 2012* (Cth) are also significant Acts for the maritime and shipping industry.

484. *International Convention for the Safety of Life at Sea* (London, UK) adopted 1 Nov. 1974, in force 25 May 1980; 1184 UNTS 2, 1983 ATS No. 22, 14 ILM 959, UKTS 46 (1980), Cmnd 7874. *International Ship and Port Facility Security Code*, Conference of Contracting Governments to the International Convention for the Safety of Life at Sea, 1974 (London, 9–13 Dec. 2002), Conference Resolution 2 (adopted on 12 Dec. 2012), SOLAS/CONF.5/34, Annex 1, Annex.

Chapter 4. Distribution

341. Gas distribution networks transport natural gas from transmission pipelines to end users. They typically consist of a backbone of high and medium pressure pipelines running between the 'city gate' (the point of connection to the transmission pipeline) and major demand centres. This network feeds low pressure pipelines, which deliver the gas to businesses and homes. Energy retailers are the distribution networks' main customers. They buy natural gas in large volumes and onsell it to consumers. Retailers arrange with gas distribution network operators for the supply of gas to end users via the distribution network.

342. The *National Gas Law* and *National Gas Rules* provide a framework for the regulation of distribution network services. As described above, the *National Gas Law* contains the principal access regime for natural gas (and, in Western Australia, LPG) distribution networks. Where any pipeline falls outside of this regime, the applicable pipeline licence may contain access conditions, and in the absence of any such conditions, any access will be a matter for commercial negotiation. As with transmission pipelines, natural gas distribution networks may also be subject to the National Access Regime under Part III of the Competition and Consumer Act, but none have been declared under that regime.

343. The AER has been the economic regulator for covered natural gas transmission and distribution pipelines in all States and Territories since 1 July 2008 (except Western Australia, where the ERA regulates the electricity, gas, water and rail freight industries in that State). Based on an assessment of the degree of competition that exists for the service, the NCC will recommend whether a distribution network should be regulated. The jurisdictional Minister is responsible for the decision whether to regulate, and the form of regulation that should apply – light or full.

344. Most gas distribution networks are subject to full economic regulation under the *National Gas Law*. For a fully regulated service, the network operator has to prepare an access arrangement for the approval by the regulator. The access arrangement includes price and non-price terms and conditions for third parties to gain access to the network. It provides a starting point for parties to negotiate access on commercial terms. In the event of a dispute, the *National Gas Rules* contain a dispute resolution mechanism.

345. The operation of a distribution network requires compliance with the licensing regime of the relevant jurisdiction, including obtaining all applicable authorisations.

Chapter 5. Consumption

§1. The Operation of Gas Markets

346. The regulation of gas markets is an important aspect of regulation of the downstream sector of the gas industry. The Australian Energy Market Operator (AEMO) has managed gas markets in Australia from 1 July 2009. While it has a number of functions, set out in section 91A of the *National Gas Law*, two key roles are to operate gas retail markets in New South Wales and the ACT, Queensland, South Australia, Victoria, and Western Australia; and to operate wholesale gas markets in southeastern Australia and, since 2015, the wholesale gas market in Western Australia.[485]

I. Wholesale Gas Markets

347. The southeastern Australian wholesale gas markets are: the Declared Wholesale Gas Market in Victoria; the Short Term Trading Market (STTM) in Adelaide, Brisbane and Sydney; and the Gas Supply Hub, with trading locations at Wallumbilla in Queensland, and Moomba in South Australia. The Victorian declared wholesale gas market (VDWGM) was established in 1999. It allows trading based on injections into, and withdrawals from, the Victorian gas transmission system (VDGTS) which links gas producers, major users and retailers.[486]

348. To be permitted to inject or withdraw gas from the VDGTS, each VDWGM participant is required to submit price/quantity pairs of bids and offers into the market. Based on these bids and offers, and subject to pipeline system security limits, AEMO will schedule each participant's injections and withdrawals, in order minimise the cost of supplying demand. Participants who are scheduled to withdraw more than they are scheduled to inject, pay the market price on the quantity of gas that they are short. Participants who are scheduled to inject more than they are scheduled to withdraw, receive a payment of the market price on the quantity of gas in excess of their withdrawal. The market price used to settle imbalance payments is set by AEMO at the start of the day.[487]

349. The high-level provisions for regulation of the VDWGM are contained in sections 91BI–BN of the *National Gas Law*. A person is prohibited from participating in a VDWGM unless they are registered in accordance with the Rules, or are exempt

485. AEMO is also a system operator of the Victorian Gas Declared Transmission System, and, since 1 Jul. 2016, is the independent power system operator for Western Australia. Its functions and powers as system operator are set out in the *National Gas Law*, ss 91B–BG.

486. AEMO, *Declared Wholesale Gas Market*, https://www.aemo.com.au/Gas/Declared-Wholesale-Gas-Market-DWGM (accessed 22 Nov. 2016).

487. Australian Energy Market Commission, *Draft Final Report: Review of The Victorian Declared Wholesale Gas Market*, 17 (14 Oct. 2016).

from registration.[488] A person participates in the VDWGM in a registrable capacity if the person is: a service provider for the VGDTS, or for declared distribution system; a producer that injects natural gas into the VGDTS; or a storage provider whose facility is connected to the VGDTS; a person who buys or sells natural gas in the VDWGM; or any person classified by the Rules as a participant.[489] AEMO makes and updates Wholesale Market Procedures, which govern the operation of the VDWGM. Among other things, these confer rights and impose obligations on registered participants, exempt participants, or other persons.[490] AEMO, and every person to whom the Retail Market Procedures are applicable, must comply with the procedures.[491]

350. The VDWGM provides an effective gas balancing service and facilitates a limited amount of trading of gas based on short-term prices. However, a review of the VDWGM by the AEMC in October 2016 found that the changes underway in the wider east coast market, in particular the growth of the LNG export industry, present new challenges for the VDWGM, and have exposed shortcomings that were 'previously obscured by its less interconnected operation and more benign market conditions'.[492] The AEMC recommended substantial reforms to the VDWGM, in particular the establishment of a 'Southern Hub' for gas trading, similar to the Gas Supply Hub established at Wallumbilla in Queensland (*see* below). Thus, the VDWGM may be abolished in the future.

351. The STTM is a market-based wholesale gas balancing mechanism established at defined gas hubs in Sydney, Adelaide and Brisbane. It runs once daily, on the day ahead, for each hub. Participants submit bids, offers, forecasts and pipeline capacities, which are used to determine schedules for gas deliveries from the pipelines which transport gas from producers to transmission users and the hubs. The market sets a daily market price at each hub, and settles each hub based on the schedules and deviations from schedules. Participants' daily transactions are settled at market prices.[493]

352. The high-level provisions for regulation of the STTM are set out in sections 91BRA–BRJ of the *National Gas Law*. The Law prohibits a person from participating in the STTM unless they are registered in accordance with the Rules, or are exempt from registration.[494] A person participates in the retail market in a registrable capacity if they are a person who supplies gas to an STTM hub, or withdraw gas from an STTM hub, or are any person classified by the Rules as a participant in the STTM.[495] AEMO is empowered to operate and administer the STTM, which includes making and updating STTM Procedures, which govern the operation of the STTM.[496] Among other things, these confer rights and impose obligations on STTM trading participants, exempt

488. National Gas Law, s. 91BJ.
489. National Gas Law, subs. 91BI.
490. National Gas Law, subss 91BM(1), (3).
491. National Gas Law, s. 91BN.
492. Australian Energy Market Commission, *supra* n. 490, Executive Summary, iv-v (14 Oct. 2016).
493. AEMO, *Short Term Trading Market*, https://www.aemo.com.au/Gas/Short-Term-Trading-Market-STTM (accessed 22 Nov. 2016).
494. National Gas Law, s. 91BRD.
495. National Gas Law, subs. 91LA(2).
496. National Gas Law, ss 91BRB, 91BRH.

participants, or other persons.[497] Section 91BRJ of the *National Gas Law* obliges AEMO and every person to whom the STTM Procedures apply to comply with the Procedures. AEMO may also trade in natural gas 'to the extent necessary or desirable to provide market operator services'.[498]

353. The Gas Supply Hubs at Wallumbilla and Moomba are wholesale gas trading exchanges, but not regulated gas markets.[499] Through an electronic platform, gas supply hub participants trade standardised, short-term physical gas products at the foundation pipelines connecting at either Wallumbilla/Moomba. AEMO's functions and powers in relation to gas trading exchanges are set out in section 91BRK of the National Gas Law. AEMO centrally settles transactions, manages prudential requirements, and provides reports to assist participants in managing their portfolio and gas delivery obligations.[500] AEMO may also trade in natural gas 'to the extent necessary or desirable for the efficient operation of a gas trading exchange'.[501]

II. Retail Gas Markets

354. The regulation of retail markets is governed by Part 7 of the *National Gas Law*, and the National Gas Rules. The *National Gas Law* prohibits a person from participating in a registrable capacity in regulated retail gas market unless they are registered in accordance with the National Gas Rules, or have an exemption.[502] A person participates in the retail market in a registrable capacity if they are classified in one of seven categories, being: a service provider; user; non-scheme pipeline user; producer; storage provider; trader or any other class prescribed by Regulation.[503] One of AEMO's key functions is to make and update Retail Market Procedures, which govern the operation of retail gas markets. Among other things, these confer rights and impose obligations on registered participants, exempt participants, users, end users or other persons.[504] AEMO and every person to whom the Retail Market Procedures apply, must comply with the procedures.[505]

355. AEMO also provides three other main gas retail market services. These are first, delivery point management, which is 'managing the customer transfer for gas delivery points and the associated market data between retailers, and between retailers and distribution businesses'; second, balancing, allocation and reconciliation management, that is, 'managing the daily allocation of gas usage to retailers to enable settlement of gas supply contracts, transmission and distribution use of system contracts';

497. National Gas Law, subs. 91BRI.
498. National Gas Law, subs. 91BRB(2).
499. National Gas Law, s. 91BRL.
500. AEMO, *Gas Supply Hubs*, https://www.aemo.com.au/Gas/Gas-Supply-Hubs (accessed 22 Nov. 2016).
501. National Gas Law, subs. 91BRK(2).
502. National Gas Law, s. 91LB.
503. National Gas Law, subs. 91LA(2).
504. National Gas Law, s. 91M, subs. 91MA(3).
505. National Gas Law, s. 91MB.

and third, operation of the central information technology systems that facilitate retail market services.[506]

§2. National Energy Customer Framework

356. The NECF is a set of national laws, rules and regulations governing the sale and supply of energy (electricity and reticulated natural gas) to consumers. The NECF includes the *NERL*, *NERR* and *National Energy Retail Regulations*. South Australia is the lead legislator, and in addition to the *NERL (SA) Act 2011* (SA) ('*NERL*') it has also enacted the *NERR* as Part 10 of *NERL* ('*NERR*') and the *NERL (Local Provisions) Regulations 2013* ('*NERL* Regulations'). Parts of the NECF are also contained in new chapters of the National Gas Rules.

357. As of 1 July 2015, the NECF had commenced in Queensland, New South Wales, the ACT, Tasmania and South Australia. The NECF is implemented by each participating jurisdiction applying the *NERL* as the law in its jurisdiction, and the *NERR* and the *NERL* Regulations made under the *NERL* are applied as law. However, individual jurisdictions have made modifications in relation to how the *NERL* and *NERR* apply in that jurisdiction, which has led to some disparity in the law. In States that have yet to adopt the NECF, State and Territory governments will remain responsible for regulating retail energy markets. Western Australia and the Northern Territory do not propose to implement the reforms.

358. The *NERL* establishes key laws and principles for the sale and supply of energy to end use customers. It operates with the Australian Consumer Law, set out in Schedule 2 to the *Competition and Consumer Act 2010* (Cth), to protect small energy customers in their electricity and gas supply arrangements. Small energy customers are residential energy users and small businesses that consume less than 100 MWh of electricity or 1 TJ of gas per year.

359. The NECF requires retailers and distributors to establish direct contracts with each of their customers. The terms and conditions of those contracts are subject to varying degrees of regulation under the *NERL* and *NERR*. Retail contract requirements mainly apply to small customers, whereas distribution contract requirements extend to all customers connected to the distributor's network. A key consumer protection under the *NERL* and *NERR* is the prohibition on retailers and distributors from entering into an agreement with a small customer to exclude their liability for failure to supply energy due to bad faith or negligence.[507]

360. The NECF prescribes the nature of scope of a retailer's contractual relationship with an energy consumer. For retailers, the contract requirement takes the form of a model standing offer.[508] The model standing offer is designed to ensure that all consumers have access to at least one energy offer where the terms and conditions of the contract are fixed and not subject to unilateral amendment by the retailer.

---

506. AEMO, *Gas Retail Markets*, https://www.aemo.com.au/Gas/Retail-markets-and-metering (accessed 22 Nov. 2016).
507. *National Energy Retail Law (SA) Act 2011* (SA), s. 316.
508. National Energy Retail Rules (Version 6) (23 Jun. 2013), r. 12. *See also* the National Gas Rules (version 32) (25 Oct. 2016), Pt. 12A, Gas Connection for Retail Customers.

361. In addition to the standing offer, the retailer can sell energy under market contracts designed to promote competition and give the retailer some flexibility.[509] The market contract allows the retailer to tailor one or more offers to target particular market segments. The market contract is subject to a minimum set of requirements including tariffs and charges, termination, cooling off periods and earlier termination charges.[510] The dual contract arrangement has been a feature of retail energy regulation in Australia for a considerable time, and jurisdiction-specific regulatory requirements are imposed on top of existing requirements. This may erode the contract flexibility given to retailers.

362. Most customers rarely deal directly with the distributor. In the case of gas, prior to the NECF small customers did not have a direct contractual relationship with their gas distributor. Under the NECF, billing and general ongoing issues relating to gas and electricity connections are managed through the retailer. The NECF imposes separate contractual requirements for supply services and physical connection services in relation to the distributor. Both large and small customers are deemed to have entered into a standard form connection contract with the distributor for the ongoing supply services. The terms and conditions of the deemed standard form connection contract are prescribed in the *NERR*, Schedule 2.

363. A major implication for gas distributors is the establishment of the direct contractual relationship with end use customers. Previously the gas distributor's relationship was with the retailer, and the retailer with the customer. This new relationship means the gas distributor is directly liable to the customer and the distributor's conduct is subject to the Australian Consumer Law. In particular, the prohibition on unfair terms in standard form consumer and small business contracts, and the consumer guarantees, apply to contracts between gas distributors and end use customers.

509. National Energy Retail Rules (Version 6) (23 Jun. 2013), r. 14. *See also* the provisions for negotiated arrangements under the *National Gas Rules* (version 32) (25 Oct. 2016), Pt. 12A, Gas Connection for Retail Customers.
510. National Energy Retail Rules (Version 6) (23 Jun. 2013), Pt. 2, Div. 7.

Part III. Regulatory Framework Concerning Petrol

Chapter 1. Production

§1. Offshore Petroleum Jurisdiction

364. The legal framework for the regulation of Australia's petroleum resources is a unique arrangement that developed in parallel with developments in international and Australian domestic law, and as a consequence of the history of Australia, particularly the establishment of independent, self-governing colonies and the Federation of Australia in 1901. Although the States/Territories are clearly responsible for the regulation of onshore petroleum exploration and production under State/Territory legislation, there are particular legislative and administrative challenges that govern the exploitation of offshore petroleum, and have influenced Australia's regulation of its offshore petroleum resources. With the six colonies becoming States, and the Commonwealth government being established, upon Federation, as well as the subsequent creation of the two Territories, there are nine separate jurisdictions, all with the constitutional capacity to make laws with respect to Australia's maritime area. As such, this makes the regulation of the offshore jurisdiction complex and at times unwieldy.[511]

365. Australia made a formal claim to its Continental Shelf in 1953, which was recognised under the Geneva Convention on the Continental Shelf 1958 and then under the United Nations Convention of the Law of the Sea (UNCLOS).[512] Under international law, jurisdiction over offshore resources is conferred under UNCLOS, and the maritime zone is divided into three zones:

(1) the territorial sea: from baseline (mean low water mark) seaward 12 nm;
(2) the EEZ from 12 nm seaward to 200 nm; and

511. *See* Daintith T, 'A Critical Evaluation of the Petroleum (Submerged Lands) Act as a Regulatory Regime', *AMPLA Yearbook 2000* 91, 93 (2000).

512. 1958 Convention on the Continental Shelf (29 Apr. 1958, Geneva, Switzerland), UKTS 39 (1964), Cmnd 2422, 15 UST 471, 499 UNTS 311 (in force 10 Jun. 1964); 1982 United Nations Convention on the Law of the Sea (10 Dec. 1982, Montego Bay, Jamaica), 1833 UNTS 3, [1994] ATS 31, 21 ILM 1261 (1982) (in force 16 Nov. 1994).

(3) the continental shelf, from 200 nm to the edge of the continental shelf, as decided by the United Nations Commission on the Limits of the Continental Shelf, to a minimum distance of 200 nm from the baseline.[513]

366. UNCLOS regulates these maritime zones. Article 2 confers sovereignty of Australia's territorial sea on the Commonwealth. Similarly, sovereignty over Australia's EEZ is conferred under Article 56. In April 2008 jurisdiction over an area of the Continental Shelf was conferred on Australia as a result of a successful submission to the United Nations Commission on the Limits of the Continental Shelf. With this extension to Australia's maritime zone, Australia attained sovereignty over the mineral and other non-living resources of the seabed and subsoil of this continental shelf area under Article 77 of UNCLOS.

367. Up until the 1960s, the Commonwealth had played a very limited role in the regulation of petroleum exploration and production in the offshore area, with the first titles granted under State law. For example, the State of Western Australia had issued permits in the offshore area under State legislation. However, there has been controversy over Australia's offshore marine territory since the discovery of petroleum in Bass Strait in the 1960s. Initial arrangements between the Commonwealth and States for the exploration and production of offshore petroleum were created under the 1967 Petroleum Agreement.[514] The Agreement did not intend to create legal relationships enforceable in a court of law. Rather, it noted that petroleum activities would be encouraged by uniform legislative measures on the continental shelf beyond territorial limits, and that the state and national governments would co-operate to ensure effectiveness of authorities over petroleum resources.[515] The legal status of the Agreement was made clear in clause 26:

> the Governments acknowledge that this Agreement is not intended to create legal relationships justiciable in a Court of Law but declare that the Agreement shall be construed and given effect to by the parties in all respects according to the true meaning and spirit thereof.[516]

---

513. UNCLOS, Pt. V, Art. 76 reads: 'The continental shelf of a coastal State comprises the seabed and subsoil of the submarine areas that extend beyond its territorial sea throughout the natural prolongation of its land territory to the outer edge of the continental margin, or to a distance of 200 nm from the base lines from which the breadth of the territorial sea is measured where the outer edge of the continental margin does not extend up to that distance.'
514. Hunt C, *The Offshore Petroleum Regimes of Canada and Australia*, 63 (Calgary Institute of Resources Law 1989). This agreement between the Commonwealth, States and affected Territories is the *Agreement Relating to the Exploration for and the Exploitation of, the Petroleum Resources, and Certain Other Resources, of the Continental Shelf of Australia and of Certain Territories of the Commonwealth and of Certain Other Submerged Land signed on 16 Oct. 1967.*
515. *Ibid.*, 64.
516. Crommelin M, 'The Legal Character of Petroleum Production Licences in Australia', in Daintith T, *The Legal Character of Petroleum Licences: A Comparative Study*, 61 (University of Dundee, Centre for Petroleum and Mineral Law Studies, 1981).

368. To achieve constitutional legitimacy, each State and Territory government legislated with respect to offshore petroleum operations in identical terms to the Commonwealth petroleum legislation, the *Petroleum (Submerged Lands) Act 1967* (Cth) ('PSLA') (known as 'mirror' legislation). In addition, all governments agreed not to make, amend or repeal regulations under the legislation except under a prior agreement to do so

369. In 1973, with the passage of the *Sea and Submerged Lands Act 1973* (Cth), the Commonwealth declared sovereignty over the continental shelf and territorial sea, raising the ire of the States. Such Commonwealth marine sovereignty was challenged by the States in the Seas and Submerged Lands Case, arguing the colonies had historical jurisdiction over the territorial sea area at Federation, and therefore continued to exert jurisdiction post-Federation.[517] In this case, the High Court held that sovereign rights in relation to the continental shelf outside the territorial waters were vested in the Commonwealth. Furthermore, with the exception of Gibbs and Stephen JJ in dissent, the Justices also concurred that the sovereignty in the territorial waters was vested in the Commonwealth. As a consequence of this decision, the States were denied property rights in the seabed and subsea terrain of the territorial waters, since their territory ended at low water mark.[518]

370. The decision in *NSW v. Commonwealth* had a major impact on the States' jurisdiction over, and income from, offshore petroleum and prompted negotiations between petroleum-producing States and Territories and the Commonwealth. The resulting negotiations, known as the OCS forever changed the regulation of, and jurisdiction over, offshore petroleum resources in Australia. Under the terms of the OCS, jurisdiction over offshore petroleum exploration and production is divided between the States/Northern Territory (NT) and Commonwealth governments. Legislation was enacted at State and Commonwealth level through mirror legislation (the Commonwealth and State/Territory Petroleum (Submerged Lands) Acts).[519] In addition, a plethora of other necessary legislation was enacted to enable the implementation of the OCS.[520] The resulting regulation of the offshore areas as outlined under subsection 5(2) of the Offshore Petroleum Greenhouse Gas Storage Act ('OPGGSA') is as follows:

- the States are responsible for regulating the waters wholly within the State, such as bays and estuaries (State or internal waters);
- the States are responsible for regulating the first 3 nm seaward from the mean low water mark (coastal waters); and

517. *NSW v. Commonwealth* (1975) 135 CLR 337.
518. Brazil P, *Offshore Constitutional Settlement 1980: A Case Study in Federalism*, 2 (Centre for International and Public Law, Australian National University, 2001).
519. *Petroleum (Submerged Lands) Act 1967* (Cth); *Petroleum (Submerged Lands) Taxation Act 1967* (NSW); *Petroleum (Submerged Lands) Act 1982* (NSW); *Petroleum (Submerged Lands) Act 1982* (Qld); *Petroleum (Submerged Lands) Act* 1982 (SA); *Petroleum (Submerged Lands) Act 1982* (Tas); *Petroleum (Submerged Lands) Act 1982* (Vic); and *Petroleum (Submerged Lands) Registration Fees Act* 1990 (WA).
520. Required Acts include *Coastal Waters (Northern Territory Powers) Act 1980* (Cth); *Coastal Waters (Northern Territory Title) Act 1980* (Cth); *Coastal Waters (State Powers) Act 1980* (Cth); *Coastal Waters (State Title) Act 1980* (Cth); and *Offshore Minerals Act 1984* (Cth).

– the Commonwealth is responsible for the waters seaward of 3 nm to the edge of the continental shelf (Commonwealth waters).

371. In addition, subsection 5(2) of the OPGGSA states that the Commonwealth, the States and the Northern Territory should try to maintain, as far as practicable, common principles, rules and practices in regulating and controlling the exploration for, and exploitation of, offshore petroleum beyond the baseline of Australia's territorial sea. The structure of the arrangement is illustrated in Figure 1 below.

Figure 1 Offshore Petroleum Scheme of Regulation

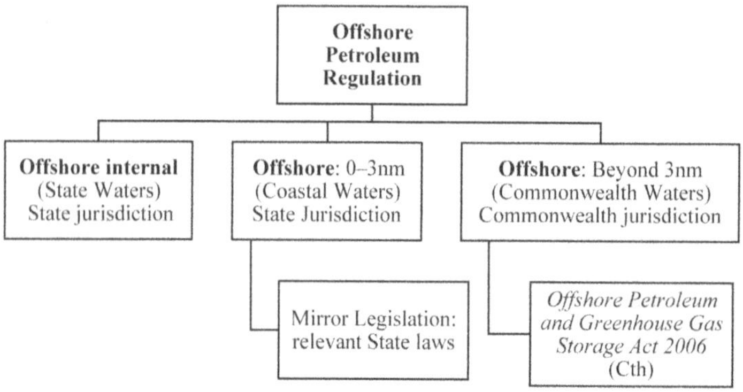

372. Onshore, jurisdiction over petroleum activities remains the responsibility of each of the States and Territories, with each jurisdiction legislating to regulate petroleum activities within its boundaries. This is because jurisdiction over onshore petroleum resources falls outside the ambit of the Commonwealth's enumerated powers in section 51 of the Commonwealth Constitution, thereby falling under the general right of a State to make laws with respect to the peace, welfare and good government of the State.

Chapter 2. Exploitation

§1. Overview of Regulatory Framework

373. Historically, the regulation of offshore petroleum activities (including the grant of petroleum licences) has been shared between the States/Northern Territory and the Commonwealth through the JA and the DA. In accordance with paragraph 5(2)(c) of the OPGGSA at the time, the States and the Northern Territory were required to share in the administration of the Commonwealth offshore petroleum legislation. As part of the shared regulation of petroleum resources, a JA for each State or Territory was established, initially under the *Petroleum (Submerged Lands) Act 1967* (Cth) ('PSLA'), and then maintained under the *Offshore Petroleum Act 2006* (Cth) (OPA) and then under Part 1.3 of the OPGGSA. The JA comprised the responsible State minister and the responsible Commonwealth minister,[521] with the Commonwealth minister having the power to decide a matter where the Commonwealth and State ministers disagree.[522] Similarly, there was a DA for each State and Territory offshore area, with the responsible minister of the State or Territory being the DA for that offshore area.

374. Under the PSLA, health and safety arrangements for offshore petroleum activities were initially shared between the Commonwealth and States/Northern Territory. However, after the Piper Alpha disaster in the UK, and ensuing Cullen Inquiry,[523] the Commonwealth recognised the need for a single offshore petroleum regulator for both Commonwealth and State offshore areas. As part of the Commonwealth commitment to establishing a national safety body, the *Petroleum (Submerged Lands) Amendment Act 2003* (Cth) was passed in order to establish the National Offshore Petroleum Safety Authority (NOPSA), and the PSLA was substantially amended. As part of the legislative reforms to the PSLA, the role of NOPSA was set out, including its structure and governance. Amendments were also made to the occupational health and safety provisions of the PSLA. Furthermore, major legislative reform to all State/Northern Territory mirror legislation was required in order to implement the roles and responsibilities of NOPSA in State and coastal waters where those States conferred upon the Commonwealth the right to regulate offshore petroleum safety in those waters.

375. As a result of the OCS and the establishment of NOPSA, multiple agencies regulated offshore petroleum activities, with differing responsibilities:

– day-to-day petroleum operations, pipelines and subsea facilities in Commonwealth waters regulated by a JA (comprising the relevant Commonwealth and State ministers); in the case of the States, the JA delegates the regulation to a DA comprising the State minister and that minister's agency;

521. OPGGSA, s. 56.
522. OPGGSA, s. 59.
523. The Hon Lord Cullen, *The Public Inquiry into the Piper Alpha Disaster* (Great Britain, Dept. of Energy, 1990).

- day-to-day petroleum operations, pipelines and subsea facilities in coastal and internal (State) waters regulated by the relevant State agency;
- environmental aspects of offshore petroleum activities in all waters regulated by the relevant State or the Commonwealth department, depending on the jurisdiction; and
- safety of all offshore facilities in all waters except Western Australian State and coastal waters regulated by NOPSA.

376. But for a serious facility integrity incident, this regulatory arrangement is likely to have continued. However, in August 2009, a blowout of the H1 Exploration well in the Montara field caused a major uncontrolled hydrocarbon release, which took over three months to contain. This incident was closely followed by the Deepwater Horizon well blowout and consequent devastating oil spill in the Gulf of Mexico in 2010. Coupled with a previous report into the regulatory burden in the offshore petroleum sector,[524] the decision was made to undertake major reform in the regulation of offshore petroleum exploration and production.

377. Amendments to the OPGGSA, which came into effect from 1 January 2012, fundamentally altered the OPGGSA regime. The peak regulatory body remains the JA for each offshore area, as constituted under section 56 of the OPGGSA, and has the extensive regulatory powers conferred by section 57 of the OPGGSA. The previously significant responsibility of the DA has been removed. Under the new regulatory structure, the JA retains responsibility for the grant of a petroleum exploration permit. The responsible minister of the relevant State or the Northern Territory continues to form part of the JA, together with the responsible Commonwealth minister. To implement the new regulatory structure, two new bodies which support the Joint Authorities were established:

(1) The National Offshore Petroleum Title Administrator (NOPTA) (referred to as the 'titles administrator' in OPGGSA) is responsible for all applications in relation to offshore titles and is responsible for assessing them. It has statutory responsibility for titles administration and data management functions in relation to offshore petroleum activities in Commonwealth waters.
(2) The National Offshore Petroleum Safety and Environmental Management Authority (NOPSEMA) is responsibile for occupational health and safety, structural integrity of facilities and platforms, environmental management and day-to-day operations for the offshore petroleum industry.

378. Under this arrangement, there are three different bodies with different regulatory functions. Consequently, the term 'regulator' can refer to the JA, NOPTA or NOPSEMA depending on the context. To assist in determining the regulatory role of each body, the new regulatory structure is illustrated below in Figure 2.

524. Australian Productivity Commission, *Review of the Regulatory Burden in the Upstream Petroleum (Oil and Gas) Sector: Research Report* (Productivity Commission, 2009).

Figure 2 Main Functions of the Offshore Petroleum Regulators

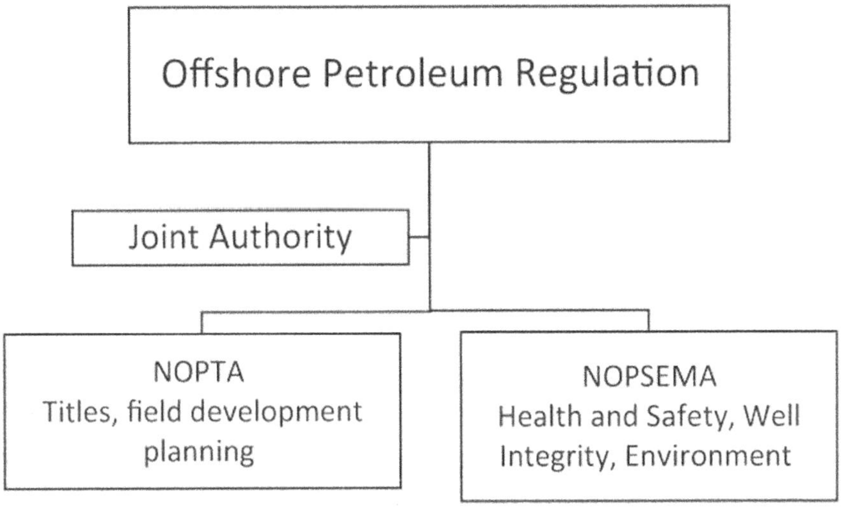

§2. Principal Legislatin: Commonwealth Waters

379. Australia's initial principal offshore petroleum Act, the PSLA (today superseded by the OPGGSA), has been described as 'a combination of painstaking detail and grand-scale delegation'[525] that was constructed as a coherent, but highly unusual system of offshore petroleum regulation, articulated by administrative rules and powers within the principal Act. It operates by prohibiting the activities it covers (e.g., extracting petroleum), and then granting companies an administrative authorisation to conduct the activity (this is known as a 'command and control' scheme of authorisation).[526] The prescriptive, rule-based, legislative structure that was created by the Commonwealth in 1967 to establish a regime for petroleum activities was necessary at that time. That command and control system is demonstrated by subsection 97(1) of the OPGGSA, where 'a person commits an offence if that person explores for petroleum and the exploration occurs in an offshore area'. It then excuses the taking of petroleum under subsection 97(1) where the taking of petroleum is 'authorised by a petroleum exploration permit, or otherwise required by or under this Act'.[527] This differs markedly from objective-based legislation, such as that in Norway, where the

525. Daintith T, *Discretion in the Administration of Offshore Oil and Gas: A Comparative Study*, 13 (AMPLA, 2005).
526. As noted in Daintith T, *supra* n. 511.
527. OPGGSA, subs. 97(2).

State merely stipulates the requirement for a licence in order to recover petroleum from an area, such as the right to recover petroleum,[528] rather than making it illegal to recover petroleum then creating conditions to make it legal.

380. Amendments to the rule-based PSLA from 1967 as a result of the changes to petroleum operations meant that there were over 1000 amendments of the Act from 1965–2005, resulting in over thirty separate compilations of the Act.[529] Industry and government alike had identified the PSLA as cumbersome, unwieldy and complex as the result of numerous amendments and updates,[530] leading to a rewrite of the PSLA in 2006. The new Act, the *Offshore Petroleum Act 2006* (Cth) (OPA), contained only changes to the structure and style of the legislation, implementing only a few minor policy changes from the regime set out in the PSLA.[531] In 2009, greenhouse gas storage provisions were added to the OPA, and it was renamed the OPGGSA.

381. The OPGGSA regulates all aspects of offshore petroleum exploration and production, and geosequestration of greenhouse gases, in Commonwealth waters, in nine chapters and seven Schedules:

- Chapter 1: Introduction;
- Chapter 2: Regulation of activities relating to petroleum, including licenses;
- Chapter 3: Regulation of activities relating to GHG substances;
- Chapter 4: Registration of transfers and dealings in petroleum, including farm-ins;
- Chapter 5: Registration of transfers and dealings in GHG titles;
- Chapter 6: Administration, including the functions and powers of the regulatory bodies;
- Chapter 7: Information relating to petroleum (including data management and data submission requirements);
- Chapter 8: Information relating to GHG (including data management);
- Chapter 9: Miscellaneous;
- Schedule 1: Scheduled areas for the states and territories;
- Schedule 2: Area that includes the area to be avoided;
- Schedule 3: Occupational health and safety (the primary safety provisions);
- Schedule 4: Petroleum production licenses to which the Royalty Act applies;
- Schedule 5: Release of technical information given to the DA before March 2000;
- Schedule 6: Transitional provisions; and
- Schedule 7: Greater Sunrise areas.

382. This OPGGSA was originally accompanied by general regulations, the Offshore Petroleum and Greenhouse Gas Storage Regulations 1985 ('OPGGSR')

528. The right for the State to regulate petroleum activities is granted under s. 1-2 of the *Petroleum Activities Act 1996* (Norway), and the right to recover petroleum is conferred under s. 3-2 of the *Petroleum Activities Act 1996* (Norway).
529. The full legislative history of the *Petroleum (Submerged Lands) Act 1967* (Cth) can be found at https://www.legislation.gov.au/ (accessed 18 Sept. 2016).
530. Explanatory Memorandum, Offshore Petroleum Bill 2005 (Cth), 2.
531. *Ibid.*

which were confined to particulars relating to a petroleum discovery, survey of wells and current rates for fees. The OPGGSA is now supported by three operational regulations:

(1) The Offshore Petroleum and Greenhouse Gas Storage (Resource Management and Administration) Regulations 2011, which set out the requirements for well operations, data and field development plans.
(2) The Offshore Petroleum and Greenhouse Gas Storage (Environment) Regulations 2009 ('OPGGS(E)R'), which regulate environmental protection.
(3) The Offshore Petroleum and GHG (Safety) Regulations ('OPGGS(S)R') which regulate facility (process) and worker safety.

383. The relationship of these regulations is illustrated in Figure 3 below.

Figure 3 Subordinate Legislation Made under the Offshore Petroleum and Greenhouse Gas Storage Act 2006 (Cth) (OPGGSA)

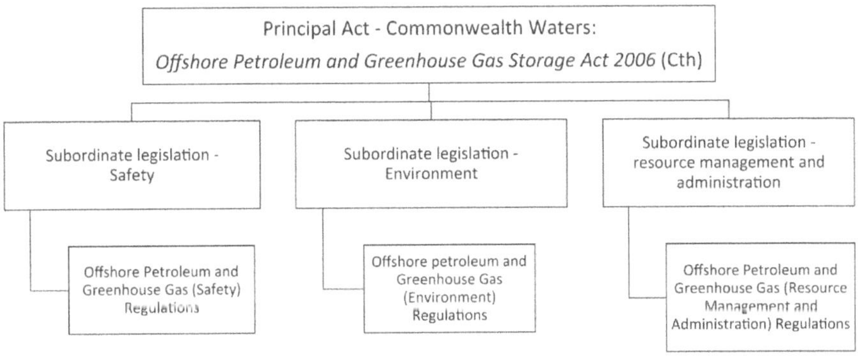

§3. Principal Legislation: Offshore State and Coastal Waters

384. The OPGGSA is an unusual Act. Whereas most petroleum regulatory regimes place the administrative details in the regulations rather than in the primary legislation,[532] the OPGGSA does not. Rather, the administrative details remain in the primary Act, a hangover from the original detailed PSLA to deal with State/Territory and Commonwealth jurisdictions. Consequently, the Act is over 1000 pages, and runs to three volumes. It has been suggested by the World Bank that the legislative structure that exists in Australia is an ineffective way of managing the change that is required

532. Daintith T, *supra* n. 511.

in petroleum regulation.[533] Indeed, the World Bank sees the role of regulations as subsidiary instruments to the petroleum legislation, not intended for legislative enactment, since this maintains maximum flexibility to respond to current petroleum developments which require changes in the regulation of petroleum operations.

385. The principal legislation for the regulation of offshore petroleum activities in coastal waters (i.e., those areas up to 3 nm that are regulated by the relevant State) is required under the OCS to 'mirror' the principal Commonwealth petroleum act, the OPGGSA. The principle of mirror legislation is that the law of the States reflects, or 'mirrors' that of the Commonwealth law in that subject area. Since the implementation of the OPGGSA, most jurisdictions have made alterations to the existing petroleum legislation. Only Victoria has made a serious attempt to alter the existing legislation to mirror the Commonwealth OPGGSA. While it might be argued that the key underlying principles in the existing State/Northern Territory Acts remain the same, the differences in the shape and drafting of the legislation make it increasingly difficult, from a practical and operational perspective, to say they are identical.

386. The relevant legislation for each State for offshore petroleum activities in internal waters and coastal waters is outlined in Table 5. The inclusion of onshore State legislation, as well as offshore State legislation, is necessary since in some States petroleum activities occur in internal waters, which are regulated under the State onshore petroleum Act. This is illustrated by a number of significant petroleum titles in Western Australia, particularly around Barrow Island, that are regulated under the *Petroleum and Geothermal Energy Resources Act 1967* (WA) and the *Petroleum Act 1936* (WA).

Table 5 State/Territory Legislation Regulating Petroleum Activities[534]

Jurisdiction	*Legislation*	
	Onshore and Internal Waters	**Coastal Waters**
New South Wales	– Petroleum (Onshore) Act 1991 – Petroleum (Onshore) Regulation 2016	– Petroleum (Offshore) Act 1982 – Petroleum (Offshore) Regulation 2016
Northern Territory	– Petroleum Act (no date) – Schedule of Onshore Petroleum Exploration and Production Requirements 2016	– Petroleum (Submerged Lands) Act 2016 – Petroleum (Submerged Lands) Regulations 2013

533. Onorato W, *Legislative Regimes Used to Foster Petroleum Development*, World Bank Policy Research Working Paper WPS 1420, 4 (World Bank, 1995).

534. From T Hunter and J Chandler, *Petroleum Law in Australia,* 140 (LexisNexis Butterworths, 2013) (updated).

Queensland	– Petroleum Act 1923	
	– Petroleum and Gas (Production and Safety) Act 2004 – Petroleum and Gas (Production and Safety) Regulation 2004 – Petroleum Regulation 2004 – Mineral and Energy Resources (Common Provisions) Act 2014 – Mineral and Energy Resources (Common Provisions) Regulation 2014	– Petroleum (Submerged Lands) Act 1982
South Australia	– Petroleum and Geothermal Energy Act 2000 – Petroleum and Geothermal Energy Regulations 2013	– Petroleum (Submerged Lands) Act 1982 – Petroleum (Submerged Lands) Regulations 2005
Tasmania	– Mineral Resources (Development) Act 1995	– Petroleum (Submerged Lands) Act 1982 – Petroleum (Submerged Lands) (Management of Environment) Regulations 2012 – Petroleum (Submerged Lands) (Diving Safety) Regulations 2008 – Petroleum (Submerged Lands) (Management of Safety on Offshore Facilities) Regulations 2008 – Petroleum (Submerged Lands) (Occupational Health and Safety) Regulations 2008 – Petroleum (Submerged Lands) (Pipelines) Regulations 2008
Victoria	– Petroleum Act 1998	– Offshore Petroleum and Greenhouse Gas Storage Act 2010

	– Petroleum Regulations 2011 – Pipelines Act 2005 – Pipelines Regulations 2007	– Offshore Petroleum and Greenhouse Gas Storage Regulations 2011
Western Australia	– Petroleum Act 1936* – Petroleum and Geothermal Energy Resources Act 1967 – Petroleum and Geothermal Energy Resources Regulations 1987 – Schedule of Onshore Petroleum Exploration and Production Requirements 1991 – Petroleum and Geothermal Energy Resources (Management of Safety) Regulations 2010 – Petroleum and Geothermal Energy Resources (Occupational Health and Safety) Regulations 2010 – Petroleum Pipelines Act 1970 – Petroleum Pipelines Regulations 1970 – Petroleum Pipelines (Management of Safety of Pipeline Operations) Regulations 2010 – Petroleum Pipelines (Occupational Health and Safety) Regulations 2010	– Petroleum (Submerged Lands) Act 1982 – Petroleum (Submerged Lands) Regulations 1990 – Petroleum (Submerged Lands) (Diving Safety) Regulations 2007 – Petroleum (Submerged Lands) (Management of Safety on Offshore Facilities) Regulations 2007 – Petroleum (Submerged Lands) (Occupational Health and Safety) Regulations 2007 – Petroleum (Submerged Lands) (Pipelines) Regulations 2007

* Repealed but continues to apply to the Barrow Island Lease.

§4. Ownership of Petroleum

387. According to the common law maxim *cuius est solum eius est usque ad coelum et ad inferos* (to whomsoever the soil belongs, he owns also to the sky and to the depths), there is a presumption that a land owner owns all minerals on or beneath the surface of the land.[535] This common law presumption was subject to the Royal Prerogative on Royal Metals (gold and silver). Until the enactment of the first mining laws in 1851, control over minerals and other natural resources vested with the British government.[536] Under a colonial grant of land title prior to 1851, ownership of resources under the ground (including the minerals) passed to the landowner (the grantee) in accordance with common law concepts, unless those rights were reserved from the grant. The ownership of underground resources excluded the precious metals of silver and gold, which were vested in the Crown by virtue of the Royal Prerogative.[537]

388. The common law presumption of ownership has been significantly altered or reversed as a result of statutory enactments. The Constitutions of New South Wales and Victoria vested control over Crown Lands in right of the State in 1855, thereby vesting ownership of minerals in the Crown. Since then, ownership of minerals in all Australian jurisdictions has altered, with respective Mineral Acts in Australian States and Territories vesting ownership of mineral resources in the Crown.

389. Today, in all States and Territories, ownership of petroleum resources in Australia is vested in the Crown. Crown ownership of petroleum (except oil shale) in Tasmania is vested in the Crown, unless it was held prior to the declaration of Crown ownership.[538] Similarly, ownership of petroleum is vested in the Crown in Queensland under section 9 of the *Petroleum Act 1923* (Qld) and section 26 of the *Petroleum and Gas (Production and Safety) Act 2004* (Qld). In New South Wales, ownership in petroleum existing in a natural state on or below the surface of any land in the State is the property of the Crown.[539] Petroleum that is found either on the surface or below the land is also owned by the State in Western Australia, whether or not alienated in fee simple.[540] On Commonwealth and Territories land, ownership of onshore petroleum resources is reserved for the Crown in right of the Commonwealth.[541]

390. Each State is generally recognised as having proprietary rights in the seabed of the territorial sea adjacent to its coast, and this is supported by Article 2 of UNCLOS. Beyond the Territorial Sea, the Commonwealth has sovereign rights over the seabed forming part of its continental shelf, rather than proprietary rights. In addition, rights conferred under UNCLOS grants sovereignty with respect to the natural resources of

535. For a discussion of this *see* Bradbrook A, 'The Relevance of the Cuius est Solum Doctrine to the Surface Landowner's Claims to Natural Resources Located Above and Beneath His Land', 11 *Adel LR* 462 (1988).
536. Hunt M, *Minerals and Petroleum Law, supra* n. 56, 8.
537. *Ibid.* Royal Prerogative refers to the customs, privileges and immunities at common law conferred on the Sovereign.
538. *Mineral Resources Development Act 1995* (Tas), s. 6.
539. *Petroleum (Onshore) Act 1991* (NSW), subs. 6(1).
540. *Petroleum and Geothermal Energy Resources Act 1967* (WA), s. 9.
541. *Atomic Energy Act 1953* (Cth); *Minerals Acquisition Act 1981* (NT), s. 3.

the seabed and subsoil, living or non-living in the EEZ and continental shelf.[542] As such, the control of the development of offshore petroleum is vested in the Commonwealth.

391. As the owner of in situ petroleum resources,[543] the relevant government has the unfettered right to award proprietary rights in its petroleum resources in order to exploit those resources as articulated in Article 1 of United Nations General Assembly Resolution 1803 (XVII) of 14 December 1962, *Permanent Sovereignty Over Natural Resources*.[544]

§5. Access to Petroleum

392. Where ownership or sovereignty over petroleum resources is vested in the Crown in respect of the relevant State or the Commonwealth, the Crown grants access to petroleum resources pursuant to the relevant statute. This access to petroleum resources in Australia is by way of a grant of a petroleum title, which confers in a legal sense an authorisation or right to the licensee to take petroleum. By awarding a petroleum title, the State 'fetters' its ownership rights, because the State is unable to transfer its ownership rights over the resource area for the period of the title. However, once the title has expired or has been handed back, the State is free to grant another title or transfer proprietary rights in the acreage to others. Thus, the rights conferred by the award of a petroleum title are conditional rights, dependent on a condition to be satisfied for the right to be either possessed or exercised. The conditions of the grant of a petroleum licence are usually outlined either within the legislative framework, or in administrative guidance notes that accompany a release of acreage for licensing.

393. In an economic (rather than legal) sense, the award of a petroleum title by a State confers property rights on the licensee.[545] These rights may be exclusive or non-exclusive rights over the title area, depending on the type of title awarded. These rights may also be proprietary in the sense that they are transferable, and can be sold, as is the case with other proprietary rights in property.

394. Given the number of offshore petroleum jurisdictions in Australia, this section will refer to the offshore Commonwealth jurisdiction. The process and type of licence is similar in all Australian jurisdictions.

395. Permits are not granted via an 'over-the-counter' system, which allows applicants to approach the regulator to negotiate the issue of a permit. Rather permits (both cash and work-programme bidding) are subject to competitive bidding following an annual release of blocks. Each year in the annual acreage release round, the government releases a selection of offshore areas for competitive bidding. The Commonwealth Resources and Energy Minister, generally coinciding with the Australian

542. UNCLOS, Arts 2, 56 and 77.

543. The Crown retains in situ rights over natural resources for two primary reasons: the resources provide the State with high economic value and the ownership of petroleum resources enables the government to have control over the development of those resources.

544. Adopted by General Assembly Resolution 1803 (XVII) of 14 Dec. 1962.

545. Property rights in this context are those rights pertaining to the permissible (socially sanctioned) use of resources, goods and services: D W Pearce (ed), *The MIT Dictionary of Modern Economics* 364 (The MIT Press, 1986).

Petroleum Production and Exploration Association Conference each year, launches the annual acreage release, and is supplemented by the annual *Offshore Petroleum Exploration Acreage Release Information Package*. Section 279 of the OPGGSA gives the regulator power to reserve blocks and, while a declaration remains in effect, various rights to such blocks will not be granted. The size of each exploration permit may vary from one block to up to 400 blocks.

396. The Australian Commonwealth offshore petroleum licensing system is one of administrative authorisations backed up by penalties. Access to petroleum in Australia is through the grant of an exploration permit, which confers the right to explore for petroleum in the Commonwealth's offshore zone under section 98 of the OPGGSA. While the Act does not expressly confer exclusive rights over the permit area, the exclusivity of those rights are implied rights since petroleum exploration offshore is prohibited under subsection 97(1) of the OPGGSA, unless the activity is authorised by the grant of an exploration licence under subsection 97(2).

397. The petroleum exploration permit gives its holder the exclusive right to explore in the permit area. Subject to compliance with the OPGGSA, this permit will also transition to a production licence. Where the permit holder makes a commercial discovery of petroleum a production licence will be issued, authorising the licensee to recovery petroleum from the licence area and granting the permit holder property rights in the petroleum recovered.[546]

398. The OPGGSA makes it an offence to carry out petroleum operations without the requisite authorisation in the form of a permit, lease, licence or authority. For example, section 97 of the OPGGSA provides that a person commits an offence if the person explores for petroleum in an offshore area unless authorised by a petroleum exploration permit or otherwise by the OPGGSA. The penalty is imprisonment for up to five years. It is therefore essential to have the appropriate permit, lease or licence in order to undertake any petroleum activity.

399. Chapter 4 of the OPGGSA provides for the titles administrator to keep a register of all petroleum titles. 'Title' is defined in section 467 of the OPGGSA to apply in Chapter 4 of the OPGGSA to mean a petroleum exploration permit, a petroleum retention lease, a petroleum production licence, an infrastructure licence, a pipeline licence or a petroleum access authority. The first reason why becoming the registered holder is important is that the rights under a petroleum title (such as property in petroleum recovered) belong to the registered holder. The second is that it is with the registered holder that the regulator will deal in relation to the requirements of the OPGGSA. So if a petroleum company wishes to receive notices in relation to its petroleum title (e.g., a notice relating to possible termination) and deal with the regulator about them, it will need to be the registered holder. The third reason is that dealings with existing titles require approval and registration under Chapter 4 of the OPGGSA to be effective to create or assign an interest in the title.

400. Petroleum exploration permits are generally granted through work-programme bidding, as required under section 104 of the OPGGSA. Work-programme bidding requires the applicant to outline proposals for work and expenditure, both within the

546. Section 98 of the OPGGSA confers the right to explore. Section 285 of the OPGGSA states that petroleum recovered in the licence area becomes the property of the petroleum production licensee.

mandatory 'primary' period of the first three years of the permit, as well as an indication in the 'secondary' period of the last three years of the six-year permit period. If there are multiple applicants, section 106 of the OPGGSA provides that the regulator may give an offer document under section 105 to whichever applicant, in the regulator's opinion, is most deserving of the grant of the petroleum exploration permit. In determining this, the regulator must have regard to criteria made publicly available.[547] For the purposes of section 106, the regulator may rank the applicants, and exclude applicants not considered to be deserving.[548]

401. In the event that the regulator cannot choose a winning applicant on the basis of the work programme proposed for the first three years (the primary work programme), the amount and timing of work proposed under the secondary work programme will be assessed under the criteria. The titles administrator, on behalf of the regulator, can seek clarification of the application and under subsection 258(2) of the OPGGSA seek supplementary information. The applicant can be invited to attend an interview. Under subsection 106(6) of the OPGGSA, if two or more applicants are in the opinion of the regulator equally deserving of the grant of an exploration permit, the regulator may invite them to propose additional work and expenditure.

402. The regulator has a wide discretion in its decision on whether to award a permit. It is not required to grant a permit to the most deserving applicant, but may do so. The JA also has discretion if there is only one applicant, with the discretion being reinforced in section 105 by the alternative that the JA may refuse to grant a permit to the applicant.

403. This approach to the award of access to petroleum is altering, as a result of the reintroduction of cash bidding in 2014. Under the system of cash bidding, a permit is awarded for a price, rather than bidding to carry out exploration work. A bid process determines the price paid by the successful applicant, where the highest bidder is awarded the licence, thereby generating revenue for the government. Although cash bidding had not been used since 1993, it was reintroduced in 2014 to allocate acreage in mature areas and in areas containing known petroleum accumulations. The existing work programme bidding system will be maintained for all other areas.

404. A transfer of a title is authorised under sections 472–474 of the OPGGSA, and executed under sections 3–4 of the *Offshore Petroleum and Greenhouse Gas Storage Regulations* (OPGGSR) as prescribed in Schedule 4 of the Regulations. The transfer of property in petroleum that has been extracted to a permittee, licensee or lessee is dealt with in subsection 285(2) of the OPGGSA.

---

547. OPGGSA, subs. 106(4).

548. The regulator is only required to have regard to the criteria when subsection 106(3) applies, and not when refusing an application or where there is a single applicant. For a fuller discussion of challenging a decision, *see* Warman T and Goldblatt L, 'The Work Program Bidding System for Exploration Permits under the Petroleum (Submerged Lands) Act 1967 (Cth)', 27 *ARELJ* 178 (2008).

§6. Safety Regulation

405. In 2008 and 2009, two potentially lethal petroleum facility incidents occurred, leading to sweeping changes in the regulation of safety, well integrity and environment in Commonwealth waters, as well as being the catalyst for the regulatory structure described above.

406. The first event was the Varanus Island gas pipeline explosion, which occurred at the Varanus Island offshore gas facility off the northwestern Western Australian coastline. It resulted from the rupture of a gas pipeline, cutting the supply of gas to Western Australia by 30%. Investigation into the incident indicated that the pipe rupture and explosion could have been avoided if facility integrity had been managed by a single agency rather than jointly by the NOPSA and the Western Australian Department of Mines and Petroleum, since a single regulator would have been responsible for the facility and the pipelines carrying the gas from the production platform to markets onshore.[549]

407. The second incident, arguably far more serious, was the Montara H1 Well Blowout and subsequent oil spill on 21 August 2009.[550] The findings of the Montara Commission of Inquiry, convened to investigate the incident, included that the failure of the operator, the company PTTEP Australasia, to use pressure containment caps as a secondary well control barrier in conjunction with the failure of the cement barrier, effectively left the well suspended without a satisfactorily tested and verified barrier, as well as the absence of other well control barriers.[551] The Montara Commission of Inquiry also noted that this practice did not constitute 'good oilfield practice', the standard required for the maintenance of well integrity at the time of the event, and blamed the blowout and consequential oil spill on the failure of the operator to adhere to the systems design, and the failure of the regulator in its role of ensuring compliance with the safety case regime and maintaining good oilfield practice.[552]

408. Prior to these incidents, the Australian Productivity Commission had considered regulation of the offshore jurisdiction in its 2009 *Review of Regulatory Burden on the Upstream Petroleum (Oil and Gas) Sector.*[553] It criticised the regulatory arrangements of the regime as unnecessarily 'complex', with 22 petroleum and pipeline laws applied at both the Commonwealth and State/Northern Territory levels and more than 150 statutes governing upstream petroleum activities in such areas as occupational health and safety, native title and environmental protection.[554] Most importantly, the report identified that well over fifty Commonwealth, State and Territory government agencies regulate upstream petroleum activities, incorporating the regulation of health

549. Bills K and D Agostini D, *Offshore Petroleum Safety Investigation: Varanus Island Incident Investigation* (Government of Western Australia, 2009).
550. All other major oil spills in Australia have been the result of ship-sourced pollution. For details of all major oil spills in Australia's waters in the last 30 years, refer to Australian Maritime Safety Authority, *Major Historical* Incidents, https://www.amsa.gov.au/environment/protecting-our-environment/major-historical-incidents/ (accessed 21 Sept. 2016).
551. Borthwick D, *Report of the Montara Commission of Inquiry* (Government of Australia, 2010).
552. *Ibid.*, 16–17.
553. Australian Productivity Commission, *supra* n. 524, at 34.
554. *Ibid.*, xxiii.

and safety, facility integrity, resource management, well operations and environmental issues.[555] One of the major areas of inconsistency Western Australia was regulation of wells drilled from offshore petroleum platforms, with regulatory responsibilities for well and platforms were divided between the Designated Authorities and the NOPSA, even though the risk of well blowout poses the greatest threat to the integrity of a platform.

409. The call by the Productivity Commission for a single offshore regular, combined with the findings of the Montara Commission of Inquiry, provided impetus for the establishment of an integrated Commonwealth regulator for safety, calling for the enlargement of NOPSA to encompass wells (which had been transferred to NOPSA in the aftermath of Montara) and the environment.

410. The recommended changes were implemented in January 2012 after a raft of legislative reform, creating a new regulatory structure as outlined above. The reforms created the National Offshore Petroleum Safety and Environmental Management Authority (NOPSEMA), responsibility for all aspects of safety. This includes responsibility for the safety of the platform is located above the sea and from which petroleum operations occur, and the integrity of the well that is being drilled subsea, as well as environmental management of the petroleum activity. As a consequence of the reforms, one body – NOPSEMA – is responsible for the regulation of all three areas. However, because no State/Territory is yet to confer regulation of their coastal or State waters on NOPSEMA, NOPSEMA's regulation of all three areas is confined to Commonwealth waters only.

411. The regulation of safety under NOPSEMA comprises two aspects: facility safety and integrity, and well integrity. The regulation of these aspects is accomplished through the use both legal (enforceable) and non-legal (unenforceable) tools:

Legal tools	Non-legal tools
Acts	Policy
Regulations	Guidelines
	Advices
	Guidance Notes

I. The Heart of Regulation: The 'Safety Case' Regime

412. The regulation of petroleum facilities such as platforms and wells is undertaken through the use a management plan (safety management plans (SMP) for facilities and well operations management plans (WOMPs) for wells) which is a permissioning document that the operator (the duty holder) is required to produce to demonstrate that the safety of the facility/well is managed through an assessment of and reduction of risks. The management plan is submitted to NOPSEMA, who will either accept the plan, if it demonstrates that risks have been identified and mitigated,

555. *Ibid.*

or rejects the plan. Once the management plan has been accepted, the plan dictates how safety of the facility/well will be preserved.

413. At the heart of the SMP is the safety case, a permissioning document that is prepared, submitted and 'owned' by the operator of the facility.[556] The legal requirement for the safety case is set out in Schedule 3 to the OPGGSA. Clause 9(1) outlines the duty of the operator to 'take all reasonably practicable steps to ensure that the facility is safe and without risk to the health of any person at or near the facility', and that 'all work and other activities carried out at the facility are carried out in a manner that is safe and without risk to the health of any person at or near the facility'.

414. A requirement of the safety case is that it addresses all aspects of the facility, including the, construction, installation, modification and maintenance of the facility, and considers all activities that will occur at the facility. As part of the SMP all standards that have been applied or will apply at the facility must be specified and complied with.

415. The safety case is assessed by NOPSEMA, which accepts the safety case if satisfied that the control arrangements set out in the document demonstrate that the risks on the facility will be reduced to 'as low as is reasonably practicable' ('ALARP'). Although a definition of ALARP is elusive, and does not appear in the OPGGSA or regulations, the concept of reasonably practicable was considered in *Edwards v. National Coal Board*:

> 'Reasonably Practicable' is a narrower term than 'physically possible' and seems to me to imply that a computation must be made by the owner in which the quantum of risk is placed in one scale and the sacrifice involved in the measures necessary for averting the risk (whether in money, time or trouble) is placed in the other; and that if it is to be shown that there is a gross disproportion between them – the risk being insignificant in relation to the sacrifice – the defendants discharge the onus on them.[557]

416. Therefore, ALARP is the point where the sacrifice required to reduce the impact and risk of the activity any further would be grossly disproportionate to the benefit gained.

417. The principle of the safety case was outlined by Lord Cullen in the Piper Alpha Inquiry, stating that those who create the risk must manage the risk. Therefore, the safety case is prepared by the operator of the facility, (the risk creator) rather than the regulator. It is the operator's job to assess the processes, procedures and systems on the facility to identify and evaluate the risks, and then implement appropriate controls. This is because it is the operator who has the greatest in-depth knowledge of the facility, and not the regulator. Given that the workers of the facility are those who are exposed to and create/control the risk, the involvement of the workforce in the preparation of the safety case is essential. Furthermore, worker involvement is necessary so that they understand what happens on the facility and why. This involvement

---

556. NOPSEMA, *The Safety Case in Context: An Overview of the Safety Case Regime*, Guidance Note *N04300-GN0060 Revision 6*, June 2013, 1.
557. [1949] 1 KB 704, 712 (Asquith LJ).

makes it more likely that workers will do the right thing, since they are undertaking the behaviour to reduce risk, rather than complying with a 'rules-based' culture.

418. Regulation of safety under the SCR is predicated on four pillars:

(1) Assessment of the SCR that is rigorous and targeted (challenges the operator to question: Have we done enough?).
(2) Inspection of the facilities that is thorough and targeted against the accepted permissioning document (challenges the operator to question: Are we doing what we said we would do?).
(3) Investigation of incidents by independent inspectors to determine what went wrong and determine whether enforcement or prosecution is required (challenges the operator to question: What was not done? What can we learn?).
(4) Enforcement – take action within powers conferred under the OPGGSA and regulations to secure compliance with the regulatory regime.

§7. Regulation of the Environment

419. The regulation of the environmental effects of offshore petroleum activities is shared between the States/Northern Territory and the Commonwealth. The Commonwealth regulates the environment in Commonwealth waters, through NOPSEMA, and States/Northern Territory regulate the environment in coastal and State waters.

420. The regulation of environmental aspects of petroleum activities in State or internal waters in each jurisdiction occurs under State/Northern Territory onshore legislation, applicable to petroleum licences within State waters or coastal waters. There are no petroleum titles in State waters in Queensland or New South Wales, with some titles in South Australian and Victorian waters. By far the largest numbers of titles in State waters occur in Western Australia. The Western Australian State waters include Barrow Island and the petroleum titles in the vast State waters from Exmouth to Dampier.

421. The regulation of the environment in coastal waters in each jurisdiction is undertaken under the mirror legislation utilising the environment plan system, unless the jurisdiction confers its regulatory powers on the Commonwealth. As at April 2016, no States/Northern Territory had conferred regulation of the environment on the Commonwealth.

422. In Western Australia, the Petroleum (Submerged Lands) (Environment) Regulations made under the *Petroleum Submerged Lands Act 1982* (WA) ('PSLA (WA)') mirror the onshore environmental regulations under the *Petroleum and Geothermal Energy Resources Act 1967* (WA) ('PGERA'), which were modelled on the Commonwealth offshore environmental regulations. The idea of modelling the Commonwealth regulations is to ensure consistency in the regulation of the onshore and offshore environment. As a result, the regulation of the environment in Western Australia's coastal waters is the same as that onshore and in State waters, with minor adjustments where necessary. Project proponents utilise the Guidelines for the Preparation and Submission of an Environment Plan, which apply to both the PGERA environment regulations and the PSLA (WA) environment regulations.

I. Commonwealth Waters

423. NOPSEMA regulates three areas of offshore petroleum activities: facilities safety, well integrity and environmental management. The regulation of safety and well integrity was considered above. This section considers the environmental management regulations.

424. Environmental management in Commonwealth waters is predicated on a system of environmental assessment and approvals. An offshore petroleum activity must usually undergo two environmental approval processes: assessment and approval under the OPGGSA and accompanying regulations, and assessment and approval under the *Environmental Protection and Biodiversity Conservation Act 1999* (Cth) ('EPBC Act').

A. Environment Approvals under the OPGGSA

425. The Commonwealth Environment Regulations ensure that petroleum operations are carried out in a manner consistent with the principles of ecologically sustainable development and in accordance with an Environment Plan (EP) that has appropriate environmental performance objectives, standards and measurement criteria that determine whether the objectives and standards have been met.[558] Thus an operator requires an accepted EP prior to the commencement of a petroleum activity. The OPGGS(E)R regulates EPs, based on four principles. Environment Plans are:

(1) objective-based, setting out general requirements, where the operator is then responsible for determining their approach to meet these objectives;
(2) risk-based, where the central basis of the EP is the assessment and management of the environmental impacts and risks of the petroleum activity to as low as is reasonably practicable;
(3) performance-based, where appropriate environmental performance objectives and environmental performance standards are in place that have measurement criteria to determine if they are being met; and
(4) system-based, where a structures risk management process is applied to developing the EP which shows the continual and iterative steps that are followed to assess and manage environmental impacts and risks effectively.[559]

426. The content of an EP required for approval is outlined in the OPGGS(E)R and must include all the elements specified in the Environment Regulations. It is usual for the operator to submit a draft management plan to NOPSEMA for the activities that are going to be undertaken. NOPSEMA then assesses the plan under an objective-

558. OPGGS(E)R, reg. 3.
559. NOPSEMA, *Environment plan content requirements*, Guidance Note N04750-GN1344, Revision No. 3, 1 Apr. 2016.

based system utilising the concepts of ALARP. Similar to the safety regulation system under the SMP, NOPSEMA will then either accept the EP, or will send the plan back to the project proponent for redrafting.

427. As part of the EP process, the operator is required to carry out the following assessments:

- describe the activity, environment, regulatory and other requirements, and acceptable levels for the impacts and risks;
- detail environmental impacts and risks for the activity;
- evaluate and demonstrate that impacts and risks are of an acceptable level;
- evaluate and demonstrate that the impacts and risks are reduced to as low as is reasonably practicable; and
- define environmental performance objectives, environmental performance standards and measurement criteria that capture performance and monitoring requirements.

428. Similar to the safety case, the EP which comprises the environmental assessment (or planning) phase, and the implementation (or operational) phase, is owned by the operator rather than the NOPSEMA. The role of NOPSEMA in the management of environment is twofold. First, NOPSEMA is an assessor of the EP, either accepting or refusing the operator's Environment Plan in the planning phase. NOPSEMA accepts an EP if there are reasonable grounds for believing that the EP meets the criteria outlined in regs 10 and 11 of the OPGGS(E)R. NOPSEMA's second role is that of monitoring once the Environment Plan has been accepted and petroleum activities have commenced, to ensure the operator's continued compliance with the Environment Plan during the operational phase.

B. Approvals under the EPBC Act

429. In addition to undergoing environmental assessment and approval under the OPGGSA, projects that affect MNES, as defined under the EPBC Act, will be referred to the relevant government agency for assessment under the EPBC Act. Under this Act, an action will require approval from the Environment Minister if the action has, will have, or is likely to have a significant impact on a matter of national environmental significance (MNES).

430. Under section 523 of the EPBC Act, an action is defined broadly to include a project, a development, an undertaking, an activity or a series of activities, or an alteration of any of these things. A 'significant impact' is defined as 'an impact which is important, notable, or of consequence, having regard to its context or intensity. Whether or not an action is likely to have significant impact depends on the sensitivity, value and quality of the environment which is impacted, and on the intensity, duration, magnitude and geographic extent of the impacts.'[560]

431. *MNES* include:

560. *Booth v. Bosworth* (2001) 114 FCR 39, 64 (Branson J). *See also Matters of National Environmental Significance: Significant impact guidelines 1.1, Environment Protection and Biodiversity Conservation Act 1999*, 2 (Australian Government, Dept of the Environment, 2013).

- the world heritage values of declared World Heritage Properties;
- the National Heritage Values of National Heritage places;
- the ecological character of a declared Ramsar wetlands of international importance;
- listed threatened species and ecological communities;
- listed migratory species protected under international agreements;
- nuclear actions (including uranium mining);
- the Commonwealth Marine environment;
- the Great Barrier Reef Marine Park; and
- water resources, in relation to CSG and large coal mining developments.

432. To determine whether an action requires approval by the Minister, a project that includes an MNES is referred (usually self-referred by the Operator, but can also be referred by a third party) to the relevant government agency, the Commonwealth DEE, for assessment as to whether the proposed development is a 'controlled action'. The Commonwealth Environment Minister will determine whether the action is a controlled action, that is, one which requires environment assessment and approval by the Environment Minister (with assistance of the DEE) under the EPBC Act, as it may pose a significant risk to an MNES.

433. After a process of Strategic Environment Assessment in 2014, the Commonwealth government recently 'streamlined' the environment assessment and approvals process for offshore petroleum projects, by giving NOPSEMA the power to assess projects under the EPBC Act, rather than the Commonwealth Environment Department.[561] Thus, NOPSEMA now assesses offshore petroleum projects under both the OPGGSA and the EPBC Act.

561. *Program Report - Strategic Assessment of the environmental management authorisation process for petroleum and greenhouse gas storage activities administered by the National Offshore Petroleum Safety and Environmental Management Authority under the Offshore Petroleum and Greenhouse Gas Storage Act 2006* (Australian Government, 7 Feb. 2014); *Notification of Decision to Endorse the Program to Streamline Offshore Petroleum and Greenhouse Gas Activity Environmental Approvals* (Australian Government, Dept of the Environment, 7 Feb. 2014); *Final Approval Decision for the Taking of Actions in Accordance with an Endorsed Program Under the Environment Protection and Biodiversity Conservation Act 1999 (Cth) (EPBC Act)* (Australian Government, Dept of the Environment, 27 Feb. 2014).

Chapter 3. Transportation and Distribution

§1. Transportation at Sea

434. Transport of petroleum at sea comprises two main methods: via pipeline, or through the use of tankers. The transport of petroleum via pipelines is regulated under the OPGGSA in Commonwealth Waters, and, in coastal and State waters, the relevant State/Northern Territory Petroleum (Submerged Lands) Acts (or, in the case of NSW and Victoria, the *Petroleum (Offshore) Act 1982* (NSW) and the *Offshore Petroleum and Greenhouse Gas Storage Act 2010* (Vic)) and regulations made under those Acts.[562] These Acts and regulations regulate the construction and operation of pipelines through a licensing regime. The movement of oil and gas by ship is regulated by Commonwealth and State shipping legislation in accordance with international instruments, and is largely directed at protection of the environment from oil spills.[563]

§2. Transportation on Land

435. Land transportation of crude oil includes the use of pipelines that are utilised primarily for gas. State Acts regulate the construction and operation of pipelines through licensing schemes established under State legislation, including the *Pipelines Act 1967* (NSW); *Energy Pipelines Act 2015* (NT); *Petroleum and Geothermal Energy Act 2000* (SA); *Petroleum and Gas (Production and Safety) Act 2004* (Qld); *Gas Pipelines Act 2000* (Tas); *Pipelines Act 2005* (Vic); and the *Petroleum Pipelines Act 1969* (WA). The majority of refined products are transported by road using trucks. Road transport is regulated under a set of model laws that form the basis of road rules of each Australian State and Territory for the transport of dangerous goods, although not all provisions have been copied exactly.[564]

562. *Petroleum Offshore Regulation 2016* (NSW); *Petroleum (Submerged Lands) Pipelines Regulations 2013* (NT); *Petroleum (Submerged Lands) Pipelines Regulations 2005 (SA)*; *Offshore Petroleum and Greenhouse Gas Storage Regulations 2011* (Vic); *Petroleum (Submerged Lands) Pipelines Regulations 2008* (Tas); *Petroleum (Submerged Lands) Pipelines Regulations 2007* (WA).
563. For example, the *Protection of the Sea (Prevention of Pollution from Ships) Act 1983* (Cth) implements the international regime for preventing marine pollution by ships established under the *International Convention for the Prevention of Pollution from Ships* (London, 1973), as modified by the 1978 and 1997 Protocols ('MARPOL 73/78'). The Australian States enacted legislation to implement MARPOL in State coastal waters. The *Protection of the Sea (Civil Liability) Act 1981* (Cth) implements international law regarding civil liability for damage for oil pollution from ships.
564. National Transport Commission (Model Legislation - Transport of Dangerous Goods by Road or Rail) Regulations 2007.

Chapter 4. Consumption

436. Distribution and consumption of refined petrol products in Australia are matters for the States and Territories. In Australia, the consumption of petroleum is not regulated, nor is there any pricing or quantity control regarding the consumption of petroleum. Taxes in petroleum are levied by the Commonwealth government and some States, and vary wildly between jurisdictions.

§1. Petrol Pricing

437. There are a number of unique, if suspicious, features of the Australian petrol market. One is the apparent 'same price' for petrol. The Australian Consumer and Competition Commission undertook an investigation of petrol pricing, and found that there is intense competition but no apparent evidence of gouging or collusion.[565] The second feature of the Australian market is that of *sawtooth pricing*, where there are daily, weekly and seasonal fluctuations in demand, all of which impact on the price of petrol in the marketplace. In particular, there are lower prices at the beginning of the week, higher prices at the weekend. This form of pricing has radically altered the price of petrol over the course of the week, triggering 'price wars', with prices varying by up to 30 cents per little in a week.

438. The price of petrol in Australia is influenced by a number of issues aside from the obvious influence of the fluctuating price of crude. Other influences include the following:

- Movements in Australian petrol prices follow international benchmarks for refined oil rather than crude. Australian petrol prices move in line with the spot price of Singapore Mogas 95, which is refined oil from Singapore, rather than crude oil. Singaporean refined oil is used since Singapore is the closest major petroleum refining and marketing centre to Australia. Furthermore, Australia does not have the refinery capacity or sale volume to warrant it being used as an international benchmark. The price of Singapore Mogas 95 is variable since it incorporates refinery costs.
- Activities in the northern hemisphere have an impact on the price of crude oil, and therefore petrol. Cold weather in Europe can influence crude prices due to high demand for heating fuels. This increases demand for refined petroleum products, thus driving the price of petrol up in the marketplace.
- High demand in the Asia-Pacific region to fuel fast growing economies has a huge influence on the price of Australian petrol. The fastest developing economies in the world are located close to Australia, especially China and India. These consumers also demand Singapore Mogas, thereby placing pressure on Australia's

565. Australian Consumer and Competition Commission, *Petrol Prices and Australian Consumers: Report of the ACCC Inquiry into the Price of Unleaded Petrol* (Commonwealth of Australia, 2007).

source of refined oil, and compete with Australia for refined oil products. Market forces then drive up the price of Singapore Mogas remains relatively high.

439. Although petroleum is an internationally traded commodity, with externalities contributing to domestic oil prices, there are also domestic factors which influence domestic oil prices. Major domestic influences include:

- *Consumer behaviour.* Consumers actively seek out cheap fuel prices, and in doing so drive strong competition between petrol retailers. This exacerbates the 'sawtooth' price cycle.
- *Taxes and tariffs.* The price of petrol only accounts for about 60% of the pump price, with the balance comprising: (a) federal taxes and excise (excise around 26%, plus Goods and Services Tax (GST) of 10%); and (b) additional State taxes added in some. Fuel excise is discussed further in Part VI: Energy and Tax.
- *Location-city v. country.* Retail margins (pump price less wholesale price) are typically higher in the country compared with major capital cities, since there are lower fuel volumes and shop sales over which to spread service station operating costs. In addition, freight and haulage is typically 1.5–3c per litre greater for country than city delivery. Distribution costs may be significantly higher for country also.
- *Other production costs.* These include refining, transport, storage, insurance and wharfage.[566]

440. In the 2006 Senate Report from the Standing Committee on Economics, *Petrol Prices in Australia,* the Australian Government considered evidence from the public, companies and other relevant parties in relation to petrol prices.[567] The report found no evidence of price collusion, and suggested that a number of options, including, monitoring, community education and wholesale price regulation, could be utilised to establish and maintain relatively stable and low petrol prices in Australia. To date none of these have been implemented.

§2. Fuel Standards and Labelling

I. Fuel Consumption Standards

441. Australia does not have mandatory carbon dioxide emission standards requirements for either cars or light commercial vehicles. As early as 1991, the Commonwealth Ecologically Sustainable Development Transport Working Group recommended that mandatory fuel economy standards be introduced. However, this has not occurred. The government has instead preferred to negotiate with the automotive industry regarding the establishment of voluntary standards. In 2003 the Australian

566. Australian Parliament, Senate Legislative and General Purpose Standing Committee, *Petrol Prices in Australia,* 35 (Senate Standing Committee on Economics, 2006).
567. *Ibid.*

Government and Federal Chamber of Automotive Industries (FCAI) agreed a voluntary fuel-efficiency target of 6.8L/100 km for new petrol passenger cars by 2010.[568] In 2005, the industry adopted a voluntary target to reduce average emissions for all new light vehicles from 245 to 222 g CO_2/km by 2010, a target which was achieved two years early and not extended.[569]

442. More recently, in May 2007, the COAG requested the Australian Transport Council (ATC) and the Environment Protection and Heritage Council (EPHC) to prepare a joint report on a package of vehicle fuel efficiency measures designed to move Australia towards international best practice. The Final Report of the joint ATC/EPHC Vehicle Fuel Efficiency Working Group recommended that the Australian Government 'undertake a detailed Regulatory Impact Statement to assess the costs and benefits of introducing CO_2 emission standards for light vehicles'.[570] On 2 July 2009, COAG considered the recommendations of the Report, and, in the National Energy Efficiency Strategy, agreed to 'develop a package of measures to improve the fuel efficiency of the Australian vehicle fleet', including by assessing the costs and benefits of introducing carbon dioxide emission standards for light vehicles.[571] COAG subsequently requested the Department of Infrastructure and Transport to undertake a detailed regulatory impact analysis for introducing carbon dioxide emission standards for light vehicles.[572]

443. Despite the Gillard Labor government promising in 2011 to introduce mandatory carbon dioxide emissions standards for new cars from 2015,[573] after which the Department of Infrastructure and Transport prepared in Discussion Paper on the topic,[574] the government did not do so. In June 2014, the Climate Change Authority recommended the introduction of mandatory CO_2 emissions standards,[575] but this recommendation has not been implemented by the current Coalition government. In October 2015, the Turnbull government established a Ministerial Forum on Vehicle Emissions to review the issue of Australia's vehicle emissions.[576] In February 2016,

568. Lyster R and Bradbrook A, *Energy Law and the Environment* (Cambridge University Press, 2006) 107; Matthew L James, *Vehicle Fuel Efficiency Standards*, Parliamentary Research Paper (28 Jun. 2013).
569. Climate Change Authority, *Light Vehicle Emissions Standards for Australia: Research Report* (Climate Change Authority, 2014).
570. Australian Transport Council and the Environment Protection and Heritage Council, Vehicle Fuel Efficiency Working Group, *Final Report,* 26 (2009).
571. Council of Australian Governments, *National Strategy on Energy Efficiency* (2 Jul. 2009, updated July 2010).
572. Department of Infrastructure and Transport, *FINAL REGULATION IMPACT STATEMENT FOR REVIEW OF EURO 5/6 LIGHT VEHICLE EMISSIONS STANDARDS* (November 2010).
573. Anthony Albanese (Minister for Infrastructure and Transport), *New Pollution standards for vehicles*, Media Release, 11 Jun. 2011 http://anthonyalbanese.com.au/new-pollution-standards-for-vehicles-2 (accessed 28 Oct. 2015).
574. *Light vehicle CO_2 emissions standards for Australia, Key Issues Discussion Paper* (Australian Government, Department of Infrastructure and Transport, 2011).
575. Climate Change Authority, *supra* n. 569.
576. Australian Government, Department of Infrastructure and Regional Development, *Ministerial Forum on Vehicle Emissions*, https://infrastructure.gov.au/roads/environment/forum/ (accessed 25 Sept. 2016).

the Forum released a Vehicle Emissions Discussion Paper for public consultation, which again considered the issue of vehicle emissions standards.[577] A Regulatory Impact Statement for the measures contained in the latest Discussion Paper is expected to be released in 2017.

II. Fuel Labelling

444. Australia has had a mandatory national labelling scheme for fuel consumption of motor vehicles since 1 January 2004. This scheme is implemented through the Australian Design Rules (3rd ed), made under section 7 of the *Motor Vehicle Standards Act 1989* (Cth), which permits the Minister to determine national standards for road vehicles. The latest instrument requiring fuel labelling is ADR 81/02.[578] This Rule makes it mandatory for a fuel consumption label or energy consumption label to be placed in a bottom corner of the front windscreen on the inside of the windscreen of all new model vehicles produced on or after 1 October 2008, and all vehicles produced on or after 1 April 2009 that are not new models. For vehicles powered by an internal combustion engine only and hybrid electric vehicles which are not externally chargeable, the label must contain fuel consumption and CO_2 emission results. Pure electric vehicles and hybrid electric vehicles which are externally chargeable are required to have energy consumption labels. The requirements apply to all M and N category vehicles with a gross vehicle mass (GVM) not exceeding 3.5 tonnes, which are essentially passenger cars and pick-up trucks.

445. The Australian Government Department of Infrastructure and Regional Development also maintains an online *Green Vehicle Guide*, which rates all new Australian passenger, four-wheel drive and light commercial vehicles based on fuel consumption, and greenhouse and air pollution emissions, thereby assisting prospective purchasers to choose a more efficient model, and reducing fuel consumption.[579]

577. *Vehicle Emissions Discussion Paper* (Australian Government, Department of Infrastructure and Regional Development, 2016).
578. *Vehicle Standard (Australian Design Rule 81/02 – Fuel Consumption Labelling for Light Vehicles) 2008.*
579. Australian Government, Department of Infrastructure and Regional Development, *Green Vehicle Guide* https://www.greenvehicleguide.gov.au/ (accessed 18 Sept. 2016).

Part IV. Regulatory Framework Concerning Coal

Chapter 1. Production

446. Coal is Australia's largest and cheapest energy resource, with resources located close to sources of energy demand. Australia has large deposits of brown coal and high quality black coal. Anthracite, which has the highest rank, is used mainly in steel and cement manufacturing. Bituminous coal is used for power generation, metallurgical applications and general industrial use, including cement manufacture.[580] Lignite and lower rank sub-bituminous coals are used predominantly for domestic power generation. Coal is used to produce about 80% of Australia's electricity, and the coal mining industry provides significant employment, attracts significant capital investment and is a major source of domestic income and export revenue.[581]

447. At the end of 2014, Australia's recoverable Economic Demonstrated Resources of black coal were estimated at 63.3 Gt, comprising 9% of the world's recoverable economic demonstrated resources of black coal. Australia was ranked fourth in the world's recoverable reserves of black coal and fourth in world production of black coal.[582] Australia has significant reserves of both thermal (steaming) coal, which is black coal mainly used to generate electricity in power stations, and metallurgical or coking coal, suitable for making coke, which is used in the production of iron.[583]

448. The overwhelming majority (96%) of Australia's EDR of black coal occur in Queensland (58%) and New South Wales (38%).[584] The major coal-producing basin in Queensland is the Bowen Basin, which covers an area of approximately 120,000 km^2. Both metallurgical and thermal coals are produced from the Bowen Basin, predominantly for export markets.[585] There are also significant black coal resources

580. Geoscience Australia and the Bureau of Resources and Energy Economics, *Australian Energy Resource Assessment* (2nd ed, 2014) (interim update 2016), http://www.ga.gov.au/aera/coal (accessed 29 Sept. 2016).
581. Geoscience Australia, *Coal Resources*, http://www.ga.gov.au/scientific-topics/energy/resources/coal-resources (accessed 29 Sept. 2016).
582. *Ibid.*
583. *Ibid.*
584. Britt A, Whitaker A, Cadman S, Summerfield D, Kay P, Champion D, McKay A, Miezitis Y, Porritt K, Schofield A and Jaireth S, *Australia's Identified Mineral Resources 2014*, 4 (Geoscience Australia, Canberra, 2014).
585. Geoscience Australia and the Bureau of Resources and Energy Economics, *Australian Energy Resource Assessment* (2nd ed, 2014), 136-7.

in the Surat, Clarence-Moreton and Galilee Basins.[586] The Surat Basin covers an area of 270,000 km^2 in Queensland and New South Wales, and is a significant source of thermal coal for domestic and export markets. The Clarence-Moreton Basin, which straddles the state border between southeast Queensland and northeast Queensland, is a source of coal for domestic electricity and generation and industrial use in Queensland and for export, although coal is not mined in that part of the basin within New South Wales.[587] The Galilee Basin, which covers an area of 247,000 km^2, is known to contain significant resources of black coal, with recoverable EDR estimated 6.3 million tonnes of black coal.[588] As of 30 September 2016, no large coal mines had yet been constructed in the Galilee Basin, although three major projects have received development approval from the Queensland government.[589]

449. In New South Wales, most of the State's known recoverable coal resources are contained within the Sydney and Gunnedah Basins, with smaller deposits in the Gloucester and Oaklands Basins.[590] The Sydney and Gunnedah Basins cover areas of 35,000 km^2 and 15,000 km^2 respectively, while the Gloucester Basin is approximately 300 km^2.[591] No coal is currently mined from the Oaklands Basin, which covers approximately 3,800 km^2 in the Riverina district of southern NSW, despite extensive exploration.[592]

450. Some black coal is located in South Australia, Tasmania and Western Australia, and relatively small amounts of coal are produced in those States. In Western Australia, black coal from the Collie Basin is currently mined for that State's domestic electricity generation. Deposits have also been identified in the southwest of WA in the Perth, Wilga and Boyup Basins, and in the northwest of WA in the Canning Basin. In South Australia, black coal from Leigh Creek is currently mined for state electricity generation, while major resources have been identified in the Ackaringa Basin in central SA. In Tasmania, the Cornwall colliery produce most of the black coal required for Tasmania's domestic electricity generation.[593]

451. As well as significant reserves of black coal, approximately 8% of the world's recoverable brown coal is found in Australia.[594] Brown coal, known as lignite, is of lower rank than black coal. As at 31 December 2014, Australia's EDR of brown coal were estimated at 62 Gt. All of these reserves are located in the State of Victoria, with approximately 93% in the La Trobe Valley in the Gippsland Basin.[595] Brown coal

---

586. Britt et al., *supra* n. 584 at 4.
587. Geoscience Australia/BREE, *supra* n. 580 at 137.
588. *Ibid.*
589. The Alpha coal mine project, the Kevin's Corner mine (adjacent to the Alpha coal mine) and the Adani Carmichael coal mine, which have been approved with conditions, were all the subject of (ultimately unsuccessful) legal challenge. Adani's Carmichael coal mine in particular has been, and remains, particularly controversial in Australia.
590. Britt et al., *supra* n. 584 at 4.
591. Geoscience Australia/BREE, *supra* n. 580 at 137.
592. NSW Department of Industry, Resources and Energy, *Oaklands Basin*, http://www.resourcesandenergy.nsw.gov.au/miners-and-explorers/geoscience-information/nsw-geology-overview/sedimentary-basins/oaklands-basin (accessed 29 Sept. 2016).
593. Geoscience Australia/BREE, *supra* n. 580 at 137.
594. Geoscience Australia/BREE, *supra* n. 580.
595. Britt et al., *supra* n. 584 at 4.

production was estimated to be around 73 Mt in 2013.[596] As it is generally not seen as suitable for export, brown coal is used exclusively for domestic electricity generation within Victoria. In addition to EDR of brown coal, there are large sub-economic and inferred resources of brown coal in the Gippsland, Murray and Otway Basins.[597] Total identified recoverable resources of brown coal, including subeconomic and inferred categories, are estimated at 218 Gt. At 2014 production levels, Australia has approximately 112 years of recoverable black coal EDR and 1022 years of brown coal EDR.[598]

452. Energy production in Australia is nearly three times domestic energy consumption, reflecting the fact that Australia is a large net energy exporter. Production of black coal accounted for 63.1% of Australia's total energy production in 2013–14, with production increasing 8% from 2012–2013 as a result of increased production at a number of sites, and the completion of new capacity.[599] Brown coal accounted for 3.3% of Australia's total energy production in 2013–2014, with production decreasing 3% from 2012–2013, reflecting the decline in brown coal-fired electricity generation.[600] In 2013–2014, Australia exported 375 million tonnes of black coal, including both metallurgical coal and thermal coal.[601] Coal exports grew 5% per year over the decade to 2014 as strong global demand for coal, particularly from China, has stimulated investment in the coal industry.[602]

453. Australia's production of metallurgical coal is forecast to have declined to 188 Mt in 2015–2016 from 194.1 Mt in 2014–2015, but is expected to increase in 2016–2017.[603] Exports of metallurgical coal increased in volume in 2015–*20*16 from 2014–*20*15, driven by increased exports to China.[604] Australia's thermal coal production rose from 247.1 Mt in 2013–2014 to 251.5 Mt in 2014–2015.[605] Thermal coal exports remained strong in 2014–2015, buoyed by demand in key markets such as Japan, South Korea and Chinese Taipei. However, thermal coal production is expected to have declined to in 2015–2016 and to decline further in 2016–2017, with suspension or cessation of production at a number of mines.[606] Exports volumes are also expected to have declined in 2015–2016 because of lower exports to key markets such as China, Japan and Taiwan, and are forecasted to decline further in 2016–2017.[607]

454. Although exports have remained steady, low world prices led to a decline in coal exploration expenditure in Australia from a record AUD 809 million in 2011 in the mining boom, to USD 210 million in 2015.[608] Coal exploration expenditure was

596. *Ibid.*
597. Geoscience Australia/BREE, *supra* n. 580 at 140.
598. Geoscience Australia/BREE, *supra* n. 580.
599. Australian Government, Department of Industry and Science/Office of the Chief Economist, *Australian Energy Update 2015*, 18–19 (Commonwealth of Australia, 2015).
600. *Ibid.*
601. *Ibid.*, 23.
602. *Ibid.*
603. Australian Government, Department of Industry and Science/Office of the Chief Economist, *supra* n. 599 at 39, 41.
604. *Ibid.*, 40.
605. *Ibid.*, 50.
606. *Ibid.*, 48 and 50.
607. *Ibid.*
608. Geoscience Australia/BREE, *supra* n. 580.

around USD 23 m in the March quarter 2016, down 63% on the December quarter 2014 and 46% on the March quarter 2015, and at its lowest level since the March quarter 2004.[609]

609. Australian Government, Department of Industry and Science/Office of the Chief Economist, *supra* n. 599 at 47.

Chapter 2. Exploitation

455. The exploitation of onshore minerals, including coal, is regulated by the Australian State and Territory governments. The exploration for, and production of, coal is regulated under a complex mix of State mining law, planning and environmental law, and native title and heritage legislation. While each State has its own mining, planning and environmental legislation, the fundamentals are similar.

456. Mining legislation reserves ownership of minerals, including coal, to the Australian States. Legislation prohibits any mining activities from occurring without the requisite authorisation, such as an exploration licence, retention lease or production/mining lease. Common provisions concerning tenements such as the area, term, and provisions concerning the application for, grant, renewal, surrender and cancellation of exploration licences and mining leases, are dealt with under the State Mining Acts. Ownership of the mineral is transferred to the person/entity authorised to produce the mineral upon payment of royalty to the State government.

457. The mining Acts usually grant administration of the legislation, including the grant, renewal, surrender and cancellation of tenements, and the imposition of tenement conditions, to the relevant government Minister for resources and energy, whose powers are then delegated to the relevant government department for resources and energy. The legislation deals with a range of other issues including the transfer of rights and interests; registers, such as commercial and environmental registers; surface rental and fees for application; and compliance and enforcement mechanisms. Provisions regarding access to private land, in particular the negotiation of agreements between land owners and/or occupiers and mining companies including the payment of compensation, are a key feature of the legislative schemes.

458. State mining legislation seeks to protect the environment in various ways, in particular through the requirement of environmental impact assessment and mitigation, environmental plans, provisions for rehabilitation, and the imposition of conditions on mining tenements. The mining Acts work in conjunction with a range of State environmental and planning laws, and the interaction between legislation can be complex. For example, proposals for large mining projects can be pulled out of the mining Act procedures and assessed under general State planning and development procedures for major projects, contained within State planning legislation. The provisions of the various State Mining Acts also have to be read in the context of State environmental legislation dealing with specific environmental issues, including (but not limited to) pollution laws, legislation regarding protected areas (such as national parks) and protected species, native vegetation clearance, the protection of water resources, and heritage protection.

459. In addition, the provisions of relevant Commonwealth law must be observed, most notably, in the context of natural resource projects, the environmental assessment and protected areas and species provisions of the *Environment Protection and Biodiversity Conservation Act 1999* (Cth); and the rights of Indigenous Peoples under the national *Native Title Act 1993* (Cth) and the *Aboriginal and Torres Strait Islander Heritage Protection Act 1984* (Cth).

460. As it is beyond the scope of this Part to look at all State and Territories, it will focus on relevant Commonwealth law, and given an overview of some of the key features of the laws of Queensland and New South Wales, where over 96% of coal production occurs.

§1. COMMONWEALTH

I. Environment Protection and Biodiversity Conservation Act 1999 (Cth)

461. The *Environment Protection and Biodiversity Conservation Act 1999* (Cth) establishes Commonwealth requirements for environmental impact assessment and approval. The Act prohibits a person from undertaking a 'controlled action' unless certain processes have been followed and/or certain approvals have been obtained,[610] prescribing civil and criminal penalties for persons undertaking development contrary to the provisions of the Act, as well as making available other remedies such as applications for injunctions.

462. One type of controlled action is an action that has, will have, or is likely to have, a significant impact on one of nine 'matters of national environmental significance' (MNES) identified in the Act.[611] If an action has, will have, or is likely to have, a significant impact on one of the nine MNES, then the proponent must refer the proposal to the Commonwealth Environment Minister.[612] This is 'triggering' the Act. Once a proposed action has been referred to the Minister, the Minister (whose functions are delegated to the Commonwealth Department for the Environment) will determine whether assessment and approval is required under the Act, and if so, the environmental assessment procedure that should be followed. The Minister may approve developments subject to conditions put in place on the approval to protect the environment.

463. Eight of the nine MNES are:[613] the world heritage values of a declared World Heritage property; the National Heritage values of a National Heritage place; the ecological character of a declared wetland of international importance under the Ramsar Convention;[614] a listed threatened species or listed ecological community; a listed migratory species; a nuclear action; a Commonwealth marine area; and the Great Barrier Reef Marine Park. Thus, any coal mining project or activity that has, will have, or is likely to have, a significant impact on one of these eight MNES must be referred to the Commonwealth Minister for assessment and approval.

610. *Environment Protection and Biodiversity Conservation Act 1999* (Cth) s. 67A.
611. *See also* provisions regarding actions on Commonwealth land (ss 26–27A); Commonwealth heritage places (ss 27B–27C); and actions by Commonwealth agencies (s. 28).
612. *Environment Protection and Biodiversity Conservation Act 1999* (Cth), s. 68.
613. Sections 12–24C.
614. Convention on Wetlands of International Importance especially as Waterfowl Habitat, Ramsar (in force 21 Dec. 1975) 996 UNTS 245; TIAS 11084; 11 ILM 963 (1972).

464. Of specific application to the coal mining industry is the ninth matter of national environmental significance, known as the water trigger, which commenced on 22 June 2013.[615] The effect of the water trigger is that any action that has, will have, or is likely to have, a significant impact on 'a water resource, in the case of large CSG projects and large mining developments' requires federal assessment and approval. A 'large coal mining development' is defined to mean 'any coal mining activity that has, or is likely to have, a significant impact on water resources (including any impacts of associated salt production and/or salinity): (a) in its own right; or (b) when considered with other developments, whether past, present or reasonably foreseeable developments'.[616] Whether a proposed coal mining activity is a large coal mining development is thus defined according to its impact on a water resource, and not according to the size of the development.

465. 'Water resource' has the same meaning as in the *Water Act 2007* (Cth).[617] A water resource is: '(a) surface water or ground water; or (b) a watercourse, lake, wetland or aquifer (whether or not it currently has water in it); and includes all aspects of the water resource (including water, organisms and other components and ecosystems that contribute to the physical state and environmental value of the water resource)'.[618] A 'significant impact' is an impact which is 'important, notable, or of consequence, having regard to its context or intensity'.[619] Although there is no statutory definition of a 'significant impact' on a water resource, the Department of the Environment has issued Guidelines to proponents to assist in determining whether an action is likely to have a significant impact on a water resource, which will be if:

> there is a real or not remote chance or possibility that it will directly or indirectly result in a change to:
>
> - the hydrology of a water resource; or
> - the water quality of a water resource,
>
> that is of sufficient scale or intensity as to reduce the current or future utility of the water resource for third party users, including environmental and other public benefit outcomes, or to create a material risk of such reduction in utility occurring.[620]

466. Only the impacts of activities that form part of the process of extracting coal need to be referred under the water trigger. Where they involve extraction of coal, actions involved in exploration, appraisal and pilot developments may need to be referred to the Minister.[621] A development of associated infrastructure, such as transport

615. *Environment Protection and Biodiversity Conservation Act 1999* ss 24D–24E.
616. Section 523.
617. Section 523.
618. *Water Act 2007* (Cth), s. 4.
619. *Booth v. Bosworth* (2001) 114 FCR 39, 64.
620. Commonwealth Department for the Environment, *Significant impact guidelines 1.3: Coal seam gas and large coal mining developments—impacts on water resources* (Commonwealth of Australia, 2013), 16.
621. *Ibid.*, 7.

infrastructure, office/housing and amenity construction and environment protection, monitoring and associated land management activities, 'which is not sufficiently proximate that it can be said to involve the extraction of coal', does not need to be referred for its impacts on a water resource.[622] However, as the Act requires the assessment of a referred action as a whole, where a large coal mining development includes the extraction of coal and the development of associated infrastructure, the significance of the impact of on water resources of the whole of the referred action would be considered at the assessment stage.[623]

467. Where large coal mining developments are referred by a proponent to the Commonwealth Minister for the Environment under the EPBC Act, the Minister must seek the advice of the IESC on CSG and Large Coal Mining Development (IESC) before deciding whether or not to approve the development.[624] This Committee was established by the Australian Government as a statutory committee under the EPBC Act in 2012 in response to community concerns about CSG and coal mining. The IESC provides expert scientific advice on the impact that CSG and large coal mining development may have on Australia's water resources.[625]

468. State government regulators who are party to the National Partnership Agreement on CSG and Large Coal Mining Development (NPA) must also refer proposals to the IESC.[626] Under the NPA, the signatory governments of Queensland, New South Wales, South Australia and Victoria, committed to amending their laws and regulations to ensure decision-makers seek the Committee's advice at appropriate stages of the approvals process for a CSG or large coal mining development that is likely to have a significant impact on water resources, and to ensure that decision-makers take account of that advice in a transparent manner.[627]

469. The Committee provides written advice for consideration by the Commonwealth/State decision-maker. The advice is scientific in nature; the Committee does not make decisions about whether or not a large coal mining development proposal should be

622. *Ibid.*, 8.

623. *Ibid.*

624. *Environment Protection and Biodiversity Conservation Act 1999* s. 131AB.

625. Sections 505C–505D.

626. *National Partnership Agreement on Coal Seam Gas and Large Coal Mining Development*, An Agreement between the Commonwealth of Australia and the States and Territory, being the State of New south Wales, the State of Queensland, the State of South Australia, the State of Victoria, and the Northern Territory of Australia (COAG, 2012). The NT did not sign the Agreement. Although the NPA expired after 30 Jun. 2014, the legislative and regulatory arrangements put in place by the Australian and State governments ensure that its objectives continue to be met.

627. Pursuant to Part 4, cl. 18(b) of the NPA, the signatory State governments produced protocols that describe how they will seek the Committee's advice: *Queensland Protocol for referral of projects to the Independent Expert Scientific Committee: in accordance with clause 18(b) of the National Partnership Agreement on Coal Seam Gas and Large Coal Mining Development* (2012); *Victorian Protocol made under the National Partnership Agreement on Coal Seam Gas and Large Coal Mining Development* (2012); *South Australian Protocol for the referral of project applications to the Independent Expert Scientific Committee on Coal Seam Gas and Large Coal Mining Development* (2013). In NSW, referral occurs as part of the 'Gateway' process for planning applications: *see* Chapter 2 §3 [III] [E] below.

approved. The advice must be provided to the Minister/Department for the Environment within no more than two months of receiving a request.[628] Where the Committee provides advice to a State or Territory regulator, it must also provide this advice to the Commonwealth Environment Minister at the same time.[629]

470. The EPBC Act allows for the Commonwealth and States to enter into bilateral agreements, the purposes of which is are, in essence, to ensure 'efficient, timely and effective processes for environmental assessment and approval' and to minimise duplication. Under a bilateral agreement, the assessment of a controlled action (under an 'assessment bilateral agreement') and/or approval of a controlled action (under an 'approvals bilateral agreement') takes place not by the federal Department of the Environment, but under State processes which have been accredited by the federal government. The Commonwealth Environment Minister may enter into a bilateral agreement only if satisfied that it: accords with the objects of the EPBC Act; and meets specific requirements of the EPBC Act for bilateral agreements to be made; and meets any other requirements prescribed by the Regulations.

471. As of 30 September 2016, all the Australian States and Territories had entered into assessment bilateral agreements with the Commonwealth government. New South Wales, Queensland, South Australia, Tasmania, Western Australia and the ACT had draft bilateral agreements relating to environmental approval, while Victoria and the Northern Territory had issued a notice of intent to enter into an approval bilateral agreement. Once both an assessment and approval bilateral exists, both the assessment and approval of controlled actions under the EPBC Act – including the impact on water resources of large coal mining developments – will be conducted by the State government under State assessment and approval procedures accredited in the bilateral agreements, and not the federal Environment department. The State government regulators who are party to National Partnership Agreement on CSG and Large Coal Mining Development will continue to referring proposals for large coal mining developments to the IESC as part of the terms of the bilateral agreements

472. The EPBC Act also restricts mining in certain protected areas (such as Kakadu National Park) and protects listed animals and plants, making it an offence to take, injure, destroy, trade in, or otherwise harm various threatened species and ecological communities, and migratory species, listed under the Act, without a permit.[630]

II. Native Title

473. The State government and mining proponents must comply with the provisions of the *Native Title Act 1993* (Cth).[631] Native title recognises a set of rights and interests over land or waters held by Aboriginal and Torres Strait Islander people, who have maintained a continuing connection to the land, through the practice of

628. *Environment Protection and Biodiversity Conservation Act 1999*, s. 505D.
629. Environment Protection and Biodiversity Conservation Regulations 2000 (Cth) reg. 15.01A.
630. *Environment Protection and Biodiversity Conservation Act 1999*, ss 196–196F (listed threatened species and ecological communities) and ss 211–211F (listed migratory species).
631. Native title was first recognised by the High Court of Australia in *Mabo and Others v. Queensland (No. 2)* (1992) 175 CLR 1, after which the federal Parliament passed the Native Title Act.

traditional laws and customs that existed prior to the establishment of British sovereignty. As well as establishing the legal procedures by which native title is recognised in Australia, the Native Title Act requires certain procedures to be followed where a 'future act' may affect native title rights and interests. A future act – which includes the grant of a mining exploration or production tenement (a 'right to mine') – will be invalid to the extent it affects native title unless it complies with the procedures set out in the Native Title Act.[632]

474. There are three main procedures available for ensuring native title holders/claimants are consulted about the grant of mining tenements and proposed mining activity, and to ensure that all reasonable efforts are made to secure the agreement of native title holders to development proposals that will affect their native title rights. These procedures are the 'right to negotiate; procedure; the negotiation of an Indigenous land use agreement (ILUA); and the 'expedited procedure'.[633]

475. The right to negotiate procedure enables registered native title parties to negotiate with mining tenement applicants, and to reach agreement over matters such as the payment of compensation. The Act does not give a native title party the right to veto the grant of a tenement, but requires that all parties negotiate in good faith. If agreement is reached – which may occur with the help of mediation by the National Native Title Tribunal (NNTT) – a copy of the agreement is lodged with the NNTT and the tenement may be granted.

476. If the parties cannot reach agreement after six months, the parties may request the NNTT to make a 'future act determination'. Before the Tribunal starts the arbitration, it may be asked to determine whether a non-native title party has negotiated in good faith. If the Tribunal finds it has not, the arbitration cannot proceed, and good faith negotiations must take place. If negotiations were conducted in good faith, the NNTT will determine whether or not the tenement can be validly granted, and if so, whether it will be subject to conditions to protect native title.

477. The Expedited Procedure is a fast-tracking procedure for the grant of a mining tenement that is expected to have minimal impact on native title.[634] Usually the procedure will apply only to mining tenements such as exploration licences that do not cause major disturbance to land or waters. If the government believes the expedited procedure applies, this is stated in a 'section 29 notice' published by the government, and the right to negotiate procedure will not apply. If there is no objection by a native title party to the expedited procedure within four months, the mining tenement may be granted. If there is an objection, then the NNTT will determine whether or not the expedited procedure applies. If it applies, the tenement may be granted; if it does not, the full right to negotiate procedure will apply. In making its decision as to whether the expedited procedure applies, the Tribunal will consider

632. *Native Title Act 1993* (Cth), s. 24OA; National Native Title Tribunal, *About Future Acts*, http://www.nntt.gov.au/futureacts/Pages/default.aspx (accessed 30 Sept. 2016).

633. The right to negotiate provisions are set in the *Native Title Act 1993* (Cth), ss 25–44; the expedited procedure provisions are set in the *Native Title Act 1993* (Cth), s. 32; the indigenous land use agreement provisions are set in the *Native Title Act 1993* (Cth), ss 24BA–24EC.

634. The relevant State mining legislation may contain provisions authorising the grant of a special 'low impact' licence that may be approved under the *Native Title Act*, s. 26A; *see* , for example, *Mining Act 1992* (NSW), ss 32A–32G; *Mineral Resources Act 1989* (Qld), Sch. 1A, ss 540–549.

whether the grant of the tenement is likely to: 'interfere directly with the community or social activities of the native title party; interfere with areas or sites of particular significance to the native title party; or involve major disturbance to land or waters'.[635]

478. An ILUA is a voluntary agreement negotiated between native title holders/ claimants and other parties, such as mining companies, addressing how land and waters will be used and managed in the future. ILUAs are flexible and can cover a broad range of matters such as compensation for mining activities, employment and training. An ILUA registered with the NNTT binds all parties to the agreement.

§2. QUEENSLAND

I. Ownership of Coal and Coal Mining Tenements

479. Coal is owned by the government on behalf of the State.[636] Although there is some private ownership of coal in Queensland, as in the other Australian States, this is an historical anomaly, in Queensland dating back to grants of land in fee simple before 1 March 1910, where the grant of land did not reserve ownership of the coal to the Crown.[637] The property in minerals passes to the person who holds a mining lease and who lawfully mines the minerals under the authority of a mining lease, upon the payment of royalty.[638]

480. Coal exploration and production is undertaken by private entities who have obtained the necessary statutory authorisations. Mining tenements are granted under the Mineral Resources Act 1989 (Qld) and Mineral Resources Regulation 2013. While the Mineral Resources Act grants regulatory functions pertaining to mining tenements to the State Minister, these functions are delegated to the Department of Natural Resources and Mines.

481. There are three mining tenements or 'resource authorities' relevant to coal, these being the coal exploration permit, mineral development licence, and the mining lease. Tenements are granted over 'sub-blocks'. A block, defined in terms of latitude and longitude, is comprised of twenty-five sub-blocks.[639]

482. A coal exploration permit is required to explore for coal. A permit authorises the holder to use vehicles, vessels, machinery and equipment necessary or expedient

635. *Native Title Act*, s. 237; National Native Title Tribunal, *Expedited Procedure Objections*, http://www.nntt.gov.au/futureacts/Pages/Expedited-procedure-objections.aspx (accessed 30 Sept. 2016).
636. *Mineral Resources Act 1989* (Qld), para. 8(2)(a).
637. *Mineral Resources Act 1989*, para. 8(2)(b). Notwithstanding the private ownership of a mineral, no person may grant a lease or enter into an agreement or arrangements for the exploration or production of a mineral, with the exception of certain agreements entered into prior to the Mining Act Amendment Act 1976: *Mineral Resources Act 1989* (Qld), subss 9(1), 320(2). Thus, the Crown is exclusively entitled to grant mining tenements. Furthermore, the Crown may grant a mining tenement even if the mineral is not the property of the State: *Mineral Resources Act 1989*, subs. 9(3).
638. *Mineral Resources Act 1989*, s. 310.
639. Section 126.

for the purpose of exploration, and includes such activities as prospecting, conducting geophysical surveys, drilling, and sampling and testing materials.[640] The term is up to five years.[641] The permit may be granted over an area of up to 300 sub-blocks.[642] Applicants may only apply for a coal exploration permits through a call for competitive tenders.[643] The government publishes an annual exploration programme, which provides a forward schedule of acreage release for competitive tenders.[644]

483. A mineral development licence is issued to allow the holder to evaluate the development potential of the resource, and is granted to the holder of a coal exploration permit where there is a mineral occurrence of possible economic potential.[645] Activities permitted under the licence include geoscientific programmes such as drilling and seismic surveys, mining feasibility studies, metallurgical testing and marketing, and environmental, engineering and design studies.[646] The term of the licence is up to five years,[647] and there is no size restriction on the area of the licence.

484. A mining lease is required to conduct larger-scale mining operations, essentially for the commercial production of coal. A mining lease authorises the holder to mine coal and conduct other activities associated with coal mining or promoting the activity of coal mining.[648] The applicant must hold either a coal exploration permit or a mineral development licence over the relevant area.[649] There is no specified term for a mining lease, as this will depend on identified reserves and the projected life of the mine. There are no statutory restrictions on the area of the lease in the Mineral Resources Act, although there may be restrictions in specific ‘restricted areas’, such as national parks.

485. The Act sets out the details and requirements for applications for tenements.[650] Among other things, an applicant for a coal resource authority must demonstrate they have the financial and technical capability to ensure planned mining activities are sufficiently funded. Also, the applicant must provide a statement of the work programme (for an exploration permit and, if work is proposed to be done for, a mineral development licence) or, in the case of a mining lease, a mining programme or statement of the proposed use of land, with the application. Applicants must pay a security deposit or provide another other form of financial assurance to ensure they will comply with the provisions of the Act and rectify any damage that may be caused by mining activities.[651] Applicants must also apply for an environmental authority under the Environmental

640. Section 129 and Sch. 2.
641. Section 141.
642. Subsection 127(4) and Mineral Resources Regulation 2013, reg. 9.
643. Sections 136B–136L.
644. Queensland Government, *Annual exploration program*, https://www.business.qld.gov.au/invest/investing-queenslands-industries/mining/exploration-incentives-opportunities/annual-exploration-program (accessed 30 Sept. 2015).
645. *Mineral Resources Act 1989*, ss 179, 181.
646. Section 181.
647. Section 192.
648. Section 234.
649. Section 232.
650. Sections 136E, 183, 245.
651. Sections 144, 190 and 277.

Protection Act (*see* Chapter 2, §2 III below) before or at the same time as the application for a mining tenement.

486. Applications for mining leases are assessed by Department of Natural Resources and Mines to ensure the applicant is eligible to apply for a mining lease, and that the requirements for application are satisfied. The Department will issue a written mining lease notice, which the proponent must provide to each 'affected person', including the owners of land the subject of the proposed lease, and owners of adjoining land; and which the applicant must publish in an approved newspaper, to provide an opportunity for consultation and objection.[652] If the objection relates to an application for an environmental authority under the Environmental Protection Act, then unless the objection is withdrawn, the Environment Protection Authority must be notified and the objection will be referred by the Chief Executive of the Department of Natural Resources and Mines to the Land Court of Queensland. The Land Court must recommend to the Minister that the application be granted or rejected in whole or in part, or if the land is over a reserve (*see* Chapter 2, §2 II C below), whether the Governor-in-Council should consent to the grant; and any conditions to which the grant should be subject.[653]

487. The Act regulates a range of other issues including: the criteria for grant of mining tenements; rules and procedures regarding the renewal, surrender, abandonment, termination and cancellation of tenements; provisions for resolving competing applications; registration and transfer of dealings; compliance and enforcement provisions; and appeals. Annual surface rental is payable on coal exploration permits, mineral development licences and mining leases, as per the amounts set out in the Mineral Resources Regulation 2013.[654] Royalty is payable on coal that is mined.[655] The Mineral Resources Regulation 2013 sets out the rate of royalty for coal, which differs according to whether the average price per tonne of coal sold, disposed or used is AUD 100, AUD 100–AUD 150 or over AUD 150.[656] Tenement holders must comply with any general statutory obligations, common statutory conditions on tenements (such as the payment of rental, the payment of royalty, and the payment of security) and any specific conditions placed on their resource authority.

II. Access to Land

488. Prior to September 2016, the legislative provisions concerning access to land and compensation that applied to applicants for coal exploration permits and mineral development licences were contained in Schedule 1 to the Mineral Resources Act 1989. New provisions for access onto private land that apply to resource authorities under all onshore mining and petroleum legislation were introduced by the Mineral and Energy Resources (Common Provisions) Act 2014 (Qld) ('Common Provisions Act'), which commenced on 27 September 2016. However, not all of the new provisions

652. Sections 252–252C.
653. Sections 265, 269.
654. Sections 138, 193 and 290; Mineral Resources Regulation 2013, reg. 98 and Sch. 4.
655. Sections 311, 320. There are certain exceptions for coal that is not the property of the Crown: subs. 320(2).
656. Mineral Resources Regulation 2013, Sch. 3 cl. 5.

apply to all resource authorities. With the exception of the restricted land access provisions, which apply to all coal mining tenements (*see* Chapter 2, §2 II D below), the land access provisions of the Common Provisions Act apply only to coal exploration permits and mineral development licences, and not to coal mining leases. Land access for coal mining leases is still regulated under the Mineral Resources Act. Thus, the Common Provisions Act must be read in conjunction with the Mineral Resources Act.

A. Restricted Areas and Constrained Land

489. An application for a mining tenement cannot be accepted over 'unavailable land', which is defined to be land over which a mining tenement cannot be granted.[657] This includes land that is part of a 'restricted area', if the mining tenement is a prohibited mining tenement for that restricted area. Restricted areas are declared to be so by the Minister by publication in the Queensland Government Gazette.[658] Restricted areas are listed with areas of constrained land, which permit mining activity but have conditions limiting certain exploration or production activities. Restrictions are imposed for a range of reasons, for example to protect resources, allow for future urban development or to protect infrastructure such as dams and water facilities.[659]

490. Areas of unavailable land include land that is part of a 'protected area', such as a national park and conservation parks constituted under the *Nature Conservation Act 1992* (Qld); high preservation areas and nominated waterways, including declared wild rivers;[660] and land that has been excluded from the application of the Act by a law of the Commonwealth.

B. Entry onto Land: Public Land

491. For coal exploration permits and mineral development licences, entry onto 'public land' is regulated under the Common Provisions Act. A tenement holder must not enter public land to conduct authorised mining activities unless the tenement holder has given a 'periodic entry notice' to the public land authority, or the relevant public land authority has waived the requirement for an entry notice to be given.[661] Notification or waiver are not required if an activity is one that may be carried out by a member of the public without requiring specific approval of the public land authority for the land, or if entry is needed to preserve life or property or because of an emergency.[662] The public land authority may, for the entry period stated in the notice, impose reasonable

---

657. Mineral Resources Regulation 2013, reg. 97.

658. *Mineral Resources Act 1989*, s. 391.

659. A list of restricted areas is available from https://www.business.qld.gov.au/industry/mining/applications-compliance/land-constraints (accessed 1 Nov. 2016).

660. The river systems in Queensland that were declared under the Wild Rivers legislation (now repealed) have been rolled into the *Regional Planning Interests Act 2014* framework as Strategic Environmental Areas (SEAs).

A regional interests development approval will be required for resource activities, broadacre cropping and water storage dams proposed within SEAs.

661. *Mineral and Energy Resources (Common Provisions) Act 2014* (Qld), ss 57, 58.

662. Section 58.

and relevant conditions on the resource authority holder about the entry to the public land or the carrying out of the authorised activity.[663]

492. A resource authority holder is liable to compensate each owner and occupier of public land that is in the authorised area of, or is access land for, the resource authority, for any 'compensatable effect' of carrying out authorised mining activities.[664] The statutory provisions regarding rights to compensation, and the negotiation of Conduct and Compensation Agreements (CACA), which are explained in detail below at Chapter 2, §2 [II][E], in relation to access to private land, also apply to public land.

493. The Common Provisions Act also sets out specific provisions regarding the power of public road authorities to issues directions for the 'notifiable road use' of a public road.[665] The Act makes particular provision for compensation to be paid for cost, damage or loss as a result of notifiable road uses, and allows public road authorities and resource authority holders to enter into road compensation agreements.[666]

C. Entry onto Land: Reserves

494. For mining leases, where mining activities are over the surface of a 'reserve', the consent of the owner of land, as defined in the Act, must be obtained to enter the land or the Governor-in-Council must consent to the grant over the reserve.[667] A 'reserve' is defined in the Act and includes but is not limited to roads; rail corridor land; a regional park (resource use area) under the *Nature Conservation Act 1992* (Qld); State forests, timber or resource reserves under the *Forestry Act 1959* (Qld); land within the wet tropics World Heritage area; and certain Aboriginal or Torres Strait Islander lands. If the owner of land refuses to give consent, or if they do not give consent within a reasonable time, or if the conditions the landowner asks for are so harsh as to be unreasonable, the holder of the permit may apply to the Minister who may either refuse the application or recommend to the Governor-in-Council that consent be given. Any terms under which entry to reserve is given, either by the owner or Governor-in-Council, form part of the terms and conditions of the relevant resource authority.[668]

D. Entry onto Land: Restricted Land

495. For coal exploration permits, mineral development licences and coal mining leases granted under the Mineral Resources Act, the consent in writing of the landowner or occupier of land must be obtained to enter 'restricted land'.[669] This is land within 200 m laterally of a permanent building used: as a residence or for business purposes; as a childcare, hospital or library; for community, sporting or recreational purposes, or as a place of worship. 'Restricted land' also includes land within 200 m laterally of

663. Section 59.
664. Section 81.
665. Sections 61–65.
666. Sections 93, 94.
667. *Mineral Resources Act 1989*, s. 271A.
668. Paragraph 276(1)(g).
669. *Mineral and Energy Resources (Common Provisions) Act 2014*, s. 70.

an area used for a school, or for certain prescribed activities under the Environmental Protection Act, such as aquaculture, pig keeping or poultry farming. It also includes land within 50 m laterally of any of the following features: a principal stockyard; an artesian well, bore, dam or other water storage facility; or a cemetery or burial place.[670] Consent may be given on conditions, and if so, these conditions of consent will become conditions of the resource authority/tenement. Landowners, occupiers, and holders of resource authorities may apply to the Land Court for an order declaring whether land is restricted land.[671]

496. If a coal exploration permit or mineral development licence has been granted over private land, the landowner or occupier can continue to make improvements to the land and, if these fall within the definition of 'restricted land', will be protected by the restricted land provisions. However, in the case of coal mining leases, land is only 'restricted land' if the use of the area, building or structure started before the mining lease application was made.[672] Any improvements a landholder makes to the land after that date do not attract the protection of the restricted land provisions.

E. Access to Private Land: Negotiation and Compensation

1. Coal Exploration Permits and Mineral Development Licences

497. The Mineral Resources Act allows titleholders entry onto land for conducting certain activities under an exploration licence or a mineral development licence, providing the holder of the tenement observes the requirements of the Common Provisions Act.[673] The Common Provisions Act sets out provisions concerning access to land and compensation that apply to applicants for coal exploration permits and mineral development licences.[674]

498. First, the Common Provisions Act prohibits entry onto private land to conduct authorised mining activities, unless the resource authority holder has given each owner and occupier a notice of entry ten business days before entry. The Act contains provisions concerning exemptions and waiver of the requirement to give notice, while the Common Provisions Regulation sets out the requirements for a valid entry notice.[675]

499. Second, before a person enters private land to conduct 'advanced activities', the resource authority holder and the landholder must enter into a CACA, a Deferral Agreement, or an Opt-Out Agreement (OOA).[676] 'Advanced activities' are those that are not preliminary activities, that is, are activities with more than a minor impact on

670. *Mineral Resources Act 1989*, Sch. 2; *Mineral and Energy Resources (Common Provisions) Act 2014*, s. 68.
671. *Mineral and Energy Resources (Common Provisions) Act*, s. 72.
672. Subsection 68(3).
673. *Mineral Resources Act 1989*, paras 129(1)(a), 181(4)(b).
674. *Mineral and Energy Resources (Common Provisions) Act 2014*, ss 36–101.
675. *Mineral and Energy Resources (Common Provisions) Act*, ss 38–42; Mineral and Energy Resources (Common Provisions) Regulation 2014, reg. 17.
676. *Mineral and Energy Resources (Common Provisions) Act*, s. 43.

the business and land-use activities of the owner or occupier of land on which the activity is to be carried out.[677]

500. A CACA is the main type of negotiated agreement between mining companies and landholders regarding access to land. A CACA must address the general statutory liability of a resource authority holder, contained in section 81 of the Common Provisions Act, to compensate landholders for the 'compensatable effects' of mining activities carried out on the land.[678] 'Compensatable effects' means: deprivation of the possession of the surface of land; diminution of the value of land or the use of land or any improvements on it; severance of any part of the land; and any 'cost, damage or loss arising from the carrying out of activities' pursuant to the mining tenement. The tenement holder is also liable to pay and accounting, legal or valuation costs the land holder necessarily and reasonably incurs to negotiate or prepare the agreement.[679]

501. CACAs must also address a range of other issues identified in the Common Provisions Regulation, such as how and when entry will be effected, and how mining activities will be carried out, and may address a range of discretionary factors. The CACA must be consistent with the Common Provisions Act, the Mineral Resources Act, a condition of a mining tenement, and the mandatory provisions of the Land Access Code.[680] The Act sets out statutory rules for the negotiating process, including the use of alternative dispute resolution processes to help achieve agreement.[681] Where a mining company and landowner(s) cannot reach agreement, either may apply to the Land Court of Queensland to resolve the impasse. The Land Court may determine the tenement holder's liability to pay compensation, and may make any order it considers appropriate to meet or enforce its decisions, including the payment of non-monetary as well as monetary compensation.[682]

502. A Deferral Agreement is a legal agreement in which a landholder and tenement holder agree to enter a CACA after the resource company has accessed the land to undertake the advanced activities.[683] An OOA is a legal agreement in which the landowner or occupier chooses to 'opt-out' of the requirement to enter into a CACA or Deferral Agreement.[684] Under an OOA, the resource authority holder is still liable to pay compensation, but no notice of entry is required, and the statutory negotiation procedures do not apply, including the option of applying to the Land Court for resolution.[685]

503. CACAs and OOAs run with the land and are not affected by a change in ownership of land or by a change in the holder of the mining tenement. The resource

677. *Mineral and Energy Resources (Common Provisions) Act*, s. 8 and Sch. 2; *Mineral Resources Act 1989*, s. 7A, 7B.
678. *Mineral and Energy Resources (Common Provisions) Act*, s. 83; Mineral and Energy Resources (Common Provisions) Regulation 2014, reg. 30.
679. *Mineral and Energy Resources (Common Provisions) Act*, subs. 81(4).
680. Subsection 83(2).
681. Sections 84–91.
682. Sections 96–101.
683. Section 44.
684. Section 45.
685. Department of Natural Resources and Mines, *A Guide to Land Access in Queensland: For the exploration and development of Queensland's mineral and energy resources on private land*, 18 (State of Queensland, September 2016).

authority must give notice to the Registrar of Land Titles to register a CACA or OOA on the title of the property.[686]

504. It is a condition of a coal exploration permit and a mineral development licence that the permit holder and any other person authorised to conduct activities under the permit comply with the mandatory conditions of the Land Access Code.[687] The mandatory provisions concern the conduct of authorised mining activities on land. They address matters such as induction training; access points, roads and tracks; minimising disturbance of livestock and property; preventing the spread of declared pests; location of camps; gates, grids and fences; and the control of items brought onto the land. Resource companies must notify landholders of any breaches of the mandatory conditions of the Code, and must repair any damages associated with access to, and use of, the private land. The Code also sets out non-binding guidelines for communication and negotiation between mining tenement holders and the owners and occupiers of land.[688]

505. Finally, the Common Provisions Act also regulates access to private land which lies outside the area of the tenement, which it is reasonably necessary to allow a resource authority holder to cross in order to enter the area of the tenement. This land is called 'access land', and the provisions apply to the holders of coal exploration permits, but not mineral development licences or coal mining leases. To enter the land, a coal exploration permit holder must enter an Access Agreement with the landholder. Landholders cannot unreasonably refuse to make an Access Agreement. Where a dispute arises, either the company or landholder may apply to the Land Court for resolution of the dispute. The mandatory conditions of the Land Access Code also apply to Access Agreements.[689]

2. Coal Mining Leases

506. A mining lease cannot be granted or renewed unless compensation has been determined either by agreement or by determination of the Land Court.[690] It is condition of a mining lease that the holder will make all payments of compensation and comply with all terms of any agreement or determination relating to compensation.[691] The matters for which the Land Court may order compensation to be paid are set out in section 281 of the Act. The Land Court also has the power to review compensation arrangements where there has been a material change in circumstances for the mining lease.[692]

686. *Mineral and Energy Resources (Common Provisions) Act 2014*, s. 92.
687. *Mineral Resources Act 1989*, ss 141, 194.
688. The State of Queensland, Department of Natural Resources and Mines, *Land Access Code*, v.2 Sept. 2016, made pursuant to s. 36 of the *Mineral and Energy Resources (Common Provisions) Act 2014* and reg. 16 of the Mineral and Energy Resources (Common Provisions) Regulation 2014.
689. Sections 46–54.
690. *Mineral Resources Act 1989*, s. 279.
691. Section 276.
692. Section 283B.

F. Regional Planning Interests Act 2014 (Qld)

507. In 2014, the Queensland government enacted the *Regional Planning Interests Act 2014* (Qld) and *Regional Planning Interests Regulation 2014* to assist in resolving potential disputes that may arise between competing land users, in particular the mining and agricultural industries in regional areas. The Act prohibits a person from carrying out a resource activity – which includes an activity authorised under a coal exploration permit, mineral development licence and coal mining lease granted under the Mineral Resources Act – in an 'area of regional interest' unless the person holds, or is acting under, a 'regional interests development approval' ('RIDA').[693] The Act defines four areas of regional interest. These are priority agricultural areas, priority living areas, strategic cropping areas and strategic environmental areas.[694]

508. The Act exempts certain resource activities carried out within a priority agricultural area or a strategic cropping area from requiring an RIDA. An approval is not required where a CACA has been reached between the mining tenement holder and the landowner, and complied with by the tenement holder, and the activity is not likely to have a significant impact on the priority agricultural area or strategic cropping area, and is not likely to have an impact on land owned by a person other than the landowner. Approval is also not required where the land owner has voluntarily entered into a written agreement with the authority holder and the carrying out of the activity is consistent with the agreement. Exemptions also exist for resource activities carried out on a property for less than one year, and for pre-existing resource activities.[695]

509. Applications for regional interests development are made to, and assessed by, the Chief Executive of the Department of Infrastructure, Local Government and Planning (whose functions are delegated to the Department of Infrastructure, Local Government and Planning) and may also be assessed by an assessing agency. Depending on the area of regional interest that the activity is located within, and the impact the activity will have, the assessing agency will be: the Department of Agriculture and Fisheries, the Department of Natural Resources and Mines, the relevant local government, and/or the Department of Environment and Heritage Protection.

510. As part of their application, applicants must demonstrate that they have consulted with the land owner of properties the subject of an application for development in a priority agricultural area or a strategic cropping area about the application. Where an application in an area of regional interest is 'notifiable' under the Act, any person, including land owners of properties that are the subject of an application, may lodge a submission expressing their concerns or support for an application.[696] Appeals against

693. *Regional Planning Interests Act 2014* (Qld), s. 19.
694. Sections 7–11.
695. Sections 22–24. The 'owner of land' means (a) the person for the time being entitled to receive the rent for the land or who would be entitled to receive the rent for it if it were let to a tenant at a rent; or (b) the lessee of a lease issued under the *Land Act 1994* (Qld) for agricultural, grazing or pastoral purposes: s. 6 and Sch. 1.
696. An application is notifiable if the area of regional interest in which the resource activity is proposed to be carried out is a priority living area: *Regional Planning Interests Act 2014*, s. 34, Regional Planning Interest Regulation 2014, reg. 13.

decisions can be made by the applicant, the owner of land covered by the application, or an affected land holder, and are heard by the Planning and Environment Court.[697]

511. An approval runs with the land, despite any change of ownership.[698] If there is a conflict between the condition of a resource authority/mining tenement, then the condition on the RIDA will prevail.[699]

III. Environmental Authorities

512. A resource authority/mining tenement cannot be granted under the Mineral Resources Act unless an applicant holds an appropriate environmental authority, granted by the Department of the Environment and Heritage Protection under the *Environmental Protection Act 1994* (Qld). The Environmental Protection Act requires the proponent of an 'environmentally relevant activity' to apply for an environmental authority. A 'resource activity' under the Mineral Resources Act is an environmentally relevant activity for the purposes of the Environmental Protection Act, thus requiring an environmental authority.

513. Ancillary activities, such as chemical storage, that are listed in Schedule 2 of the Environmental Protection Act, and which are conducted within the area of the mining tenement, can be included as part of the application for an environmental authority for a resource activity. However, an activity such as chemical storage that is undertaken outside the area of the tenement is a 'prescribed environmental activity', and a separate environmental authority is required. Once environmental authorities are granted, they can be combined as a single environmental authority.

514. The environmental authority application process has different levels of assessment according to the level of environmental risk. A proponent may apply to the Co-ordinator General to have an eligible major coal mining project declared a 'co-ordinated project' under the *State Development and Public Works Organisation Act 1971* (Qld). While the relevant tenements and approvals must still be obtained, a co-ordinated project undergoes a separate environmental assessment procedure involving whole-of-government co-ordination.

515. 'Standard applications' have been developed for low-risk activities. A proponent may apply for a standard application for an environment assessment if the environmentally relevant activity is not declared to be a 'co-ordinated project' under the State Development and Public Works Organisation Act, and if it complies with both eligibility criteria for the activity and standard conditions.[700] If an activity meets

697. *See Regional Planning Interests Act 2014*, ss 71–78.

698. Section 58.

699. Section 59.

700. Queensland Government, Department of Environment and Heritage Protection, *Eligibility criteria and standard conditions for exploration and mineral development projects—Version 2*, ESR/2016/1985 (31 Mar. 2016) and *Eligibility criteria and standard conditions for mining lease activities—Version 2*, ESR/2016/2241 (31 Mar. 2016). From 21 May 2014 to 30 Mar. 2016, the eligibility criteria and standard conditions were contained in the *Code of environmental compliance for exploration and mineral development projects,* v.1.1 (31 Mar. 2013) and the *Code of environmental compliance for Mining Lease Projects*, v 1.1 (31 Mar. 2013).

the eligibility criteria but the proponent wishes to change one or more of the standard conditions to meet their needs, then the proponent must lodge a 'variation application' for environmental assessment, which requires the provision of additional information. If a proposed activity does not meet the eligibility criteria, the proponent must apply for a 'site-specific application', which requires the provision of detailed information about the activity and its potential environmental impacts.

IV. Mine Safety

516. The major laws governing safety and health in coal mining are the *Coal Mining Safety and Health Act 1999* (Qld) and the Coal Mining Safety and Health Regulation 2001 (Qld). The Minister may make recognised standards under subsection 72(1) of the Coal Mining Safety and Health Act, 'to provide ways of achieving an acceptable standard of risk for people working in coal mines. Operators can manage the risk in a different way, but must be able to show that the method used is at least equivalent to the method in the recognised standard'.[701] The government also publishes Guidance Notes for the coal industry to help the industry meet its health and safety obligations. As of 15 March 2016, eleven recognised standards and nine Guidance Notes had been published under the Act.[702] The Mines Inspectorate may also issue directives under the Coal Mining Safety and Health Act, which usually apply to a group of mines (such as underground coal mines) and letters, which usually to all mines or a group of mines.[703]

517. The Mines Inspectorate, which is part of the Department of Natural Resources and Mines, is the government entity responsible for ensuring acceptable safety and health standards are established and observed within the mining industry. Its functions include establishing safety and health legislation and standards, and undertaking audits and inspections.

518. The Commissioner for Mine Safety and Health advises the Minister for Natural Resources and Mines of mine safety and health matters generally, and monitors and reports to the Minister and to Parliament on the administration of health and safety provisions under the Coal Mining Safety and Health Act. The Commissioner is also the chairperson of the Coal Mining Safety and Health Advisory Committee, which provides advice and makes recommendations to the Minister about promoting and protecting the safety and health of persons at coal mines, and regularly reviews the effectiveness of the relevant coal mining health and safety legislation.

701. Queensland Government, *Recognised standards, guidelines and guidance notes* (15 Mar. 2016), https://www.business.qld.gov.au/industry/mining/safety-health/mining-safety-health/legislation-standards-guidelines/recognised-standards-guidelines-guidance-notes (accessed 1 Nov. 2016).
702. *Ibid.*
703. Queensland Government, *General directives and letters* (15 Jun. 2016), https://www.business.qld.gov.au/industry/mining/safety-health/mining-safety-health/legislation-standards-guidelines/general-directives-letters (accessed 1 Nov. 2016).

§3. New South Wales

I. Ownership of Coal and Coal Mining Tenements

519. Although there is still some private ownership of minerals in New South Wales, coal is a 'publicly owned mineral', having been acquired by the Crown through legislation in 1981.[704] The property in coal passes to the person by whom or on whose behalf it is lawfully mined at the time the material from which it is recovered is extracted from the land.[705]

520. The *Strategic Statement on NSW Coal*, published in August 2014 set a high-level framework to guide the development of the coal sector. A key government objective set out in the Statement is the development of coal resources to deliver economic benefits, including export income and regional growth, while balancing potential competing land-use conflicts between coal mining and urban growth, agriculture and the environment; another is to provide a clear and transparent planning and regulatory framework for the development of coal.

521. The *Mining Act 1992* (NSW) prohibits prospecting, mining, and activities carried out for the purpose of mining, without the necessary authorisation.[706] Coal exploration and production is undertaken by private entities who have obtained the necessary statutory authorisations. Mining tenements are granted and regulated pursuant to the *Mining Act 1992* (NSW) and the Mining Regulation 2016. The three mining tenements or 'resource authorities' relevant to the exploitation of coal are the exploration licence, the assessment lease, and the mining lease. While the Mining Act grants regulatory functions pertaining to mining tenements to the State Minister for Resources and Energy, these functions are delegated to the Resources and Energy Division of the Department of Industry (DRE).[707]

522. An exploration licence is required to explore for coal.[708] A licence gives the holder the exclusive right to explore for coal.[709] An exploration licence cannot be granted over land over which an existing mining tenement is held or over which an application for a tenement has been made, without the written consent of the tenement holder.[710] A range of exploration activities are authorised by an exploration licence, including geological mapping, geochemical surveys, geophysical surveys (including airborne surveys, ground-based surveys and drilling) and bulk sampling operations.

---

704. *Coal Acquisition Act 1981* (NSW).
705. *Mining Act 1992* (NSW), s. 11.
706. Sections 5, 6.
707. Section 363.
708. Following the report and recommendations of the Independent Commission Against Corruption into the allocation of coal resources, the Coal Exploration Steering Group was established in 2014 to provide advice to the government on improving the quality and transparency of the procedures used to allocate coal exploration licences. These were reformed and new provisions in relation to the grant of exploration titles came into effect after 1 Jul. 2015.
709. *Mining Act 1992*, s. 29.
710. Section 19.

The maximum term is six years.[711] The area for a coal exploration licence may be of any size and shape.[712]

523. For mineral groups within a Mineral Allocation Area, the Minister's consent is required prior to lodging an application for an exploration licence.[713] For coal, the whole of the State of New South Wales has been constituted as a Mineral Allocation Area, thus the Minister's consent will always be required to lodge an exploration licence application. As a mineral within a Mineral Allocation Area, the Minister may invite tenders for an exploration licence for coal,[714] although to date exploration licences have been issued directly by the DRE, which is the determining authority for coal exploration licences.

524. An application for an exploration licence for coal must be lodged within six months from the date of receiving Ministerial consent to apply for an exploration licence. A public notice must be published within forty-five days from lodgement of the application.[715] For coal, a procedure for public submissions on the application is open for twenty-eight days, after which the DRE will assess and either approve or reject the application.[716] Once an exploration licence is granted, low intensity exploration activities that are not in sensitive areas, and have minimal environmental impact, can be carried out without further approval from the DRE. However, for exploration activities of a higher intensity, or activities in sensitive areas, or with the potential to affect threatened species or ecological communities, the proponent must prepare and submit a Review of Environmental Factors, which addresses all potential impacts on the community and environment, for approval before undertaking mining activities (*see* II below). Rehabilitation and environmental performance conditions are attached to exploration licences.

525. An assessment lease is issued to allow the holder to retain rights over a permit area in which significant mineral deposit have been identified, when mining activities are not currently commercially viable in the short term but there is a reasonable prospect they will be viable in the longer term.[717] An assessment lease authorises the holder to prospect for coal.[718] The term of the licence is up to six years.[719] As coal is within a Mineral Allocation Area, an application for an assessment lease in relation to coal may only be made by the holder of an existing exploration licence or mining lease for coal over that land, or with the consent of the Minister.[720]

526. A mining lease is required to conduct larger-scale mining operations, essentially for the commercial production of coal. A mining lease authorises the holder

711. Subsection 27(b).
712. *Mining Act 1992*, s. 25; Mining Regulation 2016, reg. 16 and Sch. 1.
713. Subsection 13(3). Mineral allocation areas are constituted by order of the Governor, published in the Government Gazette: s. 368.
714. Subsection 14(1)(2). Tenders cannot be invited for an exploration (mineral owner) licence for the exploration for privately owned minerals: subs. 14(2).
715. Subsection 13A; Mining Regulation 2016, reg. 15.
716. NSW Department of Trade & Investment, Division of Resources and Energy, *Public Comment Process: For the exploration of coal and petroleum, including coal seam gas*, 3 (October 2011).
717. *Mining Act 1992*, s. 47, Note.
718. Section 47.
719. Section 45.
720. Subsection 33(3).

to prospect and mine for coal, as well as carrying out primary treatment operations to separate minerals from the material from which they are recovered, and carry out other activities for the purpose of mining.[721] Mining leases may be granted for up to twenty-one years.[722] As coal is within a Mineral Allocation Area, an application for a mining lease in relation to coal may only be made by the holder of an existing exploration licence or assessment lease for coal over that land, or with the consent of the Minister.[723]

527. All new large-scale coal mining production projects require assessment and approval (a 'development consent') under State planning legislation, namely the *Environmental Planning and Assessment Act 1979* (NSW) and the *Environmental Planning and Assessment Regulation 2000*, before a mining lease may be granted (*see* II below).[724] The NSW Department of Planning and Environment is the consent authority for large-scale mining and petroleum production projects.

528. A prospective applicant for a mining lease must submit a Conceptual Project Development Plan to the DRE before applying for development consent under the Environmental Planning and Assessment Act and a mining lease under the Mining Act. The purpose of the Plan is to demonstrate the project is 'practical, feasible, optimises resource utilisation and can be achieved within known environmental and mining production constraints'.[725] In-principle support of the DRE is required to initiate the development assessment and approval processes with other government agencies, including notification of the consent authority – the Department of Planning and Environment – to ensure all necessary consents/approvals are obtained.

529. It is a condition of a mining lease that companies submit a Mining Operations Plan, including a rehabilitation plan, before commencing operations. Conditions – including rehabilitation and environmental performance conditions – are imposed on all coal mining leases to minimise potential environmental impacts.[726] It is a condition of exploration licences, assessment leases and mining leases that the holder of the tenement provide a security deposit which covers the cost of liability for obligations that may arise, including for the costs of rehabilitation.[727] Annual Environmental Management Reports are also required.[728] The management of mine subsidence related to underground coal mining requires the approval of a Mining Lease Extraction Plan by the Department of Planning and Environment, which must then be implemented

721. Section 73.
722. Section 71.
723. Subsection 51(3). As a mineral within a Mineral Allocation Area, the Minister may invite tenders for a mining lease for coal: s. 52.
724. Section 65.
725. NSW Department of Industry, Division of Resources and Energy, *Policy on Conceptual Project Development Plans for mining projects*, http://www.resourcesandenergy.nsw.gov.au/miners-and-explorers/applications-and-approvals/mining-and-exploration-in-nsw/project-approvals/development_plans (accessed 1 Nov. 2016).
726. NSW Government, Department of Industry, Division of Resources and Energy, *Mining leases and regulation* http://www.resourcesandenergy.nsw.gov.au/landholders-and-community/minerals-and-coal/mining (accessed 1 Nov. 2016).
727. *Mining Act 1992*, s. 261B.
728. NSW Government, Department of Industry, Division of Resources and Energy, *Conditions on titles* http://www.resourcesandenergy.nsw.gov.au/miners-and-explorers/applications-and-approvals/environmental-assessment/conditions-on-titles (accessed 1 Nov. 2016).

both as part of a development consent issued under the Environmental Planning and Assessment Act and a Mining Lease issued under the Mining Act.[729]

530. The Mining Act regulates a range of other issues in relation to all tenements, including: the matters to be taken into account by the decision-maker when deciding whether or not to grant a tenement; rules and procedures regarding the renewal, surrender, abandonment and cancellation of tenements; rehabilitation of land; provisions for resolving competing applications; registration and transfer of titles and dealings in titles; compliance and enforcement provisions; and appeals. Annual surface rental is payable on coal exploration licences, assessment leases and mining leases, as per the amounts set out in the Mining Regulation 2010.[730] Royalty is payable on coal that is mined, at a rate set under the Mining Regulation 2016.[731] Tenement holders must comply with any general statutory obligations, common statutory conditions on tenements (such as the payment of rental, royalty and security) and any specific conditions placed on their resource authority.

II. Development Consent and Environmental Assessment under the Environmental Planning and Assessment Act 1979

531. All new large-scale coal mining production projects are classified as 'State Significant Development' – that is, as projects of State or regional significance as listed in the *State Environmental Planning Policy (State and Regional Development) 2011* – and therefore require assessment and approval under Part 4 of the *Environmental Planning and Assessment Act 1979* (NSW) ('EPAA').[732] A mining lease for the production of coal cannot be granted under the Mining Act unless an applicant holds a development consent granted by the Minister of Planning (whose duties are delegated to the Department of Planning and Infrastructure) under section 89E of the EPAA. A comprehensive Environmental Impact Statement must be prepared and extensive public consultation is required before a development consent may be issued.

532. When considering whether or not to grant development consent, the Minister for Planning must consider, among other things, the public interest, whether or not the site is suitable for development, the impact of the development on the environment, local environment plans and State Environment Planning Policies. Local environment plans and State Environment Planning Policies may prohibit coal mining in a zone, partially prohibit mining (including coal mining) in a zone, or permit coal mining in a zone. Where mining activity is wholly prohibited, the Planning Minister cannot grant development consent, although the Act allows planning instruments to be amended to

729. NSW Government, Department of Industry, Division of Resources and Energy, *Subsidence Management* http://www.resourcesandenergy.nsw.gov.au/miners-and-explorers/applications-and-approvals/environmental-assessment/subsidence-management (accessed 1 Nov. 2016).

730. *Mining Act 1992*, ss 292E, 292F; Mining Regulation 2016, regs 78–85 and Sch. 9.

731. *Mining Act 1992*, ss 282–285; Mining Regulation 2016, reg. 74.

732. On State Significant Development, *see* the *Environmental Planning and Assessment Act 1979* (NSW), ss 89C–89L.

permit a prohibited activity to occur. Where mining activities are partially prohibited, development consent can be granted.[733]

533. The State Environment Planning Policy relevant to coal mining is the *State Environmental Planning Policy (Mining, Petroleum Production and Extractive Industries) 2007* ('Mining SEPP'). Part 3 of the Mining SEPP also sets out a range of matters the Minister for Planning must consider when determining an application for a development consent authority for a mine, including: the compatibility with other land uses; any applicable provisions of the NSW voluntary land acquisition and mitigation policy; the conditions that should be placed on the consent to ensure mining is undertaken in an environmentally responsible manner; transport issues; and rehabilitation.[734]

534. While coal mining is State Significant Development, coal exploration is not,[735] and many coal exploration activities will not require approval under the Environmental Planning and Assessment Act. The Mining SEPP identifies mining activities that are 'exempt development' under section 76 of the EPAA.[736] 'Exempt development' may be carried out without the need for either a development consent under the EPAA, or assessment under Part 5 of the EPAA, the latter of which applies to projects that do not require a development consent, but still need to undergo environmental assessment. Exempt development must be of minimal environmental impact; cannot be carried out in the critical habitat of an endangered species, population or ecological community;[737] and cannot be carried out in a wilderness area.[738]

535. 'Mineral exploration' under an exploration licence, which is limited to 'prospecting', is 'development permissible without consent' that is, it does not require a development consent under section 89E of the EPAA, although it does requires environment assessment under Part 5 of the EPAA.[739] Low intensity mining exploration activities with minimal environmental impact (such as geological mapping and airborne surveying, sampling and coring using hand held equipment, geophysical but not seismic surveying), carried out under a mineral exploration licence, that are not within 'an environmentally sensitive area of State significance', are classified as 'exempt development' and may also be carried out without a development consent under the EPAA.[740]

536. These minimal impact activities are identified on an exploration licence as 'exempt prospecting operations' and do not require further development approval

733. *Environmental Planning and Assessment Act 1979* (NSW), ss 89D, 89E, 89H and 79C.

734. *State Environmental Planning Policy (Mining, Petroleum Production and Extractive Industries) 2007*, cls 12–17.

735. *State Environmental Planning Policy (Mining, Petroleum Production and Extractive Industries)*, cl. 17A; *State Environmental Planning Policy (State and Regional Development) 2011*, cl. 8 and Sch. 1, cl. 5.

736. *State Environmental Planning Policy (Mining, Petroleum Production and Extractive Industries) 2007*, Part 2.

737. As defined by the *Threatened Species Conservation Act 1995* (NSW) and *Fisheries Management Act 1994* (NSW).

738. As defined by the *Wilderness Act 1987* (NSW).

739. *State Environmental Planning Policy (Mining, Petroleum Production and Extractive Industries) 2007*, cl. 6.

740. Clause 10.

before being carried out. All other exploration activities are identified on the title as 'assessable prospecting operations' and require approval from the Minister of Resources and Energy before they can be carried out.[741] The assessment and approval procedures for exploration activities that require further approval have been designed to satisfy Part 5 of the EPAA.

537. Certain types of 'assessable prospecting operations' have been identified as unlikely to have a significant environmental impact if carried out in a particular manner.[742] These activities are known as 'Common Exploration Activities', and can be assessed under a streamlined procedure if they: satisfy location requirements and impact thresholds and criteria set out in *ESG5: Assessment Requirements for Exploration Activities (2016)*; and if they can be carried out in accordance with various Codes of Practice for Exploration that set out mandatory obligations for companies undertaking exploration pursuant to an exploration licence.[743]

538. Applications to carry out coal exploration activities which do not meet the Common Exploration Activities requirements must be accompanied by additional environmental impact assessment information, being either a Targeted Review of Environmental Factors; a Guideline Review of Environmental Factors that meets the *ESG2: Guidelines for Preparing a Review of Environmental Factors* (2015); or an Environmental Impact Statement and/or a Species Impact Statement, depending upon the likely degree of impact on the environment, the environmental sensitivity of the location and the potential impact on threatened species and ecological communities.[744]

539. Certain development activities that are ancillary to the extraction of minerals including coal, for example some types of infrastructure works, are also identified in the *Mining SEPP* as exempt development if they are of minimal environmental impact and carried out on land that is the site of an approved mine.

III. Access to Land

A. *Exempted Areas*

540. Activities conducted under an exploration licence or an assessment lease cannot take place in areas that are declared to be 'exempted areas' under the Mining Act, unless the prior consent of the Minister for Resources and Energy has been

741. *Mining Act 1992*, ss 23A, 44A.
742. Prior to 1 Jul. 2015, these were known as Category 2 and Category 3 Prospecting Operations. Together, Category 2 and Category 3 Prospecting Operations and the new 'Assessable prospecting operations' are known as 'Assessable activities'.
743. *Exploration Code of Practice: Environmental Management* (Department of Industry, Skills and Regional Development, July 2015); *Exploration Code of Practice: Produced Water Management, Storage and Transfer* (Department of Industry, Skills and Regional Development, July 2015); *Exploration Code of Practice: Rehabilitation* (Department of Industry, Skills and Regional Development, July 2015).
744. NSW Government, Department of Industry, Division of Resources and Energy, *Coal and mineral exploration* http://www.resourcesandenergy.nsw.gov.au/miners-and-explorers/applications-and-approvals/environmental-assessment/exploration#_is-approval-of-exploration-activities-required__003f (accessed 1 Nov. 2016).

obtained.[745] Exempted areas include: lands reserved, dedicated, appropriated, resumed or acquired for public purposes, such as State Forests, National Parks, Travelling Stock Routes, and State Conservation Areas; land held under a lease for water supply by virtue of a special lease or otherwise; and land transferred, granted or vested in trust by the Crown for the purpose of a racecourse, cricket-ground, recreation reserve, park or permanent common, or for any other public purpose. The exempted areas provisions do not apply to mining leases.

B. Protected Areas and Other Special Areas

541. The *National Parks and Wildlife Act 1974* (NSW) prohibits exploration and mining in a National Park, historic site, nature reserve, karst conservation reserve or Aboriginal area.[746] The Mining Act does not apply to lands in these protected areas. The Act does permit exploration to be approved if it is undertaken in behalf of the government, but this requires the approval of both Houses of Parliament.[747] Wilderness areas constituted under the *Wilderness Act 1987* (WA), which are declared mainly over national parks and nature reserves, have the most secure protection against the impact of human activities, to ensure wilderness areas remain in pristine condition.

542. An exploration licence, assessment lease or mining lease cannot be granted over land that the Governor of New South Wales has declared to be a reserve pursuant to section 367 of the Mining Act, and over which the Governor has directed that no exploration licence, assessment lease or mining lease is permitted to be granted.[748]

543. The Mining SEPP has identified certain areas where open cut coal mining is prohibited, these being within certain land within the local government areas of Lake Macquarie and the Upper Hunter Shire.[749]

C. Houses, Gardens and Significant Improvements

544. The Mining Act prohibits the holder of an exploration licence and an assessment lease from carrying out prospecting activities within 200 metres of a dwelling house that is the principal place of residence of the person occupying it, 50 metres of a garden, or over any 'significant improvements', without the written consent of the owner and occupant of the dwelling house, and owner of the garden or significant improvement.[750] A 'significant improvement' is any substantial building, dam, reservoir, contour bank, graded bank, levee, water disposal area, soil conservation work or other

745. *Mining Act 1992*, ss 30 and 48.
746. *National Parks and Wildlife Act 1974* (NSW), ss 41, 54, 58O and 64.
747. *Ibid.*
748. *Mining Act 1992*, ss 18, 36, 57, 367.
749. *State Environmental Planning Policy (Mining, Petroleum Production and Extractive Industries) 2007* cl 9 and Sch. 1.
750. *Mining Act 1992*, ss 31, 49. These provisions do not apply if the dwelling house, garden or significant improvement is owned by the holder of the exploration licence, or if the holder is a corporation, by a related corporation.

valuable work or structure.[751] Any party may refer a dispute regarding this prohibition to the Land and Environment Court.

545. Similarly, a mining lease may not be granted over the surface of any land within 200 metres of a dwelling house that is the principal place of residence of the person occupying it, 50 metres of a garden, or over any 'significant improvements', without the written consent of the owner and occupant of the dwelling house, and owner of the garden or significant improvement.[752] However, the dwelling house, garden or significant improvement must be in existence by 'the relevant date', as specific in the Act.[753] In the case of an application for a mining lease for coal by the holder of a pre-existing exploration licence, for the landholder to receive protection from this section, the houses, gardens and/or significant improvements must have been in existence prior to the date on which the application for the exploration licence was made. Either party to a dispute may seek a determination of the dispute by the Land and Environment Court.

D. *Access Arrangements*

1. Exploration Licences and Assessment Leases

546. The provisions of the Mining Act that regulate access to land refer to exploration licences and assessment leases as 'prospecting titles'. The Act prohibits the holders of prospecting titles from carrying out 'prospecting operations' (namely, exploratory mining activities) otherwise than in accordance with a written access arrangement with the land holder.[754] 'Landholder' has a broad definition and includes owners and occupiers such as registered lessees.[755]

547. Access arrangements can be entered into before or after the grant of the title and may make provision for or with respect to a range of matters, including: the periods during which access to the land is to be permitted; the parts of the land in or on which activities may take place; the means by which the tenement holder may gain access to the land; the kinds of operations that may be carried out; the conditions to be observed by the tenement holder; any compensation to be paid to the landholder; and the manner of resolving any dispute arising in connection with the arrangement.[756] Access arrangements need only cover those parts of the land on which the title holder proposes to carry out exploratory activities. Separate access arrangements can be made with different landholders of the same land, for example the owner and any lessees or occupiers of the land. Separate arrangements can be made for different areas of the same landholding, or in relation to different matters.

---

751. *Mining Act 1992,* s. 4, Dictionary.
752. Section 62. These provisions do not apply if the dwelling house, garden or significant improvement is owned by the holder of the exploration licence, or if the holder is a corporation, by a related corporation.
753. *Mining Act* 1992, subs. 62(4)(5).
754. Section 140.
755. Section 4, Dictionary.
756. Section 141.

548. Holders of prospecting titles who wish to enter into access arrangements may serve written notice on each landholder in order to notify them of their intention to seek an access arrangement.[757] If an access arrangement cannot be agreed to within twenty-eight days, the tenement holder may send a notice in writing to the landholder(s) requesting they agree to the appointment of an arbitrator. If the parties are unable to agree on the arbitrator, either party can apply to the Director-General to appoint an arbitrator from the Minister's panel of arbitrators.[758] The arbitration process is set out in sections 143–158 of the Mining Act.

549. If the holder of a prospecting title contravenes an access arrangement, a landholder may deny them access to the land until the titleholder ceases the contravention, or until the contravention is remedied to the reasonable satisfaction of, or in the manner directed by, an arbitrator appointed by the Secretary of the Department of Industry.[759]

550. On the granting of an exploration licence or assessment lease, landholders are entitled to compensation for any 'compensable loss' suffered, or likely to be suffered, as a result of the exercise of rights conferred by the title.[760] This provision applies to landholders regardless of whether their land is within the area of the title or not. Compensation provisions may be included in an access arrangement agreed between the titleholder and landowner. An access arrangement that is determined by an arbitrator must specify the compensation to which the landholder is entitled under the Act. If a situation arises that is not covered by an access arrangement, landholders are entitled to seek further compensation under the Act. The titleholder and landholder may enter into an agreement in writing, and signed by both parties, as to the amount of compensation payable.[761] If agreement cannot be reached, the landholder may seek a determination by the Land and Environment Court.[762]

2. Mining Leases

551. Once a mining lease has been granted, the title holder may not exercise any rights under the lease on the surface of any land without a valid compensation agreement or unless an assessment as to compensation has been made by the Land and Environment Court.[763] On the granting of a mining lease, landholders are entitled to compensation for any compensable loss suffered, or likely to be suffered, as a result of the exercise of rights conferred by the mining lease.[764] This provision applies to landholders regardless of whether their land is within the area of the title or not. The holder of the mining lease and the landholder may enter into an agreement in writing, and signed by both parties, as to the amount of compensation payable. If agreement cannot be reached, the landholder may seek a determination by the Land and Environment Court.

757. Section 142.
758. Established under s. 139.
759. Subsection 141(4).
760. Sections 263, 264. 'Compensable loss' is defined in s. 262.
761. Sections 263, 264.
762. Section 276.
763. Section 265.
764. Sections 263, 264. 'Compensable loss' is defined in s. 262.

E. Agricultural Land

1. Agricultural Land: Individual Landholders

552. A landholder may object to the grant of a mining lease on the basis some or all of the land is 'agricultural land',[765] as defined in the Mining Act.[766] The objection will be referred to the Primary Industries Division of the Department of Industry for determination. In the case of a coal mining lease, the date for determining whether land is 'agricultural land' is the date on which the holder of the pre-existing coal exploration licence lodged their exploration licence application.[767] This means agricultural improvements, such as sowing crops, made after that date will not be taken into account in determining whether the land is agricultural land. Primary Industries may find that only part of the land is agricultural land. If land is determined to be 'agricultural land', the coal mining lease must not be granted, except with the written consent of the landholder.[768] However, a mining lease may be granted over any part of the land if the Minister considers that the granting of the lease is necessary to give access to any other part of the land to which the mining lease applies.[769]

2. Strategic Agricultural Land

553. The government has established a special 'Gateway process' to assess proposals for State Significant mining projects on 'strategic agricultural land'. 'Strategic agricultural land' is comprised of (a) 'biophysical strategic agricultural land', which is land with high quality soil and water resources capable of sustaining high levels of productivity; and (b) 'critical industry clusters', which are concentrations of highly productive agricultural industries within a region that are related to each other, contribute to the identity of that region, and provide significant employment opportunities. As of 1 November 2016, a total of 2.8 million hectares of biophysical strategic agricultural land' had been identified and mapped at a regional scale across New South Wales, while a number of equine and viticulture industries in the Upper Hunter have been identified and mapped as Critical Industry Clusters.[770]

554. A 'site verification process' under the *Mining SEPP* enables mining operators to verify whether or not land at the site of a potential development is classified as biophysical strategic agricultural land.[771] Where the land on which the mining activity is to be carried out is not biophysical strategic agricultural land, the proponent may

---

765. Schedule 1, cl. 22.
766. Schedule 2, cl. 1.
767. Schedule 2, subcl. 2(3).
768. Schedule 1, subcl. 23(1).
769. Schedule 1, subcl. 23(4).
770. NSW Government, Department of Planning and Environment, *Safeguarding Our Agricultural Land,* http://www.planning.nsw.gov.au/Policy-and-Legislation/Mining-and-Resources/Safeguarding-our-Agricultural-Land (accessed 1 Nov. 2016).
771. *State Environmental Planning Policy (Mining, Petroleum Production and Extractive Industries) 2007*, cls 17C–17E.

obtain a 'site verification certificate'. A coal mining proponent with a site verification certificate may proceed to apply for development consent under the EPAA.[772]

555. Where a proposed coal mine is on strategic agricultural land, the coal mining project, as State Significant Development, must be submitted to the Mining and Petroleum Gateway Panel for independent, scientific assessment of the impact on strategic agricultural land and its associated water resources, before a development consent application is submitted under the EPAA.[773] This Panel is an independent body of scientific experts constituted under the *Mining SEPP*.[774] The Panel's assessments are conducted against targeted scientific criteria.[775] Following assessment, the Panel can issue one of two types of 'Gateway Certificate': an unconditional certificate which confirms the proposal meets the scientific criteria, or a conditional certificate, which may include recommendations such as further studies or modifications to the project.[776]

556. When a coal mining project is located on biophysical strategic agricultural land, the project must also be referred to the Minister for Primary Industries for advice on the project's impacts under the government's Aquifer Interference Policy, and to the Commonwealth IESC for advice on potential impacts on water resources (*see* Chapter 2 §1 [I] above).[777] The Committee's advice must be provided to the Gateway Panel.

557. Once a coal mining proponent has a Gateway certificate, they can proceed with a development consent application under the EPAA.[778] Before determining whether or not to grant development consent, the decision-maker must consider a range of factors, including any recommendations set out in the certificate, and written advice provided by the Minister for Primary Industries and the Commonwealth IESC to the Gateway Panel.[779]

IV. Mine Safety

558. The major laws governing safety and health in coal mining are the *Work Health and Safety Act 2011* (NSW) and the *Work Health and Safety Regulation 2011*, which apply to all workplaces, including mines, and the *Work Health and Safety (Mines) Act 2013* (NSW) and *Work Health and Safety (Mines) Regulation 2014*, which support the general legislation and contain additional provisions unique to mine safety. The main statutory duties on employers in relation to workplace health and safety are contained in the general *Work Health and Safety Act 2011* (NSW) and the *Work Health and Safety Regulation 2011*.

772. Environment Planning and Assessment Regulation 2000 (NSW) cl. 50A.
773. *State Environmental Planning Policy (Mining, Petroleum Production and Extractive Industries) 2007*, cl. 17F.
774. Clauses 17N–17U.
775. These criteria are set out in cl. 17H.
776. Clause 17H.
777. Clause 17G.
778. Environment Planning and Assessment Regulation 2000, cl. 50A.
779. *State Environmental Planning Policy (Mining, Petroleum Production and Extractive Industries) 2007*, cl. 17B.

559. The Work Health and Safety (Mines) Act and Regulation, which commenced on 1 February 2015, largely cover issues related to compliance and enforcement of health and safety laws in relation to mines, for example by mandatory notification of certain serious incidents in coal mines, and provision regarding government inspections of mines. These laws are based on national model work, health and safety regulations for mining, and on additional provisions agreed between the three largest mining States of New South Wales, Queensland and Western Australia. The laws, which aim to increase harmonisation between the States and Territories, provide a single framework for regulating workplace health and safety in all mineral sectors, including coal.[780] The legislation apply to all workplaces that are mines, these being; workplaces at which mining operations are carried out, including exploration and extraction activities; and tourist mines, the latter being former mines now used solely for tourist purposes.

560. The government publishes approved Codes of practice, which are practical guides to achieving the standards of health and safety required under the legislation.[781] In most cases, following an approved code of practice will achieve compliance with statutory duties in the legislation for the subject matter of the code. Compliance can also be demonstrated by following another method, such as a technical or an industry standard, but only if an equivalent or higher standard of work health and safety than the relevant code is achieved. As of 1 November 2016, a series of codes of practice were approved under the general Work Health and Safety Act, while six of codes of practice specific to mining had been approved by the Minister for Resources and Energy. The government also publishes a range of Mining Design Guidelines for industry, Guidance Notes, and Technical References specific to coal.

561. The Department of Industry, Division of Resources & Energy, Mine Safety ('NSW Mine Safety') is the government regulator responsible for ensuring acceptable safety and health standards are established and observed within the mining industry, devising and making recommendations to the Minister, and reporting on the operation and effectiveness of the laws.[782] In the coal industry, certain powers of enforcement are also given to Industry Safety and Health Representatives and Mine Safety and Health Representatives.[783] The Mine Safety Advisory Council advises the Minister for Natural Resources and Mines on any policy matter relating to work health and safety in mines.[784]

780. The legislation replaces the *Coal Mine Health and Safety Act 2002* (NSW), the Coal Mine Health and Safety Regulation 2007, the *Mine Health and Safety Act 2004* (NSW) and the Mine Health and Safety Regulation 2007.

781. These are made under *Work Health and Safety Act 2011* (NSW) s. 274 and *Work Health and Safety (Mines) Act 2013* (NSW) s. 72.

782. *Work Health and Safety Act* 2011, s. 152 and *Work Health and Safety (Mines) Act* 2013, s. 74.

783. *Work Health and Safety (Mines) Act*, Pt. 5.

784. Sections 60–61.

Chapter 3. Transport and Distribution

562. The transportation of coal takes place through a network of road, railways and ports. The established coal-producing areas are close to the coast and are therefore able to take advantage of existing transport infrastructure.[785] The infrastructure for coal transportation is operated on a commercial basis, through commercial contracts between relevant entities such as government-owned rail and port corporations; mining companies; and private rail track owners, coal terminal owners and/or lessees, port management authorities and transport providers.[786]

§1. Ports

563. As of 1 August 2016, the coal-exporting industry in Australia is serviced by nine major coal-loading terminals located in Queensland and New South Wales. In Queensland, the railways deliver coal to six coal-exporting terminals at four major ports: the ports of Abbot Point, Hay Point, Gladstone and Brisbane.[787]

564. The Port of Abbot Point is administered by the North Queensland Bulk Ports Corporation, a statutory authority representing the Queensland government. Its sole existing coal operating terminal, the Adani Abbot Point Coal Terminal 1, is leased from the government under a ninety-nine-year lease agreement to Mundra Port Pty Ltd, a subsidiary of Adani Mining Limited. Adani Abbot Point Terminal Pty Ltd contracts the operation and maintenance of the terminal to Abbot Point Bulkcoal Pty Ltd, which is a controlled subsidiary of Glencore. In 2014–2015, 28.7 million tonnes of metallurgical and thermal coal were exported from the terminal. The increased export of coal from the Gallilee Basin may see the expansion of the existing terminal and/or construction of new terminals.[788]

565. The Port of Hay Point is also administered by the North Queensland Bulk Ports Corporation. It has two terminals which both export metallurgical and thermal coal, mined from the Bowen Basin. The Dalrymple Bay Coal Terminal is leased from the government to Brookfield Asset Management Limited, and operated under contract by a separate company Dalrymple Bay Coal Terminal Pty Ltd, owned by five of eight mining companies who put coal through the terminal. The Hay Point Services Coal Terminal (HPSCT) is a single-user terminal owned and managed by BHP Billiton Mitsubishi Alliance. HPSCT is owned by the Central Queensland Coal Associates joint venture and is operated by Hay Point Services Pty Ltd, a wholly owned subsidiary

785. International Energy Agency, *Energy Policies of IEA Countries: Australia 2012 Review*, 112 (OECD/IEA, 2012).
786. Queensland Department of Transport and Main Roads, *Coal Transport Infrastructure Development*, http://www.tmr.qld.gov.au/business-industry/Transport-sectors/Coal-transport-infrastructure-development (accessed 30 Sept. 2016).
787. *Ibid.*
788. *Ibid.*

of BHP Coal Pty Ltd. In 2014–2015, the DBCT exported 71.6 million tonnes of coal and the HPSCT exported 43.4 million tonnes of coal.[789]

566. The Port of Gladstone is administered by the Gladstone Ports Corporation, a government-owned corporation. The port exports metallurgical and thermal coal mined from the Bowen Basin. The port has three multi-user coal terminals. The RG Tanna and Barney Point Coal Terminals are both owned and managed by the Gladstone Ports Corporation. The third coal terminal, Wiggins Island Coal Export Terminal (WICET), constructed in 2015, is owned by WICET Pty Ltd, a coal industry consortium comprised of Aquila Resources, Caledon Coal, Glencore, New Hope Group, Wesfarmers Curragh and Yancoal. In 2014–2015, the RG Tanna and Barney Point Coal Terminals exported a combined 67.8 million tonnes of coal, and 0.2 million tonnes to other Australian Ports, while the WICET exported 0.5 million tonnes. Following the construction of the WICET, the Barney Point Coal Terminal is scheduled to close by September 2016.[790]

567. The Port of Brisbane is managed and developed by the Port of Brisbane Pty Ltd (PBPL), under a ninety-nine-year lease from the Queensland Government. PBPL is owned by the Q Port Holdings consortium. The port has one coal terminal, the Queensland Bulk Handling Coal Terminal, owned and operated by Queensland Bulk Handling Pty Ltd. Queensland Bulk Handling is wholly owned by the New Hope Group, an Australian-owned diversified energy company. Coal exports comprise thermal coal produced from mines in the West Moreton and Surat Basins.[791] In 2014–2015, coal exports from the Port totalled 7.3 million tonnes.[792]

568. The Port of Newcastle in NSW is one of world's largest coal-exporting facilities. Port Waratah Coal Services Limited operates the two major terminals at the Port of Newcastle, Carrington and Kooragang, which export coal from the Hunter Valley.[793] At Port Kembla, the Port Kembla Coal Terminal services mines in the southern and western coalfields of New South Wales.

§2. Rail

569. Most coal is transported to ports for export by rail. The two largest rail companies operating in the coal sector are Aurizon and Pacific National, who together service Queensland, New South Wales and South Australia.

570. In Queensland, coal for export is transported from the mines through the rail systems to the ports, by Aurizon, Pacific National and BHP Billiton Mitsubishi Alliance Rail. Aurizon owns and operates the Central Queensland coal rail network, which is comprised of the Newlands, Goonyella, Blackwater and Moura rail systems.

---

789. *Ibid.*

790. *Ibid.*

791. *Ibid.*; Port of Brisbane, *About Us*, https://www.portbris.com.au/about-us/about-us (accessed 30. Sept. 2016); Queensland Bulk Handling, *About*, http://www.qbh.com.au/content/about (accessed 30. Sept. 2016).

792. Queensland Department of Transport and Main Roads, *supra* n. 786.

793. Minerals Council of Australia, *Australia's Coal Industry: Ports and Transport*, http://www.minerals.org.au/resources/coal/exports/ports_and_transport (accessed 30 Sept. 2016).

The West Moreton rail system in the southeastern Queensland is owned by the statutory authority Queensland Rail.[794] Coal is also transported by rail to the electricity power stations at Stanwell and Gladstone, as well to various industrial users.

571. Aurizon Holdings Limited, formerly QR National, is Australia's largest coal rail transporter, operating in all major coal regions in Queensland and New South Wales. QR National was established in 2004/05 to operate the freight services of Queensland Rail (QR), the government-owned rail owner and operator. QR's freight business was privatised in 2010, when QR National was floated on the stock exchange. QR National was rebranded as Aurizon in December 2012 and is now Australia's largest rail freight company.

572. In New South Wales, Pacific National delivers coal from the Hunter Valley and southern and western coalfields to the Port of Newcastle and Port Kembla for export, as well as delivering domestic coal to power stations and steelworks in NSW.

§3. OTHER

573. Other forms of coal transport include the use of overland conveyer systems to transport coal from coal mines built close to power stations, and road transport, which is used by a number of mines located away from rail facilities. However, in general, trucks are used only for shorter hauls to port or rail loading facilities.[795]

794. Queensland Department of Transport and Main Roads, *supra* n. 786.
795. Minerals Council of Australia, *supra* n. 793.

Chapter 4. Consumption

574. Historically, coal has been one of the largest primary fuels consumed in Australia, reflecting its dominance as a fuel in Australia's electricity generation. In 2013–2014, coal remained the second largest primary fuel consumed in Australia, accounting for 31.7% of Australia's total energy consumption, behind oil (38.4%) but ahead of gas (24%) and renewables (5.9%). However, coal consumption was at its lowest share of primary energy consumption since the early 1970s, reflecting its declining use in electricity generation, and declining output in the iron and steel sectors.[796]

575. Although coal remained the largest source of fuel for electricity generation in Australia in 2013–2014, with 61% of electricity generated from coal, its share decreased from 79% in 2003–2004, accounting for much of a decline in total electricity generation in Australia over the period.[797] Coal-fired generation declined in all States in 2013–2014, except for Western Australia, dropping to the lowest levels since 1996–1997, although the rate of decline for brown coal generation reduced significantly in 2013–2014 compared to 2012–2013, most probably because of the abolition of the CPM, which increased the relative costs of coal-fired generation. In contrast, natural gas-fired electricity generation and renewable-sourced electricity increased in 2013–2014.[798]

576. With increasing concerns over the impact on climate change of GHG emissions from coal-fired power stations, the Australian Government has stated that 'the capacity to store CO_2 will be critical to Australia's continued reliance on coal-fired power stations'.[799] The Australian Coalition government has remained committed to supporting the coal industry, because of the abundance of coal as a low-cost fuel in Australia; the opportunity to earn royalties, export income, and tax revenue; and the centrality of the coal to the Queensland and NSW economies. Thus, investment in the development of carbon capture and storage technology will be a focus of the Australian Coalition government to enable the continued export and consumption of coal, while attempting to meet climate change commitments.[800] The government has also recognised that developing and disseminating new low-missions coal technologies will be vital to the continuing existence of the coal industry.[801] The regulation of carbon capture and storage is discussed in Part V.

796. Australian Government, Department of Industry and Science/Office of the Chief Economist, *supra* n. 599 at 11.
797. *Ibid.*, 20.
798. *Ibid.*, 20–21.
799. Australian Government, Department of Industry and Science, *2015 Energy White Paper*, 57 (Commonwealth of Australia, 2015).
800. *Ibid.*
801. *Ibid.*; Geoscience Australia/BREE, *supra* n. 580 at 149–155.

Part V. Interaction Between Energy Law and Environmental Law

Chapter 1. General

577. As development, energy projects require environmental assessment and approval. This takes place largely under State planning, environmental and mining/petroleum laws, and, in the particular circumstances where federal approval is required, under the *Environment Protection and Biodiversity Conservation Act 1999* (Cth). The relationship and interaction between each State's onshore and offshore resource laws and myriad planning and environmental laws, as well as federal laws, is far too complex to examine in any detail in this Part, thus only a brief overview will be offered. Then, this chapter will focus on climate change law. As energy is the major industry responsible for GHG emissions, energy use and climate change are inextricably intertwined.

578. Environmental assessment and approval under general State planning and environment laws is required for renewable energy developments such as wind farms and solar energy installations. As coal is a mineral, coal exploration and mining requires assessment and approval under the relevant State mining act and/or the relevant State planning and environment law (*see* Part IV above). Activities for the onshore exploitation of petroleum, geothermal energy, and unconventional fuels such as shale gas and CSG, require environmental assessment and approval under the relevant petroleum law and/or State planning and environment law (*see* Parts II and III above). Petroleum exploitation in State coastal waters requires assessment and approval under the relevant State's offshore petroleum legislation, while petroleum exploitation in Commonwealth waters requires assessment and approval under Commonwealth petroleum legislation (*see* Part III above).

579. The impact of energy developments on a range of environmental and cultural matters must be considered, and conditions will be placed on the development authorisation to protect the environment. In the case of coal mines or petroleum and gas projects, specific conditions on authorisations to protect the environment will address a range of matters, including rehabilitation and decommissioning. For other energy projects such as wind energy facilities assessed under general planning law, a range of conditions may be placed on the planning permit, regarding impacts such as noise, visual impact, and impacts on birds and bats.

580. Mining and petroleum law will generally require the resource Minister to consider the objectives of specified environmental legislation when administering petroleum/mining legislation, for example, when making decisions such as granting or renewing licences, or placing conditions on licences. There may be a statutory requirement that the resource Minister 'considers the environment' when administering petroleum/mining legislation. Mining or petroleum law may place statutory duties on the holder of the mining/petroleum authorisation, for example, a duty to protect the environment, or to clean up oil spills as soon as possible.

581. As well as a planning or mining/petroleum authorisation, proponents will need to obtain authorisations for energy projects under a range of environment and heritage legislation, such as: water resources law; pollution laws; native title laws; Aboriginal heritage laws; State and national heritage laws; legislation regulating the clearance of clear native vegetation; protected areas and protected species legislation; and soil conservation laws. Mining, petroleum or general planning legislation will usually require the referral of energy/resources projects to other Ministers who are responsible for the administration of certain specified environment Acts, for example, the Minister administering protected areas or protected species legislation.

Chapter 2. Climate Change Law

582. Approximately 76% of Australia's GHG emissions come from the energy sector. Stationary energy accounts for 52% of total emissions, transport 17%, and fugitive emissions from fuel accounts for 7% of total emissions.[802] Although Australia emits a fraction of the world's total emissions of greenhouse gases, the country has a very high rate of emissions per capita.

§1. International Obligations

583. Australia is a party to both the UNFCCC and the Kyoto Protocol to the UNFCCC, having ratified the Convention on 30 December 1992 and the Protocol on 12 December 2007.[803] Australia has obligations under both legal instruments.

I. Framework Convention on Climate Change

584. At the 17th Conference of the Parties to the UNFCCC, held in Durban 2011, the Parties to the Framework Convention agreed to develop and adopt 'a protocol, another legal instrument or an agreed outcome with legal force under the Convention applicable to all Parties', to apply from 2020, that would achieve the Convention's objective of stabilising GHG concentrations in the atmosphere at a level that will prevent dangerous interference with the climate system.[804] The Conference of the Parties launched the Ad-hoc Working Group on the Durban Platform for Enhanced Action to develop this legal instrument for adoption at the 21st Conference of the Parties, held in Paris, December 2015. Australia's long-term target, expressed in its Nationally Determined Contribution (NDC) under the Paris Agreement,[805] is to reduce GHG emissions to 26–28% below 2005 levels by 2030. Australia ratified the Paris Agreement on 9 November 2016.

---

802. Australian National Greenhouse Accounts, *National Inventory Report 2013*, Vol 1 (May 2015).
803. United Nations Framework Convention on Climate Change, Adopted 14 Jun. 1992, UNCED Doc A/CONF.151/5/Rev.1, (Vol I), Annex I, 13 Jun. 1992, 31 *ILM* 874 (1992); Kyoto Protocol to the United Nations Framework Convention on Climate Change, *Report of the Conference of the Parties at its Third Session, 1-11 Dec. 1997*, U.N. Doc FCCC/CP/1997/7/Add.1, 18 Mar. 1998, Annex.
804. United Nations Framework Convention on Climate Change *Report of the Conference of the Parties on its seventeenth session, held in Durban from 28 November to 11 December* 2011, FCCC/CP/2011/9/Add.1, 15 Mar. 2012, Decision 1/CP.17, 'Establishment of an Ad Hoc Working Group on the Durban Platform for Enhanced Action'.
805. United Nations Framework Convention on Climate Change, Report of the Conference of the Parties at its Twenty First Session, 30 Nov.–11 Dec. 2015, FCCC/CP/2015/L.9/Rev.1, 12 Dec. 2015, Annex.

II. Kyoto Protocol

585. Australia's commitment for the first period of the Kyoto Protocol (2008–2012) was to reduce its emissions to 108% of its 1990 emissions of greenhouse gases. Australia's current pledge for the reduction of GHG emissions, as set out in the Doha Amendment to the Kyoto Protocol, has two parts.[806] The first is an unconditional target to reduce its emissions of greenhouse gases by at least 5% by 2020 compared with levels in 2000. The second part is a conditional target: to reduce its emissions of greenhouse gases by up to 15% by 2020 if there is a global agreement, which falls short of securing atmospheric stabilisation at 450 ppm CO2-e, but under which major developing economies commit to substantially restrain emissions and advanced economies take on commitments comparable to Australia's; or to reduce its emissions of greenhouse gases by up to 25% by 2020 if there is a global agreement to secure atmospheric stabilisation at 450 ppm CO2-e, under which major developing economies commit to substantially restraining their emissions and advanced economies take on commitments comparable to Australia's.

586. As of 1 July 2016, Australia had not ratified the Doha Amendment to the Kyoto Protocol, nor was the Amendment in force, although Prime Minister Malcolm Turnbull announced at the 9th Conference of the Meeting of the Parties held in Paris, December 2015, that Australia would ratify the Doha Amendment.[807]

§2. National Initiatives to Address Climate Change

587. A range of measures to reduce GHG emissions exist at the Commonwealth and State level. Given the diversity and range of measures across the various governments, this Part will focus on a few key initiatives relevant to reducing emissions from the energy sector, including the following:

- the GHG and energy reporting scheme;
- emissions trading schemes (such as the recently abolished CPM), which, by putting a price on carbon dioxide (CO_2) emissions, makes CO_2-emitting fuels more expensive, and improves the cost competitiveness of alternative energy sources;
- the ERF, under which the Australian government pays polluters for reducing GHG emissions below a business-as-usual trajectory, and the Safeguard Mechanism to ensure emissions do not exceed certain baselines;
- mandated market policies to increase the uptake of renewable energy in electricity generation, which may be mandatory *quantities* electricity retailers must purchase

806. Kyoto Protocol to the United Nations Framework Convention on Climate Change, Conference of the Meeting of the Parties, Decision 1/CMP.8, FCCC/KP/CMP/2012/13/Add.1, *Amendment to the Kyoto Protocol pursuant to its Art. 3, para. 9 ('the Doha Amendment').*

807. The Climate Institute, 'The Paris climate deal: What it means for Australia and its policies', *Reneweconomy*, 15 Dec. 2015, http://reneweconomy.com.au/2015/the-paris-climate-deal-what-it-means-for-australia-and-its-policies-61728 (accessed 3 Feb. 2015).

(the Commonwealth RET), or mandatory *prices* for renewable-sourced electricity, such as the States' feed-in tariffs;

- certain demand-side measures to encourage energy conservation and efficiency, including standards, labelling and State market-based tradeable certificate schemes; and
- the regulation of carbon capture and storage.

588. The main initiatives of the Commonwealth government, discussed below, are administered by the CER, including the GHG and energy reporting scheme; the national registry of emissions units; the RET; the ERF; and, before it was abolished, the CPM. Other key independent national bodies, with different roles in relation to climate change and renewable energy, include: the Climate Change Authority, a statutory authority which provides independent, expert advice to the Australian Government on climate change mitigation initiatives;[808] the Clean Energy Finance Corporation, created to leverage private sector funding for renewable energy and clean technology projects and identify and remove barriers to the financing of projects;[809] and the Australian Renewable Energy Agency (ARENA), a statutory body with an AUD 3 billion budget to co-ordinate existing grant funding programmes supporting R&D in renewable energy.[810]

I. National Greenhouse Gas Emissions Reporting Requirements

589. The *National Greenhouse and Energy Reporting Act 2007* (Cth) ('NGER Act') introduced a single national reporting framework for energy and emissions reporting to ensure the accurate, transparent, verifiable and complete measurement and reporting of GHG emissions.[811] The Act imposes a statutory requirement for defined corporations to monitor and report on their GHG emissions, energy production and energy consumption to: inform government policy formulation; inform the Australian public; meet Australia's international reporting obligations; assist Commonwealth, State and Territory government programmes and activities; and avoid duplication of similar reporting requirements across the States and Territories.[812]

590. The NGER Act applies to 'constitutional corporations', that is, trading, financial and foreign corporations within the meaning of paragraph 51(xx) of the

808. http://climatechangeauthority.gov.au/ (accessed 28 Sept. 2016).
809. http://www.cleanenergyfinancecorp.com.au/ (accessed 28 Sept. 2016).
810. http://arena.gov.au/ (accessed 28 Sept. 2016).
811. The National Greenhouse and Energy Reporting Regulations 2008 set out the details that establish compliance rules and procedures for administering the NGER Act. The *National Greenhouse and Energy Reporting (Measurement) Determination 2008* describes the methods, standards and criteria to be applied when estimating greenhouse gas emissions, and energy production and consumption. The *National Greenhouse and Energy Reporting (Audit) Determination 2009* sets out requirements for preparing, conducting and reporting on greenhouse and energy audits. The *National Greenhouse and Energy Reporting (Auditor Registration) Instrument* 2012 specifies the qualifications an auditor must have to be registered under the NGER Act.
812. *National Greenhouse & Energy Reporting Act 2007 (Cth)* s. 3.

Commonwealth Constitution. The statutory obligations apply to 'controlling corporations'. A controlling corporation is a constitutional corporation that does not have a holding company in Australia.[813] It is generally the corporation at the top of the corporate hierarchy in Australia. Foreign corporations may also be controlling corporations.

591. From 1 July 2008, all controlling corporations must apply to register if, each financial year ending on or after 30 June 2009, they emit greenhouse gases, or produce energy or consume energy, above certain thresholds over a financial year.[814] There are two thresholds. The first is the 'corporate group threshold', where a controlling corporation's corporate 'group', whose members have operational control over facilities, emit 125 kt CO_2-e greenhouse gases or more, or produce or consume 500 TJ or more of energy, in total from the facilities.[815] The second threshold is a 'facility threshold', where an entity within a controlling corporation's group has operational control over a facility that emitted 25 kt or more greenhouse gases, or produced/consumed 100 TJ or more of energy, in a financial year.[816]

592. A 'facility' is an activity or series of activities that 'involve greenhouse gas emissions or produce or consume energy'; form part of a single undertaking or enterprise (i.e., occur at a 'single site'); are part of a process to produce products or services; and are attributable to a single industry sector.[817] A controlling corporation's corporate group includes subsidiaries as well as the controlling corporation, or may consist of only the controlling corporation itself.[818] A corporation has 'operational control' over a facility if it has authority to introduce and implement operating, health and safety, and environmental policies. Only one corporation can have operational control over a facility at any time.[819]

593. Once on the National Greenhouse and Energy Register, companies must report their energy consumption, energy production and GHG emissions through the Emissions and Energy Reporting System.[820] Energy production and consumption thresholds are not aggregated. Each must be exceeded separately for a corporation to be obliged to register and report. However, if any one threshold is met – GHG emissions, or production or consumption of energy – then the corporation must register and report all greenhouse gases emitted, produced and consumed. Direct and indirect emissions are aggregated for reporting.

594. 'Emissions' means the release of greenhouse gases into the atmosphere. 'Greenhouse gases' are the six gases originally included in the Kyoto Protocol: carbon dioxide, methane, nitrous oxide, perfluorocarbons, hydrofluorocarbons and sulphur hexafluoride.[821] The obligation to report covers both 'direct emissions ('Scope 1 emissions') and or 'indirect emissions' ('Scope 2 emissions'). Scope 1 emissions from

813. Section 7.
814. Section 12.
815. Section 13. The corporate group threshold was introduced progressively over three years; these amounts are from 2010–2011.
816. Section 13.
817. Section 9; National Greenhouse and Energy Reporting Regulations 2008, regs 2.15–2.22.
818. Section 8.
819. Section 11; National Greenhouse and Energy Reporting Regulations 2008, reg. 2.14.
820. Section 19.
821. Section 7A.

a facility are emissions released to the atmosphere as a direct result of an activity, or series of activities that constitute the facility. Scope 2 GHG emissions are emissions released to the atmosphere as a direct result of one or more activities that generate electricity, heating, cooling or steam that is consumed by a facility, but that do not form part of the facility.[822] Scope 2 emissions are released from the indirect consumption of an energy commodity, for example, indirect emissions come from the use of electricity produced by the burning of coal in another facility.

595. The National Greenhouse and Energy Register lists the following information: the names of registered corporations and the members of their corporate groups; the trading names of the registered corporations and group members; identifying details of each registered corporation and its group members; the section of the NGER Act under which the corporations are registered; information about the corporation's compliance with the Act; and information about greenhouse and energy audits carried out in relation to the corporation.[823] It may include corporations that do not meet a reporting threshold for the first year in which they are registered. If corporations included on the Register do not meet the thresholds for a reporting year, they must submit a nil report.[824] The Regulator may disclose the contents of part or all of the Register to the public.

596. The Act contains a range of monitoring, compliance and enforcement mechanisms. These include the appointment of authorised officers with broad powers to conduct authorised investigations to monitor compliance,[825] and greenhouse and energy audits of registered corporations, undertaken by registered auditors, to determine the extent to which corporations have or have not complied with the Act.[826] The Act also includes a range of enforcement mechanisms, most notably civil penalties for breaching the statutory obligations under the Act, but also civil penalties for continuing contraventions, infringement notices, enforceable undertakings, and pecuniary penalties for contravening civil penalty provisions.[827]

II. Emissions Trading

597. The issue as to whether Australia should price carbon through a cap-and-trade emissions trading scheme has had a long and tortuous history. As far back as the 1980s, the Labor government under the Prime Ministership of Bob Hawke discussed introducing of a carbon tax to price carbon, but did not do so, given the expected opposition of the community to a new tax and higher prices for energy.

598. At the beginning of 2006, the introduction of a price on carbon through an emissions trading scheme seemed unlikely. The Liberal government under Prime Minister John Howard had long opposed mandatory measures to address climate change. However, 2006 and 2007 saw climate change become an issue of significant

822. Section 10; National Greenhouse and Energy Reporting Regulations 2008, regs 2.23, 2.24.
823. Section 16; National Greenhouse and Energy Reporting Regulations 2008, reg. 3.04.
824. National Greenhouse and Energy Reporting Regulations 2008, reg. 4.32.
825. *National Greenhouse and Energy Reporting Act* 2007, ss 57–72.
826. Sections 73–75A.
827. Sections 29–48.

public, and hence political, concern, with the release of the *Stern Review on the Economic Impacts of Climate Change* in the UK in 2006, and the *Fourth Assessment Report* of the Intergovernmental Panel on Climate Change, in February 2007. In December 2006, John Howard established a joint government-business Task Group on Emissions Trading, the Final Report of which was published in May 2007, recommending the establishment of an Australian emissions trading scheme.[828] Some months later, the National Emissions Trading Taskforce, a multi-State taskforce, released its final report in December 2007, on establishing an emissions trading scheme between the Australian States.[829]

599. With the federal election approaching in November 2007, public pressure on the Howard government to take action on climate change increased, and the government announced it would introduce a cap-and-trade emissions trading system (ETS). The Liberal government was, however, removed from office in November 2007. The incoming Labor government, under Prime Minister Kevin Rudd, stated its intention to have a national emissions trading scheme in place by 2010. An important input into Federal Labor government policy on emissions trading was the review undertaken by respected economist Professor Ross Garnaut, which published a number interim reports and discussion papers releasing its Final Report on 40 September 2008.[830] The Federal Government's response to interim papers and advice of the Garnaut Review was the release of the 'Carbon Pollution Reduction Scheme' (CPRS) Green Paper on 16 July 2008. Following the release of the Garnaut Review Final Report, and public submissions on the Green Paper, a White Paper was released on 15 December 2008, presenting the Government's policy decisions on critical design issues of the CPRS.[831]

600. The CPRS initially had bipartisan support from the leader of the Liberal Party, Malcolm Turnbull. However, this vanished when Tony Abbott became leader of the Liberal Party. Tony Abbott resigned from his frontbench position in November 2009 in protest against Malcolm Turnbull's support for emissions trading. Forcing a leadership ballot on the subject, Tony Abbott defeated Malcolm Turnbull by 42 votes to 41, being elected Leader of the Liberal Party. A climate change sceptic, Tony Abbott strongly opposed the pricing of carbon through an ETS. The CPRS legislation, introduced to Parliament on 14 May 2009, failed to pass the Senate for the third time on 27 April 2010.[832] After this, it was abandoned by the government.

601. By June 2010 Keven Rudd had lost the confidence of the Labor Party, and Julia Gillard became Prime Minister, promising the electorate her government would

828. Prime Ministerial Task Force on Emissions Trading, *Report of the Task Force on Emissions Trading* (Australian Government, 2007).
829. National Emissions Trading Taskforce, *Possible design for a national greenhouse gas emissions trading scheme: Final framework report on scheme design* (NETT, 2007).
830. Garnaut R, *Garnaut Climate Change Review: Final Report* (Cambridge University Press, 2008). For the latest version *see* Garnaut R, *The Garnaut Review 2011: Australia in the Global Response to Climate Change* (Cambridge University Press, 2011).
831. Australian Government, Department of Climate Change, *Carbon Pollution Reduction Scheme, Green Paper, July 2008* (Commonwealth of Australia, 2008); Australian Government, Department of Climate Change and Energy Efficiency, *Carbon Pollution Reduction Scheme—Australia's Low Pollution Future, White Paper*, (Commonwealth of Australia, 2008).
832. *Carbon Pollution Reduction Scheme Bill 2010* (Cth).

not introduce a carbon tax. In September 2010, a Multiparty Climate Change Committee (MPCCC) was established to explore options for the implementation of a carbon price and help build consensus on how Australia would tackle the challenge of climate change. On 21 December 2010, the MPCCC released a *Communiqué,* in which it concluded that a *CPM* would be the most cost-effective and economically responsible way of reducing Australia's carbon pollution, and setting out eleven principles to guide discussions on a *CPM.*[833] The first broad proposal for the CPM was released on 24 February 2011 for discussion and consultation, with a more detailed Carbon Price package released on 10 July 2011. Eventually, with the support of the Greens and Independents in the Senate, the CPM was established through the *Clean Energy Act* (Cth) 2011, forming a central element of the Gillard government's 'Clean Energy Package' of 2011.

602. Although called a 'carbon tax' by Tony Abbott, the CPM was not a tax or levy on the quantity of greenhouse gases generated, but rather, a forerunner to a fully flexible cap-and-trade emissions trading scheme, operating with a fixed price per tonne of CO_2-e of greenhouse gases from 2012–2015.[834] Under the CPM, liable entities had to buy, or be allocated with, carbon units, and relinquish one carbon unit for each tonne of carbon pollution produced each year through the surrender of 'eligible emissions units' to the regulator. Liability entities who failed to surrender sufficient units had to pay an emissions charge or 'unit shortfall charge' in the fixed price period of 1.3 times the fixed price per unit. In the flexible price period, this was to be double the annual average price of units.

603. Liable entities with obligations under the scheme were first, a person with operational control of a facility that emitted over 25,000 tonnes of scope 1 emissions of CO2-e greenhouse gases annually; and second, retail suppliers of natural gas. About 500 of the biggest polluters were liable under the CPM. The scheme applied to four of the GHGs covered by the Kyoto Protocol, these being carbon dioxide, methane, nitrous oxide, and perfluorocarbons.

604. Sectors covered by the scheme included: stationary energy; industrial processes; fugitive emissions; emissions from non-legacy waste. Rail, domestic aviation, and shipping transport fuels were covered by an equivalent carbon price through separate legislation. Sectors excluded were: agricultural and land sector emissions; emissions from the combustion of biofuels and biomass (including CO2-e emissions from the combustion of methane from landfill facilities); ethanol, biodiesel and renewable diesel; fuel used for transport by households and light on-road commercial vehicles; fuel used in the agricultural, forestry and fishery industries; international aviation fuel; fugitive emissions from decommissioned coal mines; missions from legacy waste; and on-road use of LNG, LPG and CNG.

605. Various assistance packages were offered to 'emissions-intensive trade-exposed' (EITE) and other affected industries, including the Jobs and Competitiveness Program for EITE industries, under which free permits would be allocated to entities engaged in EITE activities; the Energy Security Fund; to provide transitional assistance to promote the transformation of the electricity generation sector from high to low-

833. Multiparty Committee on Climate Change, *Third Meeting Communiqué* (21 Dec. 2010).

834. The CPM is described in detail in Damien Lockie, *Clean Energy Law in Australia* (LexisNexis Butterworths, 2012).

emissions generation; the Coal Sector Jobs Package, targeted at mines most affected by the carbon price; and the Steel Transformation Plan, to provide structural adjustment assistance to the steel industry. Households were given tax cuts.

606. From 1 July 2015, when the fixed price period finished, an economy-wide cap was to be put on the emission of greenhouse gases – and hence the number of permits available – consistent with Australia's international obligations of a 5% reduction in GHG emissions by 2020 based on 2000 levels, and 80% reduction by 2050 based on 2000 levels. Caps for the years 2015–2018 would be set by 31 May 2014, with rolling pollution caps for each further year set annually by 30 June of the preceding year. The price was to become fully flexible.

607. During the fixed price period, 'eligible emissions units' included carbon units purchased from the Australian Government at the fixed price or obtained for free as part of an allocation under an assistance programme, and, to a limit of 5% of its total liability, Australian Carbon Credit Units (ACCUs) issued under the Carbon Farming Initiative, a separate scheme aimed at encouraging carbon offsets through sequestration and emissions avoidance activities in the agricultural/land-use sector under the *Carbon Credits (Farming Initiative) Act 2011* (Cth). In the flexible price period from 2015, 'eligible emissions units' were to include carbon units purchased from the Australian Government at auction, or obtained through free allocation under assistance programmes, or purchased under the secondary market for permits; ACCUs obtained from the Carbon Farming Initiative; and, with a 50% limitation until 2020, international emissions units created under the Kyoto Protocol or under recognised regional/national schemes such as the European and New Zealand emissions trading schemes. A treaty for a two-way link with the European Union emissions trading scheme was to have been agreed by 1 July 2015 and implemented no later than 1 July 2018.

608. The CPM was abolished in 2014 by the Coalition government, under Prime Minister Tony Abbott, after winning office in September 2013. Tony Abbott remained implacably opposed to the CPM, and the promise to repeal the carbon 'tax' was a fundamental plank of the Liberal Party's 2013 election campaign. However, this has not necessarily seen the end of emissions trading in Australia. In order to get the Direct Action Plan through the Senate, the Coalition government was forced to agree to an inquiry into an emissions trading scheme. Thus, in December 2014, the Minister for the Environment requested the CCA to conduct a Special Review into Australia's policies and future targets for reducing GHG emissions, in the context of its international commitments and the action of other countries. The terms of reference for the Review include whether Australia should have an emission trading scheme, and the conditions under which such a scheme should be established.

609. The final report of the Special Review, *Towards a Climate Policy Toolkit*, was released on 31 August 2016.[835] The report recommends a number of policies Australia should adopt to meet its international GHG reduction commitments. As part of the Special Review, the Authority evaluated several emissions reduction policies for Australia's electricity supply sector. A detailed explanation of the Authority's electricity sector analysis is contained within the *Policy options for Australia's electricity*

835. Climate Change Authority, *Towards a Climate Policy Toolkit: Special Review on Australia's Climate Goals and Policies* (Climate Change Authority, 2016).

supply sector—Special Review Research Report.[836] The CCA did not recommend an economy-wide cap-and-trade emissions trading scheme should be reintroduced as part of Australia's *Climate Policy Toolkit*. Rather, the Authority recommended the government expand the current ERF and Safeguard Mechanism (discussed at C below).

610. Given the recommendations of the CCA, and the resistance to emissions trading schemes by the Liberal Party/Coalition government, it seems extremely unlikely emissions trading will be re-established in Australia in the near future. While it remains a policy commitment of the opposition ALP, one of Australia's two major political parties, to reintroduce an emissions trading scheme as a priority for tackling climate change,[837] it is too difficult to predict whether politically this would be achievable should the Labor Party win the next election in three years, given the hostility of the general population and the Liberal Party to emissions trading.

III. Emissions Reduction Fund

611. The ERF is the centrepiece of the Direct Action Policy instituted by Prime Minister Tony Abbott's Coalition Government in place of the abolished CPM. Established through amendments to the *Carbon Credits (Farming Initiative) Act 2011* (Cth) on 24 November 2014,[838] the ERF comprises a government fund to purchase emissions reductions, and a safeguard mechanism 'to ensure that these reductions are not displaced by a significant rise in emissions above business-as-usual levels elsewhere in the economy'.[839]

A. Fund for Purchasing Emissions

612. The first element of the ERF is the AUD 2.55 billion fund for purchasing emission abatements. The ERF is a voluntary 'baseline and credit' scheme. A baseline for GHG emissions for companies is set at according to a 'business-as-usual' trajectory. Companies who register with the CER may seek credits – ACCUs – for emission reductions below the baseline, arising from specific 'eligible offsets projects' registered with the Regulator. There are two types of eligible offsets projects for which ACCUs may be credited. These are sequestration offsets projects, which are largely relevant to land-use sectors such as agriculture and forestry; and emissions avoidance offsets projects, which are of relevance to the abatement of CO_2-e greenhouse gases from energy use.[840]

---

836. Climate Change Authority, *Policy options for Australia's electricity supply sector—Special Review Research Report* (Climate Change Authority, 2016).
837. Australian Labor Party, *National Platform: a smart, modern, fair Australia* (2015), 61.
838. *See also* the *Carbon Credits (Carbon Farming Initiative) Regulations 2011* and the *Carbon Credits (Carbon Farming Initiative) Rule 2015*.
839. Australian Government, Department of the Environment and Energy, *Emissions Reduction Fund Safeguard Mechanism*, http://www.environment.gov.au/climate-change/emissions-reduction-fund/about/safeguard-mechanism (accessed 28 Sept. 2016).
840. *Carbon Credits (Farming Initiative) Act 2011* (Cth), ss 16, 18.

613. To receive Australian carbon credits units for a project, entities must open an account in the Australian National Registry of Emission Units;[841] apply for a declaration that a project is an eligible offsets project; apply for and obtain a certificate of entitlement from the CER; and apply for credits for the 'eligible carbon abatement' achieved by the offsets project.[842] ACCUs can then be sold to generate income, either to the federal Government through a carbon abatement contract,[843] or in the secondary market for ACCUs. A project proponent may secure a carbon abatement contract with the federal government by participating in an auction, either before the project commences, or after registering and starting a project. The Clean Energy Regulatory uses a sealed bid 'reverse auction process' to acquire abatement projects at least cost on behalf of the government. Projects that have a price greater than a benchmark price will not be selected. The CER will select the lowest-cost projects until the budget for the ERF is exhausted.[844]

614. Only specific types of approved projects, called 'methods', are eligible for credits under the ERF. The Minister has published various methodology Determinations under the *Carbon Credits (Farming Initiative) Act* that apply to these specific kinds of projects, and which set out the requirements that must be met for the project to be an eligible project.[845] Specific projects fall within one of two types of emissions reduction methods: 'activity methods' for specific emissions reduction actions, such as landfill gas capture, energy efficiency and land sector projects; and 'facility methods', which can aggregate emissions reductions from multiple activities at large facilities for which data are reported under the National Greenhouse and Energy Reporting Scheme. Methods or projects of particular relevance to reducing emissions from the energy sector include: a generic method for emissions reductions at facilities reporting under the National Greenhouse and Energy Reporting Scheme;[846] the capture and destruction of coal mine fugitive emissions;[847] fugitive emissions from oil or gas;[848] reductions in emissions-intensity of transport;[849] energy efficiency projects for

841. Established under the *Australian National Registry of Emission Units Act 2011* (Cth).
842. *Carbon Credits (Farming Initiative) Act 2011*, ss 11, 12, 15, 22 and 27.
843. Section 20B.
844. Section 20F–20G.
845. Section 106.
846. *Carbon Credits (Carbon Farming Initiative—Facilities) Methodology Determination 2015.*
847. *Carbon Credits (Carbon Farming Initiative—Coal Mine Waste Gas) Methodology Determination 2015.*
848. *Carbon Credits (Carbon Farming Initiative—Oil and Gas Fugitives) Methodology Determination 2015.*
849. *Carbon Credits (Carbon Farming Initiative—Aviation) Methodology Determination 2015*; *Carbon Credits (Carbon Farming Initiative—Land and Sea Transport) Methodology Determination 2015.*

commercial, industrial and aggregated small users of energy;[850] and the capture and combustion of landfill gas.[851]

615. To date, the CER has held three auctions, in April 2015, November 2015 and April 2016. Cumulatively, the CER has awarded 309 carbon abatement contracts covering 348 projects for a total value of AUD 1.733 billion, covering 143 million tonnes of abatement at an average price of AUD 12.10 per tonne.[852] A clear majority of contracts have covered abatement through vegetation projects (98.5 million tonnes), followed by landfill and alternative waste treatment methods (21.8 million tonnes), agriculture (8.8 million tonnes) and savanna burning (8 million tonnes). Energy efficiency projects accounted for 4.2 million tonnes of abatement (a mere 2.93% of abatement), transport 1.2 million tonnes, and industrial fugitives 0.77 million tonnes of abatement.

B. *Safeguard Mechanism*

616. From 1 July 2016, the voluntary emissions abatement projects of the ERF have been complemented by the ERF Safeguard Mechanism. The safeguard mechanism works though the *National Greenhouse and Energy Reporting Act* 2007, using data reported under the National Greenhouse and Energy Reporting System.

617. The safeguard mechanism is designed to ensure large businesses do not increase emissions above historical levels by requiring them to keep their emissions below a set baseline. Baselines will be set for individual facilities, to reflect the highest level of reported emissions for a facility over the period 1009–1010 to 2013–2014. Facilities who emit above the historical baseline – that is, have 'excess emissions' – must surrender credits to offset their emissions above the baseline. ACCUs may be used to satisfy obligations under the Act.[853] The safeguard mechanism applies only to 'designated large facilities', these being businesses with direct emissions of CO_2-equivalent greenhouse gases ('scope 1 emissions') over 100,000 tonnes per financial year (the 'designated large facility threshold').[854] The mechanism will apply to a variety

850. *Carbon Credits (Carbon Farming Initiative – Aggregated Small Energy Users) Methodology Determination 2015*; *Carbon Credits (Carbon Farming Initiative—Commercial Buildings) Methodology Determination 2015*; *Carbon Credits (Carbon Farming Initiative—Commercial and Public Lighting) Methodology Determination 2015*; *Carbon Credits (Carbon Farming Initiative—Industrial Electricity and Fuel Efficiency) Methodology Determination 2015*.

851. *Carbon Credits (Carbon Farming Initiative—Landfill Gas) Methodology Determination 2015*.

852. Clean Energy Regulator, *Combined results for auctions 1,2 and 3, Emissions Reduction Fund* (5 May 2016) http://www.cleanenergyregulator.gov.au/DocumentAssets/Documents/Emissions%20Reduction%20Fund%20-%20Cumulative%20auction%20results.pdf (accessed 14 Sept. 2016).

853. *National Greenhouse and Energy Reporting Act* 2007, ss 22XK–22XN.

854. Section 22XJ; *National Greenhouse and Energy Reporting (Safeguard Mechanism) Rule 2015*, r. 8. It has been estimated that safeguard mechanism will apply to some 261 facilities above the designated large facility threshold; that of these, 85 facilities run by 30 companies will exceed their historical baselines; and that it is unlikely any of the top twenty emitting facilities (including electricity generation facilities) will face financial penalties: Baker & McKenzie, *Australia's Emission Reduction Fund Safeguard Mechanism: Top 10 Considerations for Companies*, (4 Mar. 2016) http://bakerxchange.com/rv/ff0025da75c818a6b56f37f4274e80bd27bd7af1 (accessed 14 Sept. 2016).

of 'persons' or business entities, including corporations, partnerships, trusts, and local councils. Consistently with the NGER Act reporting framework, the entity with 'operational control' of a designated large facility, referred to as the 'responsible emitter', will be responsible for meeting safeguard requirements.[855]

618. The mechanism will allow baselines to be temporarily or permanently adjusted. Baselines may be temporarily increased in any year where facility operators who exceed their baseline can demonstrate an improvement in emissions intensity. Baselines may be permanently increased to accommodate a 'significant expansion' in production capacity.[856] If a facility exceeds or expects to exceed its baseline due to a significant expansion before 1 July 2020, the operator may apply for the baseline to be revised using the 'independent assessment approach'. Under this approach, the Regulator may make a 'calculated-emissions baseline determination', revising the baseline based on an audited emissions forecast provided by the facility operator. If a facility exceeds or expects to exceed its baseline due to a significant expansion after 1 July 2020, the Regulator may make a 'benchmark-emissions baseline determination', revising the facility's baseline using a best practice benchmark approach based on benchmark-emissions intensities.[857]

619. In the period to 2025, to accommodate variability associated with the extraction of natural resources, such as natural gas, baselines may be adjusted using the independent assessment approach. Where the operation of a facility is associated with the extraction of a natural resource or reserve, facility operators can apply for an adjustment where: the properties of the resource or reserve have a direct effect on the emissions performance of a facility; the facility has a limited cost-effective ability to control for such emissions; and the natural resource properties are the primary reason for facility emissions exceeding or being expected to exceed their baseline the facility is a natural gas processing or liquefaction facility that is associated with the extraction of natural gas from a natural gas reserve.[858]

620. If facilities expect to exceed their baseline in the first year of operation of the Safeguard Mechanism, the Regulator may increase the baseline, using the independent assessment approach.[859] Such an adjustment would be made where historical emissions are not a good indicator of future business-as-usual emissions performance, for example, low production in the baseline period due to depressed economic conditions following the global financial crisis.

621. There are also specific provisions regarding the calculation of baselines for new facilities, for there is inadequate historical data to establish historical baselines. The Regulator will set baselines for new investments that are covered before 1 July 2020 using the calculated-emissions baseline approach, and will apply the benchmark-emissions baseline approach to new investments that are covered after 1 July 2020.[860]

---

855. *National Greenhouse and Energy Reporting Act 2007*, s. 22XH.
856. *National Greenhouse and Energy Reporting (Safeguard Mechanism) Rule 2015*, rr 22, 24.
857. Rule 32.
858. Rules 22, 25.
859. Rules 22, 26.
860. Rules 22, 23, 32, 33.

622. A special approach will be taken to the electricity sector, with one sectoral baseline applying to all 'grid-connected electricity generators'.[861] This includes the following five electricity grids (the 'designated electricity network'): the NEM, the South West Interconnected System, the North West Interconnected System, the Darwin-Katherine Interconnected System, and the Mount Isa–Cloncurry Supply Network. The sectoral baseline, which is equal to 198 Mt CO_2-e GHG emissions, has been calculated as the sum of the sector's emissions in the 2009–2010 financial year. Emissions from grid-connected electricity generators are not covered as long as the sector aggregate emissions do not exceed the sectoral-baseline. If the sum of emissions exceeds the electricity sectoral baseline, grid-connected generators will then be required to keep emissions below individual facility-level baselines, set at each facility's highest annual emissions between 2009–2010 and 2013–2014.[862]

623. There is a range of compliance and enforcement mechanisms under the Act. Responsible emitters must report emissions to the CER, who will issue a notice to a responsible emitter whose net emissions exceed their baseline in any given year. The responsible emitter may apply for multi-year monitoring, which allows a facility to exceed its baseline in one year if its average emissions over two or three years are below the baseline.[863] If the facility's average emissions over the monitoring period remain above the baseline, the Regulator has a number of enforcement options. These include: issuing infringement notices; accepting enforceable undertakings; seeking an injunction; court-imposed civil penalties; and an ongoing obligation on facility operators to rectify any emissions exceedance.[864]

C. *Future of the ERF and Safeguard Mechanism*

624. In the recent report of its Special Review on Australia's climate policies, the CCA made a number of recommendations for establishing a set of policies and measures to deliver its international obligations on GHG emissions reductions. The Authority concluded that to meet its emission reduction commitments, Australia's emissions will need to decline more steeply than in the past.[865] While a number of policies have been recommended, including measures related to improving energy

---

861. *National Greenhouse and Energy Reporting Act* 2007, s. 22XI; *National Greenhouse and Energy Reporting (Safeguard Mechanism) Rule 2015*, rr 4, 7(1)I, 13 (1)(a). *See also* Australia Government, Department of the Environment, *The safeguard mechanism - Electricity sector*, http://www.environment.gov.au/climate-change/emissions-reduction-fund/publications/factsheet-safeguard-mechanism-electricity-sector (accessed 28 Sept. 2016).

862. If the sum of emissions exceeds the electricity sectoral baseline, the Regulator must publish a statement to that effect by 28 Feb. of the following financial year. The years up to and including the year the electricity sectoral baseline has been exceeded, and the financial year following that in which the Clean Energy Regulator publishes its statement, are 'sectoral-baseline financial years'. Individual grid-connected generators do not have obligations to meet individual baselines in sectoral-baseline financial years. However, after the conclusion of the sectoral-baseline financial years, grid-connected generators will be required to keep emissions below their individual facility-level baselines.

863. *National Greenhouse and Energy Reporting Act 2007*, s. 22XG.

864. Part 5; *National Greenhouse and Energy Reporting (Safeguard Mechanism) Rule 2015*, Pt. 4.

865. Climate Change Authority, *supra* n. 569 at 49.

efficiency measures in transport, perhaps the most fundamental recommendation, which lies at the heart of the Report, is that the Australian government retain and build upon the ERF and the Safeguard Mechanism.[866] The primary justifications for this are stability and predictability in energy policy; and because the 'public interest' suggests the retention and expansion of Direct Action, which offers a 'pragmatic' approach to achieving reductions, mainly because it keeps electricity price rises lower than a cap-and-trade scheme would do.[867]

625. First, for the electricity supply industry, from 2018, the CCA recommended expanding the Safeguard Mechanism into a baseline-and-credit emissions trading scheme with a declining emissions intensity baseline, whereby a baseline for emissions intensity per kWh would be set, reducing to zero before 2050. Eligible energy efficiency credits from State energy efficiency schemes (*see* §2 [VI][B] below) could be used to meet obligations, but international credits and permits could not.[868] Second, for the 'direct combustion, fugitive gases and industrial processes' sectors, the CCA recommended an 'enhanced' version of the existing Safeguard Mechanism.[869] Liable entities in these sectors would be prohibited from exceeding their baselines, but there would be no credits for emitting below the baseline. The CCA recommended that the threshold for liability under the Safeguard Mechanism should be reduced from 100,000 tonnes of CO_2-e GHG emissions to 25,000 tonnes; that baselines for all facilities should decline at a uniform rate; there should be no further baseline revisions; and that the use of international credits and permits should be permitted to meet obligations.[870]

626. The CCA report is not a consensus report, as two members of the CCA disagreed with a number of the recommendations, in particular the reliance on the ERF and Safeguard Mechanism as the main policy tools for achieving GHG emissions targets.[871] Research has already shown that since the CPM was abolished and replaced with Direct Action, Australia's largest emitters 'lost focus on carbon matters, abandoned energy projects, and lost interest in long-term strategic action on reducing emissions'.[872] A number of the criticisms of the ERF relate to the general disadvantages of a baseline and credit scheme, in comparison to a cap-and-trade scheme. Particular criticisms are that it: is an 'immense drain' on the federal budget, as polluters are paid not to pollute, compared to a cap-and-trade scheme which raises revenue; makes achieving GHG emission targets reliant on fiscal policy; replaces the 'polluter-pays principle' with a 'pay the polluter' principle, which is 'bad economics, bad ethics and bad policy'; requires a vast bureaucracy to evaluate and monitor projects; and it raises 'serious and continuing concerns' about the permanence and additionality of emissions reductions.[873]

866. *Ibid.*, 3.
867. *Ibid.*, Ch. 4.
868. *Ibid.*, 6–8.
869. *Ibid.*, 9.
870. *Ibid.*
871. Professor Clive Hamilton and Professor Karoly, *The Climate Change Authority's Special Review on Australia's Climate Goals and Policies: Towards a Climate Policy Toolkit: Minority Report*, 5 Sept. 2016, http://www.climatecouncil.org.au/cca-minority-report (accessed 28 Sept. 2016). The 'Minority Report' has no official status as a report of the CCA.
872. *Ibid.*, 11.
873. *Ibid.*, 12–13.

627. Furthermore, the minority CCA members also argued that the proposed emissions intensity baselines and Safeguard Mechanism in the electricity industry: will not require a firm whose output and emissions are growing to buy credits from companies whose emission are declining, as they may have the same emissions intensity; does not require polluters to pay the full costs of damage; and is unlikely to be able to be linked to emissions trading schemes around the world. The enhanced Safeguard Mechanism Scheme is described as a 'dog's breakfast, with a complex array of incentives and regulatory requirements that covered entities would have to negotiate', with significant difficulties with setting credible baselines; no incentive for liable entities to reduce emissions below their baselines.[874]

628. As of 28 September 2016, the Australian Government was yet to respond to the Report of the Climate Change Authority.

IV. Measures to Encourage Renewable Energy in Electricity Generation

A. Commonwealth Renewable Energy Target

629. The RET is a market-based mechanism established under the *Renewable Energy (Electricity) Act 2000* (Cth). The major aim of the RET is to encourage the additional generation of electricity from renewable energy sources (RES-E), to reduce emissions of greenhouse gases from the electricity sector.[875]

630. The RET is comprised of two sub-schemes, the Large-scale Renewable Energy Target (LRET) and the Small-scale Renewable Energy Scheme (SRES), both of which are administered by the CER. The SRES and LRET apply to all electricity retailers and wholesale electricity purchasers ('liable entities'). The CER issues Renewable Energy Certificates (RECs) – either Large-Scale Generation Certificates (LGCs) or Small-Scale Technology Certificates (STCs) – for the generation of electricity from eligible renewable energy sources. Liable entities must submit the required number of RECs to the CER to meet their liability under the Act. Their liability to meet the RET depends on their market share. If the liable entity submits an insufficient number of RECs, they must pay a shortfall charge.

1. Large-Scale Renewable Energy Target (LRET)

631. The LRET creates a financial incentive for the generation of renewable energy from large-scale renewable power stations, such as wind, solar and hydroelectric power stations. It places a statutory obligation on 'liable entities' to purchase and

874. *Ibid.*, 10–12.

875. *Renewable Energy (Electricity) (Charge) Act 2000* (Cth), s. 3. The first version of the scheme, the Mandatory Renewable Energy Target (MRET), was introduced in 2001. The name was changed to the Renewable Energy Target (RET) and the scheme was split into the LRET and SRES in 2009. The Renewable Energy (Electricity) Regulations 2001 provide more details on a number of issues, such as eligibility criteria for renewable energy sources and criteria for accreditation of power stations.

surrender a certain number of large-scale generation certificates (LGCs) in order to meet an annual target of renewable energy generated, the RET. To 2015, the RET was an additional 41,000 GWh of RES-E from 2020, with interim annual targets. Following amendments in force from 25 June 2015, the RET and interim annual targets are as set out in the table below:[876]

Renewable Energy Target 2015–2030	
Year	**Target (GWh)**
2016	21,431
2017	26,031
2018	28,637
2019	31,244
2020 (to 2030)	33,000

632. 'Liable entities' – which are mainly electricity retailers and large electricity generation companies – are required to meet the target in proportion to their market share, that is, in proportion to the amount of wholesale electricity they purchase.[877] A 'liable entity' is defined as a person who, during a year, makes a 'relevant acquisition' of electricity.[878] There are two types of 'relevant acquisitions'. The first is being wholesale acquisitions of electricity, either from the AEMO (i.e., a purchase from the national electricity pool) or an acquisition from a person who did not acquire it from another person (i.e., directly from a renewable energy generator). The second type of 'relevant acquisitions' is a 'notional' wholesale acquisition of electricity, which covers self-generation by large electricity users.[879]

633. Liable entities meet their liabilities by surrendering LGCs annually. One LGC is equivalent to 1 MWh of eligible RES-E generated above the '1997 eligible renewable power baseline'.[880] This historical baseline was introduced to ensure RECs are only created for electricity generated from renewable energy sources (RES-E) that

876. *Renewable Energy (Electricity) (Charge) Act 2000*, s. 40.
877. The liability of an entity – or amount of renewable source electricity required under the scheme – is worked out by taking the amount of electricity acquired by the entity, less any exemptions, and multiplying this by the 'renewable power percentage' for an entity, which is calculated using a formula set out in section 39 of the Act.
878. *Renewable Energy (Electricity) Act 2000* (Cth), s. 35.
879. Sections 31–33. Subsection 31(2) defines acquisitions that are not relevant acquisitions, including where: the electricity was delivered on a grid that that has a capacity of less than 100 MW and is not, directly or indirectly, connected to a grid that has a capacity of 100 MW or more; or the self-generation of electricity, where either (I) point of generation is less than 1 kilometre from the point at which the electricity is used; or (ii) the electricity is transmitted or distributed between the point of generation and end use on a line that is used solely from transmitting electricity between those two points (ie is not connected to the grid).
880. *Renewable Energy (Electricity) Act* 2000, s. 17C.

are new or additional to the amount of renewable energy generated before the Act came into effect. Renewable generation assets existing before 1 January 1997 are only eligible to earn certificates if they can demonstrate an increase in output from these assets above the 1997 eligible renewable power baseline. The 1997 baseline for each power station is determined by the Regulator, and is the average of the annual electricity generated from eligible energy sources in 1994, 1995, and 1996. Power stations generating electricity for the first time after 1 January 1997 have a baseline of zero.[881]

634. Large-Scale Generation Certificates may only be created by persons registered under section 10 of the Act. To create a LGC, renewable energy must be from an accredited power station.[882] A power station may be accredited if some or all of the power generated by the power station is generated from an 'eligible renewable energy resource'.[883] Eligible renewable energy resources are listed in the Act and are: hydro, wave, tide, ocean, wind, solar, geothermal aquifer, hot dry rock, energy crops, wood-waste, agricultural waste, waste from processing of agricultural products, food waste, food processing waste, bagasse, black liquor, biomass-based components of municipal solid waste, landfill gas, sewage gas and biomass-based components of sewage, and any other energy source prescribed by the regulations.[884] Fossil fuels or materials or wastes derived from fossil fuels are not eligible renewable energy sources, although waste coal mine gas may be eligible in certain circumstances.[885]

635. Certificates are not valid until registered by the Regulator.[886] Large-Scale Generation Certificates are negotiated and paid for outside the REC Registry and transferred within the REC Registry. Market price is not fixed, but depends on market supply and demand. LGCs are retired – that is, they expire – after surrender.[887]

2. Small-Scale Renewable Energy Scheme (SRES)

636. The SRES creates a financial incentive for owners to install small-scale renewable installations. Eligible systems are entitled to a certain number of STCs based on the amount of RES-E the system generates or conventional-source electricity it displaces. Renewable energy must be sourced from: eligible solar water heater installations installed on or after April 2001; air source heat pumps; or 'small generation units', these being small-scale photovoltaic systems, wind systems, micro hydroelectric systems installed on or after April 2001.[888]

637. STCs are created at the time of installation. There is no target for the SRES, and no cap on the number of certificates that may be created. The number that can be created depends on the date of installation of the system, and the amount of electricity measured in MWh that the system is expected to produce or displace. For small-scale solar panel, wind or hydro systems, the number of RECs depends on the amount of

881. Section 14; Renewable Energy (Electricity) Regulations 2001, reg. 5 and Sch. 3.
882. *Renewable Energy (Electricity) Act* 2000, s. 18.
883. Subsection 14(2).
884. Section 17.
885. Subsection 17(2) and s. 17 A.
886. Section 26.
887. Section 29.
888. Sections 21 and 23A; Renewable Energy (Electricity) Regulations 2001, regs 3(2) and 3A.

electricity generated over the course of an expected lifetime of up to fifteen years. For solar water heaters or heat pumps, the number of RECs depends on the amount of conventionally sourced electricity the system is estimated to displace over the course of an expected lifetime of up to ten years.[889] Generally speaking, one STC equals 1 MWh of eligible RES-E either generated or 1 MWh of displaced conventionally sourced electricity.[890]

638. Liable entities that have a statutory obligation to surrender certificates under the LRET also have a legal requirement under the SRES to buy STCs and surrender them to the CER. Once surrendered, STCs expire and cannot be reused.[891] The REC Registry facilitates the creation, validation, auditing and transfer of STCs. Once created and validated, STCs can be sold either directly to other individuals and businesses or through the REC clearing house operated by the CER.[892] Owners of renewable energy systems are entitled to create and sell STCs themselves, but in practice, system installers usually offer a discount on the price, or a cash payment, in return for assignment of the right to create the STCs, which can then be sold to liable entities under the LRET.[893] The price of STCs is driven by supply and demand of the REC market and fluctuates daily. There is a fixed price of USD 40 per certificate for STCs sold through the STC clearing house, but these will only sell when a buyer is available.[894]

3. Assistance to EITE Industries

639. To June 2015, there was a partial exemption from LRET and SRES liability for electricity used in prescribed EITE activities. From June 2015, electricity used in prescribed EITE activities will be fully exempt from liability under the scheme.[895] Over fifty activities are defined in Schedule 6 of the *Renewable Energy (Electricity) Regulations 2001* (Cth) as prescribed EITE activities, including petroleum refining and the production of LNG.

4. Compliance and Enforcement

640. A range of monitoring, compliance and enforcement mechanisms exist under the Act. These include investigations by authorised officers, including site visits, outreach visits, monitoring warrants and compliance visits, and audits of eligible and liable parties.[896] The Regulator may apply to the Federal Court for an injunction under

889. *See* Renewable Energy (Electricity) Regulations 2001, regs 19–20AAA; *Renewable Energy (Electricity) Regulations 2001 - STC Calculation Methodology for Solar Water Heaters and Air Source Heat Pump Water Heaters – Determination, March 2012.*
890. Renewable Energy (Electricity) Act 2000, s. 23B.
891. Section 29.
892. Part 2A.
893. Section 23C.
894. Section 30LA.
895. Section 38A and 38B.
896. Parts 11 and 11A.

the Act to prevent a breach of the Act.[897] The Regulator may accept written undertakings, and apply to the Federal Court for enforcement of undertakings.[898] The Act creates a range of offences under the statute, for example, for the improper creation of certificates.[899] Punitive provisions include civil penalties, for example, for the improper creation of certificates or the provision of false information resulting in improper creation of certificates;[900] civil penalty orders (pecuniary penalties) for reaching civil penalty provisions;[901] and powers of suspension by the Regulator, including suspension of registration, or accreditation of a power station.[902]

641. A liable entity that fails to comply with the obligation to submit the required number of RECs is liable to pay a shortfall charge. Liable entities who do not surrender sufficient STCs to cover their liability under the SRES will incur a small-scale technology shortfall charge.[903] Liable entities with a LGC shortfall that is greater than 10% of their liability under the LRET incur a large-scale technology shortfall charge.[904] Whether an entity has a shortfall is essentially determined by calculating the required number of LGCs the entity must surrender for the year, adding any shortfall or subtracting a surplus from the previous year, then subtracting the value of surrendered LGCs. If the result is greater than zero, there is a LGC shortfall. If result is less than zero, there is a carried forward surplus.[905] Whether an entity has a small-scale technology shortfall calculated on a quarterly basis under a procedure set out in the Act.[906] The amount payable for any shortfall is the amount of the shortfall multiplied by a fixed charge of AUD 65 per megawatt hour.[907] The Regulator has the power to publish the names of liable entities with shortfalls.

642. In 2014, two independent reviews of the RET were conducted, one by an Expert Panel established by the federal Government, and the other by the Climate Change Authority.[908] While there have been criticisms of the RET, these Reviews have found it has been successful in promoting additional generation from renewable sources, with renewable energy generation almost doubling from 2001 to 2013.[909] Over the period 2001–2014, more than 400 renewable power stations with a total capacity of over 5,000 MW were installed, equivalent to about 10% of Australia's current grid-

897. Section 154S.
898. Sections 154Q, 154R.
899. Section 24.
900. Sections 24A, 24B.
901. Section 154B.
902. Sections 30, 30A, 30D, 30E.
903. Section 38AB.
904. Section 36.
905. Section. 38.
906. Section 38AD-AE.
907. Sections 37, 38AC. The amount of the charge is specified in the *Renewable Energy (Electricity) (Large-Scale Technology Shortfall Charge) Act 2010* (Cth) s. 6 and the *Renewable Energy (Electricity) (Small-Scale Technology Shortfall Charge) Act 2010* (Cth) s. 3.
908. D Warburton, B Fisher, S In't Veld and M Zema, *Renewable Energy Target Scheme, Report of the Expert Panel* (Commonwealth of Australia, 2014); Climate Change Authority, *Renewable Energy Target Review Report* (Climate Change Authority, 2014).
909. Warburton et al., *supra* n. 908 at 14.

connected capacity.[910] However, significant uncertainty from recurring two yearly reviews of the RET,[911] 'lukewarm' federal government support and in 2015, abolition of the CPM, has undermined investment. From 25 June 2015, there will no longer be two yearly reviews of the RET.

B. *State Renewable Energy Targets*

643. In addition to the Commonwealth RET, some of the Australian States and Territories have committed to their own renewable energy targets. In 2009, the South Australian Government committed to increasing the State's renewable energy production target to 33% of electricity generation by 2020. This target was achieved in 2013–2014.[912] In 2014, a new target of 50% by 2025 was set, subject to national renewable energy policy being retained. In 2016, the ACT Government legislated a long-term RET of 100% of electricity used in the ACT to be sourced from renewable energy by 30 June 2050, with an interim target of reducing GHG emissions to 40% less than 1990 emissions by 30 June 2020.[913] The Victorian Government has committed to Victorian renewable energy generation targets of 25% by 2020 and 40% by 2025, which will feed into the development of a Victorian Renewable Energy Action Plan.[914] Queensland has committed to generating 50% of its electricity needs from renewable energy by 2030.[915]

644. As of 1 September 2016, WA and NSW did not have a RET, although NSW has a Renewable Energy Action Plan published in September 2013, to guide renewable energy development.[916] Tasmania is nearly at 100% renewable energy already, given its vast reliance on hydropower, and the construction of wind energy facilities.

---

910. Climate Change Authority, *supra* n. 908 at 11.

911. *See* , for example, the many changes to the RET at Australian Government, Department of Environment and Energy, *Updates to the Renewable Energy Target (RET) scheme* http://www.environment.gov.au/climate-change/renewable-energy-target-scheme/updates (accessed 28 Sept. 2016).

912. RenewablesSA, http://www.renewablessa.sa.gov.au/ (accessed 1 Sept. 2016).

913. *Climate Change and Greenhouse Gas Emission Reduction Act 2010* (ACT), ss 6, 7.

914. The Hon Daniel Andrews MP, Premier, State of Victoria, *Renewable Energy Targets To Create Thousands Of Jobs*, Media Release, 15 Jun. 2016, http://www.premier.vic.gov.au/renewable-energy-targets-to-create-thousands-of-jobs/ (accessed 14 Sept. 2016); Victorian Government, Department of Energy and Resources, *Victo'ia's Renewable Energy Roadmap*, http://www.energyandresources.vic.gov.au/energy/sustainable-energy/victorias-renewable-energy-roadmap (accessed 14 Sept. 2016).

915. Queensland Government, Department of Energy and Water Supply, *Renewable Energy Expert Panel*, https://www.dews.qld.gov.au/electricity/solar/solar-future/expert-panel (accessed 24 Sept. 2016); Giles Parkinson, *Queensland commits to 50% renewable target by 2030*, 14 May 2015, http://reneweconomy.com.au/2015/queensland-commits-to-50-renewable-target-by-2030 (accessed 1 Nov. 2015).

916. New South Wales Government, Department of Industry, Resources and Energy, *NSW Renewable Energy Action Plan*, http://www.resourcesandenergy.nsw.gov.au/energy-consumers/sustainable-energy/renewable-energy-action-plan (accessed 14 Sept. 2016).

V. Feed-In Tariffs

645. In Australia, FiT schemes have been operated only by the States/Territories, not the Commonwealth government, and many of the generous schemes, introduced in the mid-late 2000s, have been closed to new entrants or scaled-back. This is because in December 2012, the COAG agreed the revised *National Principles for Feed-in Tariff Arrangements*.[917] Two of these principles are that all residential and small business consumers with grid-connected micro generation are to receive a 'fair and reasonable' value for their exported electricity, and all decisions to 'legislate rights for micro generation consumers to receive more than the value of their energy' must be closed to new participants by 2014.[918] Consistently with these Principles, each State has now closed premium FiT schemes to new participants and has determined new 'fair and reasonable' values for exported electricity for new FiT customers. However, electricity retailers may voluntarily pass on a higher FiT amount as part of their unregulated market offers.

646. This means the States' FiT schemes now generally operate as a minimum rate that an electricity retailer must pay to its customers for electricity they generate, to ensure that small renewable energy generators receive a fair and reasonable rate for the electricity they supply.[919] Most existing schemes are 'net' feed-in tariffs, which means the consumer is only credited for the excess renewable-sourced electricity they export to the national electricity grid over and above their own consumption. In contrast, 'gross' feed-in tariffs pay consumers for all the electricity generated by their renewable energy system, including power generated for their own consumption. A number of existing schemes apply to solar systems only.

647. In Victoria, every licensed electricity retailer with more than 5,000 electricity customers is required to publish and offer generally available renewable energy feed-in terms and conditions, including a FiT that must not be lower than a minimum tariff determined by the Victorian Essential Services Commission.[920] The Commission determines the minimum FiT for each calendar year before the end of August of the previous year. The FiT for 2016 is 5.0 c/kWh.[921] The tariff applies to 'small renewable energy generation facilities', which defined to be a 'wind, solar, hydro or biomass energy facility (or other facility specified by order in council), connected to a distribution system, that generates electricity and has an installed or name-plate generating capacity of less than 100 kilowatts'.[922] From July 2013, proponents of distributed 'low-emissions' generation technologies of less than 100 kw in capacity, who meet a carbon emissions

917. Council of Australian Governments, *National Principles for Feed-in Tariff Arrangements* (7 Dec. 2012) http://www.coag.gov.au/node/507 (accessed 14 Sept. 2016). These revised the CoAG *National Principles for Feed-in Tariff Schemes* (29 Nov. 2008), http://www.coag.gov.au/node/243 (accessed 14 Sept. 2016).
918. Principles 1 and 2.
919. Victorian Essential Services Commission, *Minimum Electricity Feed-in Tariff to Apply from 1 Jan. 2016 to 31 Dec. 2016: Final Decision*, (C/15/11121), 1 Aug. 2015.
920. *Electricity Industry Act 2000* (Vic). Previous schemes are now closed to new members but will continue to provide rates to those who are already scheme members. The premium feed-in tariff will continue to apply to existing members to 2024.
921. Victorian Essential Services Commission, *supra* n. 919 at 1.
922. *Electricity Industry Act 2000* (Vic), s. 40F.

intensity threshold of 0.4 t CO_2-e/MWh, are able to apply for the FiT scheme, through annual application rounds.[923]

648. In Western Australia, there is no retail electricity competition, so all rates are set by the relevant regional utilities in conjunction with government regulators. The government has introduced a Renewable Energy Buyback Scheme,[924] pursuant to which the government-owned retailers – Synergy and Horizon Power – must offer to purchase renewable source electricity, under an approved contract, from an eligible customer who wishes to sell such electricity to the corporation.[925] A 'small renewable energy system' means a system of photovoltaic arrays; or a system of wind turbines; or a hydropower system; or another system for the generation of electricity from a renewable energy source that has a generating capacity exceeding 500 W but not exceeding 5 kW.[926] An 'eligible customer' is: a residential customer who consumes not more than 50 MWh of electricity per annum, or a customer that is a school, university or other educational institution, or a customer that is a non-profit-making organisation.[927] Retailers may also voluntarily accept customers who do not meet the minimum requirements of the regulations. The retailers establish their own terms and conditions, including rates, for buying back excess electricity, although these must be approved by the Public Utilities Office.[928]

649. In South Australia, from 30 September 2013, an applicant seeking permission to connect a solar system to the grid who meets the eligibility requirements will be eligible for the solar 'minimum retailer payment'.[929] This is a minimum amount that must be paid by electricity retailers to their eligible solar customers who consume less than 160 MWh per annum with a solar system up to 10 kVA (single phase) or 30 kVA (three phase), for any excess electricity they export to the grid. The payment is credited on solar customers' electricity bills. The ESCOSA determined that the minimum retailer

---

923. *Energy Legislation Amendment (Feed-in Tariffs and Other Matters) Act 2013* (Vic).
924. System owners who are also part of the WA residential feed-in tariff scheme are paid an additional rate for 10 years by the WA Government for electricity they export. The feed-in tariff scheme was open to applications from 1 Jul. 2010 to 1 Aug. 2011. After the first 10 MW of new generation, the Government introduced a capacity cap of 150 MW. When the cap was reached, the scheme was closed to new applicants. Government of Western Australia, Treasury Department, *Frequently Asked Questions: Feed-in Tariff Scheme*, https://www.treasury.wa.gov.au/Public-Utilities-Office/Solar-PV/Household-Renewable-Energy/ (accessed 1 July 2017).
925. The Electricity Industry (Licensing Conditions) Regulations 2005 (WA), reg. 6.
926. Regulation 3.
927. Regulation 6.
928. Government of Western Australia, Finance Department, *Renewable Energy Buyback Scheme*, https://www.finance.wa.gov.au/cms/Public_Utilities_Office/Energy_Initiatives/Renewable_Energy_Buyback_Scheme_-_Residential.aspx (accessed 14 Sept. 2016).
929. This payment is in addition to any feed-in-tariff which a customer is entitled to receive under the Solar Feed-in Scheme, which began on 1 Jul. 2008 and closed to new entrants on 30 Sept. 2013. Small customers in 'customer group 1', who received permission to connect received by 31 Aug. 2010, with the system fully installed and connected by 29 Jan. 2012, are entitled to an FiT of 44 c/kWh exported to the grid, until 30 Jun. 2028. Government of South Australia, *Solar feed-in tariff scheme*, http://www.sa.gov.au/topics/water-energy-and-environment/energy/rebates-concessions-and-incentives/solar-photovoltaic-systems/solar-feed-in-scheme (accessed 14 Sept. 2016).

payment applying from 1 January 2015 until 31 December 2016 is 6.8 c/kWh, excluding GST. All electricity retailers who contract with eligible solar customers must provide at least this minimum amount to solar customers, although a higher payment may be made.[930]

650. In Queensland, the Solar Bonus Scheme is open to Queensland households and businesses located in regional areas. A government-mandated FiT is available for eligible customers (who operate a solar PV system with a maximum inverter capacity not exceeding 5 kw and consume less than 100 MWh of electricity a year) in regional Queensland, where competition is not yet strong enough to ensure the market delivers a fair feed-in rate to solar customers. For customers who apply after 10 July 2012, the FiT rate is set by the Queensland Competition Authority (QCA), and is 7.448 c/kWh for 2016–2017.[931] There is no mandatory minimum FiT rate for southeastern Queensland (Brisbane area). Instead, these solar customers must approach their electricity retailer to obtain a market-based payment for solar power exported back to the grid. Electricity retailers must publish their FiT rate in their energy price fact sheets, and these rates are displayed on the QCA's online electricity price comparator.[932]

651. Tasmania's electricity utility, Aurora Energy, offers a net feed-in-tariff.[933] From 1 January 2014, the Tasmanian Economic Regulator determines a 'fair and reasonable' value for net exported electricity that is fed into the Tasmanian electricity network by residential and small businesses customers, and reviews the FiT rate on an annual basis. The rate applies to all new qualifying installations occurring on or after 31 August 2013. A qualifying system is a system that: generates electricity from either solar, wind or water; complies with Australian Standard AS4777; and, if the system installed at the premises has a single phase inverter, has a maximum generating capacity of 10 kVA, or where the system installed at the premises has a three phase inverter, has a total generation capacity of not more than 30 kVA.[934] The regulated rate

930. *Ibid. See also* ESCOSA, *Solar feed-in tariff scheme*, http://www.escosa.sa.gov.au/consumers/energy/solar-feed-in-tariff-scheme (accessed 14 Sept. 2016).
931. Queensland Government, Department of Energy and Water Supply, *Feed-in tariff for regional customers*, https://www.dews.qld.gov.au/electricity/solar/installing/benefits/regional (accessed 14 Sept. 2016). Customers who applied for the Queensland Solar Bonus Scheme feed-in tariff before 10 Jul. 2012 receive 44 c/kWh until 1 Jul. 2028: Queensland Government, Department of Energy and Water Supply, *Solar Bonus Scheme 44c feed-in tariff*, https://www.dews.qld.gov.au/electricity/solar/installing/benefits/solar-bonus-scheme (accessed 14 Sept. 2016).
932. Queensland Government, Department of Energy and Water Supply, *The benefits of solar*, https://www.dews.qld.gov.au/electricity/solar/installing/benefits (accessed 14 Sept. 2016).
933. Customers who applied for Aurora Energy's Net Metering Buyback Scheme before midnight on 30 Aug. 2013 will continue to receive the following FiT rates until 1 Jan. 2019: a flat residential rate of 28.283 c/kWh (including GST); and a small business 38.577 c/kWh (including GST) for first 500 kWh supplied during each billing period, and 28.319 c/kWh (including GST) for each kWh supplied after the first 500 kWh during each billing period. Office of the Tasmanian Economic Regulator, http://www.energyregulator.tas.gov.au/domino/otter.nsf/elect-v/30 (accessed 14 Sept. 2016).
934. *Electricity Supply Industry Act 1995* (Tas) s. 44B.

for standard FiT customers for 1 July 2016 to 30 June 2017 is 6.671 c/kWh (excluding GST).[935]

652. There is currently **no mandatory minimum FiT rate in** New South Wales. The Solar Bonus Scheme, which commenced on 1 January 2010 and operates until 31 December 2016, is now closed to new applicants.[936] Instead, individual electricity retailers offer a market-based payment to solar customers for solar power exported back to the grid. Each year, the Independent Pricing and Regulatory Tribunal (IPART) sets a benchmark range to guide retailers and solar customers as to the likely value of electricity generated from solar PV units and exported to the grid in the next year.[937] On 9 June 2016, IPART set the benchmark range for voluntary solar feed-in tariffs for 2016–2017 at 5.5 to 7.2 c/kWh.[938]

653. In the Northern Territory, following the split of the government-owned Northern Territory Power and Water Corporation into three corporations on July 2014, the retailer Jacana Energy now administers electricity tariffs and charges for most consumers, not including remote communities. The renewable energy FiT pays eligible Northern Territory households for the excess electricity they generate from small-scale solar (photovoltaic or PV), wind turbine or hydro systems. The buy-back rates applicable from Jacana energy from 1 January 2016 are: a flat buy-back rate for domestic customers of 25.54 c/kWh; a standard flat rate for commercial customers of 29.72 c/kWh; and a customised rate negotiated for solar PV systems greater than 30 kVA and for customers consuming greater or equal to 750,000kWh.[939]

654. There is **no mandatory minimum FiT rate in the ACT.** Instead, individual electricity retailers assign a value to exported solar power as they see fit. However, under the *ACT Electricity Feed-in (Large-scale Renewable Energy) Act 2011*, renewable energy generators may be granted a FiT through a competitive process known as a reverse auction. In January 2012, the Government issued a Request for Proposals to support the development of up to 40 megawatts of large-scale solar generation capacity

935. Calculated in accordance with the formula in: Office of the Tasmanian Regulator, *Regulated Feed-In Tariff Rate Determination For Standard Feed-In Tariff Customers* (5 May 2016), made under subs. 44G(1) of the *Electricity Supply Industry Act 1995* (Tas).

936. *Electricity Supply Act 1995* (NSW) and the Electricity Supply (General) Regulation 2001. The Scheme provides a feed-in tariff of 20 cents per kilowatt hour (c/kWh) or 60 c/kWh for eligible customers with small-scale solar or wind generators that are connected to the grid. New South Wales Government, Department of Industry, Resources and Energy, http://www.resourcesandenergy.nsw.gov.au/energy-consumers/solar/solar-bonus-scheme (accessed 14 Sept. 2016).

937. *Electricity Supply Act 1995* (NSW), s. 43ECB.

938. IPART, *Solar feed-in tariffs: Retailer contribution and benchmark range from 1 Jul. 2016, Energy — Determination June 2016*, https://www.ipart.nsw.gov.au/Home/Industries/Energy/Reviews/Electricity/Review-of-Solar-feed-in-tariffs-from-1-July-2016?qDh=2 (accessed 14 Sept. 2016).

939. Jacana Energy, *Solar Photovoltaic (PV) systems*, http://jacanaenergy.com.au/sustainability_and_environment/photovoltaic_pv_solar_systems (accessed 28 Sept. 2016).

in the ACT through a solar auction.[940] As of 14 September 2016, three projects of 20, 13, and 7 MW respectively had been awarded a grant of FiT entitlement each.[941]

655. The ACT has run two reverse auctions for wind energy, one in 2014 and one in 2015. In March 2014, an independent Wind Auction Advisory Panel was appointed by the Minister for the Environment, to oversee the assessment process and make recommendations for the awarding of a grant of an FiT entitlement. **Three successful proponents were announced on 6 February 2015 for Wind Auction I, totalling 120 MW capacity, while two wind projects totalling 200 MW capacity were awarded** FiT entitlements following Wind Auction II.[942]

VI. Demand-Side Mechanisms: Energy Conservation and Efficiency

656. The 2009 COAG *National Partnership Agreement on Energy Efficiency* provides overarching direction and objectives for COAG's ten-year *National Strategy on Energy Efficiency*, adopted in 2009.[943] The aim of the Partnership is to provide 'a nationally consistent and co-ordinated approach to energy efficiency, recognising the need for flexible approaches, and encouraging co-operation on innovative measures to improve the efficiency of energy generation, supply and use'.[944] The measures of the *National Strategy on Energy Efficiency* are based on improving energy efficiency in four key areas: 'assisting households and businesses to transition to a low carbon future; reducing impediments to the uptake of energy efficiency; making buildings more energy efficient; and governments working in partnership and leading the way'.[945] The Select Council on Climate Change oversees implementation of the Agreement and the Strategy across the Australian States. The various Commonwealth and State initiatives regarding energy efficiency that will be described in this Part are based on achieving the principles and recommendations of the *National Strategy on Energy Efficiency*.

940. The RFP was issued in relation to the Solar Auction determined in the *Electricity Feed-in (Large-scale Renewable Energy Generation) FiT Capacity Release Determination 2012 (No 1)*, made under the *Electricity Feed-in (Large-scale Renewable Energy Generation) Act 2011*.
941. Australian Capital Territory, Environment and Planning Directorate, *Large-Scale Solar*, http://www.environment.act.gov.au/energy/cleaner-energy/large-scale-solar (accessed 14 Sept. 2016).
942. Australian Capital Territory Government, Environment and Planning Directorate, *Wind Power*, http://www.environment.act.gov.au/energy/cleaner-energy/wind_power (accessed 14 Sept. 2016).
943. Council of Australian Governments, *National Strategy on Energy Efficiency* (2 Jul. 2009, updated July 2010) http://www.coag.gov.au/sites/default/files/nsee_update_july_2010.pdf (accessed 14 Sept. 2016).
944. Council of Australian Governments, *Water, Climate Change and the Environment*, http://www.coag.gov.au/water_climate_change_and_the_environment (accessed 14 Sept. 2016). The Partnership Agreement is available at http://www.curtin.edu.au/research/jcipp/local/docs/NP_energy_efficiency.pdf (accessed 14 Sept. 2016).
945. Council of Australian Governments, *National Strategy on Energy Efficiency*, *supra* n. 571 at 5.

A. *Minimum Performance Standards and Energy Rating Labels*

1. Greenhouse and Energy Minimum Standards Act 2012 (Cth)

657. By reducing demand for energy, Minimum Energy Performance Standards (MEPS) for electrical appliances and products, and Energy Rating Labels (ERLs), can help to reduce emissions of greenhouse gases from electricity consumption. MEPS 'specify the minimum level of energy performance that appliances, lighting and electrical equipment must meet or exceed before they can be offered for sale or used for commercial purposes'.[946] ERLs provide consumers with information regarding the energy performance of certain regulated products at the point of sale. They help consumers to compare similar products and choose the most efficient model, by comparing the estimated annual energy consumption and star rating of different models of a similar size and capacity.

658. Until 2012, requirements for minimum performance standards and labelling were dealt with under State and Territory legislation, but a national, Commonwealth framework for product energy efficiency in Australia was created in 2012 through the *Greenhouse and Energy Minimum Standards Act 2012* (Cth) ('GEMS Act').[947] Under the Act, various products must meet certain regulatory requirements – MEPS, ERLs, or both – before they can be supplied or sold in Australia. The MEPS and labelling requirements are set out in Greenhouse and Energy Minimum Standards Determinations, which are specific to various product types. The requirements are set out either directly in the relevant GEMS Determination, or the GEMS Determination incorporates a product Standard published individually, or jointly, by the national standards organisations Standards Australia and Standards New Zealand.[948]

659. MEPS are mandatory for a range of products, including (as of 26 October 2015) clothes dryers, household refrigerators and freezers, computers and computer monitors, televisions and set top boxes, power adaptors, single phase and three phase air conditioners, close control air conditioners (computer rooms), compact fluorescent lamps, ballasts for fluorescent lamps, linear fluorescent lamps, incandescent lamps, electric storage water heaters, gas storage water heaters, instantaneous gas water heaters, commercial chillers, refrigerated display cabinets, refrigerated storage cabinets, three phase electric motors, distribution transformers, and transformers and converters for halogens. As of 26 October 2015, ERL requirements applied to single phase air conditioners, televisions, clothes washing machines and dryers, dishwashers, refrigerators, freezers, and computer monitors.[949]

946. Government of Australia, *Energy Rating*, http://www.energyrating.gov.au/suppliers/legislation (accessed 14 Sept. 2016).
947. *See also* the various regulations and instruments made under the GEMS Act, including the Greenhouse and Energy Minimum Standards Regulation 2012, and various Determinations.
948. Government of Australia, *Energy Rating*, *supra* n. 946.
949. *Ibid.*

660. Regulated products must be tested to prove their energy performance,[950] comply with the applicable MEPS and/or labelling requirements, and be registered through an online register before they can be sold in Australia.[951] Products that are registered and comply with the regulations are listed on a Registration Database.[952] The Greenhouse and Energy Minimum Standards Regulator is responsible for administering the legislation. The Regulator is empowered to undertake a range of compliance activities, including inspection, monitoring and investigation, and has a range of enforcement powers, including suspending or cancelling a model's registration, accepting enforceable undertakings, issuing infringement notices, publicising certain offences, contraventions and adverse decisions, and applying for civil penalty orders and injunctions. The GEMS Act also sets out a range of offences and criminal penalties for suppliers who do not comply with the performance and labelling obligations.

2. Building Standards

661. Residential energy efficiency standards for new buildings have existed in the National Construction Code (NCC) since 2003. The NCC is an initiative of COAG, and sets out minimum requirements for the design, construction and performance of buildings throughout Australia in one code. The NCC for 2016 was adopted by the States and Territories on 1 May 2016. The NCC has legal effect through State and Territory legislation, which prescribes the NCC to fulfil any technical requirements that must satisfied when undertaking building work. It is administered by the Australian Building Codes Board.

662. The energy efficiency requirements for housing are contained in Volume 2 of the NCC. The Performance Requirements for new housing take into account both the performance of the house and performance of its domestic services. Performance Requirements can be met by meeting the 'Deemed-to-Satisfy (DtS) Provisions', which include prescriptive examples of materials, products, design factors, construction and installation methods; or by implementing a 'Performance Solution', which is any solution that can meet the Performance Requirements, other than a DtS solution, as long as it can be successfully demonstrated how the Performance Requirements will be met.[953]

950. Test methods and conditions are outlined in the Greenhouse and Energy Minimum Standards (Authorisation Requirements for Testing GEMS Products) Instrument 2013. Testing may be undertaken using a company's own test laboratory, an appropriate third party test facility, or an accredited third party testing laboratory. Accreditation is provided by the National Association of Testing Authorities (NATA).

951. Registration fees are set out in the *Greenhouse and Energy Minimum Standards (Registration Fees) Act 2012* (Cth), the *Greenhouse and Energy Minimum Standards (Registration Fees) Instrument 2015* and the *Greenhouse and Energy Minimum Standards (Variation of a Model's Registration - Application Fees) Instrument 2014*.

952. The Registration Database can be searched at http://reg.energyrating.gov.au/comparator/product_types/ (accessed 14 Sept. 2016).

953. Australian Building Codes Board, *NCC 2016: A Performance Based Code*, http://www.abcb.gov.au/Resources/Publications/Education-Training/A-Performance-Based-Code (accessed 14 Sept. 2016).

663. As regards performance requirements for the house, there are two main options for compliance using the DtS Provisions. The first is to achieve a minimum energy rating equivalent to 6-stars on a 10-star scale for new residential construction. The required energy rating for reducing heating and cooling loads must be verified by approved software, such as that accredited through the Nationwide House Energy Rating Scheme (NatHERS).[954] Also, the design must comply with specific energy saving features, for example, the testing and installation of insulation and building sealing. The second option is to comply with all the relevant NCC Volume 2 DtS Provisions for the house, which include requirements for: building fabric, for example, walls, floors and roofs; external glazing and shading; sealing of the building; and effects of air movement.[955]

664. For the performance of a house's domestic services, the relevant Performance Requirement can also be met by complying with all the DtS Provisions, which include requirements for insulation and sealing of ductwork and central heating water piping, space heating, artificial lighting, and the heating and pumping of swimming pools and spas.[956]

665. The NCC also contains energy performance requirements for new multi-residential, commercial and public buildings. The energy efficiency requirements are contained in Vol 1 of the NCC, and for most of these buildings, also take into account both the performance of the building and performance of its services. The DtS Provisions include requirements for the: performance of the building fabric, for example, walls, floors and roofs; glazing and shading; sealing of the building; performance of the heating, ventilation and air-conditioning systems; artificial lighting; heating and pumping of swimming pools and spas; ability to access services that rely on maintenance to continue to perform; and facility to monitor energy use.[957]

666. In addition to the NCC requirements, the Commercial Building Disclosure Program, which has been in operation since 2010, requires large commercial offices to receive a building efficiency rating and energy performance to be disclosed at the point of sale or lease. The aim is to improve energy efficiency by ensuring prospective buyers and tenants are informed of the energy efficiency performance of commercial buildings and thereby choose a more efficient alternative.[958] The Program was developed by the Australian, State and Territory governments as part of the COAG *National Strategy on Energy Efficiency*. It is established by the *Building Energy Efficiency*

954. NatHERS is administered by the Commonwealth Department of the Environment and Energy on behalf of the States and Territories: www.nathers.gov.au. In NSW, parts of the NCC building regulations pertaining to the energy efficiency of residential buildings are varied, and the Building Sustainability Index 'BASIX', not NatHERS applies. *See* https://www.planningportal.nsw.gov.au/planning-tools/basix (accessed 14 Sept. 2016).
955. Australian Building Codes Board, *Handbook: NCC Volume Two Energy Efficiency Provisions* (3rd ed, 2016) 21, 27–28, http://www.abcb.gov.au/Resources/Publications/Education-Training/NCC-2019-Energy-Efficiency-Provisions-development-process (accessed 14 Sept. 2016).
956. *Ibid.*, 21.
957. Australian Building Codes Board, *Handbook: NCC Volume One Energy Efficiency Provisions* (4th ed, 2016) 24, http://www.abcb.gov.au/Resources/Publications/Education-Training/NCC-Volume-One-Energy-Efficiency-Provisions (accessed 14 Sept. 2016).
958. Australian Government, Department of Environment and Energy, *What is CBD?*, http://cbd.gov.au/overview-of-the-program/what-is-cbd (accessed 14 Sept. 2016).

Disclosure Act 2010 (Cth) and is managed by the Commonwealth Department of Environment and Energy.[959]

667. The Program requires most building owners who are selling or leasing office space with a net lettable area of 2,000 square metres or more, and most tenants who are sub-leasing part of their tenancy with a net lettable area of 2,000 square metres or more, to obtain a Building Energy Efficiency Certificate (BEEC) before the building goes on the market for sale, lease or sublease. From 1 July 2017, the mandatory disclosure threshold will be lowered to 1,000 square metres.[960] Only accredited assessors can apply for BEECs on behalf of building owners or lessors.[961] BEECs are valid for up to twelve months and must include: the building's Energy star rating under the National Australian Built Environment Rating System (NABERS), which measures the environmental/energy performance of Australian buildings, and a lighting energy assessment of the relevant area of the building.[962]

668. The Act requires BEECs to be provided to potential buyers or lessors when requested at the time of sale, lease or sublease; and to be made publicly available on the Building Energy Efficiency Register.[963] The Act also requires the energy efficiency rating be included in any advertising material for the sale, lease or sublease.[964]

3. Motor Vehicle Fuel Efficiency

669. *See* Part III for a discussion of motor vehicle fuel consumption standards and labelling.

B. State Energy Efficiency Targets and Schemes

670. The Australian States and Territories have established their own State targets and market-based schemes for improving energy efficiency. The Victorian, NSW, SA and ACT schemes are quite similar in nature, although there are differences between the schemes. State Ministers attending the Jurisdictional Meeting on Climate Change on 4 May 2015, agreed to harmonise the delivery of energy efficiency schemes and improve consistency across States and Territories from 2016.

959. *See also* the Building Energy Efficiency Disclosure Regulations 2010; Building Energy Efficiency Disclosure (Disclosure Affected Buildings) Determination 2016 (Minister's Determination); Building Energy Efficiency Disclosure Determination 2016 (Secretary's Determination).

960. *Building Energy Efficiency Disclosure Act 2010* (Cth), s. 11; Building Energy Efficiency Disclosure (Disclosure Affected Buildings) Determination 2016, cl. 6.

961. Australian Government, Department of Environment and Energy, *What is CBD?, supra* n. 958.

962. *Building Energy Efficiency Disclosure Act 2010*, s. 13A; Building Energy Efficiency Disclosure Determination 2016 (Secretary's Determination), cl. 6. NABERS is run by the NSW Office of Environment and Heritage on behalf of the Australian, State and Territory governments: NABERS, https://nabers.gov.au/public/webpages/home.aspx (accessed 15 Sept. 2016).

963. *Building Energy Efficiency Disclosure Act 2010,* s. 14.

964. Section 15.

1. Energy Efficiency Target Act 2007 (Vic)

671. In 2009, Victoria established a market-based scheme to encourage energy efficiency, known as the Energy Saver Incentive scheme, or the Victorian Energy Efficiency Target scheme. It is administered by the Victorian Essential Services Commission.[965] The scheme sets a state-wide target for energy savings, which results in a range of energy-efficient products and services being made available to Victorian homes and businesses at a discount. Businesses that are accredited persons can create Victorian Energy Efficiency Certificates through the provision of energy-efficient products and services.[966] These Certificates are purchased and surrendered by energy retailers ('relevant entities') to meet their liabilities under the mandatory annual State GHG emissions target, imposed through the *Victorian Energy Efficiency Target Act 2007* (Vic) and the *Victorian Energy Efficiency Target Regulations 2008* (Vic).[967] The number of certificates generated is based on the carbon dioxide equivalent GHG savings associated with the eligible product or service. 'Greenhouse gases' are carbon dioxide, methane, nitrous oxide, sulfur hexafluoride, hydrofluorocarbons and perfluorocarbons.[968] The targets for 2016–2020 are set out in the table below. Targets for the years 2021–2025 will be set by Regulation no later than 31 May 2020, and for 2026–2029, no later than 31 May 2020.[969]

Victorian Energy Efficiency Targets 2016–2020	
Year	**Target (tonnes of carbon-dioxide equivalent greenhouse gas abatement) = Amount of Victorian Energy Efficiency Certificates**
2016	5.4 million
2017	5.9 million
2018	6.1 million
2019	6.3 million
2020	6.5 million

2. NSW Energy Savings Scheme

672. The Energy Savings Scheme (ESS), established under Part 9 of the *Electricity Supply Act 1995* (NSW) and Part 8 of the *Electricity Supply (General) Regulation 2014* (NSW), started on 1 July 2009. The ESS sets mandatory annual energy savings targets for Scheme Participants.[970] These are electricity retailers and other parties, such

965. *Victorian Energy Efficiency Target: Home*, https://www.veet.vic.gov.au/public/Public.aspx?id=Home (accessed 15 Sept. 2016).
966. *Victorian Energy Efficiency Target Act 2007* (Vic), ss 9, 15, 16.
967. Sections 30, 31.
968. Section 3.
969. Section 300.
970. Section 103 and Sch. 5.

as electricity generators, who supply direct to a customer, and market customers who buy or sell electricity in NSW.[971] Scheme Participants are required to meet individual energy savings targets based on the size of their share of the electricity market.[972] Targets must be met through the creation and surrender of Energy Savings Certificates (ESCs).[973] Scheme Participants who fail to meet their targets must pay a penalty for their 'energy savings shortfall'.[974]

673. ESCs are created by companies who become Accredited Certificate Providers[975] and carry out Recognised Energy Savings Activities, as defined in the *Energy Savings Scheme Rule of 2009*.[976] These include activities such as the replacement and installation of common electrical appliances, high efficiency lighting and other energy saving devices, the efficiency rating of buildings, changes in industrial processes and changes in electricity consumption, and gas savings. Compliance is managed by IPART as Scheme Administrator and Regulator.[977]

3. SA Retailer Energy Efficiency Scheme

674. The Retailer Energy Efficiency Scheme (REES) commenced on 1 January 2015 and will operate to 2020. It builds on the Residential Energy Efficiency Scheme, which operated from 2009 to 2014.[978] The Scheme is established in Part 4 of the *Electricity (General) Regulations 2012*, made under the *Electricity Act 1996* (SA), and Part 4 of the *Gas Regulations 2012*, made under the *Gas Act 1997* (SA).

675. The REES establishes mandatory energy efficiency and audit targets that must be met by electricity and gas retailers. Energy retailers that exceed certain thresholds are set annual targets for the delivery of energy efficiency activities to households and/or businesses. Retailers with larger residential customer bases are also set targets to ensure a certain amount of the energy-efficiency activities they deliver are provided to 'priority group' (low-income) households, and are set targets for providing energy audits to low-income households.[979]

676. The REES consists of two three-year stages: 2015–2017 and 2018–2020.[980] The Minister for Mineral Resources and Energy sets annual targets at the beginning of each stage. These are then apportioned to each liable energy retailer by ESCOSA,

---

971. *Electricity Supply Act 1995* (NSW), s. 101. Some Trade-Exposed Emissions Intensive industries are partially exempt from the Scheme*: Electricity Supply Act 199*, ss 119, 121.
972. Sections 102, 106.
973. Sections 127–133.
974. Section 112.
975. Section 134.
976. The Energy Savings Scheme Rule of 2009 and the Energy Savings Scheme (Amendment No 1) Rule 2016, as published on 8 Apr. 2016.
977. *Electricity Supply Act 1995* (NSW), ss 151, 154.
978. The Retailer Energy Efficiency Scheme, which replaced the Residential Energy Efficiency Scheme in 2015, was expanded to include small business.
979. South Australian Government, Department of Premier and Cabinet, *Retailer Energy Efficiency Scheme*, https://www.sa.gov.au/topics/water-energy-and-environment/energy/rebates-concessions-and-incentives/retailer-energy-efficiency-scheme-rees (accessed 15 Sept. 2016).
980. These are Stages 2 and 3. The Residential Energy Efficiency Scheme, which operated from 2009–2014, comprised Stage 1.

which administers the scheme.[981] Energy retailers that retail 27,000 MWh or more of electricity or 100,000 GJ or more of gas in a year to South Australian households and businesses are set a target for the delivery of energy efficiency activities to households and businesses. Retailers with 5000 or more residential customers are set targets for the delivery of energy efficiency activities to households and business, and the delivery of energy efficiency activities and energy audits to priority group households.[982] Retailers must report to the ESCOSA, and penalties apply to those who fail to achieve their target.

677. Each energy retailer participating in the scheme decides on the mix of energy efficiency activities it will undertake to meet its targets from among a list of eligible activities. The Minister for Mineral Resources and Energy is empowered to maintain and amend the list of eligible activities or measures.[983] These include the installation of energy-efficient lighting, water efficient shower heads, stand-by power controllers, insulation and energy-efficient water heating in homes, and the installation of commercial energy-efficient lighting and water efficient shower heads. General and minimum specifications apply to all approved REES energy efficiency activities from January 2015.[984] The Minister for Mineral Resources and Energy has also set minimum specifications for energy audits that energy retailers can deliver to meet any energy audit targets.[985]

4. ACT Energy Improvement Scheme

678. The *Energy Efficiency (Cost of Living) Improvement Act 2012* (ACT) introduced an Energy Efficiency Improvement Scheme (EEIS) for the ACT, similar to the schemes operating in SA, Victoria and NSW. The key elements of the scheme are regulated under the Act, regulations and various disallowable instruments made

---

981. ESCOSA carries out its functions as administrator in accordance with a Retailer Energy Efficiency Scheme Code (REES Code), made by the Commission under section 28 of the *Essential Services Commission Act 2002* (SA).
982. ESCOSA, *Targets*, http://www.escosa.sa.gov.au/industry/rees/targets (accessed 15 Sept. 2016). Key elements for the operation of the scheme for the period 2015 to 2017 were gazetted by the Minister on 11 Dec. 2014: *South Australian Government Gazette*, 11 Dec. 2014, p. 6648. *See also* South Australian Government, Department of State Development, *Retailer Energy Efficiency Scheme: Final Decisions on Thresholds and Targets* (December 2014). Individual targets for 2016 are set out at ESCOSA, *Targets 2016 - individual retailer*, http://www.escosa.sa.gov.au/industry/rees/targets/targets-2016-individual-retailer (accessed 15 Sept. 2016).
983. Electricity (General) Regulations 2012, reg. 28; Gas Regulations 2012, reg. 22.
984. *South Australian Government Gazette*, 18 Dec. 2014, p. 6787. *See also* South Australian Government, Department of State Development, *Retailer Energy Efficiency Scheme: Final decisions on Activity Specifications and Ministerial* Protocol (December 2014). For more information, *see* South Australian Government, Department of Premier and Cabinet, *Retailer Energy Efficiency Scheme*, *supra* n. 979.
985. The Energy Audit Specification describes the competency requirements for persons undertaking an REES energy audit and the way in which the audit is to be conducted: *Energy Audit Specification, Retailer Energy Efficiency Scheme (REES): Minimum Specification for an Energy Audit* (January 2015).

under the Act by the Minister for the Environment and Sustainable Development.[986] Although the Act initially provided for the scheme to run until 31 December 2015, the ACT Government amended the Act to extend the EEIS to 2020.[987]

679. The Act requires the Minister to establish an energy savings target for the ACT.[988] The energy savings target for 2016 to 2020 is 8.6% each year. Mandatory obligations are imposed on individual electricity retailers to meet the target in relation to their retail electricity market share. Electricity retailers must thus achieve individual targets in relation to electricity and gas emissions reductions, expressed in tonnes of carbon dioxide equivalence.[989] The Minister determines the eligible activities that electricity retailers may undertake to promote energy efficiency.[990] Eligible activities include a range of listed activities relating to building envelopes, space heating and cooling, hot water service, residential and commercial lighting, and appliance activities.[991] Retailers can subcontract the provision of eligible activities, and can transfer 'credits' generated from undertaking eligible activities between each other with approval from the Scheme Administrator.

680. Tier 1 electricity retailers are required to undertake a specified proportion of their energy efficiency activities in ‘priority’ (low-income) households, to meet a ‘priority household target’ set by the Minister.[992] Tier 1 electricity suppliers are those with at least 5,000 customers in the ACT, and who sell at least 500,000 MWh of electricity to customers in the ACT annually.[993] A simplified obligation has been established for smaller ‘Tier 2’ suppliers, who can either undertake eligible energy savings activities or discharge their obligations through an Energy Savings Contribution fee equal to the estimated cost of participation of a Tier 1 supplier.[994]

681. Retailers must report annually on their compliance with scheme rules. Retailers that fail to meet their obligations under the Act must pay a penalty in relation to each tonne of carbon dioxide equivalence shortfall, and make good the shortfall.[995]

VII. Carbon Sequestration and Storage

682. The development of CCS technologies has strong federal government political support in Australia, largely to enable the continuing consumption and export

986. These are listed on the ACT Legislative Register at http://www.legislation.act.gov.au/a/2012-17/di.asp (accessed 15 Sept. 2016).
987. For general information on the scheme, *see* ACT Government, Environment and Planning Directorate, http://www.environment.act.gov.au/energy/smarter-use-of-energy/energy_efficiency_improvement_scheme_eeis, accessed 15 Sept. 2016.
988. *Energy Efficiency (Cost of Living) Improvement Act 2012* (ACT), subs. 7(1).
989. Sections 13–14.
990. Section 10.
991. Energy Efficiency (Cost of Living) Improvement (Eligible Activities) Determination 2016, made under *Energy Efficiency (Cost of Living) Improvement Act 2012*, section 10 (eligible activities), 22 Jul. 2016.
992. Section 8.
993. Section 3 and Dictionary.
994. Section 11.
995. Sections 20, 20A–20C, 21, 22.

of coal. Legislation to regulate carbon storage has been enacted by the Commonwealth, Victorian, Queensland and South Australian governments, using the Ministerial Council on Mineral and Petroleum Resources' *Regulatory Guiding Principles for Carbon Dioxide Capture and Geological Storage* to facilitate a nationally consistent approach.[996] These *Regulatory Guiding Principles* set out principles to guide the development of legislation in relation to six key aspects of carbon dioxide injection and storage, these being: assessment and approvals processes; access and property rights; transportation issues; monitoring and verification; liability and post-closure responsibilities; and financial issues. The legislative schemes do not regulate the capture or transportation of greenhouse gases to the storage site, which are dealt with under other legislation, but rather regulate issues relevant to injection and storage management.

683. The *Offshore Petroleum and Greenhouse Gas Storage Act* 2006 (Cth) ('OPGGSA') provides the legal framework for offshore carbon storage under the seabed in Commonwealth waters.[997] As with petroleum, the Australian Government releases acreage for greenhouse gas activities, over which proponents can seek to obtain title. The first offshore GHG storage assessment acreage was released in 2009. One GHG permit has been awarded, in 2012, to the CarbonNet CCS project in Commonwealth waters off the Victorian Coast.[998]

684. The OPGGSA establishes a system of authorisations much like those for the mining and oil and gas industries, whereby it is an offence to carry out certain GHG activities unless the appropriate authorisation is obtained.[999] A GHG assessment permit is required to explore in the permit area for potential GHG storage formations and injection sites. If an eligible GHG storage formation is identified, the Commonwealth Minister may declare that the formation is an identified GHG storage formation. The permittee may then apply for a GHG holding lease or a GHG injection licence. A GHG injection licence authorises the licensee to inject and store greenhouse gases in the licence area. A GHG holding lease – similar in concept to a petroleum retention licence – may be obtained to enable a proponent to maintain rights over a site, and conduct certain activities, when a greenhouse gas storage formation has been identified and is wholly situated in the lease area, and the applicant is not currently in a position to

996. Ministerial Council on Mineral and Petroleum Resources, *Carbon Dioxide Capture and Geological Storage: Australian Regulatory Guiding Principles* (MCMPR, 2005). The Council, comprised of the Australian, State and Territory Ministers with responsibility for minerals and petroleum, no longer exists. For a discussion of carbon capture and storage in Australia, *see* Samantha Hepburn, *Mining and Energy Law* (Cambridge University Press, 2015), Ch. 7.

997. *See also* the Offshore Petroleum and Greenhouse Gas Storage (Management of Greenhouse Gas Injection and Storage) Regulations 2011, Offshore Petroleum and Greenhouse Gas Storage (Environment) Regulations 2009, Offshore Petroleum and Greenhouse Gas Storage (Safety) Regulations 2009, Offshore Petroleum and Greenhouse Gas Storage (Resource Management and Administration) Regulations 2011, and the Australian Government, Department of Resources, Energy and Tourism, *Guidelines for injection and storage of greenhouse gas substances in offshore areas* (December 2011).

998. Australian Government, Department of Industry, Innovation and Science, *Carbon Capture and Storage legislation and regulation*, http://www.industry.gov.au/resource/LowEmissionsFossilFuelTech/Pages/Carbon-Capture-Storage-Legislation.aspx (accessed 28 Sept. 2016).

999. *Offshore Petroleum and Greenhouse Gas Storage Act 2006* (Cth), s. 289. The system of authorisations is set out in Ch. 3 of the Act.

inject and permanently store a GHG substance but is likely to be in such a position within fifteen years.

685. Other titles are: the GHG search authority, which authorises the holder to carry on operations in the authority area relating to the exploration for potential GHG storage formations or potential GHG injection sites, but not to make a well; a GHG special authority, which authorises the holder to carry on certain operations in the authority area (but not to make a well); and GHG research consents, which authorise the holder to carry on GHG related operations in the course of a scientific investigation.

686. The Act sets out the matters that are usually dealt with in a system of licensing, including the application process, and the grant, variation, surrender and cancellation of authorisations. The Minister is empowered to place any conditions he or she thinks is necessary upon a permit or licence, and a titleholder must seek the Minister's approval before conducting GHG operations activities under their title. The Act also establishes a system of registration of GHG titles and regulates transfers and dealings in GHG titles.[1000] The Act addresses particular matters of concern in relation to CCS, including environment assessment and protection, public consultation, monitoring of injected gases, site closure and long-term liability, and the potential conflict between GHG activities and the offshore oil industry and other users of the sea.

687. The CCS legislation of certain Australian States also establish a system of authorisations or licences to regulate GHG injection and storage operations within each State's jurisdiction, as well as vesting ownership of onshore subsurface storage spaces/geological formations for carbon storage in the State.[1001] These Acts address similar matters including environment assessment and protection, monitoring of injected gases, site closure and long-term liability, and the potential land-use conflicts. In Victoria, the *Greenhouse Gas Geological Sequestration Act 2008* (Vic) regulates the onshore large-scale underground storage of captured greenhouse gas emissions, while the *Offshore Petroleum and Greenhouse Gas Storage Act 2010* (Vic) regulates CCS offshore in Victorian coastal waters. Queensland enacted specific legislation to regulate onshore CCS, namely the *Greenhouse Gas Storage Act 2009* (Qld). South Australia introduced provisions regulating CCS by amendments to the *Petroleum Act 2000* (SA).

688. In Western Australia, the Petroleum and Geothermal Energy Legislation Amendment Bill 2013 (WA), was presented to Parliament and debated, but has not yet received Royal Assent or Proclamation. However, Western Australia has enacted project-specific legislation to govern the Gorgon CO_2 Injection Project.[1002] As of September 2016, neither New South Wales nor Tasmania had CCS-specific legislation.[1003]

1000. *Offshore Petroleum and Greenhouse Gas Storage Act 2006*, Ch. 5.

1001. *Greenhouse Gas Geological Sequestration Act 2008* (Vic), subs. 14(1); *Greenhouse Gas Storage Act 2009* (Qld), subs. 27(1). The Commonwealth and Victorian offshore legislation do not vest ownership in the Crown, because of international law regarding sovereignty over the seabed and waters of the exclusive economic zone and continental shelf.

1002. *Barrow Island Act* (WA) 2003.

1003. The *Greenhouse Gas Storage Bill 2010* (NSW), introduced to the NSW Legislative Assembly in November 2010, was not passed before Parliament was prorogued for the State government elections in March 2011 and therefore lapsed.

689. Although the Commonwealth and State legal regimes have been developed in accordance with the *Regulatory Guiding Principles*, and therefore regulate the same fundamental issues in relation to CCS, the legislation is not mirror legislation, and differences do exist between the various regimes, such that there is not one, uniform or harmonised regime across the country. Nonetheless, in its global assessment of national legal and regulatory regimes, published in September 2015, the Global CCS Institute recognised that the regulatory frameworks were 'largely consistent' across Australia, and gave Australia's federal and State regimes the highest ranking as the 'most comprehensive models of regulation across the project lifecycle' in the extent that they address most (but not all) the relevant issues concerning siting, design, capture, transport, storage, closure and monitoring for potential releases of stored carbon dioxide.[1004]

1004. Global Carbon Capture and Storage Institute Ltd, *Global CCS Institute CCS Legal and Regulatory Indicator: A Global Assessment of National Legal and Regulatory Regimes for Carbon Capture and Storage* (Global Carbon Capture and Storage Institute Ltd, 2015).

Part VI. Interaction Between Energy Law and Tax Law

Chapter 1. Introduction

690. The State, Territory and Commonwealth Parliaments have concurrent legislative powers to make taxation laws. The legislative power of the Commonwealth to make laws with respect to taxation is set out in section 51(ii) of the Australian Commonwealth Constitution, which empowers the Commonwealth Parliament to make laws with respect to taxation, 'but so as not to discriminate between State or parts of States'.[1005] Australia has a vast and complex array of taxes and charges, levied by the Commonwealth, State and Territory governments, and local councils. Although the States and Commonwealth have concurrent legislative power in the field of taxation, there are some major taxes which are only levied by the Commonwealth Parliament, most notably income tax, capital gains tax (CGT), fringe benefits tax (FBT) and the goods and services tax (GST). The main sources of taxation revenue for the States are payroll tax and stamp duties.

691. The existing division of taxation between the States and Commonwealth reflects the provisions of the Commonwealth Constitution. For example, section 90 of the Commonwealth Constitution provides the Commonwealth Parliament with exclusive power to impose duties of customs and of excise, and to grant bounties on the production or export of goods. Duties of excise are taxes on any step before consumption in the production, manufacture, sale or distribution of goods, whether of domestic or foreign origin.[1006] The States are able to impose royalties on resources such as petroleum, gas and coal, as the Courts have held these are not duties of excise,

1005. Other relevant provisions in the Constitution are: s. 99 (prohibition on tax preferences); s. 53 (Senate may not introduce or amend tax laws); s. 55 (laws imposing taxation are to deal only with the imposition of taxation and only with one subject of taxation); s. 114 (prohibits the States from imposing tax on property of any kind belonging to the Commonwealth without the Commonwealth's consent, and prohibits the Commonwealth from imposing tax on property of any kind belonging to a State without the State's consent); and s. 96 (Commonwealth has legislative power to grant financial assistance to any State). Where there is an inconsistency between Commonwealth and State law, the Commonwealth law will prevail, to the extent of the inconsistency (s. 109).

1006. *Ha & Anor v. State of New South Wales & Ors* (1997) 189 CLR 465.

but are a price for the right to produce or extract resources, or a charge for the acquisition of a right to property.[1007]

692. The division of taxation also reflects political realities. For example, although at the time of Federation in 1900 the States levied income tax, the Commonwealth was able to force the States from the field of income tax from 1942 after the enactment of four Acts which together introduced the 'Uniform Tax Scheme'.[1008] The legislation did not prohibit the States from levying income tax, but by imposing a nationwide income tax at a substantial rate, calculated to yield the amount of tax equal to the previous tax take of the States and Commonwealth combined, the scheme made it politically and economically impossible for any State to levy income tax.[1009]

693. The energy sector is subject to the same tax laws that apply to all sectors of the Australian economy. However, there are some tax issues unique to the energy sector and/or which are of particular importance to energy. The remainder of this chapter briefly provides an introduction to the main Commonwealth taxes in Australia, and the role of the Australian Taxation Office, before examining some tax issues of particular relevance to the energy sector, most notably resource rent taxes such as the Commonwealth PRRT; royalties; various fuel schemes that operate through the system of income tax; excise and customs duty on fuels; and income tax incentives for R&D, which encourage the development of clean energy technology.

§1. Introduction to the Major Commonwealth Taxes

I. Income Tax

694. The Commonwealth government levies income tax on taxable income pursuant to the *Income Tax Assessment Act 1997* (ITAA97) and the *Income Tax Assessment Act 1936* (ITAA36). Income taxes are levied upon individuals and corporations. Australian companies are liable to remit income tax at a flat rate of 30% on their taxable income as their Business Activity Statement (BAS) falls due. For companies with a turnover of more than USD 20 million this is usually every month. For small companies it may be every quarter. Taxable income is Assessable Income less Deductions. Once tax rates have been applied to taxable income, the Basic Income Tax Liability can be determined. However, there may be a range of offsets that are applicable to reduce tax liability. The term 'offset' under the ITSA97 generally incorporates what were formerly known as tax rebates and credits in the ITAA36.

1007. *Harper v. Minister for Sea Fisheries* (1989) 168 CLR 314.

1008. *Income Tax Act 1942* (Cth); *Income Tax Assessment Act 1942* (Cth); *States Grants (Income Tax Reimbursement) Act 1942* (Cth); and *Income Tax (War-Time Arrangements) Act 1942* (Cth).

1009. Woellner R, Barkozcy S, Murphy S, Evans C and Pinto D, *Australian Taxation Law* (26th ed, 2016) ¶1-600.

II. Capital Gains Tax

695. Australia does not have a separate capital gains tax. Rather, from 20 September 1985, capital gain has been included as 'income', and income tax is levied on it. Thus, the taxing of capital gain is regulated by income tax legislation, namely Part 3–1 of the ITAA97. The ITAA97 identifies events known as 'CGT events, which trigger a liability to assess the value of the capital gain. The most common of these is the 'CGT event A1' which applies when an asset is sold. The profit or loss associated with assets sold as trading stock, or in the ordinary course of business, are dealt with as ordinary income and do not fall within CGT event A1. Assets that are sold and do fall within 'CGT event A1' may give rise to a capital gain, or to a capital loss, or neither a gain nor a loss. The taxable value[1010] of the net capital gain is added to income and taxed with the other ordinary income at the relevant rates.

III. Fringe Benefits Tax

696. The FBT aims to prevent employers from avoiding tax by providing common ('fringe') benefits to their employees as part of a salary package instead of money wages/salaries. The main fringe benefits are identified in Part III of the *Fringe Benefits Tax Assessment Act 1986* (Ct) and include: living-away-from-home allowances; free holidays, travel, parking and free motor vehicles; low-interest mortgages; and various entertainment benefits. The legislation does not prohibit companies from providing these benefits, but requires companies to keep track of them so that tax can be levied upon the employer.

IV. Goods and Services Tax

697. The Federal government introduced the GST in 2000. It is levied at a rate of 10% on the supply of most goods and services with a connection to Australia. It is a value added tax, so business entities are entitled to receive credits for tax paid on the input side to be set against the tax collected on the outward side. There are a number of important exceptions, including exports. GST is collected when the BAS is due to be completed.

§2. Role of the Australian Tax Office

698. The Australian Tax Office (ATO) is the federal body charged with administering Commonwealth tax law and collecting most federal taxes.[1011] The decisions of the ATO are made by the Federal Commissioner of Taxation or his or her delegates. To help taxpayers understand and comply with the law, the ATO issues

1010. Taxable value is determined once various exemptions, losses, concessions and discounts have been applied.

1011. *Taxation Administration Act 1953* (Cth).

advice in various forms, including the publication of Private and Public Rulings, which state the ATO's interpretation of the law, and, in the case of Private Rulings, the application of the law to the individual taxpayer's case. While the ATO is not a formal law-making body, the practice of the ATO, which is applied 'through its assessment and review procedures; day-to-day decisions in formal and informal dealings with practitioners and the public; public and private rulings and other advices; and its objection and review (litigation procedures)', is of enormous practical significance and influence, to the extent that it can be seen as a de facto or informal source of law.[1012] This is because 'many practitioners and their clients use the Rulings as a source of law, viewing them as authoritative, and accept ATO practices and rulings without formal challenge, and structure their affairs accordingly'.[1013]

1012. Woellner et al., *supra* n. 1009, at ¶1-320. This is despite the Federal Court cautioning against the use of Rulings as a 'kind of "defacto law"': *BHP Billiton Direct Reduced Iron Pty Ltd & Anor v. DFC of T* (2007) ATC 5071, 5095 (French J), cited in Woellner et al., *supra* n. 1009, at ¶30-000.

1013. Woellner et al., *supra* n. 1009, at ¶1-320. For more information on Rulings, *see* Woellner et al. at ¶30-010–¶30-052.

Chapter 2. The Interaction Between Tax Law and Energy

§1. Resource Rent Taxes

699. Australia has levied a profits-based PRRT since 1987.[1014] It was introduced by the Commonwealth government to replace royalties and crude oil excise in most offshore areas under Commonwealth jurisdiction. The PRRT originally applied only to offshore oil projects, with the exception of the North West Shelf project in Commonwealth waters off the coast of Western Australia, and the Joint Petroleum Development Area ('JPDA') in the Timor Sea (where administration is shared by Australia and Timor-Leste). Oil from the Bass Strait project has been subject to the PRRT since 1990. The PRRT was extended from 1 July 2012, following recommendations of the *Australia's Future Tax System Review* (the 'Henry Tax Review'),[1015] and it now covers all Australian onshore oil and gas projects, including oil shale and CSG projects, and all offshore oil and gas projects except projects in the JPDA in the Timor Sea.

700. The PRRT is levied on the profits from the sale of marketable petroleum commodities from a project, including stabilised crude oil, condensate, sales gas, liquefied petroleum gas, ethane, and shale oil.[1016] It is applied at a rate of 40% to a project's 'taxable profit'.[1017] The tax is project-based, which means PRRT liability is calculated separately for each project interest held by an entity, although an entity can apply to have an interest in two or projects combined and treated as a single project if certain criteria are met (with the exception of an interest in a North West Shelf project).[1018] A petroleum project exists if a production licence is in force.[1019] Liability to pay PRRT will arise once an entity with an interest in an offshore production licence begins deriving 'assessable receipts' from the sale of petroleum. Contractors who are paid for their services and have no entitlement to receipts from the sale of petroleum are thus not liable to pay PRRT.[1020] Joint venture participants have separate, individual PRRT obligations in relation to their interest in a project.

1014. *Resources Rent Tax Assessment Act 1987* (Cth); *Petroleum Resource Rent Tax (Imposition—Customs) Act 2012* (Cth); *Petroleum Resource Rent Tax (Imposition—Excise) Act 2012* (Cth); *Petroleum Resource Rent Tax (Imposition—General) Act 2012* (Cth); *Petroleum Resource Rent Tax (Interest on Underpayments) Act 1987* (Cth); *Petroleum Resource Rent Tax (Instalment Transfer Interest Charge Imposition) Act 2006* (Cth).

1015. Henry K, Harmer J, Piggott J, Ridout H and Smith G, *Australia's Future Tax System: Report to the Treasurer, December 2009*, Part Two, Vol 1, C – Land and resources taxes (Commonwealth of Australia, 2010).

1016. *Petroleum Resource Rent Tax Assessment Act 1987*, s. 2E; Australian Taxation Office, *PRRT Concepts* https://www.ato.gov.au/Business/Petroleum-resource-rent-tax/PRRT-concepts/ (last updated 25 Feb. 2016).

1017. *Petroleum Resource Rent Tax Assessment Act 1987*, ss 21, 22.

1018. Sections 19, 20.

1019. Subsection 19(1).

1020. Australian Taxation Office, *Petroleum Resource Rent Tax (PRRT)* (23 Sept. 2014) https://www.ato.gov.au/Business/Petroleum-resource-rent-tax/ (accessed 25 Feb. 2016).

701. An entity is only liable to pay PRRT on the 'taxable profit' in relation a project. 'Taxable profit' is defined in subsection 22(1) of the *Resources Rent Tax Assessment Act 1987* (Cth), and is calculated by deducting eligible project expenditures and transferred exploration expenditure from the assessable receipts derived from the project. Assessable receipts can be of a capital or revenue nature, and include assessable: petroleum receipts, tolling receipts, exploration recovery receipts, property receipts, miscellaneous compensation receipts, employee amenities receipts and incidental production receipts.[1021]

702. Deductible expenditure may be of a capital or revenue nature, related directly related to a petroleum project. The Act defines eligible categories, which among others, include: resource tax expenditure (payment of State and federal resource taxes/royalties); exploration expenditure (expenditure incurred in, or in connection with, exploration for petroleum); general project expenditure (expenditure incurred in preparing for or in carrying on or providing particular operations, facilities and other things comprising the project); and closing-down expenditure (such as offshore platform removal and environmental restoration).[1022] Where deductable expenditure exceeds assessable receipts, the excess undeducted amounts can be carried forward to be deducted in future years, with an 'interest uplift' to maintain their real value.[1023] The payment of PRRT is itself a deductible expense in the calculation of income tax.

703. As its name suggests, the PRRT only applies to profits from the sale of petroleum commodities, and not to the profits from the sale of mineral resources, including coal and iron ore, which have earned large profits, particularly in resource booms. In 2009, the Henry Tax Review recommended that a uniform resource rent tax should be implemented and administered by the Commonwealth government, which in addition to petroleum, would also apply to a range of minerals, including uranium and black coal.[1024] The Rudd/Gillard Labor government first announced it would introduce a broad, uniform resource rent tax on 2 May 2010, called the Resources Super Profit Tax, which, following an extensive backlash from the mining industry, was replaced by the Minerals Resources Rent Tax (MRRT).[1025]

704. Very broadly speaking, the MMRT applied an effective 22.5% tax rate to the profit of iron ore and coal mining projects with and annual group mining profit of over USD 75 million.[1026] However, after a prolonged media campaign and intensive lobbying against the MRRT by the industry,[1027] and following its federal election campaign promises in 2013 to abolish the tax, the Coalition government repealed the

1021. *Petroleum Resource Rent Tax Assessment Act*, s. 23.

1022. Division 3.

1023. Sections 32–35B; Australian Taxation Office, Australian Taxation Office, *PRRT Concepts* https://www.ato.gov.au/Business/Petroleum-resource-rent-tax/PRRT-concepts/ (last updated 25 Feb. 2016).

1024. Henry K et al., *supra* n. 1015, at 237.

1025. *Minerals Resource Rent Tax Act 2012* (Cth). *See also* the *Minerals Resource Rent Tax (Imposition—Customs) Act 2012* (Cth); *Minerals Resource Rent Tax (Imposition—Excise) Act 2012* (Cth); *Minerals Resource Rent Tax (Imposition—General) Act 2012* (Cth).

1026. Australian Taxation Office, *Minerals Resources Rent Tax (MRRT)* (23 Sept. 2014) https://www.ato.gov.au/business/minerals-resource-rent-tax/ (accessed 25 Feb. 2016).

1027. An appeal to the High Court against the constitutional validity of the MRRT failed: *Fortescue Metals Group Limited v. The Commonwealth* [2013] HCA 34.

MMRT in 2014.[1028] While the design of the MRRT has been subject to criticism, various analysts have suggested that Australia should revisit the idea of a uniform resource rent scheme, particularly in conjunction with considered reform to the system of resource royalties and company income tax.[1029]

§2. Royalties

705. In Australia, hydrocarbons and coal resources are owned by the Crown. Resources that are situated onshore, and offshore seaward to three nm, are owned by the Crown in right of the State/Territory. Resources situated offshore in Commonwealth waters (3 nm to 200 nm) or on the continental shelf from 3 nm to the outer edge of the continental shelf where that extend beyond the 200 nm limit of the EEZ are owned by the Crown in right of the Commonwealth.

706. Mining and petroleum royalties are administered and collected under State and Commonwealth legislation. Royalties are generally calculated as either a flat percentage rate of the quantity of minerals/hydrocarbons produced (the 'quantum method') or as a percentage of the total value of minerals/hydrocarbons sold ('ad valorem' method). However, they are not taxes levied on the actual production or sale of the mineral. If they were, royalties would be legally classified as a duty of excise, and under the Commonwealth Constitution, the Commonwealth Parliament has exclusive power to levy duties of excise. Rather, royalties are recognised as a charge levied by the owner of the resources – the Crown in right of the State, or the Crown in right Commonwealth – on the right to extract, dispose of, or use minerals and hydrocarbons.

I. Petroleum Royalties

A. State Government Royalties

707. Royalties are imposed on onshore petroleum production under State onshore petroleum legislation.[1030] For petroleum production in State/Northern Territory coastal

1028. *Minerals Resource Rent Tax Repeal and Other Measures Act 2014* (Cth).

1029. Murray I, 'The Minerals Resource Rent Tax Is Dead, Long Live Resource Rent Taxes?' 40 *UW Aust LR* 111 (2015); Villios S, Blissenden M, Kenny P and Xynas L, 'Reducing the Company Tax Rate and Abolishing the MMRT: A Step Forward or Back?', 1(6-10) *Tax* 109 (2014).

1030. *Petroleum (Onshore) Act 1991* (NSW), s. 85; *Petroleum (Onshore) Regulation 2007* (NSW), regs 23, 24, 24AA; *Petroleum Act* (NT), subs. 84(1); *Petroleum and Gas (Production and Safety) Act 2004* (Qld), subs. 155(1), ch. 6; *Petroleum and Gas (Production and Safety) Regulation* 2004, reg. 147C; *Petroleum and Geothermal Energy Act 2000* (SA), s. 43; *Mineral Resources Development Act 1995* (Tas), s. 102; *Mineral Resources Development Regulation 2006*, reg. 7 and Sch. 1, Item 1 (petroleum) and Item 2 (coal seam gas); *Petroleum Act 1998* (Vic), ss 149–150; *Petroleum and Geothermal Energy Resources Act 1967* (WA), ss 52, 142.

waters (low water mark seaward to 3 nm), royalties are imposed under State offshore petroleum legislation (*see* Table 6).[1031]

Table 6: State Petroleum Royalty Rates, Australia (As at 29 February 2016)

	Onshore	*Offshore*
New South Wales	For petroleum (including natural gas and coal seam gas) recovered on or after 1 January 2013 – 10% of the value at the well-head of the petroleum	10% of the value of the petroleum at the well-head. Where there is a primary and secondary production licence: not less than 11% or more than 12.5% of the value at the well-head of the petroleum.
Northern Territory	10% of the value at the well-head of the petroleum	10% of the value of the petroleum at the well-head. Where there is a primary and secondary production licence: not less than 11% or more than 12.5% of the value at the well-head of the petroleum.
Queensland	10% of the value at the well-head of the petroleum	10% of the value of the petroleum at the well-head. Where there is a primary and secondary production licence: not less than 11% or more than 12.5% of the value of the petroleum at the well-head.
South Australia	10% of the value at the well-head of the petroleum	10% of the value of the petroleum at the well-head. Where there is a primary and secondary production licence: not less than 11% or more than 12.5% of the value of the petroleum at the well-head

1031. *Petroleum (Offshore) Act 1982* (NSW), ss 143, 43; *Petroleum (Submerged Lands) Act 1982* (NT), ss 142, 42; *Petroleum (Submerged Lands) Act 1982* (Qld), ss 143, 42; *Petroleum (Submerged Lands) Act 1982* (SA), ss 142, 41; *Petroleum (Submerged Lands) Act 1982* (Tas), ss 142, 41; *Offshore Petroleum and Greenhouse Gas Storage Act 2010* (Vic), s. 690; *Petroleum (Submerged Lands) Act 1982* (WA), ss 143, 42.

Tasmania	AUD 12 for each AUD 100 of the gross value of petroleum at the well-head	10% of the value of the petroleum at the well-head. Where there is a primary and secondary production licence: not less than 11% or more than 12.5% of the value of the petroleum at the well-head.
Victoria	10% of the value at the well-head of the petroleum	10% of the value of the petroleum at the well-head
Western Australia	Petroleum recovered under a petroleum exploration permit, petroleum drilling reservation or petroleum retention lease: 10% of the value of the petroleum Primary production licence: between 5.0% or 10.0% of the value at the well-head of the petroleum. Secondary production licence: Tight gas: between 5% and 12.5% of the value at the well-head of the petroleum. Petroleum that is not tight gas: between 10.0% or 12.5% of the value at the well-head of the petroleum.*	10% of the value of the petroleum at the well-head. Where there is a primary and secondary production licence: not less than 11% or more than 12.5% of the value of the petroleum at the well-head.

* Exception: the *Barrow Island Royalty Variation Agreement Act 1985* (WA) applies a royalty rate of 40% to resource rents calculated on a similar basis to the PRRT: section 6. *See also* Barrow Island Lease, clause 2(4).

Note: the ACT does not levy any royalties on petroleum.

708. 'Petroleum' is generally defined to include any naturally occurring hydrocarbon (whether in a gaseous, liquid or solid state); or any naturally occurring mixture of hydrocarbons (whether in a gaseous, liquid or solid state); or any naturally occurring mixture of one or more hydrocarbons (whether in a gaseous, liquid or solid state); and one or more of the following: hydrogen sulphide, nitrogen, helium or carbon dioxide. Thus, royalties are payable in respect of conventional gas resources as well as liquid petroleum. CSG is charged at the same rate as petroleum in Queensland, NSW, WA and SA. In Victoria, CSG is subject to an ad valorem royalty rate of 2.75%. In Queensland, no royalty is payable for CSG that is: (a) flared or vented; or (b) for incidental CSG mined under a mining lease, or CSG mined under a mineral hydrocarbon mining lease – used beneficially for mining the coal that produced the gas.[1032]

1032. *Mineral Resources Regulation 2013* (Qld), subs. 49(1).

B. Commonwealth Government Royalties

709. Commonwealth revenues from offshore petroleum are levied through the PRRT (described above) and under the *Excise Tariff Act 1921* (Cth) (*see* below), and not through royalties paid on the value of petroleum at the well-head. However, there are two exceptions.

1. Well-Head Royalty: North West Shelf Project Area

710. The *Offshore Petroleum (Royalty) Act 2006* (Cth) imposes a royalty on the value of all petroleum and gas recovered from the North West Shelf project area off the coast of Western Australia.[1033] Section 5 imposes liability to pay a royalty on the registered holder of a North West Shelf exploration permit, or a North West Shelf retention lease, or a North West Shelf production licence, on all petroleum recovered by the holder in the permit area, lease area or licence area. This covers petroleum production from fields covered by permits WA-1-P and WA-28-P, which are within Commonwealth jurisdiction (i.e., within Commonwealth waters).[1034]

711. The rate of royalty on petroleum recovered under a petroleum exploration or retention lease is 10% of the value at the well-head of the petroleum. The rate of royalty on petroleum recovered under a petroleum production licence is levied at a rate of 10%, and for a 'secondary petroleum production licence', between 11 and 12.5% of the well-head value of the petroleum.[1035] Revenue collected under the *Offshore Petroleum (Royalty) Act 2006* is shared with WA, as prescribed under section 75 of the *Offshore Petroleum and Greenhouse Gas Storage Act 2006* (Cth), at a ratio of 60:40 of the royalty rate.[1036]

2. Resource Rent Royalty

712. The *Petroleum Revenue Act 1985* (Cth) allows the federal government to waive excise levied under the *Excise Tariff Act 1921* (Cth) on certain onshore petroleum projects. This may only be done where a State or Territory government (a) enters into a resource rent royalty agreement ('RRRA') for the project with the holder of the petroleum production licence, and (b) makes a revenue-sharing arrangement with the Commonwealth government.[1037] The rate of royalty under an RRRA is 40% of the

1033. This Act reenacts the *Petroleum (Submerged Lands) (Royalty) Act 1967* (Cth) with certain modifications.

1034. *Offshore Petroleum (Royalty) Act 2006* (Cth), s. 4 and *Petroleum Resources Rent Tax Assessment Act* 1987, ss 2, 19(1B).

1035. For rates of royalty, *see Offshore Petroleum (Royalty) Act 2006* (Cth), ss 5–7. A 'secondary petroleum licence' is defined in the *Offshore Petroleum and Greenhouse Gas Storage Act 2006* (Cth) Sch. 4, cl 1, cl 2(2) and cl 4(2), and is a petroleum production licence granted to the holder of an exploration licence or retention lease, over a number of blocks that is less than the number of blocks over which the applicant is statutorily entitled to apply for a production licence.

1036. *Offshore Petroleum and Greenhouse Gas Storage Act 2006*, subs. 75(1); *see also* Government of Western Australia, Department of Mines and Petroleum, *Petroleum Royalties* http://www.dmp.wa.gov.au/Petroleum/Royalties-1578.aspx (accessed 22 Feb. 2016).

1037. *Petroleum Revenue Act 1985* (Cth), s. 6.

accumulated net receipts from the petroleum disposed of in a financial year, but no other royalty or charges imposed by the State is payable on that petroleum.[1038] The Act determines the ratio by which revenue must be shared between the State/Territory and Commonwealth governments.[1039]

713. One RRRA is currently in existence, and applies to production from Barrow Island, Western Australia.[1040] It is a royalty based on a percentage of net cash flow. Some key aspects are that: excess income over a threshold rate is charged at a rate of 40%; the revenue is shared at a ratio of 75:25 between the Commonwealth and the State, with the higher Commonwealth share reflecting the larger proportion of Commonwealth entitlements under the previous royalty and excise regime; and as a primary tax before income tax, the royalty is deductible against income tax.[1041]

II. Mineral Royalties: Coal and Uranium Oxide

714. Royalties on onshore minerals production are imposed on onshore production under State onshore mining legislation.[1042] The State governments may also enter into State agreements with corporations covering large mines/projects of economic, social and environmental significance, which are ratified by specific legislation (often known as Indenture Acts), and which may have project-specific royalty provisions,[1043] or may simply refer to existing royalty provisions under State legislation.[1044]

715. Coal has been a major export earner in a number of States, and it is subject to a specific royalty rate (*see* Table 7).[1045]

1038. Schedule 1, Item 1(d). This Schedule sets out a formula to calculate 'accumulated net receipts': Item 4.

1039. Schedule 2, Item 1(b).

1040. *Barrow Island Royalty Variation Agreement Act 1985* (WA) (as of 11 Sept. 2010).

1041. Government of Western Australia, Department of Mines and Petroleum, *Petroleum Royalties* http://www.dmp.wa.gov.au/Petroleum/Royalties-1578.aspx (accessed 23 Sept. 2016).

1042. There is no offshore production of coal.

1043. For example, the *Uranium (Yeelirrie) Agreement Act 1978* (WA), First Sch., cl. 25.

1044. For example, the *Collie Coal (Griffin) Agreement Act 1979* (WA), Sch., cl. 26; *Collie Coal (Western Collieries) Agreement Act 1979* (WA), Sch. 1, cl. 26.

1045. *Mineral Royalty Act 1982* (NT), s. 10; *Mining Act 1992* (NSW), ss 291, 291A, 292; Mining Regulation 2010 (NSW), reg. 63; *Mineral Resources Act 1989* (Qld), ss 320–321, Mineral Resources Regulation 2013 (Qld), s. 46, Sch. 3, and Queensland Office of State Revenue, *MRA001.1—Determination of coal royalty* (14 Oct. 2015); *Mining Act 1971* (SA), ss 17, 17A; *Mineral Resources Development Act 1995* (Tas), s. 102 and Mineral Resources Regulation 2006 (Tas), reg. 7; *Mineral Resources (Sustainable Development) Act* 1990 (Vic), ss 12, 12A and Mineral Resources (Sustainable Development) Regulations 2013 (Vic), regs 6–10; *Mining Act 1978* (WA), s. 109 and Mining Regulations 1981 (WA), reg. 86.

Table 7: State Royalty Rates for Coal (As at 29 February 2016)

New South Wales	Recovered by deep underground mining: 6.2% of the value of coal recovered Recovered by underground mining: 7.2% of the value of coal recovered Recovered by open cut mining: 8.2% of the value of coal recovered
Northern Territory	20% of the net value of coal sold or removed without sale from a production unit in a royalty year, but where that net value is: AUD 50,000 or less, the royalty payable is nil; or more than AUD 50,000, the royalty otherwise payable is reduced by AUD10,000.
Queensland	Where the value of the coal sold, disposed of or used does not exceed AUD 100/t: 7%. Where the average price of the coal sold, disposed of or used is more than AUD 100/t but not more than AUD 150: an ad valorem rate worked out according to a statutory formula, whereby the royalty rate equates to 7% of value of the coal sold, disposed of or used for the first AUD 100; and 12.5% of value of the coal sold, disposed of or used for the balance. Where the average price of the coal sold, disposed of or used is AUD 150/t or more, an ad valorem royalty rate is worked out according to a statutory formula, equating to 7% of value of the coal sold, disposed of or used for the first AUD 100; 12.5% of value of the coal sold, disposed of or used for the next AUD 50; and 15% of value of the coal sold, disposed of or used for the balance.
South Australia	5% of the value of the minerals For the period of five years, royalty payable in relation to minerals (other than extractive minerals) recovered from mineral land at a new mine will be equivalent to 2% of the value of the minerals.
Tasmania	If the value of the net sales is less than AUD 100,000 for a year, the prescribed rate of royalty is 1.9% of net sales. If the value of the net sales is at least AUD 100,000 and less than AUD 600,000 for a year, the prescribed rate of royalty is 1.9% of net sales plus a figure based on the yearly profit for the immediately preceding year, to a maximum of 5.35% of net sales. Formula: $R= (0.019 \times N) + ((0.4 \times p2)/N)$ where R = royalty rate, N = yearly net sales of coal for the immediately preceding year, and p = yearly profit for the immediately preceding year.

Victoria	Brown coal (lignite): AUD 0.0588 per GJ unit of lignite produced, adjusted by CPI. A 'gigajoule unit of lignite' means a quantity of lignite which, when mined and measured at a prescribed time and in the prescribed manner, has a net wet specific energy content of 1 gigajoule. Other than lignite: 2.75%
Western Australia	Coal (including lignite), exported: 7.5% Coal (including lignite), not exported: AUD 1/t, to be adjusted each year at 30 June, in accordance with the percentage increase in the average exmine value of Collie coal for the year ending on that date, when compared with the corresponding value of Collie coal for the year ending on 30 June 1981.

716. Australia has three producing uranium mines: Ranger mine in the Northern Territory and the Olympic Dam and Beverly mines in South Australia. In the States that impose royalties on uranium oxide (yellowcake), royalty rates are generally set out in mining legislation and regulations (*see* Table 8).

Table 8: State Royalty Rates for Uranium Oxide (As at 29 February 2016)

Northern Territory	The *Uranium Royalty (Northern Territory) Act 2009* (Cth) imposes a royalty on uranium, recovered in the Northern Territory by applying the *Mineral Royalty Act 1982* (NT) as a law of the Commonwealth. Thus, the profit-based royalty regime of the Mineral Royalty Act 1982 (NT) under section 10 applies to new uranium mining operations or any expansions to existing uranium mining operations. The royalty payable is 20% of the net value of uranium sold or removed without sale from a production unit in a royalty year, but where that net value is: (a) AUD 50,000 or less, the royalty payable is nil; or (b) more than AUD 50,000, the royalty otherwise payable is reduced by AUD 10,000. If an amount of royalty is received by the Commonwealth under the *Mineral Royalty Act 1982* (NT), the Commonwealth must pay to the Northern Territory an amount equal to the received amount: *Uranium Royalty (Northern Territory) Act 2009* (Cth) section 17(1).

Queensland	The royalty rate for uranium is: (a) if the average price per kilogram of the uranium sold, disposed of or used in the return period is USD 220 or less – 5% of the value of the uranium; or (b) if the average price per kilogram of the uranium sold, disposed of or used in the return period is more than AUD 220 – the royalty rate applied to the value of the uranium sold, disposed of or used in the return period, rounded down to 2 decimal places, worked out using the following formula: RR = 5 + (((AP – 220)/AP) × 5) where: RR is the royalty rate, expressed as a percentage. AP is the average price per kilogram of the uranium sold, disposed of or used in the return period. *Mineral Resources Regulation 2013* (Qld), regulation 46 Schedule 3, clause 13.
South Australia	5% of the value of the minerals: Mining Act 1971 (SA) section 17.
Western Australia	5% of the royalty value if sold as a uranium oxide concentrate. *Mining Act 1978* (WA) section 109 and *Mining Regulations 1981* (WA) regulation 86. The *Uranium (Yeelirrie) Agreement Act 1978* (Yeelirrie State Agreement) clause 25(1) sets an ad valorem rate of 3.5% for uranium oxide sold in the first seven years after the treatment plant comes into operation. The Yeelirrie State Agreement provides a royalty review mechanism after the first seven years of operation, and every five years thereafter: clause 25(5).

III. Geothermal Energy

717. Geothermal energy is the only renewable energy resource on which royalty is payable, usually at a certain percentage rate of the well-head value (*see* Table 9).[1046]

1046. *Mining Act 1992* (NSW), ss 291 and Mining Regulation 2010 (NSW), reg. 62; *Geothermal Energy Act 2009* (NT), s. 34 and Geothermal Energy Regulations (NT) in force 1 Jan. 2015; *Geothermal Energy Act 2010* (Qld), s. 104, 105 and Geothermal Energy Regulation 2012 (Qld), regs 64, 66; *Petroleum and Geothermal Energy Act 2000* (SA), s. 43; *Mineral Resources Development Act 1995* (Tas), s. 102 and Mineral Resources Development Regulation 2006 (Tas), reg. 7 and Sch. 1, Item 3(p); *Geothermal Energy Resources Act 2005* (Vic), ss 103, 104; *Petroleum and Geothermal Energy Resources Act 1967* (WA), subs. 142(2a).

Table 9: State Royalty Rates for Geothermal Energy (As at 29 February 2016)

New South Wales	4% of the ex-mine value.
Northern Territory	The Minister may include a condition in each geothermal production lease that the lease holder must pay to the Minister a royalty in relation to all geothermal energy extracted under the lease. Although the regulations may prescribe the rate at which a royalty is payable by each lease holder, no such rate has yet been set in the Regulations.
Queensland	2.5% of the well-head value of all geothermal energy produced.
South Australia	2.5% of the well-head value of the geothermal energy produced.
Tasmania	2.75% of the value of the sale at the well-head.
Victoria	Royalty is to be paid at the rate, and in accordance with the conditions, specified in the licence under which the geothermal energy is extracted. A royalty is only payable once.
Western Australia	2.5% of the value of the geothermal energy.

§3. Special Arrangements in the Timor Sea

I. Timor Sea: Joint Petroleum Development Area

718. Australia and Timor-Leste have not been able to reach agreement on delimitation of the maritime boundary between the two nations. In 1972, Australia and Indonesia reached agreement on the boundary separating the two countries' continental shelves. At this time, Timor-Leste was under the administrative authority of Portugal. Australia and Portugal could not reach agreement on maritime boundary delimitation, and so a gap was created in the agreed boundary between Australia and Indonesia ('the Timor Gap'). In 1975, after Indonesia occupied Timor-Leste, renewed attempts to close the Timor Gap failed. Australia and Indonesia entered into the Timor Gap Treaty, which was a provisional arrangement under Article 83(3) of UNCLOS that allowed petroleum development in the Timor Gap to proceed. The Timor Gap treaty defined a 'Zone of Co-operation', with three areas.

719. Area A was subject to joint control and equal sharing in the benefits of petroleum exploitation. A single legal system, which was neither wholly Australian nor Indonesian, applied across the whole of Area A. The Taxation Code, set out in Annex D to the Treaty, dealt with the avoidance of double taxation with respect to activities in the joint area. The tax laws of each country applied in Area A. Returns had to be lodged in each country, but individuals resident in Australia were subject to Australian tax law, and vice versa for Indonesia. Area B was subject to the relevant

Australian legal regime, and Australia shared part of its tax returns from exploitation with Indonesia. Area C was subject to the relevant Indonesian legal regime, and shared part of its tax returns from exploitation with Australia.

720. The Timor Gap Treaty ceased to be in force between Australia and Indonesia on 25 October 1999. The *Memorandum of Understanding of Timor Sea Arrangements* of 5 July 2001, negotiated between Australia and the United Nations Temporary Administration in Timor-Leste when Timor-Leste was transitioning to independence, formed the basis of the Timor Sea Treaty between Australia and East Timor, adopted on 20 May 2002.[1047] The Timor Sea Treaty applies only in the area of the Timor Sea that is described by the co-ordinates for the old Area A of the Zone of Co-operation of the Timor Gap Treaty, and which is now the JPDA. Areas B and C are under the full sovereignty of Australia and Timor-Leste respectively and are no longer subject to joint development.

721. The TST sets out broad principles for the way the treaty and the JPDA is to function, and the rights/responsibilities of the Parties. Production from the JPDA is split between Timor-Leste and Australia at a ratio of 90% to Timor-Leste and 10% to Australia.[1048] Consistent with this 90/10 production split, Australia and Timor-Leste may, in accordance with their respective laws and the Taxation Code in Annex G, impose taxes on their share of the revenue from petroleum activities in the JPDA, although neither country may impose a tax not covered by the provisions of the Taxation Code in respect of or applicable to any petroleum exploration or exploitation related activity carried on in the JPDA, unless the other country consents to the imposition of that tax. The PRRT does not apply in the JPDA.

722. For the purposes of taxation law related directly or indirectly to the exploration for or the exploitation of petroleum in the JPDA, the JPDA is deemed to be, and treated by, Australia and Timor-Leste, as part of that country.[1049] The Taxation Code in Annex G provides relief from double taxation relating to petroleum activities. The Taxation Code applies to the following taxes (a) in Australia: income tax, FBT; the GST; and the superannuation guarantee charge, but not the PRRT, and (b) in Timor-Leste: income tax, the value added tax and sales tax on luxury goods ('value added tax'); and the sales tax, imposed under the law of Timor-Leste.

723. Petroleum is produced within the JPDA according to a production sharing contract, by which regulates how much petroleum the parties will receive after the recovery of a specified amount for costs and expenses.[1050]

II. Timor Sea: Greater Sunrise Unit Reservoir

724. Special provisions exist regarding PRRT payable on production from the Greater Sunrise oil and gas fields, which lie between Australia and Timor-Leste, and

1047. *Timor Sea Treaty Between the Government of Australia and the Government of East Timor*, (Dili, 20 May 2002), [2003] ATS 13 (in force 2 Apr. 2003).

1048. Article 4.

1049. Article 13.

1050. *See* the Petroleum Mining Code, developed under Art. 7 of the Timor Sea Treaty, available from http://www.anp-tl.org/webs/anptlweb.nsf/vwAll/JPDA (accessed 25 Sept. 2016).

which are estimated to contain 5.1 trillion cubic feet of LNG and 226 million barrels of condensate.[1051] Part of the Greater Sunrise unit reservoir lies within the JPDA, which is administered jointly by Timor-Leste and Australia under the Timor Sea Treaty, and part falls within Australia's exclusive jurisdiction. Under Article 7 of the 2007 Greater Sunrise Unitisation Agreement between Australia and Timor-Leste, 79.9% of production from the Greater Sunrise project is apportioned to Australia, and 20.1% to the JPDA.[1052] This means 79.9% of the amount of petroleum becomes the property of the permittee, lessee or licensee who recovered the petroleum pursuant to Australia's offshore petroleum legislation, while property in the remaining 20.1% of the petroleum is determined under the Timor Sea Treaty (which, as production from the JPDA, is split 90/10 between East Timor/Australia).[1053] PRRT is payable only on 79.9% of production from a Greater Sunrise project, which is the amount of petroleum apportioned to Australia under the Unitisation Agreement.[1054]

725. The ongoing dispute between Australia and Timor-Leste over maritime boundary delimitation in the Timor Sea, and the latter's dissatisfaction with the arrangements under the Timor Sea Treaty and the Greater Sunrise Unitisation Agreement, eventually led to the negotiation of the Treaty on Certain Maritime Arrangements in the Timor Sea in 2007.[1055] Under Article 5 of this Treaty, Timor-Leste and Australia agree to share equally in revenue derived directly from the production of petroleum lying within the Greater Sunrise Unit Area, in so far as the revenue relates to the upstream exploitation of that petroleum.

726. Australia is to make quarterly payments to Timor-Leste, equivalent to half the aggregate of the 'Australian revenue component' and the 'Timor-Leste revenue component', less the Timor-Leste revenue component. The Australian revenue component is taxation revenue collected from the PRRT; company tax (including capital gains tax); and first tranche petroleum and profit petroleum pursuant to the Timor Sea Treaty, or subsequent taxes of a similar nature. The Timor-Leste revenue component means taxation revenue collected from first tranche petroleum, profit petroleum and all profit-based income taxes calculated and levied by annual assessment pursuant to the Timor Sea Treaty, or subsequent taxes of a similar nature, but excludes Value Added Tax or

1051. Australian Government, Department of Industry, innovation and Science, *Joint Petroleum Development Area and Greater Sunrise*, http://www.industry.gov.au/resource/UpstreamPetroleum/Pages/JointPetroleumDevelopmentAreaandGreaterSunrise.aspx (accessed 25 Sept. 2016).

1052. *Agreement Between the Government of Australia and the Government of the Democratic Republic of Timor-Leste Relating to the Unitisation of The Sunrise and Troubadour Fields* (Dili, 6 Mar. 2003) [2007] ATS 11 (in force 23 Jan. 2007). *See also* Art. 9 and Annex E of the Timor Sea Treaty.

1053. *Offshore Petroleum and Greenhouse Gas Storage Act 2006* (Cth) subs. 286(1).

1054. *Petroleum Resources Rent Tax Assessment Act 1987* (Cth) subss 22(2) and 2C(2); *Offshore Petroleum and Greenhouse Gas Storage Act 2006* (Cth) s. 286 and Sch. 7.

1055. *Treaty Between the Government of Australia and the Government of the Democratic Republic of Timor-Leste on Certain Maritime Arrangements in the Timor Sea* Sydney, 12 Jan. 2006), [2007] ATS 12 (entered into force 23 Jan. 2007). In 2017, Australia and Timor-Leste are undertaking a series of dialogues under the auspices of the Conciliation Commission constituted pursuant to Annex V of the UNCLOS, following notification by Timor-Leste of its intention to terminate this Treaty.

income tax withheld monthly or similar taxes, or subsequent taxes of a similar nature.[1056] If Timor-Leste's revenue component exceeds Australia's revenue component in in a particular quarter, Timor-Leste does not make a payment to Australia; rather, subsequent quarterly payments by Australia to Timor-Leste are adjusted to take account of the earlier payment not made by Timor-Leste.[1057]

§4. Fuel Taxation: Excise

I. Brief History

727. Australia levies customs duties on the importation of fuels and petroleum products, and levies excise on fuels and petroleum products that are produced or manufactured in Australia. Fuel taxation was first introduced in Australia in 1901 by the Commonwealth government shortly after Federation, when a customs duty was applied to certain imported petroleum products to earn revenue for the new government. Excise on petrol was levied from 1929, when domestic refineries were first established. Over the course of the twentieth century, different products have become subject to excise, and at different rates, and a range of grant and rebate schemes have been introduced and abolished at various times to offset the cost of fuels taxation to various sectors and interests. To the original customs duty on imported petroleum products in 1901 and excise on petrol from 1929, excise duties were added to the following products over the twentieth century: coal tar and coke oven distillates (1931); heavy fuel oil (1940); the on-road use of diesel (1957);[1058] crude oil and including liquefied petroleum gas (LPG) (mid-1970s); heating oil, fuel oil and kerosene (1983); and refined petroleum products (1986).

728. On 1 March 2001, the Prime Minister announced that the Government would establish a Fuel Taxation Inquiry to examine the total structure of fuel taxation in Australia, as it had become apparent the structure was confused and complex.[1059] Only petroleum products were subject to fuel taxation, with the highest rate of tax being for those fuels used mainly in transport applications (petrol and diesel). Fuels subject to taxation included: in stationary energy forms, diesel, fuel oils and kerosene, and crude oil; and in mobile energy forms, petrol, diesel, aviation fuels, fuel oils, and

1056. Article 5.

1057. Article 10.

1058. Excise on diesel, introduced in 1957, did not apply to off-road users. Under the 'exemption certificate scheme' users were exempt from paying duty. The Diesel Fuel Rebate Scheme (DFRS) was introduced in 1982 to replace the exemption certification scheme. Under the DFRS, certain off-road users had to purchase duty paid fuel, with some users eligible to claim a partial or full rebate. The rebate was aimed at maintaining competitiveness in the mining and agricultural industries, as key export industries. Australian Treasury, *History of Fuel Taxation in Australia* (2001), Fuel Taxation Inquiry Background Papers, 9–10 http://fueltaxinquiry.treasury.gov.au/content/backgnd/002.asp (accessed 25 Sept. 2016).

1059. Australian Treasury, *Fuel Taxation Inquiry Terms of Reference*, http://fueltaxinquiry.treasury.gov.au/content/termsOfRef.asp (accessed 25 Sept. 2016).

kerosene. Certain petroleum substitutes, including LPG and ethanol, were excise free.[1060]

729. The complexity of the tax structure evolved from 'an incremental policy framework', as various Australian governments sought to use fuel taxation to achieve different policy objectives.[1061] From the early to mid-twentieth century, fuel taxation was earmarked to fund the development and maintenance of Australia's road network. From 1959, there was an end to the formal hypothecation of fuel excise to road funding. Fuel excise came to be treated as a general and significant source of government revenue, with road funding set as part of the budget process.[1062] Fuel taxation (in conjunction with grants, rebates and exemptions) has since been used to achieve a number of policy objectives, such as: fuel security objectives, including diversity of supply; environmental objectives, including improving air quality and reducing GHG emissions; and the development of Australian industries in direct fuel production and the manufacture of associated technology, and, associated with this, regional development and employment through industry assistance.[1063] Six monthly indexation in line with the Consumer Price Index (CPI), which was introduced in 1983, was abolished in 2001 to achieve the social objective of alleviating the impacts of high petrol prices on consumers.

730. In 2002, the Fuel Taxation Inquiry recommended that the government should design new arrangements for the application of Commonwealth fuel excise and customs duty. Among its recommendations were that excise and customs duty should apply to all liquid fuels, LPG, Liquefied Natural Gas (LNG) and Compressed Natural Gas (CNG), and that biannual CPI indexation of all fuel excise and customs duty rates should be reintroduced.[1064] These recommendations were not adopted. Nearly a decade later, in 2010, the Henry Tax Review, recommended fuel taxes as a general source of revenue should be phased out, although 'some fuel tax might be retained as a simple variable charge for variable costs of the road network that cannot be priced directly'.[1065] The Review recommended twice yearly indexation to maintain the real

---

1060. The production of LPG was first subject to excise in 1975. An excise imposed on LPG for use in vehicle propulsion was imposed between 1974 and 1979, but removed in 1979 when the Government committed to a five-year guarantee of the excise-free status of alternative fuels, including LNG and LPG. During the late 1970s and 1980s the Commonwealth Government provided excise concessions for LPG and ethanol for fuel security objectives. The excise on the production of LPG was abolished in 1993. Ethanol was given duty free status in 1980 and an exemption in 1994 from excise when blended with petrol. Australian Treasury, *History of Fuel Taxation in Australia*, *supra* n. 1058, at 25.

1061. *Ibid.*, 17.

1062. With the exception of a brief period from 1982–1988, when the government established a roads programme to be funded by a surcharge on the excise of petrol and diesel: *ibid.*, 7–8.

1063. Trebeck D, John Landels J, QC and Hughes K, *Fuel Taxation Inquiry Report*, 17 and 41 (Commonwealth of Australia, 2002).

1064. *Ibid.*, 29.

1065. Henry K et al., *supra* n. 1015, Vol 2 at 398. The Review recommended policy objectives relating to energy security should be achieved by other targeted measures, not fuel taxation; and that the reduction of greenhouse gas emissions would be best addressed by the (now abolished) Carbon Pollution Reduction Scheme (at 389 and 398).

value of fuel taxation, and extending fuels taxation to all fuels used for transport, including gaseous fuels, biodiesel and domestically produced ethanol.[1066]

731. Following the Henry Tax Review, various reforms have taken place. The *Tax and Superannuation Laws Amendment (2014 Measures No. 6) Act 2014* has aligned fuel excise and excise-equivalent customs duty with fuel tax credit rates and cleaner fuels grants scheme rates (on fuel tax credits, *see* Chapter 2, §5 below). The *Excise Tariff Amendment (Fuel Indexation) Act 2014* (Cth) and *Customs Tariff Amendment (Fuel Indexation) Act 2014* (Cth) changed the calculation of excise and excise-equivalent customs duty for fuels (other than aviation fuels); set the rate of duty at 38.6 cent per litre for liquid fuels, 10.1 cents per litre for LPG, and 21.2 cents per kilogram for CNG and LNG; and reintroduced biannual indexation of these rates in line with the CPI. These changes took effect from 10 November 2014.

II. Current Structure of Fuel Taxation

732. Under the *Excise Tariff Act 1921* (Cth), excise is levied on fuels and petroleum products that are produced or manufactured in Australia.[1067] 'Excisable goods' relevant to energy include: petroleum fuels (petrol and diesel); gaseous fuels; biofuels; crude oil and condensate; and recycled fuels and fuels products. A person who delivers fuel products into the Australian domestic market for home consumption must, in most cases, lodge an excise return and pay excise duty. Also, an excise licence from the ATO is required to manufacture excisable fuel products. The excise rates on different fuels and petroleum products are set out in the Schedule to the *Excise Tariff Act 1921* (Cth).[1068] With the exception of aviation fuels, excise rates are indexed twice a year in line with the CPI on 1 February and 1 August.[1069] Imported fuel products are 'excise equivalent good' (EEGs) and are subject to an equivalent customs duty instead of excise duty, unless (with the exception of biofuels) they are used in excise manufacture. The Australian Taxation Office maintains a table showing updated excise rates for fuel on its website.[1070]

733. Crude oil excise is imposed on eligible crude oil and condensate production.[1071] This includes 'stabilised crude petroleum oil' (SCPO) (crude oil with the volatile gases removed), 'topped crude oil' (crude petroleum that has been treated, as by distillation, to remove some of its lighter components), and condensate (a form of hydrocarbon

---

1066. *Ibid.*

1067. *Excise Tariff Act 1921* (Cth) s. 5 and Sch.

1068. These are also available online at the Australian Taxation Office website https://www.ato.gov.au/Business/Excise-and-excise-equivalent-goods/Fuel-excise/Excise-rates-for-fuel/ (accessed 1 Feb. 2016). Customs duty is levied under the *Customs Act 1901* (Cth) and *Customs Tariff Act 1995 (Cth)*.

1069. *Excise Tariff Act 1921*, s. 6A.

1070. Australian Taxation Office, *Excise Rates for Fuel*, https://www.ato.gov.au/Business/Excise-and-excise-equivalent-goods/Fuel-excise/Excise-rates-for-fuel/ (accessed 23 Sept. 2016).

1071. *Excise Tariff Act 1921*, ss 6A, 6B, 6CA and 6D and Sch., Items 20 and 21; and Sch., Item 10.

that is liquid at standard temperature and pressure).[1072] Excise is levied on production from State and Northern Territory coastal waters, onshore areas, and from the North West Shelf Project Area in Commonwealth waters.

734. SCPO and condensate attract excise duty under Items 20 and 21 of the Schedule to the *Excise Tariff Act 1921* (Cth). To ascertain the formula/rate of excise to be applied to SCPO, Item 20 distinguishes between the imposition of excise duty on 'old oil', 'new oil' and 'intermediate oil' calculated under sections 6B, 6C, and 6D of the *Excise Tariff Act 1921* (Cth) respectively.[1073] Item 21 refers the rate of excise for condensate to be calculated under section 6CA of the *Excise Tariff Act 1921* (Cth). Excise liability is calculated applying the relevant crude oil excise rate to the volume-weighted average of realised (selling) prices ('VOLWARE price') of crude oil/condensate produced from a producing field in a financial year.[1074] The first 4,767.3 megalitres of SCPO and condensate from a field (approximately 30 million barrels) are exempt from excise.[1075]

735. Crude oil and condensate from a PRRT area are not subject to excise duty under Items 20 and 21. However, petroleum condensate and SCPO also attract excise duty under Items 10.1 and 10.2 of the Schedule respectively, at a rate of AUD 0.396 per litre from 1 August 2016, unless used in the recovery, production, pipeline transportation or refining of condensate or stabilised crude oil, or as feedstock at a licensed refinery.[1076] 'Topped crude oil' attracts excise under Item 10.3 of the Schedule.

736. Excise duty applies to transport gaseous fuels that are 'delivered out of a licensed excise manufacturing or storage premises and into the Australian domestic market. Delivery into the Australian domestic market also occurs when gaseous fuels are used at the licensed premises'.[1077] Non-transport gaseous fuels are not subject to excise. Transport gaseous fuels include:[1078]

– LPG or LNG intended for use in an internal combustion engine of a motor vehicle or vessel, either directly or by filling another tank connected to such an engine;

1072. Australian Taxation Office, *Crude Oil and Condensate*, https://www.ato.gov.au/Business/Excise-and-excise-equivalent-goods/Fuel-excise/Crude-oil-and-condensate/ (accessed 25 Sept. 2016).

1073. 'Old' oil is crude oil from fields discovered before 18 Sept. 1975; 'new' oil is crude oil from fields discovered after 18 Sept. 1975; while 'intermediate oil' is crude oil from fields discovered after 18 Sept. 1975 but not developed before 23 Oct. 1984: *Excise Tariff Act 1921* (Cth), ss 6A, 6B and 6D.

1074. *Excise Tariff Act 1921*, s. 6AB. The VOLWARE price is determined under the *Petroleum Excise (Prices) Act 1987* (Cth) s. 7.

1075. *Excise Tariff Act 1921*, s. 3 and Sch.

1076. Australian Taxation Office, *Excise Rates for Fuel*, https://www.ato.gov.au/Business/Excise-and-excise-equivalent-goods/Fuel-excise/Excise-rates-for-fuel/ (accessed 23 Sept. 2016); *Excise Tariff Act 1921*, Sch., Item 10; *Excise Act 1901*, s. 77K.

1077. Australian Taxation Office, *Gaseous Fuels*, https://www.ato.gov.au/Business/Excise-and-excise-equivalent-goods/Fuel-excise/Gaseous-fuels/ (accessed 25 Sept. 2016).

1078. Australian Taxation Office, *ibid.*; *Excise Tariff Act 1921*, Sch., Item 10; *Excise Act 1901*, ss 77HA and 77HB.

- CNG for use as a fuel in a motor vehicle – excluding CNG compressed at a residential premises using equipment capable of compression at a rate not more than 10 kilograms of natural gas per hour and not for sale; and
- all gaseous fuels for mixed use (i.e., both transport and non-transport use) or where the end use is unknown.[1079]

737. The production of diesel is subject to excise duty, at a rate of AUD 0.396 per litre from 1 August 2016.[1080]

738. In relation to biofuels, excise duty is payable on blends of fuel, including blends of gasoline and ethanol, and blends of diesel and biodiesel and/or ethanol.[1081] Generally, the total volume of a fuel blend will be subject to excise duty less any customs duty or excise duty that has previously been paid on any fuel components.[1082] Thus, the amount of duty paid depends on whether (and which) components of the blended fuel have been imported and customs duty paid, and the percentage of the blend attributable to each type of component fuel. Common fuel blends are: **B5**, a blend of biodiesel and diesel that contains no more than 5% biodiesel; **B20**, a blend of biodiesel and diesel that contains no more than 20% biodiesel; **E10**, a blend of fuel ethanol and petrol that contains no more than 10% ethanol; and **E85**, a blend of fuel ethanol and petrol that generally contains more than 70% but no more than 85% ethanol.[1083]

739. The Excise Tariff Act was amended in 2015 to introduce excise duty on denatured ethanol and biodiesel from 1 July 2016.[1084] The rates of excise duty are being phased in gradually, with full rates applying from 1 July 2030 for biodiesel and 1 July 2020 for fuel ethanol, and are based on a percentage of the rates that apply to diesel (50% for biodiesel) and petrol (32.77% for fuel ethanol).[1085]

1079. Australian Taxation Office, *Gaseous Fuels*, *supra* n. 1077.

1080. *Excise Tariff Act 1921*, Sch., Item 10.10; Australian Taxation Office, *Excise Rates for Fuel*, https://www.ato.gov.au/Business/Excise-and-excise-equivalent-goods/Fuel-excise/Excise-rates-for-fuel/ (accessed 25 Sept. 2016).

1081. *Excise Tariff Act 1921*, Sch., Items 10.7 and 10.12.

1082. Australian Taxation Office, *Your excise obligations on excisable fuel blends* https://www.ato.gov.au/Business/Excise-and-excise-equivalent-goods/In-detail/Fuel/Fuel-blending/?anchor=Yourexciseobligationsonexcisableblends#Yourexciseobligationsonexcisableblends (accessed 25 Sept. 2016).

1083. Australian Taxation Office, *Biofuels* https://www.ato.gov.au/Business/Excise-and-excise-equivalent-goods/Fuel-excise/Biofuels (accessed 25 Sept. 2016).

1084. *Excise Tariff Amendment (Ethanol and Biodiesel) Act* 2015 (Cth). *See* *Excise Tariff Act 1921*, Sch., Items 10.20 and 10.2.

1085. *Excise Tariff Act 1921*, s. 6G and Sch., Items 10.7, 10.12 and 10.30 (rates for blended biofuels); s. 6H and Sch., Item 10.20 (rates for ethanol); and s. 6J and Sch., Item 10.21 (rates for biodiesel).

§5. Fuel Schemes: Fuel Tax Credits and Grants

740. 'Fuels schemes provide credits and grants to reduce the costs of some fuels or to provide a benefit to encourage the recycling of waste oils.'[1086] Various fuels schemes have been introduced in Australia in the past to reduce the costs of some fuels, in particular to ease the burden of fuel taxation, for example, the Diesel Fuel Rebate Scheme (DFRS). More recently, following the introduction of the GST and general tax reform after the Henry Tax Review, various grants schemes were introduced from 2000. These included the Fuel Sales Grant Scheme, the Energy Grants Credit Scheme (incorporating diesel fuel rebates), the Energy Grants (Cleaner Fuels) Scheme, and the Product Stewardship (Oil) Scheme.

741. The DFRS, introduced in 1982,[1087] was extended after the Henry Tax Review to include 'like fuels' and extended to rail and marine transport, and the Diesel and Alternative Grants Fuel Scheme (DAFGS) introduced, to reduce costs for road transport. A DAFGS grant was payable for diesel and alternative fuels (such as ethanol, LPG, CNG, recycled diesel and canola oil) while a DFRS rebate was only available for diesel and 'like fuels' (heavy fuel oil, light fuel oil and fuels that attract the same rate of duty as diesel, except for petrol, coal tar and coke oven distillates).[1088] In 2003, the DAFGS and DFRS were brought within the Energy Grants (Credits) Scheme (EGCS) introduced under the *Energy Grants (Credits) Scheme Act 2003* (Cth). The EGCS provided a fuel grant/offset for businesses that purchased off-road diesel and/or alternative fuels (LPG, LNG, CNG, ethanol and biodiesel) used for road transport before 1 July 2010. The *Energy Grants (Credits) Scheme Act 2003* (Cth) was repealed on 1 July 2012.[1089]

742. The Cleaner Fuels Grants Scheme, which was introduced by the *Energy Grants (Cleaner Fuels) Scheme Act 2004* and operated to 1 July 2015, aimed to encourage the manufacture or importation of fuels that have a reduced impact on the environment. Taxpayers who manufactured or imported eligible 'cleaner' fuels could claim a cleaner fuel grant to offset excise duty or customs duty payable. Eligible fuels were biodiesel, CNG, ethanol, LNG, LPG or methanol, for use as fuel in an internal combustion engine, and which met applicable fuel standards. The *Energy Grants (Cleaner Fuels) Scheme Act 2004* was repealed from 1 July 2015.[1090]

743. The Fuels Sales Grants Scheme (FSGS) was introduced to maintain regional and metropolitan price relativities on the introduction of the GST. It provided registered retailers with grants of one cent per litre in non-metropolitan zones and two cents per litre in 'remote' zones, with an additional grant of one cent per litre where the fuel price is consistently over AUD 1.21. It was repealed on 1 January 2007.[1091]

1086. Australian Taxation Office, *Fuel Schemes*, https://www.ato.gov.au/Business/Fuel-schemes/ (accessed 12 Feb. 2015).

1087. *See* n. 1058 above.

1088. *See* David Trebeck et al., *Fuel Taxation Inquiry Report* (Commonwealth of Australia, March 2002).

1089. By the *Fuel Tax (Consequential and Transitional Provisions) Act 2006* (Cth), section 23.

1090. By the *Energy Grants and Other Legislation Amendment (Ethanol and Biodiesel) Act 2015* (Cth), s. 13.

1091. By the *Fuel Tax (Consequential and Transitional Provisions) Act 2006*, s. 8.

744. These three grants schemes have been abolished and replaced by the current fuel tax credits scheme, which is now the major scheme for reducing the burden of fuel taxation on certain taxpayers (*see* below). The Product Stewardship for Oil Scheme (PSO), established from 1 January 2001 as part of the *Measures for a Better Environment* package accompanying *A New Tax System*, remains in effect. The object of the PSO is to encourage the sustainable management of used oil. Under the programme, customs and excise duty levied on petroleum-based oil or their synthetic equivalents is used to provide a benefit in cents per litre to recyclers of used oil and oils gazetted in the Product Stewardship (Oil) Regulations 2000. There are 8 categories of oil, each with a benefit rate (categories 1–7 for recycling used oil and category 8 for gazetted oils or eligible oils in a gazetted use). Taxpayers seeking to claim a benefit under the PSO must hold an excise manufacturer's licence from the ATO, and report and pay excise duty on any eligible recycled products.[1092]

I. Fuel Tax Credits for Business

745. The Australian government introduced a single system of fuel credits on 1 July 2006, through the *Fuel Tax Act 2006* (Cth). Fuel tax credits provide businesses with a credit for the fuel tax that is included in the price of fuels used in machinery, plant, equipment and heavy vehicles. Eligible businesses must be registered for GST and fuel tax credits before a claim can be made. Fuel tax credit rates change regularly, and the amount of the credit depends upon the date the fuel was acquired, the fuel that is used, and the activity for which the fuel is used.[1093]

746. Fuel that has had no fuel tax paid on it – that is, excise or customs duty – is not eligible for fuel tax credits.[1094] Eligible liquid fuels are: petrol, diesel, other fuels, such as kerosene, mineral turpentine, white spirit, toluene, heating oil and some solvents, and blended fuels, including biodiesel and ethanol blends. Fuel tax credits may be claimed for transport gaseous fuels (LPG, LNG and CNG) used in business activities and acquired from 1 December 2011.[1095] Aviation fuels (aviation gasoline and aviation kerosene) are ineligible fuels.[1096]

747. As at 30 June 2016, biodiesel or fuel ethanol were ineligible fuels, unless they were part of a blend with another fuel. From the 2016–2017 financial year, blends containing no more than 20% biodiesel (e.g., B5 and B20) are considered to be 100% diesel and eligible for fuel tax credits at the diesel rate on the entire amount, and blends containing no more than 10% fuel ethanol (e.g., E10) are considered to be 100% petrol

1092. Australian Taxation Office, *Product Stewardship for Oil Scheme*, https://www.ato.gov.au/Business/Fuel-schemes/Product-stewardship-for-oil-program/ (accessed 25 Sept. 2015).

1093. Australian Taxation Office, *Fuel tax credits – business*, https://www.ato.gov.au/Business/Fuel-schemes/Fuel-tax-credits---business/ (accessed 25 Sept. 2016).

1094. *Fuel Tax Act 2006* (Cth), ss 43-5, 43-6.

1095. Australian Taxation Office, *Eligible fuels*, https://www.ato.gov.au/Business/Fuel-schemes/Fuel-tax-credits---business/Eligibility/Eligible-fuels/ (accessed 25 Sept. 2016).

1096. *Fuel Tax Act 2006*, s. 41-30.

and eligible for fuel tax credits at the petrol rate on the entire amount. Other blends are eligible for fuel tax credits depending on the excise duty paid on them.[1097]

748. Fuel tax credits are only available for 'eligible activities'. One of these is 'road transport': the use of heavy vehicles travelling on public roads, if the vehicle is used in carrying on a business and has a GMV greater than 4.5 tonnes, which meet certain environmental criteria. Fuels used in light vehicles (4.5 tonnes GMV or less), travelling on public roads, are not eligible fuels for the heavy vehicle road transport fuel tax credit.[1098]

749. Second, fuel tax credits can also be claimed for eligible fuels used in carrying on a business, including fuels used in light vehicles travelling off public roads (for example, at work sites and mining sites), on private roads, and for non-fuel uses. A very wide range of business activities are eligible, including electricity generation by commercial generator plant, stationary generator or a portable generator.[1099]

750. Third, fuel tax credits can be claimed in relation to the packaging and supply of fuel.[1100] Fuel tax credits can be claimed when certain eligible fuels are packaged in containers of 20 litres or less for use other than in an internal combustion engine. Fuel tax credits can also be claimed for transport LPG (duty paid) when it is supplied in or into: cylinders of 210 kg capacity or less for a non-transport use; or tanks at residential premises for non-transport use at those premises. Fuel tax credits cannot be claimed for non-transport LPG as no duty has been paid on it.[1101]

751. As with rates of excise, fuel tax credit rates are indexed twice a year, in February and August. Also, the Australian government levies a Road User Charge on fuel used in heavy vehicles travelling on public roads, which is reviewed annually, and which must be included in the calculation of fuel tax credits in relation to the cost of fuels used in heavy vehicles.[1102] There are different rates for liquid, gaseous and blended fuels. On its website, the Australian Taxation Office maintains Tables showing fuel tax credit rates for business.[1103]

1097. Section 43-7; Australian Taxation Office, *Fuel blends*, https://www.ato.gov.au/Business/Fuel-schemes/In-detail/Specific-activities-for-fuel-tax-credits/Fuel-blends/ (accessed 25 Sept. 2016).

1098. *Fuel Tax Act 2006*, ss 41-20, 41-25; Australian Taxation Office, *Heavy vehicles*, https://www.ato.gov.au/Business/Fuel-schemes/In-detail/Specific-activities-for-fuel-tax-credits/Heavy-vehicles/ (accessed 25 Sept. 2016).

1099. *Fuel Tax Act 2006*, s. 41-5; Australian Taxation Office, *All other business uses*, https://www.ato.gov.au/business/fuel-schemes/fuel-tax-credits---business/eligibility/eligible-activities/all-other-business-uses/ (accessed 25 Sept. 2016).

1100. *Fuel Tax Act* 2006, s. 41-10.

1101. Australian Taxation Office, *Packaging or supplying fuels*, https://www.ato.gov.au/business/fuel-schemes/fuel-tax-credits---business/eligibility/eligible-activities/packaging-or-supplying-fuel/ (accessed 25 Sept. 2016).

1102. *Fuel Tax Act 2006,* s. 43-10. Heavy vehicle charges include registration charges for heavy vehicles administered and collected by State and Territory governments under State laws and the Road User Charge (RUC) levied by the Australian Government on the fuel used by heavy vehicles. The RUC is determined by the Transport and Infrastructure Council, a forum of Ministers from the Australian, State and Territory governments.

1103. Australian Taxation Office, *Rates –business*, https://www.ato.gov.au/Business/Fuel-schemes/Fuel-tax-credits---business/Rates---business/ (accessed 16 Feb. 2016).

II. Fuel Tax Credits for Non-business Taxpayers

752. Fuel tax credits are available for non-business taxpayers – that is, taxpayers not registered, or required to be registered, for the GST – for fuel used in generating electricity for domestic use (for use in a home, house or household).[1104] The house must be the main place of residence, and fuel tax credits cannot be claimed for electricity generated for recreational purposes. Eligible fuels are diesel and petrol; LPG, LNG and CNG upon which fuel taxation has been paid; and common blends of biodiesel and ethanol, namely B5, E10, B20 and E85. For diesel, petrol, and biodiesel and ethanol blends B5, E10, B20, the rate of fuel tax credit from 1 February 2016 is 39.6 cents per litre. The rates of credit for LPG, LNG and CNG upon which fuel taxation has been paid are zero, as the packager/supplier of LPG will have already claimed the fuel tax rebate; and LNG and CNG supplied for domestic electricity generation will rarely have excise duty levied upon it.[1105] Rates are indexed biannually in February and August, in line with the CPI.

§6. Income Tax: Deductions and Offsets

I. Deductions for Mining and Petroleum

753. Under the ITAA97, special tax concessions are available for taxpayers in the business of general mining (which is relevant to this chapter in that general mining includes coal mining) and petroleum mining.[1106] These are set out in subdivisions 40-H and 40-I of the ITAA97. The most significant are deductions for capital expenditure incurred in the course of exploration, prospecting and mining, which reduce the taxpayer's amount of taxable income. Some deductions are immediate (deductible at the time the cost is incurred); others are deductible over a period of time (e.g., the cost of depreciating assets is usually deductible over the effective life of the asset).[1107] The tax concessions for general mining and petroleum mining operate in addition to the general deductions allowed for operating expenses under the ITAA97. However, if capital expenditure is deducted under the special mining provisions of the ITAA97, it cannot be deducted under any other sections of the Act.

754. Immediate deductions may be claimed for expenditure on eligible 'exploration or prospecting' activities for minerals (which includes coal) and petroleum by 'mining operations' conducted for the purpose of producing assessable income.[1108] For coal,

1104. *Fuel Tax Act 2006*, s. 42-5. Also, not-for-profit organisations can claim fuel tax credits, for heavy emergency vehicles travelling on public roads, private roads and off-road.

1105. Australian Taxation Office, *Table 1: Fuel tax credit rates for fuels acquired from 1 Jul. 2016*, https://www.ato.gov.au/business/fuel-schemes/fuel-tax-credits---non-business/rates---non-business/from-1-july-2016/ (accessed 25 Sept. 2016).

1106. For more information, *see* Woellner et al., *supra* n. 1009, at ¶21-200–¶21-270.

1107. For immediate deductions, *see* *Income Tax Assessment Act 1997*, subdiv. 40-H; for deductions over a period of time, *see* subdiv. 40-I.

1108. Section 40-730.

'mining operations' are mining operations on a mining property for extracting the coal from its natural site. For petroleum, 'mining operations' means mining operations for the purpose of obtaining petroleum.[1109] However, an immediate deduction is not allowable for expenditure on development drilling for petroleum, or operations in the course of working a mining property or petroleum field; these may be deducted over time.[1110]

755. The type of 'exploration and prospecting' activities for which expenditure may be deducted is, for coal mining, geographical mapping, geophysical surveys, systematic search for areas containing coal, search by drilling and other means, search for ore within or in the vicinity of an ore body, and feasibility studies to evaluate the economic feasibility of mining once coal has been discovered. It also includes obtaining mining information associated with the search for, and evaluation of, areas containing minerals. For petroleum mining, the activities include: geological, geophysical and geochemical surveys; exploration drilling and appraisal drilling; and feasibility studies to evaluate the economic feasibility of mining once petroleum has been discovered.[1111] 'Petroleum' does not include coal and oil shale.[1112]

756. An immediate deduction is also available expenditure on depreciating assets acquired after 30 June 2001 – including expenditure on mining or prospecting rights and information (as intangible assets) – where the assets are first used for exploration or prospecting.[1113] At the time the asset is first used, it must not be for development drilling for petroleum, or operations in the course of working a mining property or petroleum field.

757. Immediate deductions are also allowable for expenditure on the rehabilitation of mining or petroleum sites upon which a taxpayer conducted eligible mining operations, exploration of prospecting, for activities ancillary to eligible mining operations.[1114] 'Rehabilitation' is the act of resting or rehabilitating a site or part of a site to its pre-mining condition or to a reasonable approximation of that condition, and includes the removal of offshore petroleum platforms. In certain very limited circumstances, it may also include expenditure on geological sequestration.[1115]

758. Deductions may be claimed for allowable capital expenditure on developing or operating a mine site or petroleum field, and is deductible over the estimated life of the project. Expenditure deductible over time includes expenditure incurred on carrying on eligible mining operations, as well as expenditure incurred on: preparing a site for mining operations; buildings and other improvements necessary to carry on such operations; buildings for use directly in connection with operating or maintaining plant for treating minerals produced by the operation; buildings and other improvements

---

1109. Subsection 40-730(7).
1110. Subsection 40-730(2).
1111. Subsections 40-730(4), (8). On the meaning of expenditure on 'exploration and prospecting', *see* further *Taxation Ruling* TR 98/23.
1112. *See* definition of petroleum in *Income Tax Assessment Act 1997*, subs. 40-730(6) and *Esso Australia Resources Ltd v. FC of T* (1998) 84 FCR 541.
1113. *Income Tax Assessment Act 1997*, s. 40-80, subs. 40-30(2).
1114. Subsection 40-735.
1115. *Taxation Ruling* TR 2008/6.

for storing minerals to facilitate treating them; and on housing and welfare of mining employees and their dependants.[1116]

759. Finally, capital expenditure on transport facilities and ancillary works used primarily and principally for transporting the products of mining operations away from the site of operation is deductible over the life of the project (but not the cost of a depreciating asset, which must be claimed under the general provisions).[1117]

II. Income Tax Deductions: Environmental Protection

760. Energy companies such as coal and petroleum mining companies may be able to deduct certain expenditures on environmental protection activities under general provisions in the ITAA97. The Act provides an immediate deduction for expenditure that is for the 'sole or dominant purpose of carrying on environmental protection activities'.[1118] 'Environmental protection activities' are activities carried on to prevent, fight or remedy pollution resulting from the taxpayer's earning activities, or carried on to treat, clean up, remove or store waste from the taxpayer's earning activities.[1119] An 'earning activity' is an activity carried on for the purpose of producing assessable income; for the purpose of exploration or prospecting; or for the purpose of mining site rehabilitation.[1120]

761. Expenditure on the geological sequestration of gases may be deductible, if it is done to prevent, fight or remedy pollution resulting from the taxpayer's earning activities, or is carried on to treat, clean up, remove or store waste from the taxpayer's earning activities.[1121] 'Environmental protection earthworks' are capital works that are deductible if they are constructed as part of carrying out an environmental protection activity; can be economically maintained in good working order and condition for an indefinite period; are not integral to the construction of capital works; and if the expenditure on the earthworks was incurred after 18 August 1992.[1122]

III. Income Tax: Research and Development

762. The R&D Tax Incentive took effect from 1 July 2011.[1123] It aims to 'boost competitiveness and improve productivity across the Australian economy' and encourage more companies to engage in R&D activities, particularly those activities most likely to result in public benefits in (and from) generating new information which, in the

1116. *Income Tax Assessment Act 1997*, s. 40-860.
1117. Sections 40-865–40-875.
1118. Subsection 40-755(1).
1119. Subsection 40-755(2).
1120. Subsection 40-755(3).
1121. *Taxation Ruling* TR 2008/6.
1122. *Income Tax Assessment Act 1997*, subs. 43-20(5).
1123. Division 355. This incentive replaces the previous Research and Development Tax Concession.

absence of the incentive, might not otherwise take place because of uncertain returns.[1124] The ATO and AusIndustry, on behalf of Innovation Australia, jointly administer the incentive.[1125]

763. While the incentive is of general application across the economy, it is of importance to the energy sector in general, and the clean energy industry in particular. A significant amount of R&D already occurs in the energy sector – covering the supply chain from energy generation through to retail and the consumer and encompasses energy storage, electricity generation/distribution, transport fuels and emerging renewable energy technologies – a trend that is 'likely to grow as companies seek to develop cleaner and renewable technologies for domestic and international markets'.[1126]

764. However, with the exception of energy efficiency, the capital intensity of the energy industry is a barrier to development of new technology for small to medium enterprises, particularly where R&D requires demonstration at some scale before it is considered commercially viable. Without innovation through R&D, 'alternative forms of generating and delivering energy, novel ways to monitor, manage and reduce energy consumption or ways to decarbonise existing energy sources will not secure the investment vital to driving them down the cost curve and into the commercial arena'.[1127] For energy companies, the R&D tax incentive can be 'a powerful driver to help create new products, processes and services'.[1128]

765. The tax incentive provides 'eligible entities' with a tax offset for expenditure on 'eligible R&D activities' and for the decline in value of depreciating assets used on eligible R&D activities. Generally only R&D undertaken in Australia qualifies for the incentive, although Innovation Australia can approve R&D activity to be conducted overseas if certain statutory conditions are met.[1129] 'Eligible activities' are classified as either 'core' or 'supporting' R&D activities.[1130] Core activities are essentially 'experimental activities' whose outcome cannot be known in advance, conducted on the basis of established science, for the purpose of acquiring new knowledge (including about creating new knowledge or improved materials, products, devices, processes or services), whereas 'supporting activities' are activities directly related to core R&D activities, or for certain activities, are undertaken for the dominant purpose of conducting core R&D activities.[1131]

766. Only 'eligible entities' – called R&D entities – may claim the incentive. 'Eligible entities' include corporations resident in Australia for tax purposes, foreign corporations that carry out R&D activities though a permanent establishment in

1124. Subsection 355-5(1); Australian Taxation Office, 'About the Program' (19 Nov. 2015) (accessed 2 Feb. 2016).

1125. The administrative scheme and rules for the Incentive, including the role of Innovation Australia, are set out in the *Industry Research and Development Act 1986* (Cth).

1126. Australian Government, Department of Industry and Science, *The R&D Tax Incentive: Energy Guidance*, 1 (Commonwealth of Australia, 2015).

1127. Mark Bonnar, *The R&D Tax Incentive and Australia's Energy Sector*, July 2013, http://www.business.gov.au/grants-and-assistance/innovation-rd/RD-TaxIncentive/Program-Information/July2013/Pages/RDTaxIncentiveAustraliasEnergySector.aspx (accessed 17 Feb. 2015).

1128. Australian Government, Department of Industry and Science, *supra* n. 1126, at iv.

1129. *Industry Research and Development Act 1986* (Cth) s. 28D.

1130. *Income Tax Assessment Act 1997*, ss 355-25, 355-30.

1131. Sections 355-25, 355-30.

Australia, and public trading trusts with a corporate trustee.[1132] Individuals, exempt entities and other trusts are not eligible for the tax incentive. Special rules apply to consolidated groups and R&D partnerships.

767. A minimum expenditure ('notional deductions') of AUD20,000 is required to qualify for the incentive in any given financial year.[1133] Eligible entities with an aggregate turnover of less than AUD 20 million per year (unless they are a tax-exempt entity or are majority owned or controlled by tax-exempt entities) may be eligible for a 45% refundable tax offset (equivalent to a 150% deduction).[1134] For all other eligible entities, a 40% non-refundable tax offset (equivalent to a 133% deduction) is available. For the financial years starting 1 July 2014 and ending 30 June 2024, that portion of an entity's expenditure than exceeds AUD 100 million in a financial year is reduced to an R&D tax offset rate of 30%, equivalent to the company tax rate.

768. The R&D Tax Incentive is a self-assessed programme. Companies must self-assess whether an activity forms part of core or supporting R&D activity, register R&D activities with AusIndustry within ten months of the end of the company's financial year, and claim for expenditure relating to the registered activities in the company's tax return.

769. In March 2015, and in the 2015–2016 Budget released on 12 May 2015, the Australian Government indicated that it is committed to reducing the rates of assistance to 43.5% for eligible entities with a turnover under AUD 20 million per annum and not controlled by a tax-exempt entity, and 38.5% for all other eligible entities, to apply from 1 July 2014. In launching the National Innovation and Science Agenda on 7 December 2015, the Australian Government committed to undertaking a review of the R&D Tax Incentive, to 'identify opportunities to improve the effectiveness and integrity of the programme, including by sharpening its focus on encouraging additional R&D expenditure'.[1135] The Review is comprehensive, covering among other matters, the rates and thresholds, definition of eligible R&D, and administration. The Review concluded in April 2016 and the Government was considering its response, when parliament was prorogued on 17 April 2016, pending the federal election in July 2016. As of 25 September 2016, no changes had been made on the basis of the Review.

1132. Section 355-35.

1133. With the exceptions of research performed for an R&D entity by a Research Service Provider and contributions to a Cooperative Research Centre.

1134. The rate is calculated under the *Income Tax Assessment Act 1997*, s. 355-100.

1135. Australian Government, Department of Industry, Innovation and Science, *Review of the Research and Development (R&D) Tax Incentive,* https://www.business.gov.au/assistance/research-and-development-tax-incentive/review-of-the-randd-tax-incentive (accessed 25 Sept. 2016).

Part VII. Interaction Between Energy Law and Competition Law

Chapter 1. Background

§1. INTRODUCTION

770. Australia has a comprehensive regime of competition laws aimed at enhancing consumer welfare and promoting efficiency through competition.[1136] Activities within the energy sector are regulated by both by general competition laws which apply across the economy to prohibit anticompetitive conduct, and also by energy-sector specific laws. Some aspects of Australia's competition laws aim to create a level playing field by prohibiting certain forms of anticompetitive conduct. These include, for example, the application of the *Competition and Consumer Act 2010* (Cth) (formerly the *Trade Practices Act 1974* (Cth)) to both publicly and privately owned energy businesses, and the application of the principle of competitive neutrality to publicly owned energy businesses.[1137] Other systems of regulation, such as third-party access to services provided by monopoly infrastructure, and cross-ownership restrictions, are designed to promote competitive outcomes.

771. The current application of competition laws to the energy sector is most effectively understood within the historic context in which this application came about: the National Competition Policy reforms of the mid-1990s. Fundamental structural and regulatory reform occurred through these reforms to enable a competitive energy sector.

§2. REFORM OF PUBLICLY OWNED MONOPOLIES

772. Because of Australia's constitutional structure, for most of the twentieth century until the mid-1990s, electricity and gas services were predominately provided

1136. *Competition and Consumer Act 2010* (Cth), s. 2; *National Electricity Law* (schedule to the *National Electricity (South Australia) Act 1996* (SA)), s. 7; *National Gas Law* (schedule to the *National Gas (South Australia) Act 2008* (SA)), s. 23.

1137. Competition and Consumer Act, s. 2B and Pt. IV; *Competition Principles Agreement* (11 Apr. 1995), cl. 3.

and regulated by State and Territory governments. Large vertically integrated agencies or instrumentalities of the State or Territory governments provided utility services, which in some instances extended from the fuel source to delivery to the ultimate consumer.[1138] Utility service delivery was viewed as a public service provided by governments on terms and conditions which could be influenced by political considerations (for example, subsidised pricing).[1139]

773. Both the electricity and gas sectors underwent fundamental change as a consequence of the National Competition Policy Review, which reported to the federal government in 1993.[1140] This Review resulted in a series of intergovernmental agreements focused on microeconomic reform, including the Competition Principles Agreement.[1141] The Competition Principles Agreement required State governments to review and reorganise government business enterprises, including the publicly owned electricity and gas businesses.[1142]

774. The implementation of reform across the economy, led to a liberalised energy sector. For these changes to occur, however, certain preconditions to competitive energy markets needed to be present. These preconditions, which are examined in more detail in Chapter 2 below, were:

- removal of regulatory functions from publicly owned energy businesses;
- structural reform of publicly owned energy businesses;
- competitive neutrality in the operation of publicly owned energy businesses;
- regulatory frameworks designed respectively for competitive and natural monopoly elements of the electricity and gas sectors; and
- application of anticompetitive conduct laws to publicly owned energy businesses.

775. The implementation of these preconditions supported the entry of private sector energy businesses into the Australian energy sector by removing the advantages of public sector ownership. The shift to a mix of publicly and privately owned energy businesses was accelerated through the privatisation of energy businesses in South Australia and Victoria during the late 1990s. This privatisation was an outcome of the micro-economic reforms under the National Competition Policy, but had not been mandated by that policy. While other privatisation processes have occurred over the last two decades, some States and Territories retain ownership of electricity and gas businesses.[1143]

1138. For example, the Electricity Trust of South Australia (*Electricity Trust of South Australia Act 1946* (SA)).

1139. Hilmer F, Rayner M and Taperell G, *supra* n. 135, 5.

1140. *Ibid.*

1141. *Competition Principles Agreement*, *supra* n. 136.

1142. *Ibid.*, cl. 4.

1143. Australian Energy Regulator, *State of the Energy Market 2015* (Commonwealth of Australia, 2015) (updated February 2016).

Chapter 2. Preconditions to a Competitive Energy Sector

§1. Removal of Regulatory Functions from Publicly Owned Energy Businesses

776. As agencies or instrumentalities of government, the publicly owned government energy businesses could be agents of government policy, rather than simply utility service providers. For a level playing field to develop between publicly and privatelyowned businesses, the regulatory functions of the publicly owned businesses needed to be separated from the commercial functions of these agencies. It is axiomatic that a business should not be enabled to regulate its competitors.

777. As governments reviewed monopoly businesses with a view to creating competitive markets, regulatory functions were identified and divested from the government business.[1144] The separation of regulatory from commercial or service delivery functions of the publicly owned businesses was an initial step towards ensuring competitive neutrality between these businesses and the private sector businesses that would enter the energy sector.[1145]

778. The other impact was the emergence of independent regulators established by governments to oversee the economic, technical and consumer protection regulation of the sector. For example, the South Australian Independent Industry Regulator (SAIIR) (now the ESCOSA) was established in 1999 to regulate prices and licensing, monitor service standards and provide consumer protection with respect to prescribed industries.[1146] In fulfilling these functions, the SAIIR needed to have regard to a range of matters which had their origin in competition theory. These were to:

- promote competitive and fair market conduct;
- prevent misuse of monopoly or market power;
- facilitate entry into relevant markets;
- promote economic efficiency;
- ensure consumers benefit from competition and efficiency;
- protect the interests of consumers with respect to reliability, quality and safety of services and supply in regulated industries; and
- facilitate maintenance of the financial viability of regulated industries.[1147]

779. The State and Territory energy market regulators are established by legislation, but are intended to operate independently of governments. Consequently,

1144. *Competition Principles Agreement, supra* n. 136, cl. 4(2).
1145. *Ibid.*
1146. *South Australian Independent Industry Regulator Act 1999* (SA), subs. 5(1); *Essential Services Commission Act 2002* (SA), s. 5.
1147. South Australian Independent Industry Regulator Act, subs. 5(2); Essential Services Commission Act, s. 6.

the regulators are not subject to the direction of the responsible minister.[1148] Regulatory decisions are intended to be referrable to the regulatory framework established for the industry, rather than being influenced covertly by policy or politics.

§2. Structural Reform of Publicly Owned Energy Businesses

780. Clause 4 of the Competition Principles Agreement set out the process by which States and Territories would review the operations of their government-owned monopoly businesses, prior to introducing competition into the market traditionally serviced by the monopoly. Under clause 4, the States and Territories are required to consider a range of factors prior to introducing competition into these markets. These factors are:

- the appropriate commercial objectives for the public monopoly;
- the merits of separating any natural monopoly elements from potentially competitive elements of the public monopoly;
- the merits of separating potentially competitive elements of the public monopoly;
- the most effective means of separating regulatory functions from commercial functions of the public monopoly;
- the most effective means of implementing the competitive neutrality principles set out in the Competition Principles Agreement;
- the merits of any community service obligations undertaken by the public monopoly and the best means of funding and delivering any mandated community service obligations;
- the price and service regulations to be applied to the industry; and
- the appropriate financial relationships between the owner of the public monopoly and the public monopoly, including the rate of return targets, dividends and capital structure.[1149]

781. Within the requirements of the Competition Principles Agreement, the States and Territories were able to determine their own form of, and timetable for, structural reform. Consequently, the reform of gas and electricity businesses took various forms across the various States and Territories over different timeframes.[1150]

782. A key component of this review process was analysing the merits of separating potentially competitive and natural monopoly elements of the publicly owned business. In the gas and electricity sectors, publicly owned energy businesses were typically transformed from vertically integrated businesses into distinct business units focused on a functional element of the service delivery. Consequently, publicly owned electricity entities were disaggregated into generation, transmission, distribution and retail entities; while gas businesses were disaggregated into transmission, distribution and retail businesses. In some jurisdictions, the market was of a sufficient size to

1148. South Australian Independent Industry Regulator Act, s. 7; Essential Services Commission Act, s. 7.

1149. *Competition Principles Agreement*, *supra* n. 136, cl. 4(3).

1150. *Ibid.*, cl. 4(1).

warrant the further disaggregation of the government business within a functional level. For example, multiple generators or retailers were created from the publicly owned entity.

783. Generally, the States and Territories separated competitive elements (i.e., generation and retail) from natural monopoly elements (i.e., transmission or distribution), but in Victoria 'stapled' retail and distribution businesses were established and then privatised in 1997.[1151] A different model was adopted in New South Wales for the privatisation of its publicly owned generation business in 2010 with the splitting of the physical ability to generate electricity (generators) from the right to trade the output of the generation (gentrader).[1152]

784. The National Competition Policy did not mandate that publicly owned government businesses should be privatised. Initially, only Victoria and South Australia (1998) privatised their electricity and gas businesses. Over time, however, other jurisdictions have privatised some or all of their gas and electricity businesses. Australia's energy sector, however, remains characterised by a mix of privately and publicly owned energy businesses.[1153] Competition laws, both general and sector specific, apply equally to energy businesses in Australia regardless of ownership.

§3. Application of Competitive Neutrality

785. Governments were obliged by the Competition Principles Agreement to give effect to the principles of competitive neutrality. Competitive neutrality aims to eliminate resource allocation distortions arising out of public ownership of entities engaged in significant business activities.[1154] Private sector equivalency measures are applied to significant government businesses to achieve these objectives.

786. The highest level of private sector equivalency is corporatisation. The States and Territories which retained public sector ownership of their gas and electricity businesses adopted a corporatised model for these entities. Typically, the corporatised entity's commercial objectives were expressly stated; a board was established to govern the operations of the entity; and the financial relationship between the entity and its government shareholders were regularised by making subsidies for community service obligations overt and requiring the entity to return a dividend. Where governments retain ownership of electricity businesses today, these corporatised models remain in place.[1155]

1151. *Electricity Industry (Residual Provisions) Act 1993* (Vic).

1152. New South Wales Government, *Submission in support of application for authorisation lodged by the Treasurer, the Hon. Eric Roozendaal MLC, for and on behalf of Delta Energy, Eraring Energy and Macquarie Generation in relation to the co-insurance arrangement for the Energy Reform Strategy*, 14 http://registers.accc.gov.au/content/index.phtml/itemId/904369/fromItemId/401858/display/application (accessed 1 Mar. 2017).

1153. Australian Energy Regulator, *State of the Energy Market 2015*, *supra* n. 213, 125.

1154. *Competition Principles Agreement*, *supra* n. 136, cl. 3(1).

1155. For example, *Power and Water Corporation Act* (NT).

§4. Regulatory Frameworks for Competitive Electricity and Gas Segments

787. Disaggregation gave rise to a need to determine the appropriate form of regulation for the various functional levels within the electricity and gas industries. Regulatory issues differed between the competitive (generation and retail) and monopoly (transmission and distribution) elements of the energy sectors. For the competitive functions, the prominent regulatory issues were: opening the electricity and gas retail sectors to competition; consumer protection within competitive retail markets; access to markets for both retailers and suppliers of electricity and gas; restrictions on market dominance; and technical and market requirements.

I. Opening Markets to Competition

A. Retail Markets

788. The introduction of private sector competition into electricity and gas retail markets typically occurred in stages. Timetables to achieve 'full retail contestability' (FRC) were developed by governments and entrenched in legislation.[1156] These timetables released tranches of customers defined by the customer's consumption volumes for competitive service delivery over time.[1157] The States and Territories determined their own timetables for FRC. Until a tranche of customers was released for competition, the customers were subject to monopoly service provision, either by the incumbent public-owned business or by a private sector business with a concession to provide services to non-contestable customers.[1158] Non-contestable customers generally remained subject to price regulation and standard terms and conditions of supply.[1159]

B. Supply Markets

789. Prior to the National Competition Policy reforms of the mid-1990s, there was private sector supply of natural gas.[1160] Competition between suppliers of natural gas was, however, constrained by the physical limitations of the pipelines installed to transport the gas from the area of production to consumption centres. Key issues for producers of natural gas were, therefore, access to pipeline transportation services (*see* discussion below in relation to market access) and the development of new pipelines to support supply to alterative consumption centres and eventually basin-on-basin

1156. For example, *Electricity (General) Regulations 1997* (SA) (as in operation at 13 Dec. 1998), reg. 5B.
1157. For example, *Electricity (General) Regulations 1997* (SA) (revoked), reg. 5A.
1158. For example, *Electricity Act 1996* (SA) (as applying in 2000), s. 24.
1159. For example, *Electricity Act 1996* (SA) (as applying in 2000), ss 35A, 36.
1160. For example, Indenture (schedule to the *Cooper Basin Ratification Act 1975* (SA)).

competition. Currently, gas customers in Sydney, Melbourne, Canberra, Adelaide, Perth and Darwin receive gas from multiple basins and multiple pipelines.[1161]

790. As regards electricity, the NEM was established in 1998 and operates as a wholesale market for electricity in all jurisdictions other than the Northern Territory and Western Australia. The introduction of a competitive electricity generation sector also required regulated access to transmission networks to enable electricity to be transferred to consumers (*see* discussion below in relation to market access). A national interconnected grid extending throughout southern and eastern Australia enabled generators in NEM jurisdictions to compete.

II. Consumer Protection

791. The Australian Consumer Law applies general consumer protection provisions to all Australian businesses.[1162] Actions have been taken against energy companies for breaching the consumer protections set out in this legislation (or the preceding legislation set out in Part V of the Trade Practices Act) in relation to: illegal door-to-door selling practices;[1163] forming unsolicited agreements;[1164] misleading and deceptive conduct;[1165] and false or misleading representations.[1166]

792. More specifically in respect of the energy sector, consumer protection is regulated under a mixture of State and Territory laws and a national framework for consumer protection set out in the NECF.[1167] The application of laws schemes comprising the NECF does not apply in Western Australian or the Northern Territory and only partially applies in Victoria.[1168] As a consequence of the varying regulation, compliance with consumer protection requirements can be burdensome for energy businesses operating in multiple jurisdictions.

A. Retail Pricing

793. Retail price regulation persists in the ACT, Tasmania, Western Australia, Queensland and the Northern Territory for classes of customer prescribed by the

1161. Australian Energy Regulator, *State of the Energy Market 2015*, *supra* n. 213, 98.

1162. *Competition and Consumer Act 2010* (Cth), Sch. 2.

1163. *Australian Competition and Consumer Commission v. Neighbourhood Energy Pty Ltd* [2012] FCA 1357.

1164. *Ibid.*

1165. *Australian Competition and Consumer Commission v. AGL South Australia Pty Ltd* [2014] FCA 1369.

1166. *Australian Competition and Consumer Commission v. Energy Australia Pty Ltd* [2015] FCA 274; *Australian Competition and Consumer Commission v. Origin Energy Limited* [2015] FCA 55.

1167. *See* above, Part V: Regulatory Framework Concerning Electricity.

1168. In Victoria, Ch. 5A of the *National Electricity Rules* has applied since July 2016, but the *National Energy Retail Rules* have no application: *see* Australian Energy Market Commission, *Guide to the application of the NECF* (Australian Energy Market Commission, 2016).

relevant jurisdiction.[1169] In most of these jurisdictions, retail pricing is determined by the independent regulator, but in the Northern Territory this determination is made by the Territory government. Unsurprisingly, the greatest diversity in pricing occurs in those jurisdictions which have removed retail price regulation.[1170]

794. The NECF provides that standing offer pricing must be published by electricity and gas retailers.[1171] Standing offer pricing must be notified to the AER.[1172] The manner in which both standard offer and market offer pricing is presented to consumers is regulated by guideline issued by the AER to facilitate consumers comparing offers from different retailers.[1173]

B. *Standard Contracts*

795. Standard contracts or standing offers have been a feature of the consumer protection framework which has applied since competition was introduced into the electricity and gas sectors. Conceptually, smaller customers are protected by a default contract with terms and conditions approved by an independent regulator. Smaller customers can choose to take electricity and gas on the terms of the default contract or otherwise accept a market contract from the electricity or gas retailer. The NECF requires the adoption and publication of a standard contract by energy retailers.[1174] Model terms and conditions for these contracts are set out in the *NERR*.[1175] The ability of a retailer to vary these terms is limited.[1176]

C. *Marketing Conduct*

796. Direct marketing to customers through door-to-door sales and telemarketing has been the subject of detailed regulatory scrutiny by energy regulators and the ACCC.[1177] Requirements are set out in the *NERR* with respect to: the timing of information provision to a customer relative to the formation of a contract to provide retail services; the specific information which is to be provided to the customer; the

1169. *Independent Competition and Regulatory Commission (Price Direction for the Supply of Electricity to Small Customers on Standard Retail Contracts) Terms of Reference Determination 2016* (disallowable instrument DI2016–138, made under the *Independent Competition and Regulatory Commission Act 1997* (ACT), ss 15, 16); Office of the Tasmanian Economic Regulator, *Aurora Energy Pty Ltd 2016 Standing Offer Price Determination* (2016 Price-Regulated Retail Service Price Determination) (27 Jun. 2016); *Energy Operators (Electricity Generation and Retail Corporation) (Charges) By-laws 2006* (WA); Electricity Pricing Order issued under the *Electricity Reform Act* (NT) (22 Dec. 2016); *Electricity Act 1994* (Qld), subs. 90(1).
1170. Australian Energy Regulator, *State of the Energy Market 2015*, *supra* n. 213, 21.
1171. *National Energy Retail Law*, subs. 23(1).
1172. *National Energy Retail Law*, subs. 23(6).
1173. Australian Energy Regulator, *Retail Pricing Information Guidelines* (version 4) (August 2015), effective 1 Feb. 2016.
1174. *National Energy Retail Law*, subs. 25(1).
1175. *National Energy Retail Rules*, r. 12 and Sch. 1.
1176. *National Energy Retail Law*, subss 25(4) and (5).
1177. Australian Energy Regulator, *State of the Energy Market 2015*, *supra* n. 213, 21.

application of no contact lists; and compliance with indications that a person does not want to be canvassed or receive advertising materials.[1178]

D. Retailer of Last Resort

797. A competitive retail energy sector brings with it a risk of retailer failure. To avoid consumers being stranded without a supplier, jurisdictions have implemented retailer of last resort schemes.[1179]

E. Ombudsman Schemes

798. Industry funded ombudsman schemes are also a feature of the competitive gas and electricity retail sector in Australia.[1180] These independent bodies provide an avenue for the resolution of consumer complaints in respect of the delivery of services by energy retailers.[1181]

III. Market Access

A. Generic Access Regimes

799. Where monopoly service providers operate within a supply chain (for example, electricity or gas networks) regulation is required to ensure that the competitive elements of the supply chain are able to supply their products.[1182] Part IIIA of the Competition and Consumer Act was introduced as part of the National Competition Policy reforms to provide a means of seeking third-party access to services provided by means of declared infrastructure.[1183] Aside from the Part IIIA access regime, States retained an ability to seek certification of state-based access regimes which complied with criteria set out in the Competition Principles Agreement.[1184] Once certified, the state-based access regime takes precedence over the generic regime in Part IIIA.[1185]

1178. *National Energy Retail Rules*, Div. 10, Pt. 2.
1179. *National Energy Retail Law*, Pt. 6; *see* , for example, Australian Energy Regulator, http://www.aer.gov.au/retail-markets/retailer-failure/register-of-rolrs/agl-energy-sales-marketing-limited (accessed 1 Mar. 2017).
1180. For example, the Energy and Water Ombudsman of South Australia, the Energy and Water Ombudsman Victoria and the Energy and Water Ombudsman Queensland.
1181. *See* Australian Energy Regulator, *Making a Complaint*, http://www.aer.gov.au/consumers/making-a-complaint (accessed 1 Mar. 2017).
1182. *National Competition Policy Review*, *supra* n. 135, Ch. 11.
1183. *Competition and Consumer Act 2010* (Cth), Pt. IIIA.
1184. Competition and Consumer Act, s. 44N; *Competition Principles Agreement*, *supra* n. 136, cl. 6(3).
1185. Competition and Consumer Act, para. 44H(4)(e).

The Western Australian electricity network access regime was certified for this purpose on 17 July 2006 for a period of fifteen years.[1186]

B. Specific Access Regimes: Retail Markets

800. Regulation governs the ability of retailers to access markets by connecting to distribution networks in both the gas and electricity sectors. For example, licence condition applying to transmission and distribution companies may provide obligations ensuring that customers can access electricity or gas provided through the network.[1187] Customer connections are also provided for in the National Gas Rules and National Electricity Rules, and through provisions of the NECF which define the responsibilities of retailers and distributors to facilitate customer connections.[1188]

C. Specific Access Regimes: Supply Markets

801. Regulation can also provide rights of access to networks for the purposes of ensuring that electricity or gas can be supplied to consumers. For example, licence conditions applying to transmission and distribution companies may provide obligations with respect to granting other electricity entities the right to use or have access to the entity's network on non-discriminatory terms for the purpose of transmitting or distributing electricity.[1189]

802. Other access rights are provided through the National Gas Rules and the National Electricity Rules.[1190] Prior to the inclusion of third-party access provisions in the National Gas Law, a third-party access regime operated under an application of laws scheme. Established as a component of the National Competition Policy reforms, the *National Third Party Access Code for Natural Gas Pipeline Systems* operated until 1 July 2008.[1191]

IV. Market Dominance

803. Market dominance and the vertical integration of energy businesses can undermine competition. First, to prevent the formation of business entities that may be able to exercise power to undermine competition, in general, any mergers and

1186. National Competition Council, *Western Australian access regime for electricity networks: final recommendation* (12 Oct. 2005) and *Western Australia access regime for electricity services: decision on effectiveness of access regime – reasons for decision* (no date) http://ncc.gov.au/application/western_australian_electricity_network_services_access_regime/6 (accessed 1 Mar. 2017).

1187. *Electricity Act 1996* (SA), subs. 23(1)(i).

1188. *National Gas Rules* (version 33), Pt. 12A; *National Electricity Rules* (version 89), Ch. 5A; National Energy Customer Framework (version 7), Pt. 4.

1189. *Electricity Act 1996* (SA), para. 23(1)(h).

1190. *National Gas Rules* (version 33), Pt. 11; *National Electricity Rules* (version 89), Ch. 5.

1191. *National Third Party Access Code for Natural Gas Pipeline Systems*, set out in the *Gas Pipelines Access (South Australia) Act 1997* (SA), Sch. 2; also *see* above, Part II: Regulatory Framework Concerning Gas.

acquisitions which would have the purpose or effect (or likely effect) of substantially lessening competition are regulated under section 50 of the Competition and Consumer Act (*see* Chapter 3, below). Second, specific cross-ownership restrictions relevant to the energy sector were enacted at the time of the South Australian and Victorian privatisation processes to prevent market dominance and reintegration.[1192] In South Australia, these restrictions were subject to automatic expiry.[1193] In Victoria, government reviews led to the repeal of the restrictions.[1194]

V. Technical and Market Requirements

804. The electricity and gas sectors are heavily regulated in respect of technical and market requirements.[1195] These requirements are part of the competition law framework in that they ensure common standard of technical compliance, protect assets which are pivotal to the provision of services on a competitive basis (for example, transmission pipelines and networks) and mitigate the risks of negative externalities which may arise in respect of competitive service provision.

§5. Regulatory Frameworks for Natural Monopoly Electricity and Gas Segments

805. Different regulatory issues needed to be addressed with respect to the natural monopoly elements of a disaggregated energy sector. The most prominent issues were: economic regulation; service standards; network investment; access to markets for both retailers and suppliers of electricity and gas; restrictions on market dominance; and technical and market requirements. The issues of market access, market dominance and technical and market requirements are discussed at Chapter 2, §4, above. Issues relating to economic regulation, service standards and network investment are discussed in Parts II and V above, in relation to the regulatory frameworks for electricity and gas.

1192. *Electricity Act 1996* (SA) (as in operation until 31 Dec. 2002), Sch. 1; *Electricity Industry Act 2000* (Vic) (as in operation until 14 Apr. 2013), Pt. 3.
1193. *Electricity Act 1996* (SA) (as in operation until 31 Dec. 2002), cl. 2(2), Sch. 1.
1194. *Energy Legislation Amendment (Flexible Pricing and Other Matters) Act 2013* (Vic), s. 4.
1195. *See* above, Part V: Regulatory Framework Concerning Electricity and Part II: Regulatory Framework Concerning Gas.

Chapter 3. Application of Anticompetitive Conduct Laws to the Energy Sector

§1. OVERVIEW

806. Australian businesses are subject to the anticompetitive conduct laws set out in Part IV of the Competition and Consumer Act. The object of this Act is to 'enhance the welfare of Australian through the promotion of competition and fair trading and provision of consumer protection'.[1196]

807. Government business enterprises, including energy businesses have been subject to Part IV of the Competition and Consumer Act since 1996. The application of anticompetitive conduct laws equally to public sector and private sector energy businesses occurred through the National Competition Policy reforms.[1197] The *Competition Policy Reform Act 1995* (Cth) was applied as an application of laws scheme in each Australia jurisdictions to create a 'scheduled' version of Part IV of the Competition and Consumer Act known as the 'Competition Code'.[1198] The Competition Code and supporting application of laws scheme overcame constitutional limitations in the Commonwealth's ability to legislate to apply trade practices regulation to natural persons, corporations other than constitutional trading corporations, State government and State government instrumentalities.[1199]

808. The application of Part IV of the Competition and Consumer Act to State government and State government instrumentalities is subject to a 'carrying on a business' threshold so that governmental activities which do not constitute carrying on a business are not subject to the anticompetitive conduct prohibitions.[1200] By their nature and activities publicly owned energy businesses satisfy the 'carrying on a business' threshold and are consequently subject to Part IV of the Act in the same manner as privately owned energy businesses.[1201]

1196. *Competition and Consumer Act 2010* (Cth), s. 2.

1197. The *Competition Policy Reform Act 1995* (Cth) was applied as an application of laws scheme in each Australia jurisdictions to create a 'scheduled' version of Part IV of the Competition and Consumer Act.

1198. Competition and Consumer Act, Sch. 1.

1199. For an example of the application of laws legislation *see Competition Policy Reform (South Australia) Act 1996* (SA).

1200. *Competition and Consumer Act 2010* (Cth), s. 2B. The Commonwealth Government is considering removing the 'carrying on a business' threshold: *see Australian Government Response to the Competition Policy Review* (Commonwealth of Australia, 2015) 20.

1201. *NT Power Generation Pty Ltd v. Power and Water Authority* [2004] HCA 48.

§2. General Application of Part IV

809. Part IV of the Competition and Consumer Act prohibits a wide range of anticompetitive conduct. While energy businesses are subject to each of the provisions of Part IV of the Competition and Consumer Act, some of these provisions are of greater relevance than others to the electricity and gas industries. The relevance of these provisions to particular activities in the energy sectors are described at Chapter 3, §3below. This section will provide a very brief general overview of the key anticompetitive provisions of Part IV of the Act.

I. Conduct Prohibited by Part IV of the Competition and Consumer Act

810. As a summary, Part IV prohibits the following conduct:

- cartel conduct (price fixing; restricting outputs in the production or supply chain; allocating customers, suppliers or territories; and bid rigging);[1202]
- entering into, or giving effect to, a contract, arrangement or understanding which has the purpose, effect or likely effect of substantially lessening competition;[1203]
- exclusionary provisions (conduct which leads to a boycott of a person or class of person);[1204]
- misuse of market power for a proscribed purpose;[1205]
- third line forcing (the supply of goods or services on the condition that other goods or services are acquired from an unrelated third party);[1206]
- exclusive dealing by tying (bundling) products or services from a single supplier in manner which has the purpose or effect of substantially lessening competition;[1207]
- resale price maintenance;[1208] and
- mergers and acquisitions which would have the effect of substantially lessening competition.[1209]

811. These anticompetitive conduct provisions can be conceptualised as being either: per se offences where the impact of the conduct on competition is irrelevant to determining whether or not a contravention has occurred; or offences which require a substantial lessening of competition to be proven in order to establish the offence. The concept of 'substantial lessening of competition' is not defined in the Competition and Consumer Act. Courts have interpreted this phrase to require an impact on

1202. *Competition and Consumer Act 2010* (Cth), s. 44ZZRA.
1203. Paragraphs 45(2)(a)(ii), 45(2)(b)(ii).
1204. Section 4D, paras 45(2)(a)(i), 45(2)(b)(i).
1205. Section 46.
1206. Subsections 47(6), (7).
1207. Section 47.
1208. Section 48.
1209. Section 50.

competition which is 'meaningful or relevant to the competitive process'.[1210] To determine this, courts consider a counterfactual focused on the relevant market with and without the impugned conduct.[1211]

812. The term 'market' in the Competition and Consumer Act generally refers to a market in Australia defined by reference to the goods and services which are substitutable.[1212] Australian courts adopt the following description:

> We take the concept of a market to be basically a very simple idea. A market is the area of close competition between firms or, putting it a little differently, the field of rivalry between them ... Within the bounds of the mark there is substitution – substitution between one product and another, and between one source of supply and another, in response to changing prices.[1213]

To determine substitutability, four market dimensions are considered:

(1) ***product***: identify the goods or services (as relevant) which a consumer would consider substitutable;
(2) ***geographic***: determine the geographic range in which a consumer would source a good or service (e.g., local, regional, national, international);
(3) ***functional***: determine the functional level of an industry at which the goods or services are provided (e.g., wholesale, retail); and
(4) ***temporal***: identify any temporal constraint on the substitution of goods or services (e.g., lead times for market entry or production).[1214]

813. 'Competition' is the field of rivalry between persons who are able to supply substitutable goods or services.[1215] Where provisions of Part IV of the Competition and Consumer Act require as an element of conduct an agreement between competitors, both acquisition and supply markets are relevant. For example, price fixing can occur where acquirers of goods or service agree the price of acquisition, or where the suppliers of goods or services agree the price of supply.

814. The anticompetitive provisions have a wide scope of application. First, the way that various concepts are defined in the Competition and Consumer Act broadens the application of some provisions. For example, for conduct to amount to price fixing, there needs to be an agreement between competitors with the purpose or effect of fixing, maintaining or controlling price.[1216] This includes conduct which has the purpose or likely effect of directly or indirectly fixing, controlling or maintaining

1210. *Stirling Harbour Service Pty Ltd v. Bunbury Port Authority* [2000] FCA 38, [114].
1211. *Dandy Power Equipment Pty Ltd v. Mercury Marine Pty Ltd* (1982) 64 FLR 238 at 259, cited in *Stirling Harbour Service Pty Ltd v. Bunbury Port Authority* [2000] FCA 38, [113].
1212. *Competition and Consumer Act 2010* (Cth), s. 4E.
1213. *Re Queensland Co-op Milling Assn Ltd* (1976) 25 FLR 169; approved in *Queensland Wire Industries Pty Ltd v. Broken Hill Pty Co Ltd* (1989) 167 CLR 177.
1214. Miller R, *2016 Miller's Australian Competition and Consumer Law Annotated* (38th ed, Lawbook Co, 2016) 223.
1215. *Re Queensland Co-op Milling Assn Ltd* (1976) 25 FLR 169, 188.
1216. *Competition and Consumer Act 2010* (Cth), s. 44ZZRD.

(or providing for the fixing, controlling or maintaining of) the price of, or a discount, allowance, rebate or credit for, goods or services.[1217] Second, the prohibitions under Part IV of the Competition and Consumer Act apply to 'contracts, arrangements or understandings', they are not limited to conduct which is reflected in legally binding agreements. It is sufficient for there to be a 'meeting of the minds' between relevant persons for a contravention of the Act to occur.[1218]

II. Penalties

815. Significant penalties apply for breach of the anticompetitive conduct provisions. The maximum pecuniary penalty that can apply to a body corporate for breaching a provision of Part IV of the Competition and Consumer Act is the greatest of: USD 10,000,000; three times the value of the benefit to the body corporate of engaging in the breach; or 10% of annual turnover of the body corporate for the year ending on the month in which the contravention occurred.[1219] For individuals involved in contravening these provisions of the Act, there are maximum penalties of USD 500,000.[1220] Breach of the cartel provisions can also result in imprisonment for up to ten years.[1221] Furthermore, aside from persons directly involved in the contravention, any person who: aids, abets, counsels or procures a contravention; induces a contravention by another person; is directly or indirectly, knowingly concerned in, or a party to, or conspires with others in a contravention; can be found guilty of an offence carrying the same penalties.[1222]

III. Exclusions and Exceptions

A. Notification

816. Conduct which would constitute either the private disclosure of pricing information to a competitor in contravention of section 44ZZW of the Competition and Consumer Act, or exclusive dealing in contravention of section 47 of the Act, may be notified to the regulator, the ACCC.[1223,1224] Unless the ACCC indicates that the notification is not allowed,[1225] notification provides immunity from penalty under the Competition and Consumer Act in respect of the notified conduct immediately in

1217. Section 44ZZRD.
1218. *ACCC v. Construction, Forestry, Mining and Energy Union* [2008] FCA 678, [42].
1219. *Competition and Consumer Act 2010* (Cth), s. 76(1A).
1220. Section 76(1B).
1221. Section 79(10).
1222. Section 76(1).
1223. The ACCC is required to maintain a public register of notifications, available at http://registers.accc.gov.au/content/index.phtml/itemId/6031 (accessed 1 Mar. 2017).
1224. *Competition and Consumer Act 2010* (Cth), subs. 93(1); *see* , for example, Ausgrid, Endeavour Energy and Essential Energy, *Notification of Exclusive dealing* (N98837 – N98839) (7 Jan. 2016).
1225. *Competition and Consumer Act 2010* (Cth), ss 93(3A), 93(7C).

respect of exclusive dealing (other than third line forcing) and fourteen days after lodgement for third line forcing and private disclosure of pricing information.[1226]

817. Notification can also be given of proposed collective bargaining where a contract, arrangement or understanding or proposed contract, arrangement of understanding contains a cartel provision.[1227] The collective bargaining notification process only applies where there is a reasonable expectation at the time of giving the collective bargaining notice and the entry into the relevant contract that the value of the relevant contract or contracts will not exceed USD 3 million.[1228] Immunity for notified conduct commences fourteen days after the lodgement of the notification, unless the ACCC objects to the notice.

B. Authorisation

818. The ACCC may authorise conduct which otherwise could breach the prohibitions against: cartel provisions; exclusionary provisions; contracts, arrangements or understandings which substantially lessen competition; exclusive dealing; and resale price maintenance.[1229,1230] While the authorisation is in place the authorised conduct is immune from penalty under the Competition and Consumer Act. Authorisation may be reopened and revoked by the ACCC where the ACCC considers that there has been a material change in circumstances.[1231] Mergers may be authorised by the Australian Competition Tribunal.[1232] The ACCC may also provide a formal clearance to a proposed merger.[1233] Further consideration of mergers and acquisitions is given in section 3.03.

C. Collective Acquisition Exception

819. A contract, arrangement or understanding containing a cartel provision is not subject to enforcement under the Competition and Consumer Act in so far as the cartel provision has the effect or purpose of price fixing; and the cartel provision relates to the price for goods or service to be collectively acquired, whether directly or indirectly, by the parties to the contract, arrangement or understanding.[1234] The scope of the collective acquisition exception has not been tested before a court.

1226. Section 93(7), 93(7A).
1227. Section 93AB.
1228. Subsections 93AB(4), (5).
1229. The ACCC is required to maintain a public register of authorisations, available at http://registers.accc.gov.au/content/index.phtml/itemId/6031 (accessed 1 Mar. 2017).
1230. *Competition and Consumer Act 2010* (Cth) subss 88(1A), (1), (8), (8A).
1231. Paragraph 91B(3)(c); *see Re AGL Cooper Basin Natural Gas Supply Arrangements* [1997] ATPR 41-593.
1232. *Competition and Consumer Act 2010* (Cth), s. 95AT.
1233. Section 95AC.
1234. Section 44ZZRV.

D. Statutory Exemption

820. Subsection 51(1) of the Competition and Consumer Act enables State and Territory governments to enact legislation excepting anything done in the State or Territory from being taken into regard in deciding whether or not a person has contravened Part IV of the Act. The excluded thing must be specifically identified in, and authorised by, legislation.[1235]

§3. Application of Anticompetitive Conduct Prohibitions to Energy Businesses

I. Joint Ventures

821. Given the scale of projects in the energy sector, often these projects can be delivered as joint ventures between entities which are competitors. Giving effect to joint venture arrangements may involve conduct which in the absence of an exemption would breach the Competition and Consumer Act.[1236,1237] Specific treatment of joint ventures is provided for in respect of the cartel conduct provisions. Defences are provided to criminal and civil proceedings for breach of the cartel provisions if the requirements of the legislation are satisfied.[1238] The application of the prohibition in respect of exclusionary provisions is modified in respect of joint ventures by requiring that the conduct must be for the purpose, or have the effect (or likely effect) of substantially lessening compensation.[1239]

822. Joint venturers can also seek authorisation from the ACCC for conduct that otherwise would breach the Competition and Consumer Act. For example, authorisation has been granted to companies involved in the development, production, marketing and sale of natural gas produced from the continental shelf off North-West Australia.[1240] Authorisation was granted by the ACCC to allow the participants in the joint venture to jointly discuss and negotiate common terms (including price), the

1235. *See* , for example, *Cooper Basin (Ratification) Act 1975* (SA), s. 16.
1236. For further analysis of the application of competition laws to joint ventures *see* Corones S, 'Joint Ventures and the Competition and Consumer Act', in Duncan W (ed.), *Joint Ventures in Australia* (3rd ed, Federation Press, 2012).
1237. For the definition of 'joint venture', *see* *Competition and Consumer Act 2010* (Cth), s. 4J.
1238. Sections 44ZZRO, 44ZZRP.
1239. Section 76C.
1240. BHP Billiton Petroleum (North West Shelf) Pty Ltd, BP Developments Australia Pty Ltd, Chevron Australia Pty Ltd, Shell Development (Australia) Pty Ltd and Woodside Energy Ltd, *Exclusionary provisions and associated cartel provisions: application for authorisation* (A91220 – A91123) (31 Mar. 2010).

methods by which natural gas from the North-West Shelf would be offered for sale, and enter, and give effect to, contracts containing these provisions.[1241]

II. Mergers and Acquisitions

823. Mergers or acquisitions which have the effect or would be likely to have the effect of substantially lessening competition in any market are prohibited by section 50 of the Competition and Consumer Act, unless cleared by the ACCC or authorised by the Australian Competition Tribunal.[1242]

824. Merger guidelines are published by the ACCC.[1243] An informal clearance process provided by the ACCC enables parties to a proposed transaction to request the ACCC's view as to whether the ACCC will seek an injunction from the Federal Court to stop the merger from proceeding.[1244] If the ACCC raises concerns regarding the proposed merger then there is the potential for these concerns to be addressed through court enforceable undertakings.[1245] If the ACCC denies an informal clearance and indicates that it will seek an injunction to prevent a merger from progressing, the merger proponents can seek a declaration as to whether or not the proposed merger will substantially lessen competition in contravention of section 50 of the Competition and Consumer Act.[1246]

825. A formal clearance process is also available under the Act.[1247] Where a formal clearance is granted, the parties to the transaction are immune from prosecution for breach of section 50 with respect to the transaction. Conditions on the formal clearance may be imposed by the ACCC. A right of appeal to the Australian Competition Tribunal is available if the ACCC denies an application for formal clearance.[1248] Alternatively, merger parties can seek an authorisation of the Australian Competition

1241. ACCC, *Determination Applications for authorisation lodged by BHP Billiton Petroleum (North West Shelf) Pty Ltd, BP Developments Australia Pty Ltd, Chevron Australia Pty Ltd, Shell Development (Australia) Pty Ltd and Woodside Energy Ltd* (A91220 – A91123), (8 Sept. 2010); *see also* ACCC, *Determination Application for authorisation in respect of the PNG Gas Project* (A40081) (3 May 2006).

1242. A recent review into Australia's competition policy recommended that the formal merger clearance process and the authorisation process described in this part be combined and reformed: Harper I, Anderson P, McCluskey S and O'Bryan M, *Competition Policy Review Final Report: March 2015* (Commonwealth of Australia, 2015) Recommendation 35. The Australian government supports this recommendation.

1243. ACCC, *Merger Guidelines: November 2008* (Commonwealth of Australia, 2011).

1244. *Ibid.*, [1.8] and [1.9]. *See also* ACCC, *Informal Merger Review Process Guidelines*: September 2013 (Commonwealth of Australia, 2013) and ACCC, *Public competition assessments*, http://registers.accc.gov.au/content/index.phtml/itemId/501191 (accessed 1 Mar. 2017).

1245. For example, *see* ACCC, *Elgas Limited – proposed acquisition of Wesfarmers Kleenheat Gas Pty Ltd's east coast LPG assets: Public competition assessment* (22 Dec. 2015).

1246. *Australian Gas Light Company (ACN 052 167 405) v. Australian Competition & Consumer Commission* (No 3) [2003] FCA 1525.

1247. *Competition and Consumer Act 2010* (Cth), s. 95AC.

1248. ACCC, *Merger Guidelines*, *supra* n. 1243, [1.10] and [1.11]; *see also* ACCC, *Formal Merger Review Process Guidelines* (May 2011) reproduced in Miller R, *supra* n. 1214, 2227.

Tribunal.[1249] Authorisation may be granted on basis that the merger is likely to result in such public benefits that the merger should be allowed to proceed.[1250]

III. Contract Terms to Support Investment

826. Investment for large-scale energy projects can be dependent upon securing foundation contracts with terms which can be reasonably anticipated to provide a financial return for the project. Long-term contracts or contracts which contain 'take or pay' obligations or other forms of tying obligation could be assessed in some circumstances to be arrangements which substantially lessen competition.[1251] Other investment decisions can be influenced by the manner in which capacity constraints in a supply chain can be collaboratively managed by participants within the supply chain.[1252]

827. Contracts of long duration may initially not have the effect of substantially lessening competition, but may during the term (with changing market circumstances have this effect). Authorisation of long-term arrangements in the energy sector has been granted by ACCC.[1253] The ACCC has also reopened authorisations on the basis that circumstances have materially changed during the term of arrangements.[1254]

828. Contract terms proposed to support the divestment of publicly owned generation assets have also been scrutinised through the authorisation process. In 2009 Delta Electricity, Eraring Energy and Macquarie Generation (each at the time generators owned by the New South Wales' government) applied for authorisation of 'co-insurance' arrangements. In essence, the co-insurance arrangements would have provided a right in a gentrader to call for compensation in the event that the output of a generator contracted to that gentrader fell below the contracted firm capacity.[1255] The co-insurance

1249. *Competition and Consumer Act 2010* (Cth), s. 95AT; *see*, for example, *Re Macquarie Generation and AGL Energy Ltd* [2014] AcompT 1.

1250. ACCC, *Merger Guidelines*, *supra* n. 1243, [1.13]; *see also* Australian Competition Tribunal, *Practice Direction* http://www.competitiontribunal.gov.au/__data/assets/pdf_file/0010/33787/Practice-Direction-20160923.pdf (accessed 1 Mar. 2017).

1251. For further analysis in respect of long-term contracts, *see* Pengilley W, 'Long-term Supply Contracts: Here Today, Gone Tomorrow', 6 *Trade Practices Law Journal* 203 (1998); Chiam L and Ahuja V, 'Long-term Supply Contracts – Time for Review', 25 *Australian Energy and Resources Law Journal* 149 (2006).

1252. *See*, for example, Port Waratah Coal Services Limited, Newcastle Coal Infrastructure Group Pty Limited and Newcastle Port Corporation, *Submission in support of the application for authorisation under the* Trade Practices Act 1974 (Cth) *New South Wales coal industry – Long term solution* (29 Jun. 2009), 6 http://registers.accc.gov.au/content/index.phtml/itemId/879882/fromItemId/401858/display/acccDecision (accessed 1 Mar. 2017).

1253. *See*, for example, ACCC, *Determination Applications for Authorisation lodged by Port Waratah Coal Services Limited, Newcastle Coal Infrastructure Group and the Newcastle Port Corporation in respect of the Capacity Framework Arrangements at the Port of Newcastle* (Authorisation Nos: A91147–A91149 and A91168–A91169) (9 Dec. 2009).

1254. ACCC, *ACCC action on gas authorisation* (28 Mar. 1996); on appeal, *Re AGL Cooper Basin Natural Gas Supply Arrangements* [1997] ATPR 41-593.

1255. New South Wales Government, *supra* n. 1152, 4 and 16–17.

arrangements were considered necessary to address the loss of portfolio benefits which would result from the disaggregation.[1256] The authorisation was denied on the basis that the co-insurance arrangement was not necessary to enable the energy reform strategy in New South Wales to proceed and there were other mechanism available to gentraders to hedge risk.[1257]

IV. Joint Purchasing Groups

829. The Competition and Consumer Act applies to competitors in both acquisition and supply markets. Joint purchasing groups who want to utilise their combined demand are subject to the prohibitions under the Act. Authorisation can be sought by proposed joint buying groups who intend pooling their energy demand when tendering for a supplier.[1258] Electricity market participants may also seek efficiencies through joint negotiations with their suppliers.[1259]

V. Market Operation

830. Some arrangements for the operation of energy markets are subject to authorisation by the ACCC. Historically, the National Electricity Code (forerunner to the National Electricity Rules) was subject to authorisation.[1260] No authorisation is required for the National Electricity Rules, however, market operation arrangements

1256. *Ibid.*, 23.

1257. ACCC, *Determination: Applications for authorisation lodged by Macquarie Generation, Delta Energy and Eraring Energy in respect of a co-insurance arrangement between the electricity Generators and Gentraders in NSW* (Authorisation Nos: A91198–A91199) (20 May 2010), iii – iv.

1258. For example, SACOME Electricity Purchasing Group, *Exclusionary Provisions and Associated Cartel Conduct Application for Authorisation* (Authorisation Nos: A91567–A91568) (4 Jan. 2017).

1259. For example, joint negotiation for the supply of coal: *see* ACCC, *Determination application for authorisation lodged by CS Energy and Callide Power management Pty Limited in respect of a joint negotiation for the purchase of black coal with Anglo Coal* (Authorisation No: A50027) (11 Nov. 2006).

1260. ACCC, *Final Determination: Applications for authorisation National Electricity Code* (Authorisation Nos: A90671, A90672 and A90673) (22 Dec. 1999).

outside of the NEM may require authorisation to prevent contravention of Part IV of the Competition and Consumer Act.[1261]

VI. Retail marketing

831. Certain retail marketing strategies can contravene the anticompetitive conduct provisions in Part IV of the Competition and Consumer Act. The supply of a good or service on the condition that a good or service is acquired from an unrelated entity will constitute third line forcing unless authorised or notified. Retail energy companies have offered incentives for customers to enter into market contracts which have been notified to avoid liability for third line forcing.[1262] Other types of retailers have provided incentives for the purchase of their goods or services by offering credits or rebates with energy retailers.[1263]

832. Door-to-door energy sales are regulated under consumer protection laws (*see* Chapter 2, §4 [II], above). Self-regulatory schemes may breach prohibitions under Part IV of the Competition and Consumer Act and have been the subject of authorisation by the ACCC.[1264]

VII. Uptake of Technology

833. Support by energy market participants for the uptake of technologies by consumers may contravene Part IV of the Competition and Consumer Act without authorisation or notification. For example, arrangements for the purchase of solar feed-in from consumers on the condition that the solar PV system has been purchased

---

1261. *See* , for example, ACCC, *Determination Applications for Authorisation lodged by The Independent Market operator in respect of the Market Rules to govern the wholesale electricity market in Western Australia* (Authorisation Nos: A91004, A91005 and A91006) (22 Dec. 2006); ACCC, *Determination Applications for Authorisation lodged by Stanwell Corporation Limited and Diamantina Power Station Pty Limited in respect of arrangements for participants in the NWPS to agree to rules relating to the coordination of electricity dispatch scheduled at electricity generators in the NWPS* (Authorisation Nos: A91448 and A91449) (20 Jan. 2015); ACCC, *Determination Application for Authorisation lodged by Retail Energy Market Company Ltd in respect of the Retail market Rules* (Authorisation Nos: A91136, A91137, A91138, A91170 and A91171) (26 Aug. 2009).

1262. For example, *see* IPower Pty Ltd & IPower 2 Pty Ltd t/a Simply Energy, *Notification of Exclusive Dealing* (N98987 and N98988) (10 Mar. 2016).

1263. For example, *see* Alinta Energy Retail Sales Pty Ltd, *Notification of Exclusive Dealing* (N98913) (12 Feb. 2016).

1264. ACCC, *Determination for authorisation lodged by Energy Assurance Limited in respect of a scheme to regulate door-to-door energy sales* (Authorisation Nos: A91258 and A91259) (23 Jun. 2011).

form a nominated supplier would constitute prohibited third line forcing and have been notified to the ACCC.[1265]

1265. For example, *see* IPower Pty Ltd & IPower 2 Pty Ltd t/a Simply Energy, *Notification of Exclusive Dealing* (N99431 and N999432) (15 Nov. 2016); IPower Pty Ltd & IPower 2 Pty Ltd t/a Simply Energy, *Notification of Exclusive Dealing* (N99226 and N99227) (28 Jul. 2016).

Conclusion

834. Australia is richly endowed with a variety of natural resources, including coal, gas, uranium, and an abundance of renewable energy resources. Australia is a net energy exporter, although the nation does import most of its petroleum supplies for domestic use. Because of its self-sufficiency in natural resources, security of energy supply has not been an issue for Australia to the extent, and in the same way, it is for countries that rely heavily on imported fuel supplies.

835. A number of challenges face the nation as it moves forward over the next decades. Since the 1990s, a primary focus of energy policy in the electricity and gas sectors has been the deregulation of the state-owned electricity and gas enterprises and the introduction of competition into these markets, along with the establishment of the NEM and regional gas markets. However, reform in electricity and gas reform in some States has stagnated, and the 2015 Review into Australia's Competition Policy has suggested a challenge for the future is to proceed with liberalisation of energy markets to ensure the benefits of competition are realised.

836. As with many countries, a major issue over the coming years will be decarbonisation of the economy, in order to mitigate GHG emissions and meet the challenge of climate change. This will need to be done while ensuring security and stability of electricity supply, and ensuring energy remains affordable. In recent months, it has become of increasing concern that the NEM rules, which were designed over twenty years ago to service a market characterised by coal-powered fire stations, are not sufficiently innovative and flexible to allow for the increased integration of electricity sourced from renewable energy technologies into the grid. Reform of the network rules to allow for technological developments in variable and other renewable power sources, battery storage, distributed power and micro grids, will be a key challenge.

837. In the near future, gas has been heralded as the 'cleaner' fuel to transition Australia away from coal to renewable energy sources. However, with much of Australia's existing gas contracted for sale as LPG to overseas buyers, a gas shortage is looming. While many States have introduced moratoriums on the exploration for and development of unconventional gas resources because of environmental concerns over hydraulic fracturing and methods of extracting CSG, there may be increasing pressure to remove the moratoria in the face of a domestic gas crisis.

838. With a lack of political will to address the issue of energy and climate change, and a lack of bi-partisanship from the two major political parties at both federal level and at the federal-State level, Australia does not currently have a strong energy policy that will take the country through the necessary transformation to a clean energy future. To meet the challenges for the future, developing such a policy needs to be a priority for all political parties at both the federal and State levels of government.

Selected Bibliography

Books and Articles

Bonyhady T and Christoff P (eds), *Climate Law in Australia* (The Federation Press, 2007).

Bradbrook A, 'The Relevance of the Cujus est Solum Doctrine to the Surface Landowner's Claims to Natural Resources Located Above and Beneath His Land' 11 *Adel LR* 462 (1988).

Brazil P, *Offshore Constitutional Settlement 1980: A Case Study in Federalism* (Centre for International and Public Law, Australian National University, 2001).

Daintith T, *The Legal Character of Petroleum Licences: A Comparative Study* (University of Dundee, Centre for Petroleum and Mineral Law Studies, 1981).

Daintith T, *Discretion in the Administration of Offshore Oil and Gas: A Comparative Study*, 13 (AMPLA, 2005).

Hepburn S, *Mining and Energy Law* (Cambridge University Press, 2015).

Hunt C, *The Offshore Petroleum Regimes of Canada and Australia* (Calgary Institute of Resources Law, 1989).

Hunt M, *Minerals and Petroleum Law* (Butterworths, 1996).

Hunter T and Chandler J, *Petroleum Law in Australia* (LexisNexis Butterworths, 2013).

Knight P and Hood M (eds), *Coal and the Commonwealth: The Greatness of an Australian Resource*, 46 (University of Queensland, October 2009).

Lockie D, *Clean Energy Law in Australia* (LexisNexis Butterworths, 2012).

Lyster R and Bradbrook A, *Energy Law and the Environment* (Cambridge University Press, 2006).

Miller R, *2016 Miller's Australian Competition and Consumer Law Annotated* (38th ed, Lawbook Co, 2016).

Murray I, 'The Minerals Resource Rent Tax is Dead, Long Live Resource Rent Taxes?' 40 *UW Aust LR* 111 (2015).

Peel J and Osofsky H, *Climate Change Litigation: Regulatory Pathways to Cleaner Energy* (Cambridge University Press, 2015).

Toskas E, 'A Comparative Review of Unit Development under the Commonwealth Petroleum Act' 26 ARELJ (2007).

Woellner R, Barkozcy S, Murphy S, Evans C and Pinto D, *Australian Taxation Law* (26th ed., 2016).

Wouters C, Vigar C and Van Hende K, 'Increasing consumer choice – the potential impact of prosumers on electricity market regulation', *ICER Chronicle* (ed. 3) (March 2015).

Zahar A, Peel J and Godden L, *Australian Climate Law in Global Context* (Cambridge University Press, 2013).

Reports, Reviews and Government Papers

Australian Consumer and Competition Commission, *Petrol Prices and Australian Consumers: Report of the ACCC Inquiry into the Price of Unleaded Petrol* (Commonwealth of Australia, 2007).

Australian Energy Market Commission, *Draft Final Report: Review of the Victorian Declared Wholesale Gas Market*, 17 (14 October 2016).

Australian Government, Department of Climate Change, *Carbon Pollution Reduction Scheme, Green Paper, July 2008* (Commonwealth of Australia, 2008).

Australian Government, Department of Climate Change and Energy Efficiency, *Carbon Pollution Reduction Scheme—Australia's Low Pollution Future, White Paper*, (Commonwealth of Australia, 2008).

Australian Government, Department of Industry and Science, *2015 Energy White Paper* (Commonwealth of Australia, 2015).

Australian Government, Department of Industry and Science/Office of the Chief Economist, *Australian Energy Update 2015* (Canberra, 2015).

Australian Government, Department of Infrastructure and Regional Development, *Vehicle Emissions Discussion Paper* (Commonwealth of Australia, 2016).

Australian Government, Office of the Chief Economist, *Resources and Energy Statistics 2014* (Commonwealth of Australia, 2014).

Australian Government, Office of the Chief Economist, *Resources and Energy Quarterly: June 2015* (Commonwealth of Australia, 2015).

Australian Parliament, Senate Legislative and General Purpose Standing Committee, *Petrol Prices in Australia,* 35 (Senate Standing Committee on Economics, 2006).

Australian Productivity Commission, *Review of the Gas Access Regime* (Productivity Commission, 2004).

Australian Productivity Commission, *Review of the Regulatory Burden in the Upstream Petroleum (Oil and Gas) Sector: Research Report* (Productivity Commission, 2009).

Selected Bibliography

Australian Transport Council and the Environment Protection and Heritage Council, Vehicle Fuel Efficiency Working Group, *Final Report* (2009).

Bills K and Agostini D, *Offshore Petroleum Safety Investigation: Varanus Island Incident Investigation* (Government of Western Australia, 2009).

Borthwick D, *Report of the Montara Commission of Inquiry* (Government of Australia, 2010).

Britt A, Whitaker A, Cadman S, Summerfield D, Kay P, Champion D, McKay A, Miezitis Y, Porritt K, Schofield A and Jaireth S, *Australia's Identified Mineral Resources 2014* (Geoscience Australia, Canberra, 2014).

Climate Change Authority, *Light Vehicle Emissions Standards for Australia: Research Report* (Climate Change Authority, 2014).

Climate Change Authority, *Renewable Energy Target Review Report* (Climate Change Authority, 2014).

Climate Change Authority, *Towards a Climate Policy Toolkit: Special Review on Australia's Climate Goals and Policies* (Climate Change Authority, 2016).

Climate Change Authority, *Policy options for Australia's electricity supply sector—Special Review Research Report* (Climate Change Authority, 2016).

Cullen, The Hon Lord, *The Public Inquiry into the Piper Alpha Disaster* (Great Britain, Dept. of Energy, 1990).

Garnaut R, *Garnaut Climate Change Review: Final Report* (Cambridge University Press, 2008).

Garnaut R, *The Garnaut Review 2011: Australia in the Global Response to Climate Change* (Cambridge University Press, 2011).

Geoscience Australia and the Bureau of Resources and Energy Economics, *Australian Energy Resource Assessment* (2nd ed, 2014).

Geoscience Australia and the Bureau of Resources and Energy Economics, *Australian Energy Resource Assessment* (2nd ed, 2014) (interim update 2016).

Global Carbon Capture and Storage Institute Ltd, *Global CCS Institute CCS Legal and Regulatory Indicator: A Global Assessment of National Legal and Regulatory Regimes for Carbon Capture and Storage* (Global Carbon Capture and Storage Institute Ltd, 2015).

Harper I, Anderson P, McCluskey S and O'Bryan M, Competition Policy Review Final Report: March 2015 (Commonwealth of Australia, 2015).

Henry K, Harmer J, Piggott J, Ridout H and Smith G, *Australia's Future Tax System: Report to the Treasurer, December 2009* (Commonwealth of Australia, 2010).

International Energy Agency, *Energy Policies of IEA Countries: Australia 2012 Review* (OECD/IEA, 2012).

James M, *Vehicle Fuel Efficiency Standards*, Parliamentary Research Paper (28 June 2013).

National Emissions Trading Taskforce, *Possible design for a national greenhouse gas emissions trading scheme: Final framework report on scheme design* (NETT, 2007).

Parer W, Breslin P, Sims R and Agostini D, *Towards a Truly National and Efficient Energy Market* (Commonwealth of Australia, 2002).

Parliament of Western Australia, Standing Committee On Environment and Public Affairs, *Implications for Western Australia Of Hydraulic Fracturing For Unconventional Gas*, Report 42 (November 2015).

Prime Ministerial Task Force on Emissions Trading, *Report of the Task Force on Emissions Trading* (Australian Government, 2007).

Trebeck D, John Landels J, QC and Hughes K, *Fuel Taxation Inquiry Report* (Commonwealth of Australia, 2002).

Warburton D, Fisher B, In't Veld S and Zema M, *Renewable Energy Target Scheme, Report of the Expert Panel* (Commonwealth of Australia, 2014).

Index

The numbers here refer to paragraph numbers.

Index

Index

www.ingramcontent.com/pod-product-compliance
Lightning Source LLC
Chambersburg PA
CBHW071428230926
51846CB00001B/158
9789041196293